Divorce For Dummies, 3rd Edition

Cheat Sheet

W9-AAM-398

Divorce Decisions in a Nutshell

You face many tough decisions when you're working out the terms of your divorce, especially if you and your spouse are parents of minor children. The basic decisions you must make are

- Who will have physical custody of your children?
- Who will have legal custody of your children?
- If you will have sole or primary custody of your children, what visitation rights will their other parent have?
- Will you prepare a parenting plan? If so, what will it include?
- Which parent will pay child support, how much will the payments be, and when will the payments end?
- Who will pay for your health insurance and your children's health coverage — you or your spouse?
- How will you handle child-related expenses like private school tuition, tutoring, after-school activities, summer camp, and so on?
- How will you and your spouse share the cost of your children's college educations or enrollment in a trade or career school?
- Which of you is going to claim your children as income tax exemptions?
- Will you or your spouse pay the other spousal support (also known as alimony)?
- How much will those support payments be?
- How long will the spousal support payments continue?
- What are your marital assets and marital debts?
- What percentage of the value of your marital assets are each of you entitled to?
- What portion of the property and debts will each of you take from your marriage?

Questions to Ask Before You Hire a Divorce Attorney

Hiring a divorce attorney is a critically important decision because whoever you hire can affect the cost and tenor of your divorce, not to mention the outcome. Following are some questions to ask the attorneys you meet with:

- How long have you been practicing divorce law and how many cases have you handled?
- If I hire you, will you or someone else with your firm handle my case?
- If my spouse and I can't agree on an issue in our divorce, how would you to help us break our stalemate? Would you suggest we try mediation?
- Do you practice collaborative divorce law?
- Have you ever had a case like mine? How did you handle it?
- What do you see as the strengths and weaknesses of my divorce case?
- Knowing what you know about my situation, how would you proceed if I were to hire you?
- If I call you, how quickly can I expect to have my calls returned?
- What is your hourly rate and can you give me an estimate of how much my divorce will cost?
- Will I have to pay you a retainer? If so, how much will it be?
- What sort of expenses should I expect to pay, and how much do you estimate they will be? Are there things I can do to minimize them?
- Will you provide me with an estimate of my expenses and an explanation of what those expenses may include?
- If my divorce goes to trial, will you continue to represent me or will you recommend another attorney?

For Dummies: Bestselling Book Series for Beginners

Divorce For Dummies,® 3rd Edition

Cheat Sheet

Helpful Organizations and Resources

Keep these national and local resources in a handy place as you go through your divorce.

National resources

- **American Academy of Matrimonial Lawyers** (www.aaml.org **or 312-263-6477):** Through this organization, you can find a family law attorney in your area to help you with your divorce. The site also offers useful handbooks and articles about various aspects of divorce.

- **The Institute for Divorce Financial Analysts** (www.institutedfa.com **or 800-875-1760):** This national organization certifies financial professionals as divorce planners and can refer you to a certified divorce planner (CDP) in your area. A CDP can create a specific plan for resolving the financial issues in your divorce and works hand in hand with your divorce attorney.

- **The National Center for Missing and Exploited Children** (www.missingkids.com **or 800-843-5678), Child Find of America** (www.childfindofamerica.org **or 800-I-Am-Lost), and the Polly Klaas Foundation,** (www.pollyklaas.org **or 800-587-4357):** Any of these organizations can help you locate your children if your spouse disappears with them.

- **National Domestic Violence Hotline** (www.ndvh.org **or 800-799-7233):** Hotline staffers can help you develop a safety plan if you think that your spouse may become violent or if you're in immediate danger of being attacked. They can also provide phone numbers for domestic violence resources in your area.

- **National Foundation for Credit Counseling** (www.nfcc.org **or 800-388-2227):** The agency can provide free or low-cost credit counseling, debt-management services, and financial information.

- **TherapistLocator.net** (www.aamft.org/TherapistLocator): This Web site, a public service from the American Association for Marriage and Family Therapy (703-838-9808), helps you locate a marriage and family therapist in your area who can help you and your family deal with the emotional issues of divorce.

State and local resources

- **Accountant:** A certified public accountant (CPA) can answer questions about your family's finances and advise you about the financial implications of the property settlement agreement you may be considering. If you need help finding a CPA near you, try 1-800 Accountant (800-222-6868 or www.1800accountant.com).

- **Bar associations in your community and state:** Local and state bar associations can refer you to family law attorneys in your area. They can also provide you with information about the code of ethics and standards that lawyers in your area must follow. You can find the phone numbers for your local and state bar associations in your area's Yellow Page directory or by doing a Web search.

- **Chapter of Parents Without Partners nearest you** (800-637-7974 or www.parentswithoutpartners.org): This organization can help ease the stress of being a single parent by putting you in touch with other parents in your situation.

- **Child Support Enforcement (CSE) office in your state** (www.acf.dhhs.gov/programs/cse/): This state government office can assist you if you're having trouble collecting your court-ordered child support. The Web site can take you to the CSE office for your particular state.

- **Domestic abuse shelter in your community:** A shelter can be a life-saver if you're fearful that your spouse may become violent or if your spouse has already harmed you or your children. You can find the phone number in your local Yellow Pages under listings for "crisis intervention services" or "domestic violence services." Memorize the number and keep it in a safe place.

- **Religious advisor:** Spiritual guidance and advice can help you make some of the difficult decisions you may face in your divorce and can help you stay calm and gain perspective on your failed marriage.

- **State family court in your area:** Head here if your divorce involves any hearings for temporary orders, if you go to trial because you and your spouse can't work out all of the terms of your divorce, or if you or your spouse want to change some aspect of your final agreement or the judge's divorce court order.

For Dummies: Bestselling Book Series for Beginners

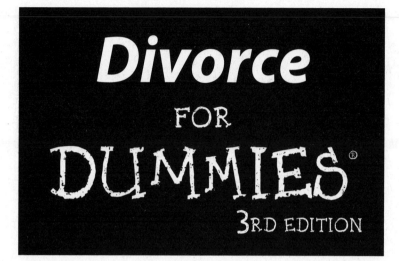

Divorce FOR DUMMIES®

3RD EDITION

by John Ventura and Mary Reed

WILEY

Wiley Publishing, Inc.

Divorce For Dummies®, 3rd Edition

Published by
Wiley Publishing, Inc.
111 River St.
Hoboken, NJ 07030-5774

www.wiley.com

Copyright © 2009 by Wiley Publishing, Inc., Indianapolis, Indiana
Published by Wiley Publishing, Inc., Indianapolis, Indiana
Published simultaneously in Canada

No part of this publication may be reproduced, stored in a retrieval system or transmitted in any form or by any means, electronic, mechanical, photocopying, recording, scanning or otherwise, except as permitted under Sections 107 or 108 of the 1976 United States Copyright Act, without either the prior written permission of the Publisher, or authorization through payment of the appropriate per-copy fee to the Copyright Clearance Center, 222 Rosewood Drive, Danvers, MA 01923, (978) 750-8400, fax (978) 646-8600. Requests to the Publisher for permission should be addressed to the Permissions Department, John Wiley & Sons, Inc., 111 River Street, Hoboken, NJ 07030, (201) 748-6011, fax (201) 748-6008, or online at http://www.wiley.com/go/permissions.

Trademarks: Wiley, the Wiley Publishing logo, For Dummies, the Dummies Man logo, A Reference for the Rest of Us!, The Dummies Way, Dummies Daily, The Fun and Easy Way, Dummies.com, Making Everything Easier, and related trade dress are trademarks or registered trademarks of John Wiley & Sons, Inc. and/or its affiliates in the United States and other countries, and may not be used without written permission. All other trademarks are the property of their respective owners. Wiley Publishing, Inc., is not associated with any product or vendor mentioned in this book.

For general information on our other products and services, please contact our Customer Care Department within the U.S. at 877-762-2974, outside the U.S. at 317-572-3993, or fax 317-572-4002.

For technical support, please visit www.wiley.com/techsupport.

Wiley also publishes its books in a variety of electronic formats. Some content that appears in print may not be available in electronic books.

Library of Congress Control Number: 2009920900

ISBN: 978-0-470-41151-3

Manufactured in the United States of America

10 9 8 7 6 5 4 3 2

WILEY

About the Authors

John Ventura was an attorney and a nationally known authority and advocate on consumer law and financial issues. As a boy, he dreamed of becoming a Catholic priest so he could help others. To prepare for that career, he spent his high school years in a seminary. After graduation, John decided he could best pursue his dream by combining journalism with the law, so he earned a degree in both from the University of Houston.

John was the Director of the Texas Consumer Complaint Center at the University of Houston Law School and an associate professor at the Law School. Prior to joining the Law School, John was the owner of four law offices in South Texas, where he provided bankruptcy services to consumers and small business owners and also worked in the area of consumer law. His goal as an attorney and as an author was to provide everyday people with the information and advice they needed to make the laws work for them, not against them.

John wrote 17 books on consumer and small-business legal and financial matters including *Managing Debt For Dummies* and *Law For Dummies* (Wiley). He wrote for *Home Office Computing* and *Small Business Computing* magazines and for many years he wrote a regular column for a Texas business journal and hosted a weekly radio program on legal issues.

John was quoted about consumer legal issues in a wide variety of publications including *Newsweek, The Wall Street Journal, Money, Kiplinger's Personal Finance Magazine, Black Enterprise, Inc., Bottom Line Personal,* and *Martha Stewart's Living,* among others. His advice was featured on such Web sites as MSNMoney.com, Bankrate.com, and Marketwatch.com. He was also interviewed on *MarketPlace Morning* (American Public Radio), *Morning Edition* (NPR), CNN, CNBC, Bloomberg Television & Radio, the Fox News Channel, the Lifetime Network and numerous national and local radio programs.

Mary Reed writes about financial and legal issues affecting consumers and small-business owners. She coauthored *Divorce For Dummies* and *Managing Debt For Dummies* (Wiley), *Good Advice for a Bad Economy* (Berkley), and *Stop Debt Collectors* (Credit.com). She has ghostwritten 13 other books for consumers and small business owners and has also written for *Good Housekeeping Magazine, Home Office Computing Magazine, Hispanic Business,* as well as for several Texas newspapers.

Mary is the owner of Mary Reed Public Relations (MR•PR), an Austin, Texas-based marketing and public relations firm (www.get-your-messsage-out.

based marketing and public relations firm (www.get-your-messsage-out.com). She counts book publishers, attorneys, financial professionals, healthcare professionals, Web-based businesses, nonprofit organizations, retailers, and restaurants among her clients.

Prior to starting MR•PR, Mary was vice president of marketing for a national market research firm, public affairs and marketing director for a women's healthcare and advocacy organization, public relations manager for *Texas Monthly Magazine,* and aide to an Austin City Council member. She also worked as a consultant to state and federal agencies while living in Cambridge, Massachusetts, and Washington, D.C.

In her free time, Mary enjoys being with her many friends and family, gardening, bike riding, reading, volunteering, and taking care of her cats.

Dedication

John's Dedication
To Lisa Taylor, the best divorce attorney I know.

Mary's Dedication
To my parents. Your words and deeds have taught me what a successful, happy marriage is all about and have provided me with a model to strive for. Thank you!

Authors' Acknowledgments

Thanks to Traci Cumbay, our project editor, for her help in reshaping the material in *Divorce For Dummies,* 3rd Edition. Her sense of humor made the editing process a pleasure and her suggestions have helped us make this edition of our book better than ever.

Publisher's Acknowledgments

We're proud of this book; please send us your comments through our Dummies online registration form located at `http://dummies.custhelp.com`. For other comments, please contact our Customer Care Department within the U.S. at 877-762-2974, outside the U.S. at 317-572-3993, or fax 317-572-4002.

Some of the people who helped bring this book to market include the following:

Acquisitions, Editorial, and Media Development

Project Editor: Traci Cumbay

(Previous Edition: Alissa Schwipps)

Acquisitions Editor: Tracy Boggier

Copy Editor: Traci Cumbay

Assistant Editor: Erin Calligan Mooney

Editorial Program Coordinator: Joe Niesen

Technical Editor: Jacqueline Chosnek

Editorial Supervisor & Reprint Editor: Carmen Krikorian

Editorial Assistant: David Lutton, Jennette ElNaggar

Cover Photos: © Darren Greenwood

Cartoons: Rich Tennant (`www.the5thwave.com`)

Composition Services

Project Coordinator: Kristie Rees

Layout and Graphics: Reuben W. Davis, Melissa K. Jester

Proofreader: Nancy L. Reinhardt

Indexer: Potomac Indexing, LLC

Publishing and Editorial for Consumer Dummies

 Diane Graves Steele, Vice President and Publisher, Consumer Dummies

 Kristin Ferguson-Wagstaffe, Product Development Director, Consumer Dummies

 Ensley Eikenburg, Associate Publisher, Travel

 Kelly Regan, Editorial Director, Travel

Publishing for Technology Dummies

 Andy Cummings, Vice President and Publisher, Dummies Technology/General User

Composition Services

 Gerry Fahey, Vice President of Production Services

 Debbie Stailey, Director of Composition Services

Contents at a Glance

Table of Contents

Part IV: Working Out the Details of Your Divorce 195

Introduction

. . . .

*N*early half of all marriages in the United States end in divorce. That adds up to more than a million divorces a year! Although you probably know at least one person who has gotten divorced, if your marriage is ending and you're like most people in your same situation, you're at a loss as to exactly what you should do first. That's totally understandable; most of us get married believing we will live happily ever after.

Unfortunately, many divorcing spouses turn what could be an amicable breakup into a cutthroat, emotionally difficult, and expensive battle because they allow anger, hurt, and fear to take over. Some of them also panic about what's happening to their marriage and make costly mistakes that affect their lives (and the lives of their young children) for years to come. They could have avoided those mistakes and minimized their emotional turmoil if they had had good information about the divorce laws in their state, knew more about their finances, and had received sensible advice about how to handle their emotions.

Getting divorced is almost never easy, but it doesn't have to be about winners, losers, and huge legal bills. With the right information and advice (and the proper attitude), most couples can work out the terms of their divorce on their own or with the help of attorneys with a minimum of expenses, hassles, and emotional upheaval. In this book, we tell you how.

About This Book

Welcome to the third edition of *Divorce For Dummies.* Like the first two editions, this book guides you through the divorce process using plain English (and not a bunch of confusing legalese). Although most of the information and advice in the previous editions is in this edition, too, we've updated everything and added new features, so we think you will find the third edition of *Divorce For Dummies* better than ever.

One of the nice features of *Divorce For Dummies,* 3rd Edition, is that you get to decide where in the book you want to begin reading. We worked hard to make sure that you don't need to have read (or remembered) the previous chapters if the information in one of the later chapters is what you most need at the moment. We define new terms wherever they show up or direct you to their definitions so that you're never at a loss for information. In other words, this is a reference that you can jump into and out of at will whenever you have a question about divorce or that you can read from cover to cover.

Conventions Used in This Book

We use the following conventions throughout the text to make things consistent and easy to understand:

- ✔ All Web addresses appear in `monofont`.
- ✔ New terms appear in *italic* and are closely followed by an easy-to-understand definition.
- ✔ **Bold** highlights the action parts of numbered steps and other important information you should know.

When this book was printed, some Web addresses may have needed to break across two lines of text. If that happened, rest assured that we haven't put in any extra characters (such as hyphens) to indicate the break. So, when using one of these Web addresses, just type in exactly what you see in this book, as though the line break doesn't exist.

What You're Not to Read

We know that reading a whole book about divorce can be a pretty overwhelming proposition, so we've made it easier for you to use *Divorce For Dummies* by separating the stuff you really need to read from the information that may be interesting but isn't essential. The shaded boxes of text called sidebars elaborate on information in the rest of the chapter, provide extra tips and advice, or highlight useful resources. You may want to return to this information after you have a clearer understanding of the basics of divorce and are ready to deepen your knowledge.

Foolish Assumptions

As we wrote this book, we made some assumptions about our readers. We imagine that you

✔ Are either going through your first divorce or made a mess of your previous divorce and want to do a better job of ending your marriage this time

✔ Don't have a lot of experience with the legal system and may feel a little intimidated by attorneys, laws and legal terms, and judges

✔ Haven't been to law school and don't read legal books for fun

✔ Want to get divorced with a minimum of angst and expense

✔ Want to protect your legal rights and get your fair share

✔ Intend to make your divorce as easy as possible on your children

If our assumptions about you are right on the money, we're sure that you'll find this book to be a valuable resource. Although it can't mend your broken heart or take away your pain and worry, *Divorce For Dummies,* 3rd Edition, can help you become more informed about divorce and give you more control over your life as you plan for the end of your marriage, go through the divorce process, and begin building a happy, fulfilling postdivorce life for yourself.

How This Book Is Organized

You can use *Divorce For Dummies,* 3rd Edition, in one of two ways: You can sit down and read it from cover to cover or pick it up when you want to read about a certain topic or need an answer to a question. For easy navigation, this book is organized into six parts; the following sections explain what information you can find where.

Part 1: When Your Marriage Is on the Rocks

If you find your thoughts are increasingly turning divorce-ward, start here. This part gives you guidance for dealing with your marriage when it's in serious trouble. To show you what may lie ahead, we introduce you to the key issues and decisions in divorce and provide an overview of the divorce process itself, whether you work out the terms of your divorce outside of court or go through a divorce trial. We review various alternatives to divorce and provide detailed information on getting separated, whether you separate in an effort to save your marriage or use the separation as a prelude to divorce. Dissolving a same-sex marriage brings unique problems, and we explain those in this part, as well.

Whether you want to stay married or plan to divorce, you need to become an informed manager of your finances, and this part shows you how. You find out about the kinds of financial skills you need, the various financial records and documents you should have access to and understand, and why — whatever the state of your marriage — you have to have a credit history in your own name and know how to build one. Finally, we offer advice and resources for maintaining your employability if you're a stay-at-home spouse so that you can earn a good living after your marriage ends.

Part II: Getting Your Divorce Going

You've made the decision. Now what? Part II tells you how to initiate a divorce, with specific advice about how to break the news to your spouse. This part also helps you set your divorce goals and priorities and begin preparing financially for the end of your marriage. For those of you who anticipate a hostile divorce, we include a chapter that provides essential advice and guidance for protecting yourself financially and we give you the specific steps you should take to protect yourself and your children if your spouse becomes violent or threatens violence.

Getting divorced tends to stir up a lot of emotion, and so we include a chapter that discusses the kinds of emotions you may feel as you move through your divorce and offers suggestions for how to handle them. In addition, we provide advice for breaking the news about your divorce to your children, prepare you to answer the kinds of questions they're likely to ask you about your divorce and give you suggestions for how you can help them cope with the effects of your divorce on their lives.

Part III: Deciding the Basic Issues in Your Divorce

You have some important and sometimes difficult decisions to make before your marriage can be officially over. For example, you and your spouse must decide how to divide the assets and the debts you acquired during your marriage. You also may need to decide about spousal support — whether you will receive it or pay it and how much the payments will be. If you and your spouse have young children, you must also figure out how to handle child custody and visitation and child support. This part of the book gives you the basic information you need to resolve these issues.

Part IV: Working Out the Details of Your Divorce

Working out the terms of your divorce on your own with your spouse, through mediation, or with the help of attorneys are much better options than going through a divorce trial. This part of the book prepares you for any of these options. We show you how to do your own negotiating, and we explain the benefits and the drawbacks of using mediation to help settle the issues in your divorce.

We also tell you how to locate an affordable divorce attorney, what you should expect from your attorney and what she expects from you, and we advise you about how you and your attorney can work together so that you end up with a good divorce agreement. In case you *are* headed for divorce court, the final chapter in this part tells you what to expect before, during, and immediately after your divorce trial.

Part V: After You're Divorced: Avoiding Problems and Handling Challenges

After your divorce is over, you still have legal loose ends and paperwork to take care of and money matters to handle. For example, you'll be totally in charge of your own finances, and so you'll probably want to revise your estate plan, or prepare one for the first time, and if you have trouble meeting all of your financial obligations, you'll have to figure out what to do. Plus, you may need to begin working outside your home for the first time or find a job that pays you more than you're making now. This part of the book helps you handle all of these responsibilities.

But money isn't the only part of your new life that requires attention. This part offers advice and guidance for how to get the emotional support you may need after your marriage has ended officially, how to begin having fun again, and how to rebuild a sense of family for yourself and your children. In addition, this part features a chapter to help you grapple with some of the most difficult problems that many people face after divorce, including problems with visitation, unpaid child support and/or spousal support, and emotionally troubled children.

Romance never dies, and so here we also offer advice for steps you can take if you marry again, like getting premarital counseling and preparing a prenuptial agreement.

Part VI: The Part of Tens

Within this part are short chapters full of quick and interesting tidbits you don't find anywhere else. Here we tell you about useful and even amusing divorce blogs you may want to check out and offer advice on helping your kids cope with the aftermath of your divorce.

Icons Used in This Book

To make this book easier to read and simpler to use, we include icons that can help you find and fathom key ideas and information.

We use this icon to draw your attention to some of the more technical but very important financial details of getting a divorce.

This icon points out important information, details you're likely to return to again and again.

We use this icon to draw your attention to aspects of divorce and family law that may differ from one U.S. state to another.

Anything especially useful that can save you time, money, or energy as you're going through your divorce is highlighted with this icon.

Stop and read this information to steer clear of common divorce-related mistakes and pitfalls.

Where to Go from Here

If you have a specific divorce-related issue that you would like to know more about, check out this book's table of contents or index to find out what to read. For example, if you're particularly concerned about child custody and child support, start with Chapters 10 and 11, or if you're worried about spousal support, turn to Chapter 9. If you would like to get an overview of the main issues in a divorce read Chapter 1. It introduces you to the key concepts and topics you find in *Divorce For Dummies,* 3rd Edition. And if you're an overachiever or just particularly hungry for information about divorce, feel free to start with Chapter 1 and read right through to the index.

Part I
When Your Marriage Is on the Rocks

The 5th Wave   By Rich Tennant

"I heard it was good to use humor when you're having an argument."

In this part . . .

*E*very marriage isn't made in heaven. If you and your spouse are not living happily ever after and you think that your marriage may be ending, this part of the book provides you with a quick overview of divorce (and alternatives to it). It introduces you to the legal and financial issues that you and your spouse must resolve before your divorce can be official and the laws that apply to divorce, and it gives you an idea of the likely cost of your divorce. It also provides an overview of what you can expect if your divorce ends up in court.

Chapter 1

Divorce Fundamentals

· ·

· ·

*T*he thought that a divorce is in your future may make your stomach churn and cause you to lie awake at night worrying about what the process will be like, especially if your only knowledge of the legal system comes from watching courtroom dramas on TV. Understandably, the prospect of dealing with lawyers, courts, and legal mumbo jumbo may intimidate you.

Like most people in your situation, you're probably also concerned about what the divorce will do to your finances. You may worry about how much you'll have to spend to get divorced and whether after your divorce is final you'll have to pay every penny you earn on spousal support and/or child support (or whether you'll receive enough spousal support or child support from your spouse). You may also lose sleep wondering about the kind of postdivorce lifestyle you will be able to afford.

And, if you have young children, you probably have worries about how your divorce will affect them. You're right to be concerned because studies show that when parents don't work together to make their children feel safe and to keep their lives as normal as possible during and after their divorce, the children are apt to suffer emotionally. Studies also show that these same children have difficulty establishing healthy relationships as adults.

After you read this book, you should sleep better at night and worry a little less because you'll be armed with the information and advice you need to help you and your children get through your divorce and prepare for life afterward.

This chapter takes you through predivorce planning, provides a peek at the divorce process, and touches on the emotional aspects of divorce. In addition, we introduce you to some of the professionals you may need to call on to help with your divorce, explain the role that mediation may play in your divorce and discuss a relatively new, non-court process for ending your marriage called a collaborative divorce.

Considering Whether You Have Cause for Concern

If your marriage is going through tough times, you may find yourself wondering whether it's an example of the "for better or for worse" your marriage vows mentioned or whether your relationship is truly on the rocks. Although no test exists that can tell you whether your problems are typical reactions to the stress and strain that most marriages experience at one time or another or whether they point to more serious issues, troubled marriages do tend to exhibit many of the same characteristics. How many of the following statements apply to your marriage?

- ✔ In your mind, your spouse just can't do anything right anymore.
- ✔ You fight constantly.
- ✔ You've lost the ability or the willingness to resolve your marital problems.
- ✔ Resentment and contempt have replaced patience and love.
- ✔ You've turned from lovers into roommates.
- ✔ One or both of you is having an affair.
- ✔ You go out of your way to avoid being together and, when you are together, you have nothing to talk about.
- ✔ Your children are reacting to the stress in your marriage by fighting more, having difficulty in school, getting into trouble with the police, abusing drugs or alcohol, or becoming sexually promiscuous.
- ✔ You have begun having thoughts about divorce.

Don't panic if you find that your marriage exhibits some of these characteristics; you're not necessarily headed for divorce court. However, you do have cause for concern; you and your spouse need to assess your options — first separately and then together — and decide what to do next.

You may be married without realizing it

In some states, you may be married in the eyes of the law if you live with someone long enough (although no state defines just how long "long enough" is) and meet other state criteria, like the two of you have been holding yourselves out as married, you file joint income taxes, or you have plans to marry eventually. Such an arrangement is called a common-law marriage and provides you and your common-law spouse all the same rights and obligations as any other couple in your state who were married formally in a civil or a religious ceremony. It also means that you must obtain a legal divorce in order to officially end your relationship.

The following states recognize common-law marriages:

- Alabama
- Colorado
- District of Columbia
- Georgia (Assuming a couple satisfied all the requirements for a common-law marriage before January 1, 1997.)

- Idaho (Assuming a couple satisfied all the requirements for a common-law marriage before January 1, 1996.)
- Iowa
- Kansas
- Montana
- Ohio (Assuming a couple satisfied all the requirements for a common-law marriage before October 10, 1991.)
- Oklahoma
- Pennsylvania (Assuming a couple satisfied all the requirements for a common-law marriage before January 1, 2005.)
- Rhode Island
- South Carolina
- Texas
- Utah

Marital problems can trigger depression, feelings of vulnerability, powerlessness, and anger, as well as sleep disturbances, any of which can impede clear thinking and sound decision-making. A mental health professional can help you or your spouse deal with these problems so that you can move forward. If your spouse is struggling emotionally, suggest that he or she get mental health counseling, assuming that you think your spouse will be receptive to advice coming from you given the state of your marriage.

Getting Prepared Financially for a Divorce

Predivorce financial planning is essential to minimizing the cost of your divorce and increasing the likelihood that when your divorce is over, you have a settlement agreement that meets your short- and long-term postdivorce financial needs. (We discuss how to prepare yourself emotionally in the "Surviving the Emotional Roller Coaster" section, later in this chapter, as well as in Chapter 7.) The amount and type of planning you need to do depends on how involved you've been in managing your family's financial life, whether you have a good credit history in your own name, and whether you have maintained a career outside your home during your marriage. See Chapter 3 for advice about evaluating your family's finances.

If your spouse totally surprises you with plans for a divorce, predivorce planning may be impossible, especially if you're clueless about your family's finances. If that's the case, your divorce teaches you a painful lesson: That not being an informed and active partner in your family's financial life is risky because you're at an immediate disadvantage if your marriage ends (or if you become widowed).

Ideally, before your divorce begins, you will have

- **Built a good credit history in your own name.** In other words, all or most of your credit should not be *joint credit* — that is, credit that you share with your spouse. Without a solid credit history of your own, you will have a difficult time qualifying for credit that has affordable terms after your divorce. You may even have a difficult time qualifying for certain kinds of jobs or promotions because some employers check your credit history or credit score as part of their decision-making process. You may also have a difficult time renting a nice place to live because some landlords review their potential tenants' credit histories or scores as part of their screening process. Finally, without good credit, you may not be able to obtain adequate insurance.

- **Cleaned up your credit history if the one you built in your own name was full of negatives.** To improve your credit history, make all future credit payments on time, don't go over your credit limits, and don't take on new debt. Within a matter of months, your credit history should begin to improve.

- **Begun to update your job skills or to develop new ones if you've been a stay-at-home parent or a full-time homemaker during your marriage.** In today's economy, having the right job skills is critical to being competitive in the job market. You may have to return to school to get the skills that you need.

- **Considered taking a part-time or full-time job while you're married.** By taking a job while you're married, you can begin adding recent work experience to your resume and begin building some professional relationships that may help you after you're out of your marriage.

- **Gotten the information you need about financial issues.** If you know next to nothing about money matters or feel that you need a refresher course, take a basic class in personal finance at your local college or university or through some other resource. Having the right money-related information and skills is essential to negotiating the financial aspects of your divorce and to managing your money wisely after you're on your own.

✔ **Created a written inventory of all your family's assets and assigned an approximate value to each one.** Going into a divorce, a complete record of everything you and your spouse own is essential so that you know what assets you have to divide between the two of you. Without a record, you may overlook an asset and not get all that you're entitled to in your divorce. When compiling your list, don't worry about items of little value; instead, focus on financially significant assets like bank accounts, real estate, stocks, antiques, and so on.

When valuing each asset on your inventory, write down its *market value* — what the asset is worth now, meaning what someone would pay for it if you were selling it right now. Market value isn't what you or your spouse paid for the asset when you first purchased it.

✔ **Inventoried all your family's debts.** Your inventory should note the name of each of your creditors and how much you owe each one. Creating an inventory of all your marital debts is just as important as inventorying all your marital assets because you have to divvy up those debts during your divorce negotiations, too.

✔ **Located all the ownership papers for your assets.** These documents include

- Deeds to property
- Titles to vehicles
- Documentation for stocks, bonds, mutual funds, and other investments
- Life insurance policies
- Estate-planning documents that you and your spouse prepared
- Information about your respective retirement plans

You need these documents for two reasons. First, you need them to help determine the value of the assets that you and your spouse are dividing between yourselves. Second, after you've divided everything, you need the documents so that you can properly transfer the titles to you or your spouse, depending on who gets what. Without the titles to the assets you're taking away from your marriage being transferred to you, you will not be their legal owner.

✔ **Obtained copies of important documents.** Have on hand documents such as your family's tax returns for the past five years and your real estate tax bills for the most current year. Also obtain a record of all your bank accounts — the accounts that you and your spouse share as well as your individual accounts — including the types of accounts, the financial institutions where the accounts are located, and the account numbers.

✔ **Have begun thinking about your postdivorce financial needs.** Start figuring out how much money and which other assets you will need to live a financially secure life after your marriage ends. Consider what trade-offs you're willing to make with your spouse to ensure that your needs are met.

Making It Official

Before your divorce can begin, you must take care of some preliminary divorce matters. For example, you must make certain that you meet the divorce requirements of the state where you want to get divorced. Also, you or your divorce attorney must file legal paperwork with the court to officially set your divorce in motion and you must decide whether you will file a no-fault or fault divorce, assuming fault divorces are permitted in the state where you're divorcing.

If you don't want to live with your spouse anymore, but you don't want to get divorced, either, you and your spouse can *separate.* You can separate temporarily while you decide what to do about your relationship or you can make your separation permanent and finalize it with a *legal separation agreement,* which addresses the same kind of issues you would address in a divorce. We discuss the pros and cons of separation in Chapter 4.

Meeting the requirements

To get a divorce, you must meet certain minimum requirements set by your state. Although those requirements vary somewhat from state to state, the most common ones are

✔ **Residing in your state for a certain period of time.** A handful of states have no residency requirement — your obvious destination for a "quickie divorce" — but most states require that one or both of you be a resident for a minimum amount of time before you can file a petition for divorce or before your divorce can be granted. Six months is the most common residency requirement, but some states' requirements are weeks, months, or even a year. Some counties have their own residency requirements.

✔ **Getting divorced in the state where you live.** You must get divorced in the state you call your permanent home — and not in the state where you got married.

✔ **Being separated.** Before you can get a no-fault divorce, some states require that you live apart from your spouse for a certain period of time — six months to a year in most of these states, but as long as two to three years in some states. The theory behind this requirement is that you and your spouse may have a change of heart and reconcile. See Chapter 4 for information about legalizing a formal separation.

Filing a divorce petition

No matter what state you live in and regardless of whether you and your spouse agree that ending your marriage is for the best, your divorce officially begins when one of you files a divorce petition with the court in your area. If you and your spouse have already hired divorce attorneys, one of the attorneys files the divorce *petition*. (See the later section in this chapter, "Involving a divorce attorney," as well as Chapters 13 and 14, for more information about working with a divorce attorney.) Otherwise, one of you can go to your local courthouse and file a divorce petition yourself.

After someone files a divorce petition, the nonfiling spouse is legally notified about the petition, which usually involves a sheriff or constable hand-delivering the notice, or the nonfiling spouse receiving the notice in the mail. If the nonfiling spouse disagrees with anything in the petition, such as the grounds for the divorce, the request by the filing spouse for sole custody of the couple's children, and so on, he or she will file an *answer* with the court, stating his or her side of those issues.

Deciding whether to file a fault divorce

Depending on the state you live in, if you initiated your divorce, you must decide whether to file a fault or a no-fault divorce. As of this writing, about 70 percent of all states allow couples to get either an old-fashioned fault divorce or a no-fault divorce, which is a kinder, simpler type of divorce.

When you file a *fault divorce,* you must provide a very specific reason, or *grounds,* for wanting to end your marriage. In other words, you must accuse your spouse of some sort of unacceptable behavior, such as adultery, physical abuse, mental cruelty, drunkenness, drug addiction, or insanity. Depending on your state, you may also be able to get a fault divorce if your spouse has been in prison for a minimum period of time or has deserted your marriage.

When you allege fault, you must also prove that the grounds actually exist. Proving fault may involve having a friend or relative who witnessed your spouse's bad behavior testify to it, hiring a detective to document your spouse's bad behavior on video, or something else. Although a fault divorce can provide the grist for a lurid soap opera, some spouses feel that the drama is worth it because if they can prove that what they allege about their partner is true, they may be able to get a better divorce settlement.

Breaking up can be hard to do for same-sex married couples

Many married gay couples face a mountain of hurdles when their relationships go south and they decide to divorce. For example, some of them have difficulty finding attorneys to represent them who understand how to apply existing laws to the issues in their divorce. Also, because divorce-related laws aren't always clear when it comes to same-sex marriages, it's not unusual for married gay couples to have to resolve some of the issues in their divorce through litigation rather than negotiation.

Massachusetts has allowed homosexuals to marry since 2004, and California began allowing same-sex marriages in 2008 (but in November of that year, voters in the state passed Proposition 8, which rescinded the right of same-sex partners to marry). Same-sex spouses who married in Massachusetts or California but reside in one of the 43 states where the law doesn't recognize their marriage or where the law is silent on the issue of same-sex marriages face other hurdles when their marriages hit the skids. Because their state of residence doesn't recognize their marriage, they must get divorced in the state where they were married, which means that they must meet that other state's divorce requirements, including living in the state for a certain period of time. (The residency requirement in Massachusetts is one year; in California it's six months.) This requirement poses economic not to mention logistical problems for many same sex couples who want to end their marriages. In fact, some of these couples have had to stay married. Others have taken legal action to try to force their home states to let them divorce there. To date, the results have been mixed, with a Rhode Island court prohibiting a lesbian couple who married in Massachusetts from divorcing in Rhode Island and a New York State court allowing a lesbian couple who married in Canada to divorce in New York. That ruling was the first of its kind.

Currently, all states recognize some form of *no-fault divorce*. If you opt for this kind of divorce, you don't have to prove that your spouse did anything to cause you to seek a divorce. Instead, all you really need to do is acknowledge that things "just didn't work out" between the two of you. Common grounds for obtaining a no-fault divorce include "incompatibility," "irretrievable breakdown," or "irreconcilable differences." Because you don't need to prove fault, this kind of divorce is usually less expensive, quicker to complete, and easier on spouses and their children than most fault divorces. As a result, no-fault divorces are much more frequent than fault divorces.

Fault used to play a major role in decisions about spousal support (or alimony), but many states no longer consider that factor. About half the states consider fault when dividing up a couple's property. In those states, fault has an impact on the final details of a couple's divorce, including the amount the spouse who's *not* at fault eventually receives in the divorce settlement. To find out whether your state permits fault divorces, call your local or state bar association or a divorce attorney in your area.

Peering Into the Divorce Process

Although the ultimate goal of every divorce is to end a marriage, divorcing couples achieve that goal by heading down one of three paths. For example, some spouses work together to define the terms of their divorce because they want the process to be as quick, easy, and inexpensive as possible. They may or may not hire attorneys to help them. Other couples are unable or unwilling to cooperate with one another and as a result, their divorce goes down a path that is characterized by conflict, anger, and a big price tag. The most difficult path a divorce can go down is the one that ends with a divorce trial. This kind of divorce is emotionally draining, time consuming, and very expensive.

If you and your spouse have been married for a very brief amount of time, have no young children from your relationship, and have amassed little or no marital property and debt, your state may have an abbreviated divorce process for which you qualify. To find out whether your state has such a process and the criteria you must meet to use it, contact your state or local bar association or a family law attorney.

Deciding which path to take

Just which path your divorce takes is up to you and your spouse. Your basic options include

- ✔ A cooperative divorce
- ✔ An uncooperative divorce
- ✔ A courtroom divorce

Sometimes a divorce that begins amicably can turn nasty and difficult. For example, initially you and your spouse may try to work out the terms of your divorce together on a friendly basis, but then one of you may become upset and the two of you stop trying to cooperate with one another. If this happens in your divorce and you and your spouse are working with attorneys, they may eventually succeed in negotiating a divorce agreement that the two of you are willing to live with; however, if your emotions are running high and you and your spouse are unwilling to compromise on one or more issues, your divorce may head to court, although the majority of divorces — even extremely contentious ones — get settled outside of court eventually. The following sections describe each divorce path in greater detail.

A cooperative divorce

A *cooperative divorce* is easiest on your pocketbook, your emotions, and on your young children. In this type of divorce, you or your spouse file a no-fault divorce petition, and the two of you work out the terms of your divorce together. (Chapter 12 provides negotiating tips.) When you've decided everything, one of you files your final divorce decree. You can also achieve a cooperative divorce if you both hire attorneys to help with the negotiations but stay committed to keeping things friendly. (You and your spouse cannot share an attorney. You both need your own.)

One way to have a cooperative divorce is to end your marriage by using the *collaborative divorce process*. This process is a relatively new option for divorcing couples, and it's not currently available in all states. We provide an explanation of the collaborative divorce process later in this chapter.

After you and your spouse have a divorce agreement that both parties feel is fair (with or without the help of attorneys), the spouse who initiated your divorce by filing a divorce petition, or one of your attorneys if you're working with attorneys, files the agreement with the court. The spouse who initiated the divorce may have to make a brief court appearance. Soon after, your divorce becomes official. From start to finish, a cooperative divorce happens relatively quickly because you and your spouse work together toward the same goal and as a result, your divorce involves less bureaucratic red tape, fewer legal procedures, and less paperwork.

An uncooperative divorce

An *uncooperative divorce* occurs when you and your spouse can't agree on all the key issues in your divorce. For example, you want sole custody of your kids, but your spouse wants to share custody. Or you want to keep the house but your spouse wants to sell it. Usually the only chance spouses involved in this kind of divorce have to end their marriage is to hire attorneys to handle the negotiations and the legal paperwork for them. An uncooperative divorce tends to take longer than a cooperative divorce, costs a whole lot more, especially if it leads to a trial, and is harder on everyone's emotions.

You may be able to avoid a trial by resolving your differences through a dispute-resolution technique such as *mediation* (discussed in Chapter 15). In fact, in many states, you will not be able to get a court date until you have tried mediation.

A courtroom divorce

A *courtroom divorce* (see Chapter 16) is an extreme version of an uncooperative divorce and tends to be much more contentious, emotional, time-consuming, and expensive than a divorce decided outside of court because it involves a lot more legal paperwork and red tape and much more of your attorney's time. Your divorce goes to court when you and your spouse are unable to resolve all the terms of your divorce; either a family law judge or a jury decides how to handle all the outstanding issues.

Although taking your divorce to court may be unavoidable in your situation, it's risky because no matter how much time a judge or jury spends trying to understand your marriage, they can never have a complete grasp of its intricacies, the needs of your children, and so on. Also, although we like to think that all judges (and juries) decide legal issues with unbiased minds, the truth is that sometimes their own prejudices, preferences, and real-life experiences color their decisions. For example, maybe the judge's daughter is a single, divorced mom who struggles to make ends meet because her ex-spouse doesn't meet his support obligations, or maybe the judge has recently gone through a divorce and feels like he or she was "taken to the cleaners." As a result, neither you nor your spouse may be happy with the outcome of your trial. In fact, research shows that spouses who resolve the issues in their divorce through a trial are less likely to be happy with the final outcome of their divorce and less committed to making the terms of their divorce work than couples who work out the details of their divorce outside of court.

A courtroom divorce can exhaust you emotionally and financially, and it can create so much animosity between you and your spouse that years pass before it abates. If you and your spouse have young children together, this animosity can be a serious problem because your anger toward one another may seriously harm their short- and long-term emotional well-being. Also, don't forget that if you both want to be actively involved in their lives after your divorce, you will run into one another at their after-school games, recitals, graduations, weddings, and so on. The last thing you want is for your estrangement with your ex-spouse to overshadow or color the important events in your children's lives.

If your divorce ends with a trial, you're more apt to revisit the final terms of your divorce in your lawyer's offices and in court. Doing so not only takes money and time, but it also means that you never really put your divorce and your failed marriage behind you. Also, you can appeal the court's decision in your divorce, but appeals are hard to win. Plus, appealing means spending more money on an attorney and then, if you win your appeal, more money on a new trial. Also, a new trial may unleash emotions that you thought you had come to terms with. No one wins when you have to litigate your divorce, so do your best to settle without a trial. Sometimes swallowing your pride and giving up a little during your divorce negotiations is the wisest thing to do.

Involving a divorce attorney

When most people think of getting divorced, they automatically assume that they need a divorce attorney's guidance from start to finish. That's the way people have handled divorce traditionally, and for many people, working hand in hand with an attorney is usually best. But you have other options, although it's almost always a good idea to consult an attorney at various stages throughout the divorce process.

Hiring a CDP to help negotiate the financial stuff

A certified divorce planner (CDP) analyzes your family's finances and helps you develop a specific plan for resolving the financial issues in your divorce, such as property settlement, spousal support, and how much child support one spouse may pay the other above and beyond the minimum amount set by your state's child support guidelines. Also, the CDP may help you figure out a way to pay for your children's college educations, their summer camp, and other expenses that go beyond child support by taking into account your earnings potential, age, lifestyle needs, and so on. A good CDP considers not only what's best for you in the immediate years after your divorce but also your financial needs in 5, 10, and 15 years.

You and your spouse can hire a CDP together if your divorce is amicable and you're both committed to working out an agreement that's fair, or you can each hire your own. For more information about how a planner can help you and for a referral to one in your area, contact the Institute for Divorce Financial Analysts, a national organization that certifies divorce planners. You can call the Institute at 800-875-1760 or visit its Web site at www.institute dfa.com.

For example, you and your spouse may negotiate all the terms of your divorce and draft a divorce agreement with the help of Chapter 12, not attorneys. If you decide to do all the negotiating yourselves, it's a good idea for each of you to meet with a divorce attorney before you begin in order to get briefed on the divorce-related laws of your state and advised about the particular issues that relate to your divorce. After you and your spouse work out your divorce agreement, the attorneys should review your draft to make sure that you haven't overlooked anything important, that your interests are protected, and that you haven't unwittingly created the potential for future problems.

If you and your spouse can hardly stand being in the same room with each other or if you don't trust one another, you need attorneys to negotiate the details of your divorce agreement from start to finish and to prepare your final agreement. Similarly, if you're afraid of your spouse, have a hard time asserting yourself, or are unsure of your ability to negotiate a good settlement for yourself, don't go it alone — let an attorney handle your divorce. (See Chapter 13 for more information about hiring a helpful divorce attorney.)

If you want specific help working out the financial aspects of your divorce but don't want to pay attorney-level prices for the assistance, you can consider hiring a *certified divorce planner* (CDP), who's a CPA or a certified financial planner who specializes in helping couples resolve the financial aspects of their divorces. A CDP will help you not only get the best settlement possible under the circumstances but will also recommend how to manage and invest the assets you end up with in your divorce so you can maximize your return on their value in the future. A CDP isn't a substitute for an attorney but is another player on your divorce team. In fact, CDPs and divorce attorneys often work hand in hand, especially when a couple owns a substantial amount of assets. Read the "Hiring a CDP to help you negotiate the financial stuff" sidebar in this chapter to find out more about the services that a CDP offers.

Exploring alternative ways to reach an agreement

Hiring attorneys to do the negotiating for you or turning your divorce over to a judge aren't the only ways to end up with a divorce agreement if you and your spouse don't want to do the negotiating on your own or if you're deadlocked on certain issues. Depending on the circumstances, you can also use mediation or the collaborative law process. Both options emphasize working things out in a civil manner and using and finding mutually acceptable solutions to the issues in your divorce.

Getting to "yes" with mediation

When you and your spouse just can't see eye to eye on some of the issues in your divorce, mediation may be able to help you move forward. Mediation relies on a trained facilitator, who may be a family law attorney, a marriage and family counselor, a psychologist, or someone else with knowledge of and understanding of the divorce laws in your state and of the ins and outs of the issues that must be resolved in a divorce. The facilitator helps create a safe environment for you and your spouse to discuss the sticky issues in your divorce, makes it easier for you to hear what the other is saying, and tries to keep your negotiations moving forward. The facilitator doesn't take sides or tell you or your spouse how to decide the issues in your divorce; instead, the facilitator helps you and your spouse identify solutions to the issues you're struggling with.

If you and your spouse are already working with attorneys but have reached a stalemate on certain issues, your attorneys may suggest giving mediation a try because it tends to be less stressful than a trial and a lot less expensive. If your mediation efforts are successful, the mediator puts everything you agreed to in writing and sends a copy to your attorney so he or she can review it. If mediation doesn't work, you and your spouse go back to the drawing board and continue working with your attorneys to figure out a resolution to your differences. You can also go to court and let a judge decide. Chapter 15 provides more information on mediation.

Capitalizing on the collaborative law process

The *collaborative law process* is a relatively new cooperative divorce option spouses can use to work out the terms of their divorce outside of court. This highly structured, future-focused process was the brainchild of an attorney who was worn out by the adversarial nature of litigated divorces and wanted to find an easier way for attorneys to help their clients come to an agreement about the terms of their divorce. Texas was the first state to legalize the collaborative law process; presently, attorneys in nearly every state in the union who practice collaborative law.

Several aspects of the collaborative divorce process distinguish it from a traditional divorce. For example

- A divorce petition might not be filed with the court until after the couple has negotiated a final divorce agreement.

- Both spouses and their attorneys must sign a participation agreement before the divorce process can get underway. The agreement spells out the ground rules that all of them abide by during the process. Among other things, they commit to

  - Not involving the court. In fact, as part of the participation agreement, both attorneys pledge that if the collaborative process fails, they will withdraw from the case.

  - Freely sharing with one another all information related to the divorce. No one can withhold anything.

  - Treating one another with respect and courtesy through the divorce process.

  - Negotiating in good faith.

  - Keeping confidential everything about their negotiations.

  - Allowing both parents to maintain loving, involved relationships with their minor children postdivorce because doing so is in the children's best interest.

The collaborative law process employs a team approach. Rather than you and your spouse each hiring your own attorneys and adopting an adversarial *you-versus-me* approach to resolving the terms of your divorce, which tends to happen in most divorces, spouses and their attorneys are on the same team in a collaborative divorce. In fact, at a series of divorce settlement meetings, or team meetings, you and your spouse sit together at the same table and work out the details of your divorce together, using mutual understanding, problem-solving, and negotiation.

Although your attorneys will have been trained in the collaborative law process and will be by your sides at each meeting, they won't do the negotiating for you. That's not to say that your attorneys won't be active members of your team. But unlike a traditional divorce where attorneys take the lead in a couple's negotiations, they play supporting roles in a collaborative divorce, helping you and your spouse identify all the issues that must be resolved before your divorce can be final, helping you brainstorm possible options for deciding each issue, answering any questions you may have, and so on.

Before the start of your negotiations, you and your spouse will meet one-on-one with your respective attorneys at least once. Your attorneys will help you understand exactly how the process works and prepare you to actively participate in it; they will also have regular meetings with each of you one-on-one before and after each team meeting.

Other professionals are likely to be part of your team, to actively participate in your divorce negotiations and communicate regularly with your attorneys. These include

✔ Financial professionals. In many cases, the spouses hire a neutral financial professional to help inventory and value their marital assets and debts and figure out the best way to divide everything, prepare postdivorce budgets, suggest creative ways to resolve financial sticky issues, help each spouse plan for his or her financial future, and so on.

✔ Divorce coaches. In some states, each spouse may also hire a *divorce coach* (a mental health professional who has been trained in the collaborative divorce process). This person helps clients handle any emotional issues that may arise and interfere with their ability to negotiate effectively, communicate effectively with the other members of the divorce team, provides emotional support throughout the process, refer them to another mental health professional for ongoing counseling if necessary, and works with everyone on the team to brainstorm solutions to the issues in the couple's divorce.

✔ In other states, couples can agree to hire one divorce coach who works with both of them on a neutral basis. In some states, these neutral professionals may also help divorcing couples with minor children prepare a written parenting plan. The plan spells out how much time each of you will spend with your children, your individual and shared rights and responsibilities in regard to them, and how you will share expenses associated with your children, among other issues.

✔ Child specialists. When couples don't share a divorce coach, they may hire a neutral *child specialist* to be part of their team. This person helps ensure that the couple makes decisions that are in their children's best interest and assists in the preparation of a parenting plan.

If the collaborative process breaks down, your attorneys may suggest that you and your spouse try mediation. But because collaborative law attorneys have pledged not to take a divorce case to trial, if you refuse mediation or if you give mediation a try and it doesn't work, and you decide that your only option is to go to trial, your attorneys withdraw from your case. In that instance, you and your spouse have to hire new attorneys, which means that your divorce is back at square one.

The collaborative law process offers some important benefits compared to a traditional divorce:

- ✔ It tends to be less stressful for everyone involved.

- ✔ It's more apt to yield creative, "outside the box" solutions to the issues in your divorce — solutions that would not occur if you and your spouse let your attorneys work out the terms of your divorce or if you took your divorce to court.

- ✔ It encourages cooperation between you and your spouse and helps build a positive foundation from which to build a postdivorce relationship, which is especially important if you have young children together.

- ✔ It may cost less than a traditional divorce — especially one that ends in court.

- ✔ It's usually a faster way to reach an agreement on the terms of a divorce.

Assuming that your state recognizes the collaborative law process, you can find an attorney who uses this method by contacting your local or state bar association or by going online to find out whether your state has a collaborative law institute. If it does, the institute may provide referrals.

Understanding the Basic Issues in a Divorce

Regardless of which kind of divorce you pursue and which path your divorce goes down, you must resolve certain issues before your divorce can be final. (If you get a legal separation before you divorce, you must work out these same issues; see Chapter 4.) The basic issues are

- ✔ **How you will divide up your marital property and debts (see Chapter 8):** Complex laws, including state property laws, federal tax laws, plus the numerous interpretations of those laws, can make deciding who gets what a complicated undertaking, especially if you and your spouse have managed to amass considerable assets. If you have debt from your marriage, you and your spouse must also decide how the debts will get paid. You may decide, for example, to sell some of your marital assets and pay off debts with the proceeds, or one of you may agree to assume all or most of the debt in exchange for more assets.

- ✔ **Whether one spouse will pay spousal support (or alimony) to the other (see Chapter 9):** If one of you will pay spousal support, you must also decide how much the support payments will be and how long they will continue. These days, a spouse rarely receives spousal support for life or until he or she remarries. Usually if spousal support is paid, the payments continue long enough to let the spouse acquire some job skills or to rebuild his or her career.

✓ **How you and your spouse will handle child custody, visitation, and child support if you and your spouse have minor children from your marriage (see Chapters 10 and 11):** Decisions related to custody and visitation are some of the most contentious and emotional in a divorce, especially when couples try to use their children as a means of getting back at one another. Although how much one spouse will have to pay the other in child support can also be a highly emotional issue, state child-support guidelines dictate the minimum amount of payment.

When deciding the issues in your divorce, certain state laws and guidelines provide a framework for your decision-making. In most instances however, these laws and guidelines also allow a considerable amount of flexibility in your decision-making, though they have some limits. When making decisions about the terms of your divorce, assuming that a family law judge is looking over your shoulder is best. What we mean is that whatever you decide should be fair to you and your spouse given the laws of your state and should reflect an appreciation of what a judge would probably decide if your divorce was to end in a trial.

So What's All This Going to Cost?

Almost as soon as your divorce begins, one thing will become painfully clear: that divorce is all about dollars and cents. In fact, the thousands of dollars you probably spent on your wedding and honeymoon may be a mere drop in the bucket compared with what your divorce could end up costing you.

Ordinarily, both parties in a divorce pay their own legal and court costs; however, you can request that your spouse reimburse you for all or a portion of your divorce-related expenses. It never hurts to ask, especially if you feel you have a strong argument for why your spouse should pay. For example, your spouse makes a lot more money than you do or your marriage is ending because your spouse was unfaithful. Whether your spouse agrees to pay your legal and court costs depends on how amicable your divorce is, his or her own financial resources, and whether your spouse thinks your request is reasonable, among other things.

The deciding factors for cost

Exactly how much you spend to end your marriage depends on a number of factors:

✓ **Whether your divorce is amicable and cooperative or bitter and contentious:** The more you and your spouse agree on, the less you have to spend on attorneys, legal fees, and court costs.

✔ **The cost of the attorney you hire to help with your divorce:** Chapter 13 reviews the key factors that influence how much you will spend on an attorney.

✔ **How many divorce decisions you and your spouse are able to work out together without the involvement of your attorneys:** The more issues in your divorce you can resolve without your attorneys' help, the less your divorce will cost.

✔ **Whether you and your spouse end up in a custody battle, which can be very expensive:** For example, in a custody battle, you may have to pay for the assistance of a social worker, a child psychologist, and other experts.

✔ **The amount and complexity of marital property and debts that you have to divide up:** Depending on the debts and assets involved, you may need to hire a real estate appraiser, art appraiser, CPA, pension expert, or other professionals to help determine a fair property settlement.

✔ **Whether you believe that your spouse is hiding any of your marital assets:** If you believe that your spouse is hiding assets, you will have to hire financial experts to try to determine what has happened to them, and that help doesn't come cheap.

✔ **Whether you and your spouse are willing to settle your divorce outside of court or whether one or both of you is determined to go to trial:** If you end up in divorce court, you can expect to pay substantially more to your attorney, not to mention the fees of any experts you may call to testify on your behalf, court fees, and a whole lot more.

✔ **The legal strategy of your attorney and your spouse's attorney:** If either of your attorneys employs an aggressive, adversarial strategy, the cost of your divorce is apt to skyrocket because your divorce will take up more of your attorney's time. Your attorney also is likely to file more legal motions and call more expert witnesses to testify, which adds more onto the price tag of your divorce. However, you and your spouse can control the strategy that your respective attorneys use by carefully screening potential attorneys to find ones who aren't attack dogs.

The least it will cost

If your divorce is extremely simple — you and your spouse have little to negotiate, no minor children, no marital property, few debts, neither of you is asking for spousal support, and you're both willing to complete most, if not all, of the legal paperwork yourselves — you can get divorced for just a few hundred dollars, maybe even less if you don't use an attorney.

Even if you own some marital property or have some debt from your marriage, your divorce may cost you no more than a few thousand dollars if you and your spouse can work out the terms of your divorce together after an upfront consultation with your individual attorneys. Your attorneys should also review your final agreement. Chapter 12 provides helpful information if you and your spouse want to do most of your negotiating.

The most it will cost

Be prepared to spend a whole lot of money on your divorce if you and your spouse fight like cats and dogs, are unwilling to give and take, or if the issues in your divorce are complicated and the active involvement of your attorneys from start to finish is essential. In this case, you may be looking at legal bills in the five figures — or even more. For example, at the end of a prolonged child-support battle, your legal bills can easily be $50,000 because your divorce will involve a lot of fact-finding, which causes your legal bills to skyrocket. If you and your spouse end up in court over the custody of your children, those bills can *triple!* Yikes!

The hourly rate of an experienced family law attorney ranges from $150 to $750 or more. If you hire an attorney, you have to pay a down payment, sometimes called a *retainer,* that's likely to be between $500 and $10,000, depending on the attorney's hourly rate.

Surviving the Emotional Roller Coaster

Even if you know that getting divorced is the right thing for you and everyone else involved and even if your divorce is amicable, you will almost inevitably experience a range of emotions as you move through the divorce process, including shock, disappointment, regret, sadness, anger, depression, and fear, among other feelings. This mix of emotions should come as no surprise given that for better or worse you're ending an important relationship in your life (see Chapter 7).

Having an idea of what's ahead and putting an emotional support system in place can help you get through the tough times you're likely to experience. Your support system may include trusted friends and/or close relatives, your religious advisor, and a mental health professional.

Consulting a therapist as soon as you know that you're getting a divorce (if not before) is a good idea; the therapist can provide you with ongoing emotional support and advice. Alternatively, you may want to consult a therapist only when you're having a particularly difficult time with a specific problem.

Controlling your emotions so you can stay on an even emotional keel is critical when you're going through a divorce. If you don't keep your emotions under control, making wise decisions about matters that can affect your financial well-being and happiness and that of your children for years to come can become difficult. Although letting your emotions take over and allowing yourself to express your anger and to say hurtful things to your spouse or trying to extract revenge from him or her because your marriage is ending may be tempting, in the end, that approach is apt to backfire and likely to hurt everyone involved, not just your spouse.

In addition to establishing a support system and getting therapy, here are some other things you can do to help yourself stay emotionally balanced before, during, and after your divorce:

- ✔ Keep a journal
- ✔ Exercise
- ✔ Take up meditation
- ✔ Begin practicing yoga
- ✔ Pursue a hobby you enjoy

Divorce can be hard on kids, too. Don't directly involve your children in your divorce — for instance, by fighting about the terms of your divorce with your spouse in front of them, by bad-mouthing your spouse to them, and so on. And don't involve them indirectly, either, by crying in front of them, by not doing the things that you've always done for your children while the terms of your divorce are being negotiated, and so on.

Although your divorce will certainly affect your children, your responsibility is to protect them as much as possible, to keep their lives as normal as you can, not to scare them, and to reassure them that you and their other parent will continue to love them after your divorce and that you and their other parent will continue to be involved in their lives. You do a grave injustice to your children if you don't give them the sense of security that every child needs, especially when his or her family life is falling apart and if you don't stay actively involved in their lives despite the distractions of your divorce. Doing everything you can to shield them from the emotions that you're feeling is critical.

Despite your best efforts to protect your children, they may begin to experience emotional problems during and after your divorce. Exactly how they express their problems depends on their ages and individual personalities; problems can range from bedwetting and temper tantrums to depression, problems in school, defiant behavior at home, among other behaviors. If you're unsure how to respond to your child, read some books about children and divorce, talk to your child's teacher or counselor, or consult a mental health professional. You may also want to consider scheduling time for your child with a child therapist. For more details on how to help your children cope with your divorce, see Chapters 6 and 21.

Chapter 2

Avoiding a Divorce

· ·

· ·

Marriages rarely die overnight. Almost always, they die little by little over time. Ideally, if serious problems begin to develop in your marriage, you and your spouse can work through them before they harm your relationship so that you can stay together. However, if you and your spouse are unable to resolve your differences, or if you don't even want to try to save your marriage, you must decide what to do about your relationship. Although divorce is the option that many couples pursue when their marriage falls apart, it isn't the only option. Some couples decide to stay married despite their troubles — maybe until their kids move out of the house — whereas others separate rather than divorce or, under certain conditions, have their marriages annulled.

When you have marriage problems, the sooner you acknowledge them and decide what to do about them, the better. Pretending that the problems don't exist doesn't make them go away. In fact, they will more than likely grow worse. Furthermore, if a divorce or legal separation is in the cards, the sooner you acknowledge that your marriage is on the rocks, the better prepared you'll be for what's to come, both emotionally and financially.

This chapter highlights the nondivorce options that you have for dealing with your relationship problems. Just knowing that you have choices can be reassuring and helpful. This chapter also addresses steps you can take if the pressures in your troubled relationship cause your spouse to turn violent, because it isn't uncommon for violence to accompany serious marital problems.

The Old-fashioned Alternative: Sticking It Out

The pressure (whether societal, religious, or economic) to stay married used to be so great that when a couple's marriage failed, divorce was almost inconceivable, no matter how miserable the couple may have been. Although times and attitudes about marriage have changed, many of today's couples also opt to stay married after their relationships have failed. They may have young children and feel that raising them in a two-parent household is important, or they may not be able to afford to get a divorce right away. Some couples experience implicit or explicit pressures from their family, friends, or church to stay together, whereas other couples come to an understanding that allows them to lead separate lives but remain under the same roof. Finally, some couples don't divorce because they're afraid of what life will be like if they were single again; fear of the unknown may motivate them to tolerate a situation that would be unbearable to others.

If you decide to stay in your marriage, you have two basic options: You can try to improve your relationship or you can grit your teeth, shut down your feelings, and grin and bear it by putting up with things the way they are. The first alternative is almost always the better choice. Three options for improving your marriage include taking a short break from one another, getting marriage counseling, and trying mediation, all of which we discuss in the following sections. None of these alternatives are mutually exclusive, so you may want to give each of them a try.

If your home is full of tension and anger because of your marital problems, you may be doing your children more harm than good by staying together. Also, if your spouse threatens to physically harm you or has already harmed you or your children, at the very least, separate and give your spouse an opportunity to get professional help. If you're fearful that leaving may trigger violent behavior in your spouse, contact your local domestic abuse shelter or the National Domestic Violence Hotline (800-799-7233; if you're hearing impaired, call 800-787-3224) for help in developing a safety plan. The end of this chapter provides additional advice for protecting yourself from a violent spouse.

Taking a short break from each other

Sometimes what you really need when you just can't get along with your spouse and your emotions are running high is a short time apart — a day or two, a month, maybe even a vacation on your own. At the end of your time apart, you may have a whole new attitude toward your relationship and a renewed commitment to it.

Use the time apart to calm your emotions, assess your situation, and put your marital problems in perspective:

- ✔ Try to assess why you and your spouse aren't getting along and your role in your difficulties.

- ✔ Analyze the kind of arguments you've been having — what you tend to argue about, whether certain issues seem to trigger your arguments, and when you tend to argue — to determine whether any patterns emerge.

- ✔ Think about whether your marital problems stem from the fact that you and your spouse have grown apart and/or whether they exist because of things one of you did to the other that caused you to lose trust in the other, to feel hurt or misunderstood.

- ✔ Ask yourself whether your problems developed because you stopped giving your spouse enough attention and affection or vice versa.

- ✔ Think about the complaints you have both voiced about the other and try to decide whether they're truly valid.

- ✔ Try to identify the changes that you'd need to make to save your marriage and the changes you would want your spouse to make. Then think about whether the two of you are capable of making those changes and also willing to make them.

Don't use your time apart to go on shopping sprees or to just have fun by going out at night and spending time with friends. Also, avoid short romantic flings, and don't try to forget your troubles by using drugs or alcohol. If you spend your time away from your spouse with a close friend or family member, choose that person carefully. If you want advice from this person, he or she should be someone who is impartial and has good judgment, so avoid anyone who dislikes your spouse or resents your marriage.

Spending even a short period of time apart when your marriage is floundering can give both of you an opportunity to clear your heads and examine how you feel about one another and your relationship. You may both conclude that you're committed to your marriage and want to save it. On the other hand, when you're away from the emotional stresses and strains of living together, one or both of you may decide that you want to make living apart a permanent thing.

Getting marriage counseling

Saving your marriage may require more than taking a break from one another. (If only it were that easy!) The two of you may need to work with a marriage counselor.

Couples helping couples save their marriages

Some couples with troubled marriages find it helpful to work with another married couple who has been trained to help strengthen floundering marriages. The Association for Couples in Marriage Enrichment (ACME), an international, nonprofit, nonsectarian organization, runs such a marriage enrichment program. Go to ACME's Web site (www.better marriages.org) or call ACME at 800-634-8325 to find out more about the organization and its marriage program and to locate a local chapter in your area.

Another option is Marriage Enrichment, Inc., a nondenominational, nonprofit Christian organization, that sponsors workshops intended to improve communication between spouses. The workshops are conducted in cooperation with local churches and other organizations. To find out more about Marriage Enrichment or to contact the organization, go to www.gbgm-umc.org/me-incoh/welcome.

The right counselor creates an environment that promotes honest discussion and mutual understanding so that you and your spouse can have a productive dialogue about what has gone wrong in your relationship, why, and what you can do to improve things. The counselor can also offer insights into your problems and even teach you new marriage skills. For example, you may need to learn new ways of relating to one another. Also, if one of you was unfaithful to the other or did something else that damaged the trust you used to have in one another, you may need help rebuilding your lost trust. However, when your marriage is in serious trouble, your emotions may run so high that a calm, rational discussion about the roots of your marital problems and what to do about them can be next to impossible.

If you decide to consult a marriage counselor, choose your counselor carefully. Although nearly all states require marriage counselors to be licensed, licensing standards for education and experience vary by state. Therefore, just because a counselor is licensed by your state, don't assume that he or she has the experience and training necessary to help you make sense of your marriage and decide what to do about the relationship. See the "Finding a qualified marriage counselor" sidebar for advice on locating a good counselor.

 If money is an issue for you, check your local phone book to see whether a Family and Child Services, Inc., office is nearby. This nonprofit organization offers counseling on a sliding-fee scale for couples, families, and individuals. You may also want to consider getting marriage counseling from your religious advisor.

If your spouse won't go with you to talk to a marriage counselor or a religious advisor, go by yourself. You may discover things about yourself as well as new relationship skills that can improve your current marriage or prepare you for a happier marriage in the future.

Finding a qualified marriage counselor

Choosing a marriage counselor is a very personal decision because you and your spouse will be sharing intimate and emotionally painful details about your relationship with this person. The right counselor can help save your marriage or, at the very least, save you and your spouse months or even years of anguish trying to decide what to do about the problems in your relationship.

We offer you the following tips for locating a qualified marriage therapist:

✔ Look for a marriage counselor or family therapist who's a member of the American Association for Marriage and Family Therapy (AAMFT). For counselors and therapists to become members of AAMFT, they must complete a rigorous training program. For the names and phone numbers of the AAMFT members in your area, call the association directly (703-838-9808), go to the association's Web site at www.

aamft.org, or look in the Yellow Pages of your local phone book under "Marriage Counselors" or "Therapists."

✔ Get a referral from a friend or family member you trust.

✔ To make sure that your medical insurance covers your counseling, ask your insurer for a list of the counselors who are preferred service providers.

After you have narrowed your list to a few potential counselors, schedule a get-acquainted meeting with each one. At these meetings, find out how long each counselor has been practicing marriage or family therapy, what courses he or she has taken in that field, and what professional licenses or certifications he or she has. Also, take note of whether the counselor makes you feel comfortable and whether you think you can open up to that person.

Your spouse's unwillingness to go to marriage counseling sessions may signal that he or she is no longer committed to your marriage, or simply doesn't believe in marriage counseling. Try to talk with your spouse about why he or she won't get counseling and if there are any circumstances under which your spouse would talk with a counselor or religious advisor about your marriage. If your spouse is adamant about not getting counseling and offers no good alternatives, it's probably time to face facts and acknowledge that your marriage is over.

Looking into mediation

Mediation involves working with a trained mediator who helps you and your spouse work together to identify mutually acceptable solutions to your problems. The mediator doesn't take sides, interject opinions, or solve your problems for you. Instead, during mediation, you and your spouse each have an opportunity to express your opinions and to explain your side of the issues in your marriage. When one of you is talking, the other is expected to listen without interrupting and to stay calm and focused. If your mediation session (or sessions) is successful, you and your spouse may end up with a written contract that spells out what you agreed on and the new terms of your relationship. (Chapter 15 discusses mediation in more detail.)

Mediation has a couple of advantages. First, it can be a good way to address very specific problems that are playing havoc with your marriage, like arguments over who should do which household chores, how to share child-care responsibilities, or what to do with your money. However, mediation is *not* appropriate if your marriage has a host of problems or if your problems are emotionally complex.

Another important advantage of mediation is its low cost. It's relatively inexpensive and considerably cheaper than getting a divorce.

But mediation isn't a substitute for therapy. In fact, you may need to spend some time in therapy by yourself or with your spouse before you can use mediation successfully. Therapy can help you get a handle on any emotions you are feeling that might make it impossible for you to use mediation — like feeling angry with your spouse or wanting revenge for something your spouse said or did to you.

Mediation is about mutual understanding, cooperation, and problem-solving; it's not about winning. But like the tango, mediation takes two. So, if one of you is unwilling to give mediation a try, it's not a viable option for trying to save your marriage.

To find a mediator who's experienced in helping couples resolve marriage-related issues, look in the business pages of your local phone book under "Mediation" or contact the Association for Conflict Resolution, which can provide you with information about mediating marital problems and refer you to family mediators in your area. Call the association at 202-464-9700 or go to www.acrnet.org to browse its mediator referral list. The names on the list have met the association's standards, which include at least two years of family mediation experience and a minimum of 60 hours of family mediation training, 20 hours of continued training each year, and two hours of domestic violence awareness training.

When Living Apart Is a Better Option

Living together while you try to resolve your marital differences and save your marriage may be an unrealistic option for some people. Instead, you may decide to separate for a while. You may also choose to separate permanently with no intention of divorcing. (Chapter 4 discusses separations in detail, including the legal issues and financial considerations you should bear in mind before you separate.)

Separating can provide you with an opportunity to find out what living alone is really like. Meanwhile, the door is still open for you and your spouse to get back together if you both decide that that's what you want to do. On the other hand, separation can be a prelude to divorce or a permanent alternative to divorce.

Before you separate for even a relatively short period of time, protect yourself by talking with a family law attorney, especially if you want spousal or child support. In addition, the attorney can warn you about anything that you can do that may jeopardize your standing in a divorce if your marriage ends. For example, dating others while you're separated usually isn't a good idea because you may leave yourself open to charges of adultery.

You can opt for either of two types of separation — an *informal separation* or a *legal separation.*

   ✔ Couples who separate informally simply begin living apart. This option may be appropriate if you and your spouse clearly anticipate that your separation is temporary and that you'll eventually reconcile.

   ✔ If you view your separation as the first step toward a divorce and have no plans for reconciliation or you intend to live apart without any plans to divorce, then a legal separation formalized with a legally binding separation agreement is best. A legal separation can be a court-approved arrangement or one that you and your spouse agree to in writing.

   In some states, if you and your spouse decide to divorce, depending on the grounds for your divorce, you may have to live apart from one another for a certain period of time first, usually from six months to a year.

A legal separation is often preferable for the following financial and legal reasons:

   ✔ You formalize the terms of your separation, including whether one of you will help support the other financially while you're living apart; how you will handle custody, visitation, and child support if you and your spouse share minor children; and how you will divide up the property that you own together as well as your joint debts.

   ✔ Having everything spelled out minimizes the potential for conflict while you're separated.

   ✔ If one of you reneges on the terms of your separation agreement, it's easier to get the court's help enforcing the terms of your separation.

   ✔ You and your spouse will have fewer issues to resolve if you eventually decide to get a divorce.

While you're married and going through a divorce, even if you're separated, you and your spouse can either file joint tax returns or individual returns. You and your spouse should talk to a CPA about which option is best and what to do about any deductions you may be eligible for.

If divorce isn't an option for you because of religious, financial, or even health insurance considerations, you can opt for a permanent legal separation, depending on your state. A legal separation means that you're still married, but you're no longer living together. If you decide to legally separate, formalizing your new living arrangement with a written separation agreement is important.

Like a divorce agreement, a separation agreement addresses the division of your marital property, child custody, child support, and spousal support, as appropriate. The process for preparing such an agreement is similar to what you'd do if you were getting divorced. For example, you and your spouse can work together to negotiate the terms of your separation or you can both hire divorce attorneys to help you negotiate the agreement and if necessary to represent you before the court if you are unable to work out all the terms of your separation.

If you and your spouse resolve the terms of your separation together without the help of attorneys, it's best to file an order with the court for the judge to sign. The order sets out all the terms of your separation. Then, if your spouse fails to do what he or she agreed to do in your separation agreement, you can go to court to get the agreement enforced. Court enforcement is especially important if your separation agreement provides you with spousal support and/or child support. In some states a separation agreement must be court ordered.

Getting a Legal Annulment

A legal *annulment* is a court action that voids your marriage and proclaims that it was never legally valid in the first place. It's like the marriage never happened. Annulments were much more common when getting divorced had more of a social stigma attached to it.

Legal annulments are available in most states, but the process for obtaining one varies. You must meet all the criteria established by your state to prove to the court that your marriage is not legally valid.

The most common criteria for a legal annulment include the following:

- ✔ Your spouse lied to you or misled you in some way and, had you known the truth, you would not have gotten married. For example, you want a family, but your spouse never told you that he is impotent, or your spouse never told you that he or she had a criminal record or has a sexually transmitted disease.

- ✔ You and your spouse never consummated your marriage.

- ✔ At the time of your marriage, your spouse was already married.

- ✔ Your spouse was not a legal adult when you got married.

- ✔ You were forced into marriage.

- ✔ Either or both of you were under the influence of alcohol or drugs at the time of the marriage.

An annulment voids your marriage but, if you have young children from that relationship, it doesn't change your parental responsibilities to your children in any way.

Some couples seek a religious annulment in addition to or instead of a legal annulment because they want to remarry in their church and can't do so without such a religious annulment. This particular kind of annulment is most commonly associated with the Roman Catholic Church. If you get a religious annulment, you don't have a legal annulment, and vice versa.

There is a specific process you must follow in order to get a religious annulment in the Catholic Church. Although the details of the annulment process vary somewhat from Catholic diocese to diocese, you can obtain general information about the process at www.idotaketwo.com. For detailed information, talk with your parish priest.

Chapter 3

Getting Your Finances in Order

*N*o matter your sex, age, or personal situation, preparing not only for the possibility that your marriage may end in divorce (in recent years between about 40 percent and 50 percent of them do), but also for the potential financial consequences of ending your marriage, makes sense. At a minimum, your preparation should include

✔ Familiarizing yourself with your family's finances

✔ Learning how to manage your money

✔ Building and maintaining a positive credit history in your own name

✔ Building and maintaining marketable job skills

If you aren't up to speed on your family's financial situation or if your credit history or job skills are lacking, this chapter can help. If you think that a divorce may be in your future, the sooner you act on the advice in this chapter, the better prepared you'll be, both financially and legally, for life on your own.

Taking care of yourself when it comes to your finances isn't selfish. Doing so helps you gain the confidence and the resources — both inner and financial — you need in order to look out for yourself (and your kids) if your marriage ends. And if you and your spouse end up staying married, becoming more financially savvy can help strengthen your relationship by making the two of you more equal financial partners. Another benefit of increasing your financial know-how is that if your spouse becomes too ill to manage your finances or passes away, your finances won't suffer as they would if you were clueless about them.

Getting Smart about Your Family's Finances

Relying on your spouse to pay your household bills, to reconcile your checkbook, to make investment decisions, and so forth isn't a good idea. At the very least, you should know

- How much money comes into your household every month and how much goes out

- Who you owe money to and the total amount of each debt

- Your monthly living expenses

- How much money is in your checking and your savings accounts

- What sources of cash are available for you and your spouse in the event of an emergency

- What assets you and your spouse own, including any life insurance policies and retirement accounts you have

- Where your money is invested

- The passwords and user names for any accounts that your spouse manages online

If you review this list of financial-ought-to-knows and come up lacking, don't panic. You can find out most of what you need to know about your family's finances in several ways.

If you and your spouse have an amicable relationship despite the fact that you are divorcing, ask him or her to sit down and explain your family's finances to you. Also ask your spouse to show you where key documents and other important records are kept and have him or her answer your questions.

If you and your spouse are no longer on speaking terms, becoming fully informed about your family's finances may be somewhat of a challenge. If you know where your family's financial records are located and you have access to them, make copies of that information. Also, talk with your family's financial advisors if you know who they are. They may include a CPA, a banker, an insurance broker, and a financial advisor and/or broker. And don't overlook information stored on your home computer; many families use personal finance software to help manage their money.

If you're able to locate little or none of your family's financial information, you will probably need a divorce attorney to help you obtain it using the discovery process (a process for obtaining information in a lawsuit). Chapter 16 describes how this process works.

Taking inventory

Taking inventory of your family's financial situation, including what you own and what you owe, gives you a good idea of your overall state of financial well-being. The upcoming section "And now for a quick lesson in marital property law," explains how the law in your state treats the assets you and your spouse acquired during your marriage. That law will also help determine how those assets will be divided up between the two of you in your divorce.

What you own

You don't have to be a CPA or a math whiz to figure out your family's financial worth. Use a notebook or your computer to list the following financial information:

- ✔ Your total household income and the sources of that income.

- ✔ The checking and savings account numbers that you, your spouse, or the both of you use.

- ✔ Your family's significant assets. An *asset* is a thing of value, such as cash, real estate, vehicles, or stocks. Depending on the type of assets you have, you can use them to purchase something, sell them, or use them as collateral to secure a loan. To help figure your family's financial worth, estimate the market value of each asset. *Market value* is what an asset is worth now — what you could sell it for, not what you bought it for. Assets can be tangible (like your car and house) or intangible (like stocks and mutual funds) and may include

  - Brokerage accounts, including stocks, bonds, and mutual funds

  - Business interests

  - Cash in the bank (savings and checking accounts) and in your money market accounts

  - Certificates of deposit (CDs)

  - Deferred compensation plans, including IRAs, SEPs, 401(k)s, stock options, and profit-sharing plans

  - Fine art, antiques, and other collectibles

  - Fine jewelry

  - Household furnishings

  - The cash value of your life insurance policy

  - Vehicles (including cars, motorcycles, and recreational vehicles, such as boats, jet skis, and snowmobiles)

  - Your home and other real estate

You should know whether your state is a community property state or an equitable distribution state when it comes to dividing up your marital property — the assets from your marriage. We describe the distinctions in the upcoming section "And now for a quick lesson in marital property law."

To make certain that your inventory list is comprehensive, look through your home safe and bank safe-deposit box for titles to property, deeds, securities, wills, or other documents related to your ownership of property. If possible, check out any financial records your spouse may maintain online. Also, if you and your spouse have applied for any loans recently, the loan applications should provide much, if not all, of the asset information that you need.

What you owe

Until you inventory and value your household debts, your family's financial portrait is only half-finished. Your debts may include:

- ✔ Credit card debts
- ✔ Home equity loans or balances on home equity lines of credit
- ✔ Mortgages
- ✔ Notes you or your spouse may have cosigned
- ✔ Other types of personal loans, including car loans, student loans, and business loans for which you or your spouse are personally liable

Next to each debt, note whether it's *secured* or *unsecured.* If a debt is secured, write down which of your assets secures the debt. An asset that secures a debt is referred to as collateral. For example, your home secures or collateralizes your mortgage and your car is the collateral for your vehicle loan. When one of your debts is secured, the creditor is entitled to take your collateral if you don't pay the debt according to the terms of your loan agreement. For example, if you fall behind on your mortgage, the lender is legally entitled to *foreclose* on your home, or take it from you.

The documents you need

In order to create as complete and accurate an inventory of your assets and debts as possible, you need to refer to a variety of financial and legal documents in addition to your checking and savings account registers and bank statements. (If you do not receive printed statements from your bank anymore, call the bank to order copies of these statements.) Those documents include

- ✔ Copies of your tax returns for the past five years.

If you don't know where your family's tax returns are filed and your spouse won't tell you, you can obtain copies by writing the IRS, assuming that you filed joint returns. The IRS has a Web site where you can download federal tax forms and publications, check on the status of your tax refund, and find out how to contact the IRS Taxpayer

Assistance Center nearest you. Check out www.irs.ustreas.gov. Your family's CPA should also be able to provide you with copies of your tax returns, assuming that he or she prepared your tax returns.

✔ Real estate tax bills.

✔ Copies of all life insurance policies that list you or your spouse as the policy owner or a primary or contingent beneficiary of the policy.

✔ Account statements for your stocks, bonds, mutual funds, and other investments.

✔ Copies of any financial statements you prepared separately or together when you applied for a loan.

✔ A copy of your will, your spouse's will, and any other estate-planning documents that you may have prepared, such as a living trust agreement.

✔ Profit-and-loss statements and balance sheets for the business that you, your spouse, or both of you own and copies of related partnership agreements or articles of incorporation.

✔ Copies of any prenuptial or postnuptial agreements you may have signed.

If you hire an attorney to help negotiate your divorce, your attorney needs all this information. The more you and your spouse willingly share with your respective attorneys, the less information the attorneys must obtain through the formal discovery process — and the more money you save. (We tell you about discovery in Chapters 14 and 16.) Making copies of all the documents you pull together on your own is a good idea, just in case your spouse takes the originals.

Other things you should know about your family's finances

Besides all the financial information this chapter has already indicated that you should have, you still need some other information before you can claim to be fully informed about your family's finances and ready for whatever may happen to your marriage. That other information includes

✔ Which of your family's bills are regularly paid online and the user name and password for each account.

✔ What your Equifax, Experian, and TransUnion credit histories say about you and your spouse. These three national companies dominate the credit-reporting industry in the United States. The "Building a Positive Credit History" section, later in this chapter, tells you how to order copies of your credit history from each company.

- ✔ Your three FICO scores represent how good a job you do at managing your credit. You find out about them later in this chapter.

- ✔ The names, street addresses, e-mail addresses, and phone numbers of your family's CPA, banker, attorney, financial advisor, and stockbroker.

- ✔ Where financial and legal documents important to your family are stored, including bank records; tax returns; wills and other estate-planning documents; titles and deeds; loan agreements; insurance policies; documentation pertaining to any IRAs, stocks, bonds, and mutual funds that you or your spouse may own; and the paperwork related to your and your spouse's retirement plans.

And now for a quick lesson in marital property law

When you get divorced, your state's marital property laws entitle you and your spouse to a share of the assets that you acquired together or separately during your marriage and to a share of the income that you both earned while you were married. Together those assets and income make up your *marital property*. Exactly how your marital property eventually gets divided depends, in part, on whether you live in an equitable distribution state or a community property state. We distinguish between these two types in the following sections.

Share and share alike

If you live in a *community property* state, each of you owns an undivided half interest in the value of your marital property, regardless of whether your income alone purchased most of what you own, whether your spouse made significantly more than you did, or whether your spouse stayed home to care for your young children throughout your marriage. However, you and your spouse can agree to something different. Also, if the court gets involved in the division of your assets, a judge (or jury) can order that you receive more or less than your half interest. (See the next section "Everything is relative when it comes to fairness.")

Most states are equitable distribution states, except for the following nine community property states:

Arizona
California
Idaho
Louisiana
Nevada

New Mexico
Texas
Washington
Wisconsin

If you live in a community property state, a creditor has the right to collect from your share of your marital property if your spouse fails to pay on the debts that he or she acquired during your marriage.

Everything is relative when it comes to fairness

Equitable distribution states use the concept of "what is fair" to decide how a couple's marital property and debts should be divided between them when they get divorced. "What is fair" varies from divorce to divorce, although each equitable distribution state uses certain criteria to guide the division of a couple's assets. The most common criteria include:

- How much each of you earns and could earn in the future

- Your current standard of living

- The value of the separate property each of you may own and the value of your marital property

- The contribution each of you made to your marriage (by the way, being a full-time homemaker or stay-at-home parent has financial value)

- The employee benefits to which each of you may be entitled

- The length of your marriage

- Your age and health

- Whether you have children from your marriage who are *minors* (children under the age of 18 or 21, depending on the state you live in) and your custody arrangements for those children

If you and your spouse are doing your own negotiating, you don't have to take into account whether your state is a community property or an equitable distribution state when you divide up your marital assets. Instead, you can divvy up your assets however you want, as long as both of you are happy with the final result.

Factors that may influence the division of your marital property

A variety of factors may come into play if you and your spouse hire attorneys to negotiate your property settlement agreement or if the court decides how your assets will be divided between the two of you.

The exact factors that apply to your divorce may depend on whether you live in a community property or an equitable distribution state. Here are a few of the factors that may apply:

- If your divorce is a fault divorce, the courts in some states consider that fact when deciding how your marital property and debt will be split between you and your spouse. For example, they may penalize the spouse who is at fault by giving him or her less of the marital assets than he or she would otherwise be entitled to.

Courts in community property states may use these same factors in determining whether divorcing spouses should leave their marriage with more or less than their presumptive half share of their marital property.

✔ If you and your spouse acquire property while living in a community property state and then move to an equitable distribution state, the property you take with you from the first state to the second is considered community property and is treated as such in your divorce. The opposite is true if you move from an equitable distribution state to a community property state. Obviously, the more often you move among equitable distribution and community property states during your marriage and the more assets you acquire in each of those states, the more complicated negotiating your property settlement agreement is if you divorce.

✔ In some equitable distribution states, a spouse's contribution to the end of a marriage plays a role in determining how a couple's marital property is divided between them. For example, if your marriage ended because you committed adultery, the court may give you less marital property than you're entitled to according to your state's property law.

✔ Community and equitable distribution states do not consider inheritances and gifts a spouse received during marriage to be marital property. It's that spouse's separate property. The same is also true for any property a spouse brings to a marriage. How a court treats a personal injury cash settlement in a divorce depends on the state; some view the money as separate property and others don't.

✔ If you *commingle* property (meaning that you mix your separate property with your spouse's or you mix your separate property with marital property), you can unwittingly convert your separate property to marital property. For example, you and your spouse open a joint bank account and you deposit your separate funds into the account. You've now commingled your funds.

Managing your financial future

Many low-cost and even no-cost sources of information and help are available if you want to improve your financial skills and know-how so that you can become a more confident and competent money manager. In this section, we highlight some of those resources.

Money management and personal investment classes are a good resource for increasing your financial skills and knowledge. Your local college or university may offer such classes for little cost. Also, many investment companies and financial advisors offer investment seminars as a way to attract new clients or to develop additional business from their current clients. These seminars are usually free, and you don't have to purchase anything if you attend. However, sometimes these advisors assume that their audience has a better-than-average knowledge of investing, not to mention better-than-average money to invest.

Another possible source of financial education is a nonprofit credit counseling office that's affiliated with the National Foundation for Credit Counseling (NFCC), most of which are known as a Consumer Credit Counseling Service (CCCS). These organizations offer low-cost to no-cost money management classes, including classes on how to develop and use a budget. If you don't find a listing for a CCCS office in your local phone directory, go to the NFCC's Web site (www.nfcc.org) or call 800-388-2227 for the name and contact information for the NFCC-affiliated credit counseling agency nearest you.

If you can't find a financial education class that fits your needs, ask your family banker, CPA, broker, or financial advisor for a referral to a class.

Here are further sources for financial information:

- ✔ Magazines such as *Money* and *Kiplinger's Personal Finance Magazine* offer solid, easy-to-understand financial information and advice on a wide variety of consumer-related subjects. Although you won't become another Warren Buffett just by reading an issue or two, over time, you can increase your consumer IQ about subjects like choosing a bank card, buying stocks and mutual funds, living on a budget, buying a car, purchasing real estate, and avoiding consumer scams.

- ✔ Bookstores are another financial education resource. Their shelves are overflowing with books about personal finance and investing. Even if you're a financial neophyte, you can find many books written for people just like you. We don't mean to be self-serving, but *Personal Finance For Dummies,* 4th Edition, by Eric Tyson (Wiley) and *Managing Debt For Dummies*, by *yours truly* (Wiley) are two darn good books.

- ✔ You can also find a good bit of money-management information and advice on television. For example, every network morning show features periodic segment on personal finance topics, and CNN and CNBC also devote airtime to personal finance and investment topics.

- ✔ If you prefer getting your financial education by staring at a computer screen rather than a TV, many excellent Web sites offer information on personal finance issues. Here are a few great sites you can check out:

  - • **Bankrate.com:** This site offers a wide variety of information on nearly every aspect of financial management, from choosing a credit card, paying down debt, buying a home, and getting a mortgage to information on insurance, investing, taxes, and much more. Subscribe to Bankrate.com's free online newsletter to discover something new about personal finance every week.

- **Credit.com:** Looking for easy-to-understand information and advice about money, credit, and loans? Then this site is for you. When you visit, check out Creditbloggers.com and sign up for "Tidbits," Credit.com's free monthly email newsletter.

- **MoneyCentral.msn.com:** At this site, you can read stories about the main financial news of the day and peruse practical articles about everyday money matters, like banking, credit, insurance, investing, and financial planning, among other things.

Keeping Your Job Skills Up-to-Date

Even though two-income families have become the norm in today's society, many women and a growing number of men choose to be full-time homemakers and stay-at-home parents for at least some time during their marriage. If you're one of them, be aware that in today's fast-changing work world, your job skills can quickly become rusty or even obsolete and that while you're staying at home, you may lose many of your professional contacts unless you make a real effort to maintain them.

If your job skills need some refreshing or if you've never worked outside the home, as soon as you begin to think that a divorce is in your future, take immediate steps to update your job skills and/or to develop new ones. Trade schools in your area as well as nearby private or community colleges and universities are all potential sources of training and education. Some of them may even offer you the opportunity to earn a degree or a certification online. (See Chapter 17 for more on these training grounds.)

At the very least, learn how to use a computer if you aren't already computer literate, and become familiar with the most popular software programs. Although different industry sectors and types of businesses vary in terms of the specific software programs their employees use, some of the most popular ones are Word, Excel, PowerPoint, and QuickBooks. If you can't make it to computer classes, check out *For Dummies* books on these popular programs. For other advice how to make the transition from being a stay-at-home parent to being gainfully employed in the work world, check out the Quintessential Careers guide at `www.quintcareers.com/stay-at-home-parents_careers.html`.

Getting a part-time job is another option for building new job skills, honing old ones, and developing a network of professional contacts. A part-time job also helps you build a resume. Plus, the money you earn can fund a checking or savings account in your own name. You may need that money to help pay a divorce attorney and to pay your bills if you and your spouse separate. You may even be able to work part-time from your home.

Get smart about your education options

If you're worried about your lack of job skills and are eager to increase your employability by getting additional education, you may decide to attend a trade school in your area or an online university. Although many of these educational opportunities are legitimate, watch out for bad apples, like:

✔ **Trade schools that overpromise the marketability of the job they train you for or the amount of money you can make in the job.** Also be alert for schools that overstate the credentials of their teachers or the quality of their facilities and equipment. For guidance on how to choose a reputable trade school, read the Federal Trade Commission's free brochure, "Choosing a Career or Vocational School," at the FTC's Web site, www.ftc.gov/bcp/consumer.

✔ **Distance-learning universities that are nothing more than frauds.** Many of these phony "universities" advertise in legitimate publications, have very impressive-looking Web sites, and claim to be accredited. Don't be duped. All that window dressing is calculated to convince you that you're dealing with a legitimate institution of higher learning. However, if you enroll in one of these schools, you get nothing in return or, at best, you get an extremely poor education that has a limited value in the work world.

Also steer clear of diploma mills. These bogus universities sell phony degrees. For extra money, you can even purchase a fake diploma stating that you graduated summa cum laude!

However, if you purchase one of these degrees and use it to get a job, you commit a fraud and can be criminally prosecuted if your scheme is found out.

Here are some sure signs that you're dealing with a phony university or diploma mill:

✔ Having a Visa or MasterCard is the only admissions requirement.

✔ The "university" claims to be unaccredited or is accredited not by the Council on Higher Education Accreditation (CHEA) but by some phony accrediting organization. You can find out whether or not a university is CHEA-accredited at www.chea.org.

✔ The university's name is similar to a university you are familiar with, but when you check more carefully, you discover that its name is slightly different from the legitimate educational institution. Many bogus universities choose names that are almost identical to legitimate schools in order to dupe unsuspecting consumers.

✔ You're instructed to fax or e-mail your resume to the university so it can review your experience and issue you a diploma based on that information alone.

✔ You can obtain your degree in just a month or so.

✔ When you visit the Better Business Bureau's Web site (www.bbb.org) you find numerous complaints about the university.

Beware of work-at-home schemes that promise you the opportunity to earn big bucks. You may have to pay a bundle upfront to purchase the supplies and equipment you need to take advantage of the "opportunity," and in return you may get nothing despite the marketer's promise of training, software, manuals, and so on. Furthermore, it's unlikely that you'll ever recoup your investment. Some work-at-home scams promise to provide you with technical training and a job in exchange for money upfront. Of course, after you've paid the money you get neither. Before you take advantage of any work-at-home offer, protect yourself by getting the details of the offer in writing and by getting all your questions answered. If the company making the offer refuses to send you written information or never provides the information or if it gives you vague answers to your questions, don't do business with it. Also, check out the company with your local Better Business Bureau (www.bbb.org), the consumer protection office of your state attorney general (www.naag.org), and the Federal Trade Commission (877-382-4357 or online at www.ftc.gov).

Being prepared to enter the work world as quickly as possible has assumed greater importance now that lifelong spousal support has virtually become a thing of the past. The more quickly you can land a good job after your divorce and earn a good living, the better off you'll be.

Building a Positive Credit History

Your *credit history* is a record of how you manage the credit accounts that are in your name or that you share with your spouse (called *joint credit*). Credit accounts may include credit cards, mortgages and other bank loans, debit cards, lines of credit, and so on. Having good credit in your own name (not just joint credit) is essential to being prepared for the possibility of divorce. In this section, we tell you why.

Your credit history

Whenever you apply for new or additional credit, a creditor reviews your credit history to make sure it doesn't contain a lot of negative information about your past use of credit, such as late payments, accounts turned over to collections, defaults, tax liens, or bankruptcy. Creditors get your credit history information from the three national credit reporting agencies, each of whom probably maintains a credit history on you in their vast computer databases: Equifax, Experian (formerly TRW), and TransUnion. If you have negative information in your credit history — you've paid your accounts late, you've exceeded your credit limits and/or you've had an account cancelled, for example — or if the creditor believes that you have too much credit relative to your income, the creditor may deny your application or give you credit at less favorable terms than it would have had your credit history been stellar.

Creditors aren't the only people who check out your credit history in order to make decisions about you. Many employers, landlords, and insurance companies also review consumers' credit histories. Here are some of the most important reasons to have good credit in your own name:

✔ If you get divorced and have a poor credit history in your own name, obtaining a bank loan or a credit card, purchasing a home, renting a place to live, renting a car, and even getting the insurance or job you need is apt to be a challenge. Although you can build a solid credit history in your own name after your divorce, the process will probably take you about two years.

✔ If, prior to your divorce, you or your spouse closed all your joint accounts and you later tell those creditors that you'd like credit with them in your own name, they can require you to reapply for the credit if your joint accounts were based on your spouse's income. If you don't already have a positive credit history with accounts in your name only, the credit company may turn you down for the credit you want or approve you for that credit, but at a high interest rate.

✔ When you and your spouse share joint credit, both of you are legally responsible for those accounts. That means that if your spouse misManages the credit you share, your credit history as well as your spouse's is damaged. However, if you have good credit in your own name, it can help counteract the bad effects of the joint credit your spouse has misManaged. The more individual credit you have, the better off you are.

Credit scores count

A *credit score* is a number derived from the information in your credit history, and it measures how well you've managed credit in the past and how well you're likely to manage it in the future. Most credit scores range from 300 to 850. The higher your score, the better.

More and more, creditors, insurance companies, employers, and landlords are checking consumers' credit scores to make decisions about them rather than reviewing their credit histories. For example, they may review a consumer's credit score to decide whether to give him or her new or additional credit, insure the consumer, offer the consumer a new job or promotion, and so on.

The *FICO score* is the gold standard for credit scores and the one that most businesses use. You actually have three FICO scores, with each one based on the information in one of your three credit histories — your Equifax, Experian, or your TransUnion credit histories. You can order all three of your FICO scores by going to the Fair Isaac Corporation's Web site, www.myfico. com. The site also offers information about the various factors that affect your FICO scores as well as advice about what you can do to raise yours.

Choosing the right credit card

All credit cards aren't alike. Their terms of credit — interest rates, grace periods, late fees, and so on — vary. So, when you're in the market for a credit card, shop for one with the terms of credit that best meet your needs, depending on how you intend to use the card. Also, be aware that certain credit card features may seem attractive but, in fact, may cost you more than a card that doesn't have those features. When you're shopping for a good deal on a credit card, follow these guidelines:

✔ If you plan to pay your full credit card balance each month, go for a card that offers you a grace period of at least 25 days. (A *grace period* is the time you have to pay the card balance before the company charges you interest.)

✔ If you expect to carry a balance on your credit card sometimes, look for a card that has a low annual percentage rate (APR). Also pay attention to how the company applies that APR to calculate your monthly balance, because some balance calculation methods cost a lot more than others.

Most companies use the *average daily balance including new purchases* method; that method works out better for them than it does for you. The most consumer-friendly balance calculation method is the *adjusted daily balance method* because you end up paying the least money in interest. The *average daily balance not including purchases* method is second best. Steer clear of cards that use the *two-cycle average daily balance method* because they cost you a bundle in finance charges. Credit card companies must include their balance calculation method in their card offers' fine print.

✔ Don't automatically go for the card with the highest credit limit. Using a credit card to pay for a major purchase is an expensive financial alternative. You're better off saving up for what you want to buy or getting a bank loan. Also, having a high credit limit can jeopardize your opportunity to obtain an important loan for other credit in the future.

✔ Don't be tempted by credit card offers touting special benefits, such as product rebates, frequent flier miles, and so on. To take advantage of these offers, you probably have to charge a lot on the credit card first, and some cards with added benefits tack on high APRs, a short grace period, or other unfavorable terms of credit.

✔ Avoid cards with a high annual fee or an annual fee that escalates after a certain period of time. Also, be aware of what other fees a card may have, including a late fee, an over-your-limit fee, a fee for every time you use your card (called a *transaction fee*), cash advance fees, and so on. The more fees a card has, the more it costs you to use it.

✔ Be cautious of credit card offers with especially low interest rates. The low rates may do nothing more than get you to agree to begin using the card or to transfer the balance on another card to the new card. Frequently, the low rate lasts for only a short period. When that period ends, the credit card company may charge you a much higher rate of interest.

✔ Steer clear of cards that increase the annual rate you pay if you're late with your payment or if you exceed your credit limit.

To obtain up-to-date, unbiased information about the best deals on credit cards, visit www.cardratings.com, www.cardtrak.com, or www.bankrate.com.

The three national credit reporting agencies also generate and sell their own consumer credit scores. However, although the credit score you can purchase at the Equifax Web site is actually a FICO score, the scores being sold at the Experian and TransUnion Web sites are not. They are *educational* credit scores not predictive scores like the FICO scores are, and therefore, they're not widely used by businesses. So if you are going to purchase your credit scores, buy the ones that really count when it comes to getting credit, buying insurance, getting a good job and renting a place to live — your FICO scores.

When you order your three FICO scores, you'll probably discover that each one is a different number. Mainly that's because the information in your three credit reports is slightly different and those differences affect your scores.

Establishing a credit history of your own

Before you begin the credit-history building process, request a copy of your credit report from each of the three national credit reporting agencies (listed in the previous section of this chapter). Review each of them so that you're familiar with their information and know whether the information is accurate. Also, make certain that each of your credit histories includes all your credit accounts — any accounts you may have in your own name and any joint credit accounts with positive histories that you and your spouse share.

If you find any problems in your credit reports, correct the problem by initiating an investigation with the credit-reporting agency that produced the report. Information about how to begin an investigation should come with your credit report. You can also initiate an investigation with the organization that reported the information to the credit reporting agency.

Knowing what's in your spouse's credit report is a good idea, too; if you live in a community property state your finances are legally intertwined with your spouse's. For example, if your spouse incurs individual debts and does not pay them, your spouse's creditor can come after your share of your marital property to collect money. However, to obtain your spouse's credit report, he or she has to agree to let you order it, and that's unlikely if there is a lot of animosity between the two of you or if your spouse has anything to hide. For example, he or she may be using credit to pay for an asset you know nothing about. However, your credit reports alone provide you with information on most of your joint debts as well as your individual ones. They just don't tell you about your spouse's individual or separate debts.

The Credit Repair Handbook, by John Ventura (Kaplan Publishing) and *The Ultimate Credit Handbook*, 2nd Edition, by Gerri Detweiler (Plume) are two good resources for understanding how to interpret the information in your credit reports, how to correct credit record problems, how to rebuild your credit history after financial trouble, and how to build a credit history in your name if all your credit is joint credit.

Requesting your credit reports from the three national credit bureaus

The federal Fair and Accurate Credit Transactions Act (FACTA) entitles you to a free annual copy of your credit report from each of the three national credit bureaus. You can obtain a credit report from each credit reporting agency by

✔ Calling 877-322-8228

✔ Visiting www.annualcredit report.com

✔ Writing to the Annual Credit Report Request Service, P.O. Box 105281, Atlanta, GA 30348-5281

If you order your copies by mail, you must request your free credit reports using a special form, which is available at www.ftc.gov/bcp/conline/include/request-formfinal.pdf. You can order all three credit reports at once or stagger your orders throughout the year.

If you want to purchase additional copies of your credit reports, the current cost in most states is $10. (You may have to pay a sales tax, too.) However, depending on your state, you may be able to obtain one or more additional credit reports each year for free or for less than $10. That deal applies in Colorado, Georgia, Maine, Maryland, Massachusetts, New Jersey, and Vermont.

To order additional copies of your credit reports, you must contact each of the national credit reporting agencies individually by calling or writing to them, or by visiting their Web sites.

Experian
National Consumer Assistance Center
P.O. Box 2104
Allen, TX 75013
888-397-3742
www.experian.com/consumer_online_products

TransUnion
Consumer Disclosure Center
P. O. Box 1000
Chester, PA 19022
800-916-8800
www.transunion.com

Equifax
Disclosure Department
P.O. Box 740241
Atlanta, GA 30374
800-685-1111
www.equifax.com

If you've ever been denied credit, employment, or insurance due in whole or in part to information in your credit report, you're entitled to a free credit report from whichever credit reporting agency provided the information. You are also entitled to a free copy from each of the credit reporting agencies if you believe that you've been the victim of identity theft and you've added a fraud alert to your credit histories as a result; if you are unemployed and intend to apply for a job within the next 60 days; or if you're receiving public assistance payments. Use the preceding contact information to find out how to order your free reports under these circumstances.

If all your credit is in your spouse's name, request that each of the three national credit bureaus establish a credit history in your own name, too (Susan Smith, not Mrs. Robert Smith, for example). If you live in a community property state, also tell each creditor that you want it to begin reporting the payment history on the credit accounts in your spouse's name that you're contractually liable for to the credit reporting agencies it reports to. Ask the creditors to begin reporting information on these accounts in your name as well as your spouse's. Assuming that these accounts have positive payment histories, having them in your credit file may help you build your own credit history.

If you used to have credit in your maiden name, make sure that this credit is a part of your credit history. If it's not, ask that the credit bureau add that information.

If some of the joint accounts in your credit history show late payments or even defaults because of your spouse's mismanagement of those accounts, try to distance yourself from that negative information by preparing a 100-word statement explaining the reason for the negatives. Send the statement to the three national credit bureaus (see the sidebar "Requesting your credit reports from the three national credit bureaus"). The statement you provide becomes a permanent part of your credit record. However, given that creditors, insurance companies, employers, and landlords are increasingly making decisions based on your FICO scores rather than the details of your credit histories, make a copy of any written explanation you may add to your credit history. Then, when you apply to one of these businesses, share your written explanation with the business.

Being an *authorized user* on your spouse's accounts will *not* help you build your own credit history. The reason being that an authorized user means you get to use the credit, but you have no legal responsibility to make payments on the account.

The federal Equal Credit Opportunity Act (ECOA) says that when creditors report information to credit bureaus about joint accounts that were opened prior to June 1, 1977, the information must be reported in both your names. That way, the information is in your credit history as well as your spouse's.

After you clear up any credit record problems and contact the credit bureaus about reporting certain accounts in your name as well as your spouse's, continue the credit-building process by applying for a small ($1,000, for example) *unsecured* bank loan. If you can't get one, apply for a *cash-secured* loan. (If you're approved for an unsecured loan, the bank's only requirement is that you promise to repay what you borrow according to the terms of the loan. But, if you can obtain only a cash-secured loan, the bank requires you to keep a certain amount of cash in a savings account at the bank or to purchase a certificate of deposit [CD] from the bank. If you don't pay off the loan, the bank can take the money in your savings account or your CD as payment.)

If the bank won't loan you money without a cosigner, don't ask your spouse to cosign the note because you end up linking your credit to your spouse's. Ask a relative or close friend to cosign instead.

After you pay off the loan, take a few more steps to secure a good credit history:

- ✔ Order a copy of your credit report from each of the three national credit reporting agencies to make sure that the reports reflect your loan payments. If they don't, ask the bank to report your payment history to the credit bureaus it works with. Next, apply for a MasterCard or a Visa card. But don't charge many purchases on the card, and make all your payments on time.

- ✔ You may have to apply for a second loan that's unsecured or isn't cosigned before you can get a credit card in your own name.

- ✔ If you don't qualify for a regular Visa or MasterCard, apply for a secured card. With a secured card, you have to collateralize, or secure, the card by opening a savings account or by purchasing a CD from the bank issuing the card. If you default on your payments, the bank can withdraw the money from your account or take cash from your CD to cover the charges. Make the secured card a stepping stone to an unsecured card by not exceeding your credit limit and by making all your account payments on time.

Chapter 4

Putting Your Marriage On Hold with a Separation

In This Chapter

▶ Knowing the advantages and disadvantages of separating

▶ Reviewing your separation options

▶ Protecting yourself legally and financially when you separate

▶ Being on good behavior during your separation

▶ Making your marriage work if you and your spouse reconcile

Separation is more than just a matter of living apart from your spouse. It's an important step that has legal, financial, and emotional ramifications, and it requires plenty of advance planning. Separation can be the beginning of the end of your marriage or the start of a better-than-ever union. Either way, don't take the decision to separate casually.

Before you and your spouse separate, you need to fully understand the pros and cons of such a change in your living arrangements. If possible, you and your spouse should also be clear about the direction you anticipate your separation will take you — toward reconciliation or to divorce court. Otherwise, you may be setting yourself up for disappointment and more heartache. But realistically, sometimes the whole reason couples separate is to figure out whether they will continue or end their marriage.

This chapter can help you analyze your reasons for separating and alert you to some potential drawbacks of living apart from your spouse while you're still married. It also explains the steps you should take to protect your legal rights and financial well-being after you separate. If you're using separation as a way to save your marriage, this chapter also provides you with sound advice about what to consider if you and your spouse decide to reconcile.

Weighing the Pros and Cons of Separating

Separation is the equivalent of marital limbo. You no longer live with your spouse, and you may even feel single again, but you're still married. To help you decide whether or not you should separate from your spouse, the following sections highlight the pros and cons of taking that step.

If you're contemplating a separation, consult with a family law attorney first in order to gain a clear understanding of the pros and cons of separating given the laws of your state and the particulars of your situation. If you and your spouse aren't certain that separating is your best move, talking with a marriage counselor, your therapist, or your religious advisor together or individually may help you decide.

Arguments for separating from your spouse

In this section, we list some of the most common advantages of separating from your spouse. The more that apply to you, the stronger your argument may be for a separation.

- ✔ You get to find out what living on your own feels like.

- ✔ You have time to assess your commitment to your marriage, away from the day-to-day stress and responsibilities of the relationship.

- ✔ You have the opportunity to get a grip on your emotions and analyze your marriage from a new and different perspective.

- ✔ You can send your spouse a strong message that things have to change if you're going to stay married. (For example, your spouse has a drug or alcohol problem and has been unwilling to deal with it.)

- ✔ You can give your spouse time to realize that living apart isn't so bad and ease your way toward a final break.

- ✔ Your spouse may miss you so much while you're living apart that divorce stops looking like an answer.

- ✔ You can get a court order for a legal separation and resolve issues such as how child custody, child support, and spousal support will be handled before you and your spouse begin living apart.

Other reasons why you may consider separating include the following:

- ✔ The law in your state requires that you and your spouse live apart for a certain period of time before you get divorced. No separation, no divorce.

- ✔ Even though you anticipate an amicable divorce, it's emotionally impossible for you and your spouse to remain under the same roof.

- ✔ You and your spouse are estranged and can no longer live together.

- ✔ Your spouse has become physically violent, and you're afraid for your safety or your children's safety.

- ✔ You have religious objections to divorce.

The drawbacks of separating

Although separating certainly has its pluses, living apart from your spouse can have its drawbacks, too. Before you agree to separate, determine whether any of the following situations apply to you. If any of them do, decide how important those drawbacks are to you. Also, consult with a family law attorney who's experienced in handling divorces and separations so you are clear about whether moving out could put you at a legal disadvantage if you and your spouse divorce subsequently.

- ✔ Your individual living expenses will increase after you and your spouse separate.

- ✔ If you're the spouse who moves out of the house, your new digs may not be nearly as plush as your family's home.

- ✔ If you view your separation as temporary and anticipate living together again, your children may have a hard time understanding that "Daddy and Mommy are just spending some time apart."

- ✔ Separating may only delay the inevitable. You may be doing nothing more than prolonging the pain of your failed marriage and postponing the process of getting on with your life.

- ✔ If you don't have your own source of income or if your family's income is limited, you may not have enough money to live comfortably apart from your spouse.

- ✔ In some states, if you separate against your spouse's wishes, you may give your spouse grounds for a fault divorce because you can be accused of abandoning your marriage.

✔ If you separate, you can still be held responsible for your spouse's debts and legal problems, even though you're no longer living together. And you can still be treated as a married couple with regard to pensions, life insurance, inheritance, and contractual obligations. However, a carefully worded separation agreement written by a family law attorney can help address these issues.

The attorney files the separation agreement with the court and asks the judge to issue a court order requiring both spouses to live up to everything in the agreement. Keep a copy of the agreement and the court's order in your files because you need those documents if your ex doesn't live up to the terms of the agreement in some way and you have to go back to court to get it enforced.

✔ If you're the one who decides to separate from your spouse, you can be charged with abandoning or deserting your marriage, which may weaken your position in your divorce negotiations and reflect badly on you if your divorce ends up in court. However, a well-worded separation agreement can effectively deal with this potential drawback, too.

State laws related to legal separations vary greatly. In fact, a handful of states don't even recognize legal separations.

✔ If your spouse agrees to pay certain marital debts while you're separated and fails to do so, your creditors may have a legal right to come after both of you for payment if the debts are joint debts, regardless of whether you live in a separate or community property state.

In a community property state, if one spouse agrees to pay certain marital debts and fails to do so, the creditors can try to collect from the other spouse's share of their marital property. Furthermore, if you live in a community property state and your spouse gets into debt while you're separated and doesn't pay the debt, the creditors your spouse owes can try to collect from your share of your marital assets, even if you have a written agreement to the contrary. The value of the agreement is that if you end up paying what your spouse was supposed to pay, you can sue your spouse for reimbursement.

✔ Depending on where you live, your separation can affect what is and isn't marital property. If you separate legally as a prelude to divorce, the property and debts you acquire during your separation may be considered yours and yours alone. If instead you're living apart but not legally separated, the property and debts you acquire during your separation may be considered marital property and debts.

Initiating a Separation

Before you separate, you and your spouse should discuss the reasons for your separation (assuming that you can have a calm and productive conversation) and you should each consult with a family law attorney. Be clear with one another about why you're separating — as a prelude to a divorce, as a last-ditch effort to save your marriage, or to sort things out so you can decide whether you want to try to stay married.

You and your spouse also need to decide whether you will have a legal or an informal separation. An *informal separation* is easy — you just begin living apart. This type of separation is probably all that you need if

- ✔ You and your spouse both earn a good living and can comfortably support yourselves. In other words, you're not asking your spouse to provide you with any money or pay any of your bills while you're separated.

- ✔ You have no minor children from your marriage, so you don't have to worry about child custody or support.

- ✔ You don't share joint accounts or jointly owe a great deal of money.

- ✔ You're confident that your separation will be relatively brief and amicable.

An *informal separation* isn't a good idea if you and your spouse have young children or if one of you wants spousal support, wants to remain on your spouse's health insurance, or has some other important financial issues that you want your spouse to help with while you're separated. It's also not a good option if you and your spouse have an extremely contentious relationship and you're concerned that your spouse won't live up to the understandings you reach regarding the terms of your time apart. In these instances, you need a court-ordered *legal separation agreement* instead, which is a formal, written statement of all the terms that you and your spouse will abide by while you're separated. That way, if your spouse doesn't comply with the terms of the agreement, you can get the court to help force him or her to do so. (In some states, you can obtain a legal separation *only* as a preliminary step to getting a divorce.)

In many states, a *legal separation* begins exactly the same way as an informal separation does — by writing a separation agreement. In these states, the key difference between an informal and a formal separation is that you file the separation agreement with the court.

However, some states require that one spouse initiate a legal separation by filing a *petition* for separation with the family court where that spouse lives. The petition is a legal document that formally asks the court for a legal separation and states what the spouse wants in terms of child custody, child support, spousal support, marital assets, debts, and so on. Filing the petition marks the official beginning of the legal separation process. The spouse who initiates the legal separation can file the petition directly or hire an attorney to do it. After the couple has negotiated the terms of their separation, which may end up being somewhat different from what the spouse who filed the petition asked for in that document, and put them in a written agreement, the agreement is filed with the court.

Even if your state doesn't require that you initiate a legal separation by filing a petition and a formal written separation agreement, it's a good idea for you and your spouse to put the terms of your separation in writing and to file your final agreement with the court. The benefits of doing so are threefold: The process helps you and your spouse get clear about your rights and responsibilities during the period of your time apart; if problems arise after your separation begins, you have your written agreement to refer to; and the court will enforce the terms of your agreement if need be.

A handful of states don't recognize legal separation agreements. Call your local or state bar association or talk to a divorce attorney to find out whether your state is one of them.

Think before you walk! Walking out in a huff definitely makes a strong statement about your feelings toward your spouse and your marriage. But if you stay away from home for an extended period of time (and just what constitutes an "extended" period depends on your state), the court may view your act of bravado as desertion or abandonment, and the spouse you left behind may have the last laugh. If you walk out, you may put yourself in a legally disadvantageous position for working out the terms of your separation or divorce, especially if a family law court decides your case. Furthermore, in some states, you forfeit your legal right to your share of marital assets if you desert your spouse. That's a hefty price to pay for making a dramatic exit.

Traditionally, the spouse who wants the separation is the one who moves out of the couple's home. However, if your spouse wants a divorce and is the primary caregiver of your young children, you should consider moving out instead so that the lives of your children are disrupted as little as possible.

Protecting Yourself When You Separate Informally

If you opt for an informal rather than a formal or legal separation, you still should work out all the terms and ground rules for your separation and commit them to paper. Putting everything in writing provides you with something to refer to if there's any confusion during your separation about exactly what one of you agreed to do or not to do. After you draft your agreement, you and your spouse should each hire your own divorce attorneys to review it. The attorneys can make certain that you didn't overlook anything that should be in your agreement and that the agreement doesn't create the potential for problems between you and your spouse down the road. Your final agreement is dated and you both sign it. Make sure that each of you gets a copy of your final signed agreement.

Ideally, your written agreement identifies any issues that may disrupt the peacefulness of your time apart and determines ahead of time the best ways to deal with those potential conflicts whenever possible. Working out solutions to possible problems in advance minimizes the potential for disagreements and misunderstandings during your separation. If problems do arise, instead of relying on your individual recollections of who promised to do what in order to resolve your differences, you can refer to your written agreement. Plus, you won't have to hammer out a solution in the heat of the moment if you already have one on paper.

When you and your spouse prepare your informal or legal separation agreement, be sure to ask yourselves the following questions:

✔ How will we share the money in our joint bank accounts?

✔ What will we do about your joint credit cards?

✔ Who, if anyone, can access the line of credit we have with our bank?

✔ Who will remain in our home?

✔ How will we pay our pre-existing debts?

✔ Who will pay the debts either of us may incur while we're separated?

✔ Will one of us pay maintenance to the other while we're separated? If so, when will the payments be due and how much will they be?

✔ How will we share responsibility for the care of our children?

✔ When will our children spend time with, and stay with, each of us?

✔ Will one of us pay child support to the other and, if so, how much will the payments be and when will they be paid?

If your spouse mismanages your finances while you're separated, your credit history and your credit score, not just your spouse's, may be damaged. For that reason, in your separation agreement, include provisions stating that during your separation, your spouse will *not* include your name on any new financial or banking accounts, will *not* sign your name on any documents whatsoever, especially financial documents, and so on.

Formalizing a Legal Separation Agreement

If you and your spouse decide to legally separate, you won't live together anymore, but you won't be divorced, either. In this section, we tell you when you should separate legally rather than informally and what you should include in your legal separation agreement.

Who should get a legal separation agreement?

A legal separation agreement (called a *temporary court order* in some states) is essential if you're separating permanently rather than getting a divorce, assuming that your state recognizes legal separations (remember, not all states do). To protect yourself, you need everything to be black and white and filed with the court so that if either of you fails to live up to the terms of your agreement, the other spouse can ask the court to enforce it.

Other instances when a legal separation agreement is essential include when

- ✔ You're separating as a prelude to divorce.
- ✔ You're so estranged from your spouse that communication and cooperation are impossible.
- ✔ You don't trust your spouse to live up to his or her verbal promises.
- ✔ One of you wants spousal support while you're living apart.
- ✔ Minor children are involved.

The longer you live apart, the greater the chances are that your relationship will deteriorate. As time goes on, you may find cooperating with each other harder to do, maybe because your spouse becomes involved in a new romantic relationship and abandons your reconciliation plans. Under the circumstances, having a written separation agreement can help prevent a total breakdown of your relationship, even if you anticipate an eventual divorce.

If you and your spouse can't negotiate a separation agreement, the family law court in your area will decide the terms of your separation.

What should be in a legal separation agreement?

A legal separation agreement should address most, if not all, of the same issues that you would cover in a divorce agreement, including how you will handle the custody of your children; how much child support one spouse will pay the other; whether one of the spouses will receive spousal support and, if so, the terms and conditions of the support; and what you will do about your marital assets and debts. If you or your children are currently covered on your spouse's insurance policy and that coverage will continue, your separation agreement should address the coverage, too. If not, your agreement should address what other means you will use to make sure that your children are insured. For an overview of these issues, turn to Chapter 1, and for greater detail, read the chapters in Part III. Although the discussions in these chapters focus on divorce, most of the discussions apply to legal separations, too. In fact, if you separate and then decide to divorce, all or some of what you include in your separation agreement can be included in your divorce agreement.

Depending on your state, the personal property that's in your possession when you're separated may become the personal property you end up with in your divorce. Therefore, if you move out of the home you share with your spouse and you plan on leaving some of your personal property in that home, you may want to include a provision in your separation agreement stating that the property will be yours if you divorce.

Hang on to your liquid assets

Ideally, your agreement should give you ready access to the *liquid assets* (cash or an asset that you can quickly convert to cash) that you and your spouse own. Certificates of deposit, cash advances on your credit cards, your checking account overdraft, a line of credit, as well as money market accounts and bond funds that allow you to write checks against your investment are all liquid assets. You may need these assets during your separation to help pay bills, to put food on the table, or to cover unexpected expenses, especially if your income is low and you won't be receiving much, if any, direct financial support from your spouse.

Try the art of compromise

When working out the terms of your separation, a give-and-take strategy usually works better than strong-arm tactics. In other words, don't expect to get everything you ask for. You can refuse to compromise in an effort to have everything your way, but that approach is likely to backfire because your spouse is unlikely to give in to you on everything, and if the two of you get stalemated, the court may have to decide the terms of your separation.

Be careful about what you sign

Question anything in a separation agreement that you don't understand. And don't agree to a provision in your agreement because "it's good enough for now" or because you "can live with the arrangement for a while." Separation agreements often become *divorce agreements,* and after something is in a separation agreement, having that provision voided or modified can be difficult, if not impossible, to change, unless you and your spouse agree to the change or any problems caused by the provision were obvious and significant.

Give yourself some room to maneuver by clearly indicating in writing that the separation agreement in no way binds you to the same terms in your final divorce agreement. Make this statement part of the agreement.

The financial benefits of having a legal separation agreement

Having a legal separation agreement can provide you specific financial benefits in addition to ensuring that if your spouse fails to live up to his or her obligations in the agreement, the court will take steps to make your spouse do what he or she agreed to. Here are some of the other benefits of having a written agreement:

✔ If one spouse pays the other spousal support, the spouse making the payments can claim them as a deduction on his or her federal tax return. Those payments must be part of a legal separation agreement or court order to be a deduction.

 If your spouse claims your spousal support payments on his or her tax return, you must report that money as income.

✔ A legal separation agreement can help limit your liability for any debts that your spouse may rack up during your separation, assuming you live in a separate property state. Spouses who live in community property states do not get this protection.

✔ The agreement helps ensure that certain financial benefits that you currently receive as a spouse continue during your separation. Those benefits could include health insurance and continued access to credit if you and your spouse share joint accounts or if you're an authorized user on your spouse's accounts.

Alimony pendente lite and *separate maintenance* are legal talk for spousal support payments during separation. You may hear your attorney use these terms or hear them in court if you look to a judge to decide some of the terms of your separation agreement.

Other things you should do when you're separating legally

Besides negotiating a legal separation agreement, if you're moving out of the residence you share with your spouse, and especially if your separation isn't amicable or if you don't fully trust your spouse, you should also protect yourself by

✔ Taking your name off the lease if you and your spouse are renters.

✔ Taking your name off your family's utility, phone, cable, Internet, lawn maintenance, and newspaper delivery accounts and so on, assuming that doing so doesn't cause a hardship for your spouse or your children. If your spouse can maintain these things alone, taking your name off the accounts is fine, but if your doing so means that your spouse and children will lack heat, phone service, and so on, don't do it. Furthermore, under those circumstances, if you end up in court, a judge will not look kindly on what you did.

✔ Contacting all the creditors you share with your spouse — your joint creditors — and putting a freeze on your joint accounts so that your spouse cannot run them up.

✔ Making copies of your family's tax returns for the years that contain information that will be helpful in your divorce negotiations.

✔ Creating a record of all your joint credit account numbers, bank accounts, insurance policies, investment accounts, and so on. Also create a record of whatever you and your spouse have stored in your home safe, safe deposit book, or bank safety-deposit boxes.

✔ Obtaining credit in your own name if all your credit is joint.

✔ Taking any personal property that's important to you and that you fear your spouse may destroy or discard out of anger.

Following Separation Etiquette

If Emily Post wrote rules of proper behavior for separated spouses, they'd have to include the following do's and don'ts. Ignoring these rules of separation etiquette can turn an amicable split into a hostile one, derail any plans for reconciliation, and even weaken your position when the time comes to negotiate your divorce.

Take heed of these separation don'ts:

✔ Don't get involved in a serious relationship, especially if the relationship means that you spend less time with your young children or that you neglect them when you and your new romantic interest are with your children. If your spouse finds out about your love affair, that information is likely to increase the hostility that he or she may already feel toward you. Also, a new main squeeze is likely to put you in a disadvantageous position when you negotiate the terms of your divorce.

✔ If you do have a new romantic interest, don't bring him or her home for the night when your children are staying with you.

- Don't bad-mouth your spouse — ever! If your children hear what you say, they may repeat your comments to your spouse. Plus, nothing short of spousal abuse will send a judge into a tirade more quickly than learning that you've been saying disparaging things about your spouse. In addition, it's not healthy for young children to hear one spouse bad-mouth the other.

- Don't do things that you know will be hurtful to your spouse or to your kids. Ultimately, the person you hurt most may be yourself.

- Avoid having sexual relations with your spouse without first understanding the potential ramifications of doing so according to the laws of your state. In some states, if you have sex with your spouse while separated and if you've already filed for a fault divorce, you may lose your grounds for divorce. Furthermore, you may mislead your spouse into thinking that you want to reconcile, which would not be fair.

While you're at it, be sure to keep these separation etiquette do's in mind:

- Do keep open the lines of communication between you and your spouse. As long as your communication is at least civil, being able to talk with one another when necessary makes your separation easier on you and on your kids.

- If your children are living with you, allow your spouse to spend plenty of time with them (unless your spouse has been abusive, you suspect that he or she has sexually molested the children, or you are concerned that your spouse may kidnap your children). If you're legally separated, your agreement should state when and where your spouse can see the children.

- Meet all your obligations to your spouse and children without fail. Besides the fact that it's only fair that you live up to your family obligations, if you don't, you can end up in court and a judge may order you to do whatever you haven't been doing or may decide to take certain rights away from you. For example, if you and your spouse share custody of your children, but you're never available when your turn comes to have your kids live with you, the judge may give your spouse sole custody of your children and let you have visitation rights. In addition, not meeting all your obligations under your separation agreement can minimize your bargaining power if you and your spouse decide to divorce eventually and you're negotiating the terms of your divorce agreement.

If You Kiss and Make Up

Some of you will breathe a huge sigh of relief after you've separated, but others of you may begin to miss certain aspects of married life. If you're the one who moved out and you now live in a smaller place surrounded by rented furniture and just a few items from your home, you may miss the old familiar comforts. If your spouse took care of most of the cooking (and boiling water sums up your culinary skills), you may quickly tire of fast food and scorched meals.

If your children are still young and aren't living with you, you'll miss having them around; if you're the parent with primary responsibility for the children while you're separated, you may feel overwhelmed without your spouse to help out. Or maybe you've determined that you truly love your spouse and are willing to do what's necessary to repair your marriage.

For any or all of the reasons we listed, you and your spouse may decide that living together is better than living apart. And, like many couples who reach that conclusion, you will reconcile and end your separation.

Be sure that you're reconciling with your spouse because you really want to, not because you feel guilty, are scared to be alone, are lonely, are tired of doing your own laundry or eating by yourself, are afraid of the future, or for other reasons that may not be the right ones. Otherwise, although initially after you've reconciled, you may feel a sense of exhilaration and renewed hope for your future as a couple, sooner or later, the old problems in your relationship are likely to resurface, and you may respond to them in the very ways that contributed to your marital troubles in the first place. Also, you may feel angry with yourself that you returned to your marriage and now have to separate and disrupt your life and your family's life all over again.

Despite your happiness at being together again, both of you may harbor negative feelings toward one another, such as anger, hurt, doubt, and distrust, as a result of your separation or because of problems that triggered your separation. Although these feelings may be quite natural under the circumstances, they can get in the way of rebuilding your marriage. Therefore, if you and your spouse are really serious about staying together and repairing your marriage, begin seeing a therapist or marriage counselor, if you aren't already doing so.

If you and your spouse get back together, you're more apt to make your marriage work if you begin therapy or counseling while you're still in the honeymoon phase of your reconciliation because you'll both be more motivated to make your relationship work.

Part II
Getting Your Divorce Going

The 5th Wave   By Rich Tennant

"My analyst said I should channel the emotions of my divorce into an activity or pastime. Matador comes to mind..."

In this part . . .

The chapters in this part provide must-have information if your marriage is definitely over and you're getting a divorce. Chapter 5 explains the legal steps involved in beginning a divorce, offers advice for breaking the news to your spouse, helps you plan for what you want out of your divorce, and provides guidance about what to do if you believe that your divorce will be hostile or your spouse may become violent. Chapter 6 offers advice for telling your kids about your divorce and for helping them cope with the news. Finally, Chapter 7 provides suggestions to help you handle the roller coaster of emotions that often go hand-in-hand with a divorce.

Chapter 5

Taking the First Steps

· ·

In This Chapter

▶ Starting the divorce paperwork

▶ Telling your spouse that you want a divorce

▶ Determining your divorce goals and priorities

▶ Planning a budget for life after divorce

▶ Protecting your assets if you anticipate an ugly divorce

▶ Keeping yourself safe from a violent spouse

· ·

*W*hen you realize that you and your spouse are headed for splitsville, you must take certain steps to get the divorce wheels in motion, including filing the proper paperwork and breaking the news to your spouse, assuming that your divorce isn't a mutual decision.

This chapter reviews the legal process that officially begins a divorce (unless you and your spouse pursue a collaborative divorce — see Chapter 1 — in which case the petition in your divorce may not be filed until after the two of you have worked out all of the terms of your divorce) and offers practical advice for how to tell your spouse that you're ending your marriage together with words of compassion for those of you who hear your spouse say, "I want a divorce." This chapter also helps you begin working out the details of your divorce agreement, regardless of whether you and your spouse do the negotiating yourselves or hire attorneys to help you. (Part IV can help you with both situations.)

To help you organize your thoughts, this chapter offers suggestions for defining your divorce goals and priorities, advises you on the financial information you should pull together before you begin working out the terms of your divorce, and discusses the importance of working with a postdivorce budget. It also offers special divorce preparation advice for those of you who anticipate that your divorce will be extremely hostile.

As part of your preparation, consider reading some issues of *Divorce* magazine, which, as its name implies, is devoted entirely to the subject of divorce. For subscription information or to sign up for the magazine's free divorce newsletter, go to www.divorce.mag.com.

Initiating the Divorce Proceedings

Every divorce officially begins when one spouse files a petition with the court. That filing marks the legal start of a couple's divorce. Next, the other spouse is officially notified of the filing of the petition for divorce, although, in many marriages, the fact that one spouse filed for divorce comes as no surprise to the other spouse.

Depending on your state and whether you're getting a *fault divorce* (a type of divorce where one spouse alleges that the other spouse has harmed their marriage by committing certain misdeeds such as adultery, mental cruelty, or physical abuse), you may need to live apart from your spouse for a period of time before you can file for divorce.

Filing a petition

No matter which state your divorce takes place in and what sort of divorce you anticipate — friendly or hostile — every divorce except many collaborative divorces starts out the same way: One spouse files a *complaint* or *petition* with the court, which initiates a divorce civil law suit. The spouse who files becomes the *plaintiff,* or the *petitioner,* in the lawsuit, and the other spouse becomes the *defendant,* or *respondent.*

If you file the petition, you use it to generally establish the facts and the issues of the divorce as you see them. You file either a *fault* or *no-fault divorce* (see Chapter 1 for a discussion about the different types of divorce) and indicate want you want from your divorce — spousal support, child support, custody of the children, and so on (see the "Planning for Life after Divorce" section, later in this chapter, to help you make these decisions).

Most couples don't work out the terms of their divorce until after one of them files a divorce petition. However, if getting divorced is a mutual decision for you and your spouse, and you and your spouse decide to negotiate a divorce agreement without the help of attorneys or if you and your spouse decide to pursue a collaborative divorce, you may work out the terms of your divorce before one of you files a divorce petition.

Serving the papers

After one spouse files for divorce, the other spouse is formally notified of the action by being served with an official notice that he or she is being sued for divorce. If you hire a divorce attorney, your attorney arranges for the service after the attorney files your divorce paperwork. If you don't hire an attorney, the clerk in the court where you file your petition can tell you what your particular service options are.

Although states vary in regard to how this notification can happen and the service requirements can be different depending on whether you and your spouse share minor children, service can occur in one of the following ways:

✔ **You deliver the paperwork to your spouse yourself.** Use this method only if you believe that your divorce is going to be amicable and especially if your spouse knows that you planned to file for divorce.

✔ **A sheriff or constable formally serves your spouse by physically delivering the notice to him or her.** You're most likely to use this method if your divorce is hostile. You pay a fee for serving your spouse this way. The amount of the fee varies depending on the part of the country you live in, but the fee is unlikely to amount to more than $150.

✔ **If you or the sheriff or constable can't find your spouse, you can hire a private process server.** Your spouse will have a tougher time eluding this person because private process servers wear street clothes, and so they aren't as easy to spot as a uniformed constable or sheriff. But hiring a private process server costs more than using a sheriff or constable. Most private process servers charge between $25 and $75 per hour.

✔ **You mail your spouse the notification.** You may be able to send the notice via regular mail, or you may have to use certified or registered mail. Not all states provide this option.

If your spouse can't be served, don't worry: You don't have to stay married forever. In most states, you can publish legal notices in the newspaper in the community where your spouse is living. The published notices inform your spouse that you have filed for divorce and outline your spouse's legal rights. If your spouse fails to respond within a certain period of time after the date of the final notice, you get a default divorce judgment from the court, which means that your divorce is granted. However, some issues in your divorce may remain unresolved until you find your spouse — for example, child support or spousal support. Ordinarily, the court can't order your spouse to pay temporary spousal or child support until your spouse has been served.

Processing the response

After your spouse is served, he or she has a certain amount of time — usually 20 to 60 days — to file a formal *response* to your lawsuit, also known as an *answer*. An answer is a legal document that states whether your spouse disagrees with anything in your divorce petition, what he or she wants from the divorce, and so on. If your spouse has a divorce attorney, the attorney takes care of preparing the response and filing it with the court.

If your spouse agrees with everything in your petition and you didn't file a fault divorce, he or she probably won't file a response. This is what happens in many divorces. In fact, if your divorce is amicable and, especially if you and your spouse see 100-percent eye-to-eye on the terms of your divorce, your spouse can sign a *waiver of service,* which means that he or she won't be formally served with your divorce paperwork. Under this scenario, your divorce will probably move forward pretty quickly because fewer legal paperwork and administrative procedures can slow it down.

If your spouse doesn't agree with what you included in the divorce petition, your spouse will file a response stating what he or she wants from the divorce. For example, maybe you asked for sole custody of your children in your petition, but your spouse wants joint custody, or maybe your spouse asked for spousal support and you don't want to pay him or her a penny. Also, if you alleged fault in your divorce petition, your spouse may counter by denying that he or she is at fault or your spouse may point the finger at you instead. If you and your spouse don't agree on the facts of your marriage and on how to end it, your divorce is likely to be complicated and expensive unless your attorneys can diffuse the bad feelings between the two of you.

If you and your spouse aren't already legally separated but plan on living apart now that your divorce has begun, having a written agreement that details your living and financial arrangements and how you will handle child-related issues during the divorce process is a good idea. (See Chapter 4 for more details on legally separating.)

Discussing Your Decision with Your Spouse

If getting divorced isn't a mutual decision, how you break the news to your spouse can have a big impact on whether your divorce will be amicable or contentious. It can also help set the tone for your postdivorce relationship, an important consideration if you have minor children. Not wanting to be married anymore is no reason to be insensitive to your spouse's feelings.

Breaking the news gently

Most couples in troubled marriages try just about everything to resolve their problems but, at some point, calling it quits becomes the obvious answer to one or both spouses. Ideally, if only one spouse reaches this conclusion, that spouse can sit down with the other spouse and explain his or her decision.

Your spouse should learn about your divorce plans from you first, not through the rumor mill (from mutual friends, relatives, or even your kids) or by being served with an official notice of the fact that you've filed. Getting the news from anyone other than you is a cruel way for your spouse to find out that his or her marriage is ending and is a sure way to make for a bitter divorce. You owe your spouse a face-to-face conversation about your divorce plans out of respect for him or her and the relationship you have shared. As difficult as having this conversation may be, it's the kindest way to convey the news. However, if you're afraid that your spouse will harm you physically after hearing the news, you should avoid a face-to-face conversation.

The following suggestions may make it easier for you to have such a difficult conversation and help your spouse accept the news as calmly as possible:

✔ Quietly tell your spouse your reasons for wanting to end your marriage. Review what you consider to be the problems in your marriage, what you've done to try to fix them — together or separately — and why you feel that those efforts haven't worked. Even if you've covered this ground many times before, go over it again patiently.

✔ As much as possible, talk in terms of how you feel, not in terms of what your spouse did or didn't do in your marriage. It's harder to argue with someone about his or her feelings, and you're less apt to put your spouse on the defensive.

✔ Avoid accusatory or derogatory language and try to steer clear of starting an argument. If your spouse tries to argue with you, calmly reiterate your feelings and intentions — over and over, if necessary.

You may need to have a few conversations concerning your intention to divorce before your spouse finally accepts the news.

If you can't tell your spouse in person or with a phone call, write your spouse a letter. It's best if the letter comes from you, not from your attorney. An attorney's letter is an impersonal way to convey such very personal news. Furthermore, your spouse will probably be hurt and angry that you didn't bother to write it yourself. You should also avoid breaking the news to your spouse via e-mail, which is an impersonal means of conveying news that is going to be emotionally upsetting to the recipient.

Waiting until your spouse is ready to begin negotiating

Don't expect to begin negotiating your divorce agreement as soon as you share your news with your spouse. Give your spouse time to let the news sink in, to begin coming to terms with what's happening, and to do some of the upfront divorce-related planning you may have already begun. Realistically, it may take weeks or even months before your negotiations can begin, so be patient and move slowly.

Pushing your spouse to begin working out the details of your divorce may backfire on both of you. For example, feelings of guilt or remorse on your part or feelings of anger or abandonment on your spouse's part may result in bad decisions that you both will regret later. You may concede too much to your spouse or be too willing to compromise, and your spouse may make unreasonable demands out of anger, spite, and hurt feelings. Also, your spouse may panic and immediately hire an attorney, possibly turning your divorce into a hostile battle when it could have been an amicable split if you had just been more patient.

But sometimes waiting for the right time to begin working out the terms of your divorce may be impossible or impractical given the particulars of your situation. Therefore, you may not be able to hold off until your spouse is ready. The truth is, if your spouse is adamantly against getting divorced, he or she may *never* be ready. Or maybe you're so estranged from one another that being civil to each other and working cooperatively is impossible.

Assuming that your spouse comes around eventually and is willing to start talking about your divorce, have a general discussion about the issues involved, particularly whether you want to do the negotiating yourselves or hire attorneys to help you work everything out. Also, try to develop a general timetable for moving forward.

Keeping your cool if your spouse initiates the divorce

Even if the writing has been on the wall for months or maybe years, finding out that your spouse wants a divorce can send you into an emotional tailspin of shock and disbelief. As time goes on, you may vacillate between feelings of anger and sadness or anger and depression.

The sooner you face the facts and move forward, the better off you'll be. Although feeling sorry for yourself is an understandable response to learning that your marriage is ending, especially if you didn't want it to end, painting yourself as a victim and wallowing in self-pity aren't healthy responses to your situation. Obsessing over "the unfairness of it all," how you've "been wronged," and "what could have been" will prevent you from working out a reasonable divorce agreement and getting on with your life. The "poor me" refrain will eventually drive away most of your friends and family members at the time when you may need them most. Also, don't get hung up on the idea that if you just do or say certain things, your spouse will have a change of heart and you can stay married. That probably won't happen.

As you work through your emotions and begin dealing with the practical realities of your divorce, avoid angry recriminations and don't insult your spouse. Also, don't go out of your way to spend time together or to remain apart; do what makes *you* feel most comfortable. If you need help understanding and handling your emotions, turn to Chapter 7.

Planning for Life after Divorce

Whether ending your marriage is your idea, your spouse's idea, or a mutual decision, getting divorced is a big step that can affect your life for years to come. Therefore, as difficult as you may find stepping back and considering what you need out of your divorce , doing so is important so that when the time comes to work out the details of your divorce settlement, you know what you want to push for and what you are willing to give up.

Evaluating your divorce goals and future financial needs

Before your divorce begins or immediately after, start thinking about what you want your life to be like after your marriage ends, what you need from your divorce to create that life, and how you want to handle issues like spousal support, child custody, and child support. Define your goals for your divorce — what do you *really* need and want from your divorce? Consider also what you're willing to give up to achieve your goals. Unless you go into your divorce negotiations with a clear idea of what you want, you're apt to end up with a divorce agreement that doesn't meet your needs and leaves you feeling frustrated and resentful toward your spouse.

When thinking about the financial aspects of your divorce, be realistic. You may wish that your postdivorce life could include a mansion, an expensive car, and a constantly cushy checking account balance, but those things may be pie-in-the-sky dreams, depending on the current state of your family's finances, your individual and joint assets, your own earning power, and how much money your spouse makes. You also don't want to ask for the moon just to hurt or upset your spouse. If you do, you risk setting yourself up for disappointment and making your divorce more difficult than it needs to be.

Be careful not to let your emotions take over when you're dealing with the financial matters of your divorce. An amicable, cooperative divorce is always easiest on your emotions and your pocketbook, and the best kind of divorce when young children are involved. However, to divorce amicably, you and your spouse must behave like reasonable adults, be open to compromise, and not bring your anger and hurt feelings to the negotiation table.

Another benefit of being clear about your divorce goals is that if you hire an attorney to help work out the terms of your divorce, you're better prepared to hire the right kind of attorney and to provide him or her with helpful direction and feedback during the divorce process. For example, if you decide that you're willing to fight your spouse on certain issues no matter what, you probably need an attorney who's aggressive and has a lot of divorce trial experience. On the other hand, if you want to avoid controversy and conflict, the attorney you hire should be great at negotiating and at creating win-win resolutions to the problems in your divorce. For advice on hiring the right attorney and getting the results you want, turn to Chapters 13 and 14.

Ask yourself the following questions to help you begin identifying practical goals for your divorce:

- How much will I need in order to pay my living expenses after I'm divorced? Develop a postdivorce budget that projects the income and expenses you anticipate. The "Developing a budget for life after divorce" section later in this chapter provides advice and information for putting a budget together.

- Will I need spousal support? If so, come up with an idea of how much you'll need and for how long. In most divorces these days, spousal support isn't a permanent thing. (See Chapter 9 to find out more about spousal support; the "Developing a budget for life after divorce" section in this chapter also helps you figure out how much support you'll need.)

- What adjustments should I be prepared to make in my life in order to be able to meet my financial needs?

- What skills do I need to get a job in today's market if I will be working outside the home after my divorce for the first time or will be returning to the work force after an absence of several years?

- Where can I get the job skills I need? How long will it take to get them and how much will the education cost? Remember to factor in educational expenses other than your tuition (like textbooks and a computer) to your postdivorce budget and any transportation and childcare costs you may incur while you're building your job skills.

- Are any particular assets from my marriage really important to me, either financially or emotionally? If so, write them down.

- What kind of child-custody arrangement do I want? Think in terms of what's best for your children. That's the criteria the court will use to decide the issue if your divorce ends up in court.

- How much child support will I need if I end up with custody of the children?

As you think about your answers to these questions, try to distinguish between your needs and your wants. Think of a *need* as something that's essential to your postdivorce life (or to your children's lives) and a *want* as something that would be nice to have, but isn't necessary. During your divorce negotiations, you may have to give up a want in order to satisfy a need. For example, you may decide that you're willing to get fewer assets in your divorce in exchange for receiving larger spousal support payments or in order to receive spousal support for a longer period of time.

After you decide on your divorce goals, write them down in order of importance and put the list away in a safe place. Later, take another look at your list. Now that some time has passed, you may find that you want to add, subtract, or reorder a few items on that list.

Pulling together all your financial information

If you haven't already followed the advice in Chapter 3 about gathering up the financial and legal documents and other information you need to work out the terms of your divorce, begin that process right away, even if you anticipate an amicable divorce and totally trust your spouse to treat you fairly. Complete and accurate financial information is essential to obtaining an equitable divorce settlement. Without it, you may get saddled with more than your fair share of your marital debts and too little of your marital assets. Also, you may not receive a reasonable amount of spousal support if you need it, and you may come up short when it comes to child support.

Trying to negotiate a settlement agreement with your spouse when you don't have all the necessary financial information is like playing poker without knowing which cards you're holding. In other words, you have a snowball's chance in hell of coming out a winner because you have to guess about when to raise the stakes, when to hold, and when to fold. Also, if you hire an attorney to help with your negotiations and you cannot provide him or her with the necessary information, your attorney has to obtain it through the discovery process, which increases the cost of your divorce. Chapter 14 describes the discovery process.

Developing a budget for life after divorce

If you want spousal support or child support, knowing exactly how much money you need will be difficult, if not impossible, if you have no idea how much your living expenses will be after your divorce. In addition, when the time comes to divvy up your marital assets and debts, you may not have the information you need in order to advocate for a fair share of both for yourself. For these reasons, as soon as your divorce begins, you should develop a budget for your life after divorce using the sample form in Table 5-1.

When preparing your budget, you may have to estimate your postdivorce income and some of your expenses. Come up with your best guesses, based on your own experience and by reviewing your checkbook register, bank statements, records of your ATM withdrawals and debit purchases, your cash receipts, and so on. As time goes on and you have more specific information, you can adjust your budget accordingly.

Developing a postdivorce budget also helps you figure out whether you should look for a better-paying job, whether you can realistically continue living in your family's home, whether you need to turn in your gas-guzzling SUV for something more economical, and so on.

For help developing and using a budget, pick up a copy of *Personal Finance For Dummies* by Eric Tyson (Wiley) or *The Budget Kit* by Judy Lawrence (Kaplan Publishing).

Table 5-1:	**Sample Form for a Household Spending and Saving Plan**
Fixed Monthly Expenses	*Dollar Amount*
Rent or mortgage	_____
Car payments	_____
Other installment loans	_____
Insurance	_____
Children's allowances/activities	_____
Day care	_____
Monthly dues	_____
Cable TV and subscriptions	_____
Internet service	_____
Total	**$_____**
Variable Monthly Expenses*	*Dollar Amount*
Groceries	_____
Utilities	_____
Telephone	_____
Gasoline	_____
Clothing	_____
Credit card payments	_____
Out-of-pocket medical/dental	_____
Magazines and books	_____
Church or charitable donations	_____

Variable Monthly Expenses*	Dollar Amount
Haircuts and grooming supplies	_____
Restaurant meals	_____
Miscellaneous	_____
Total	$_____

Estimate the entire year's expenses and divide by 12 for the monthly amount.

Periodic Expenses*	Dollar Amount
Tuition	_____
Other educational expenses	_____
Auto registration and license	_____
Insurance	_____
Taxes	_____
Household repairs	_____
Birthday and holiday gifts	_____
Entertaining	_____
Subscriptions	_____
Total	$_____

Estimate the entire year's expenses and divide by 12 for the monthly amount.

Total Monthly Household Expenses (The three previous totals from this table combined.)	$_____
Net Monthly Household Income	$_____
Surplus or Deficit (Net Household Income minus Total Monthly Expenses)	$_____
Surplus Allotted for Savings	$_____
Surplus Allotted for Investments	$_____

Safeguarding Your Money if You Anticipate a Hostile Divorce

If you suspect that your divorce will be a knock-down, drag-out fight or if you're certain that your divorce won't go smoothly, prepare to take the following steps prior to the start of your divorce. Protecting yourself from financial harm and having ready access to the financial resources you may need during your divorce is critical.

Open accounts in your own name

If you share a savings account with your spouse, withdraw some of the money in the account — maybe half, depending on your needs and the amount in the account — and deposit it in a new account in your own name at a different bank. Do the same if you and your spouse share a checking account, too.

If you don't tell your spouse what you're doing with the money in your joint accounts before you withdraw the funds, you should expect some fireworks when he or she learns what you've done. Those fireworks will probably make your divorce agreement negotiations more difficult. Also, if you withdraw an unreasonable amount of money (and just what constitutes an "unreasonable" amount is something your attorneys have to decide), you may end up getting less in your property settlement.

Also, beware of leaving too little in your checking account to cover your monthly bills and expenses, especially if the checking account you share with your spouse usually contains just enough funds to pay them. Bounced check charges and angry creditors are the last things you need right now!

Close your joint accounts

Close any joint credit card accounts you share with your spouse. Also, if you and your spouse have a line of credit with a bank or credit card, cancel or reduce it, too. Be sure to inform your spouse of what you have done.

Individual credit — that is, credit in your own name — is essential to your financial life postdivorce. But building a credit history in your own name takes time, so if you don't have individual credit when you close your joint accounts, you may have to wait several years before you have access to credit at the best terms. The sooner you begin building your own history, the better. (See Chapter 3 for more on building your own credit history.)

Stash your important personal property

If you're concerned that your spouse may try to damage, destroy, or steal some of your personal property in anger that the marriage is ending or out of a desire for revenge, find a safe place to hide your valuables. That place can be a bank safe-deposit box in your name only, the home of a trusted friend or family member, a file cabinet at your office, or any other place that your spouse can't access.

If your spouse steals or damages your personal property, you may be able to sue him or her for theft or destruction of property. Also, your attorney can use evidence of your spouse's destructive behavior as leverage during your divorce negotiations or divorce trial.

Protect your mutual assets

If your spouse is angry about your divorce or wants revenge, he or she may try to use up your joint assets rather than allow you to get a portion of them in your divorce. If you're concerned that your spouse may attempt this, consult a family law attorney right away about taking steps to safeguard your joint assets. For example, the attorney will probably advise that you avoid maintaining large cash balances in your joint checking accounts if you can. Your attorney may also file a temporary restraining order against your spouse and then request an emergency hearing on the property in question.

Identify sources of cash

Protecting your legal rights when you're involved in a hostile divorce takes money — and lots of it. So, if you anticipate that your divorce will be hostile, start identifying the financial resources you have at your disposal that you can use to pay for your divorce. Those resources may include your separate property, such as

- ✔ The cash in your individual checking or savings account
- ✔ Your stocks, bonds, or mutual funds
- ✔ Money you borrow against your retirement fund
- ✔ A second mortgage on the real estate you own
- ✔ Money you borrow from family members

Talk with a CPA or with your financial advisor about the tax consequences and other implications of selling stocks or mutual funds, borrowing against the funds in your retirement account, or taking a second loan on the real estate you own before you take any of these actions.

Taking Action if Things Turn Violent

Sometimes when a marriage falls apart, one spouse (usually the man) begins to threaten the other with physical violence or becomes physically violent. If this happens in your marriage, take the threats or the violence very seriously. Ignoring them can literally be a matter of life or death.

Important steps for addressing violence

Violence in a marriage often escalates when the wife begins to assert herself or talks about a separation or a divorce. If your spouse becomes physically violent with you, do the following:

- ✔ Call 911 for immediate help as soon as you are threatened or hurt.

- ✔ Contact your community's domestic abuse hotline or the National Domestic Violence Hotline at 800-799-7233 or www.ndvh.org.

- ✔ Go to the hospital no matter how minor your injuries. Get copies of your medical records from the hospital; they can help you if you go to court.

- ✔ Have a friend or relative take photos of your injuries and record the date that the injuries took place, what happened, and so on. Keep the photos and the written record in a safe place where your spouse can't find them. You may want a trusted friend or relative to keep them for you.

- ✔ Ask the district attorney in the area where the abuse occurred to press charges against your spouse. If the district attorney agrees, be willing to testify in court about what happened. If there is no police report about the incident, you'll need to provide the district attorney with evidence that it happened before he or she will agree to prosecute. Examples of evidence include photos of what your spouse did to you, your hospital medical records related to injuries you suffered, letters, e-mails, or voice mail messages from your spouse threatening you with abuse, and so on.

If you're reluctant to report instances of violence in your marriage, consider joining a support group. The members of the group will understand what you are going through and can help you gain the resolve to deal with your situation in a decisive manner. The people on the other end of the National Domestic Violence Hotline can help you find a group in your area (800-799-7233 or www.ndvh.orghelp/help_in_area), or you can call your local domestic abuse shelter for information.

Protecting yourself from a violent spouse

If your spouse has been violent in the past or is threatening you with violence for the first time, don't wait for the worst to happen. Take the steps outlined in the upcoming sections to minimize the likelihood that your spouse will harm you.

Get a protective order against your spouse

A *protective order,* sometimes called a *restraining order* or an *injunction,* is a court order that makes it illegal for your spouse to enter or come within a certain distance of your home, your workplace, and your children's school or day care center; to stalk you; to harass you; or to try to intimidate you; and

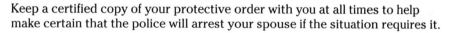

so on. Call your local police department or domestic violence center hotline to find out how to obtain a protective order. A judge, who may or may not be a family law judge, will issue the order after you apply for it.

Keep a certified copy of your protective order with you at all times to help make certain that the police will arrest your spouse if the situation requires it.

Many states have different types of protective orders, and the process for obtaining one differs depending on which type of order you want. Not only can these various orders be confusing for the spouse who's seeking a protective order, but they can also be confusing for local law enforcement officials, as well. That confusion can affect how effectively those officials enforce protective orders that are violated.

In most states, a protective order lasts for a limited amount of time — between one and three years — although some states provide for longer-lasting orders under certain circumstances. All states allow you to apply for an extension of your protective order, but, in some of those states, you must go to court and face your spouse to get the extension. A few states have authorized permanent protective orders in certain situations.

Be specific in your protective order about exactly what you do not want your spouse to do. The order won't apply to anything that you don't specifically include in it. If you've called the police in the past because of previous incidents of spousal abuse, include that information in the court order, too.

If your spouse violates the terms of your protective order, the penalty imposed on your spouse depends on the laws of your state. Possible sanctions include being charged with a misdemeanor, a felony (a type of crime that's more serious than a misdemeanor), or with contempt of court. A few states require anyone who violates a protective order to spend time in jail, whereas others require a violator to pay a fine or to pay a fine *and* go to jail. In a few states, someone who violates a protective order must receive counseling or be electronically monitored.

All states have *antistalking laws* that can help protect you if your spouse is following you, waiting for you outside your residence or your place of employment, following you in his car, using the phone or e-mail to threaten or harass you, or displaying other behaviors that are intended to intimidate and frighten you. Be sure to call the police if you're being stalked.

Reporting every incident of domestic violence, threat of violence, harassment, intimidation, or stalking by your spouse to the police is a good idea because, in some communities, getting a protective order against your spouse is easier when you've filed police reports on past incidents. The reports can also help if you file criminal charges against your spouse.

If you need immediate protection and the courts are closed because it's a weekend, evening, or holiday, your local police can issue a *temporary protective order*. However, the order stays in effect for only a few days, so you need to file the appropriate paperwork for a longer-lasting protective order as soon as possible.

Don't let your guard down just because you have a protective order. If your spouse is intent on harming you, he won't care about the order. Therefore, it's wise to also change your day-to-day habits — when you leave for work in the morning and the route you travel to get there, for example — and to develop an emergency plan of action so that you know exactly what to do if your spouse violates the protective order. The "Make yourself more secure with a safety plan" section, later in this chapter, provides advice for what should be a part of your plan.

File criminal charges

If your spouse has already been physically violent toward you, in addition to getting a protective order from the court, you should ask the district attorney in your community to file criminal assault charges against your spouse. Taking both actions provides you with different and overlapping protections. However, the district attorney won't file charges unless you have evidence of an assault. The "Important steps for addressing violence" section earlier in this chapter describes some of the evidence you can provide.

Call 911

Domestic violence is a crime in all states, although how each state deals with the crime varies. Even so, if your spouse harms you or threatens to harm you, call 911. One or more police officers will come to talk with you and will prepare a police report. Get a copy of the police report number because it may be very helpful if you end up in court. If you've obviously been abused, the police will probably arrest your spouse on the spot.

A small minority of police officers believes that domestic violence isn't a matter for the police to handle; some believe that it's a private matter between a husband and wife. Therefore, if you call the police for help and the responding officers seem reluctant to prepare a police report, calmly request that one be prepared, and get the officers' names and badge numbers. If the officers still refuse to write up a police report, this information will be helpful to have when you contact their superiors.

Head for a crisis shelter

If you're afraid to remain in your home despite having a protective order against your spouse, consider going to your local domestic abuse shelter. You can take your children with you. If you're in a crisis situation (your spouse has just beaten you or is threatening to) and you can get to a phone, call the shelter's crisis hotline. The person answering the phone can calm you down, advise you on how to handle the situation, and call the police for you. If you don't have the shelter's crisis hotline memorized, dial 911.

If you're in an abusive relationship, the excellent book *Getting Free: You Can End Abuse and Take Back Your Life* by Ginny Nicarthy (Seal Press) can help you break away.

Increase your security with a safety plan

Take the time to develop a safety plan for yourself if your spouse has been abusive in the past and you're afraid that he will harm you again or if your spouse is threatening you with violence for the first time. Know exactly what to do if violence does occur and take certain actions ahead of time, just in case. Planning ahead can mean the difference between minor injuries and very serious injuries or even life and death.

Make the following practices part of your safety plan:

- ✔ Memorize the phone number of your local domestic abuse shelter.

- ✔ Hide an extra set of keys, some money, and some clothes in a safe place in case you need to get out of your home quickly. That safe place may be at a friend's or relative's home, in the locked trunk of your car, at your office, and so on.

- ✔ Always have a safe place to go that your spouse doesn't know about. It can be your local women's shelter, a friend's home, or any other place you can count on any time of day or night.

- ✔ If you feel that you can trust one of your neighbors who lives next door, decide on a signal that you can use to let your neighbor know that you need help and that your neighbor should call 911, just in case you're not able to get to a phone. The signal could be something like turning on a specific inside or outside light or pulling the curtains together on a certain window.

- ✔ If you have children, be sure that they understand what to do if your spouse becomes violent. For example, you may want to tell them that if you say a certain code word, that's the signal for them to run to a neighbor's house for help or to call 911.

- ✔ Tell everyone you know about your spouse's abuse. Sharing this information with others diminishes the power of some abusers.

Chapter 6

Breaking the News to Your Kids

. . . .

. . . .

*P*utting your children first when you're getting a divorce can seem like an awfully tall order. After all, you have your own emotions to cope with! Plus, you may become so caught up by concerns about how you and your spouse will resolve the financial and legal issues in your divorce and what your future may be like that you may not pay close attention to how ending your marriage is affecting your kids and what you can do to help them cope with the changes in their lives.

Certainly, you have a lot on your plate. But remember, you're the parent. You have a responsibility to your children to tell them about your divorce in as caring and as sensitive a manner as possible. You also have an obligation to provide them with all the love, attention, and support that they need throughout your divorce so that you can minimize any emotional trauma that they may experience as a result. If you don't, research shows that your children may struggle as adults to lead happy, well-adjusted lives.

In this chapter, we offer guidance and advice regarding how and when to tell your kids about your divorce, and we also discuss what you should and shouldn't do after you break the news to them. In addition, we explain the importance of staying attuned to signs that your children may be having emotional problems as a result of learning about your divorce plans, and we help you anticipate the kinds of questions they may ask you.

Breaking the News

The best way to let your children know that your marriage is ending is for you and your spouse to break the news to them together, even if you have to put your animosity toward each other aside for a while. Telling them together helps reassure your kids that, although your marriage may be ending, you and your spouse can cooperate with one another as their parents, that they still have a family — just a different kind of family — and that you both will remain actively involved in their lives.

Before you tell your children about your divorce plans, you and your spouse should decide what you're going to say to them. Get your story straight so that the two of you don't convey conflicting messages to your children. If the two of you need help deciding exactly what to tell your children, schedule an appointment with a mental health professional or talk things over with your religious advisor.

You should both agree that when you talk with your children neither of you will blame the other for your breakup nor encourage your children to side with one of you against the other. Putting your kids in the middle of your divorce is unfair to them and can inflict irreparable emotional harm on your kids. Furthermore, when you criticize your spouse, your comments can backfire on you: You may encourage your children to side with the parent you maligned.

Here is some more advice you and your spouse should take to heart before you break the news to your children:

- ✔ **Be honest with your children about why you're getting divorced, but don't reveal too much.** Keep your children's ages in mind and don't share the lurid details behind your split. Tell them as much as they need to know and no more. For example, they don't need to know that Daddy or Mommy has been having an affair, if infidelity is a key cause of your divorce. If you haven't been able to hide the discord in your marriage, you may want to acknowledge what your children already know by saying something like, "We know that you've heard us fighting a lot, and here's why. . . ."

- ✔ **Don't hide the fact that life is going to be different for everyone in the family because of your divorce.** Prepare your kids for some of the changes to come. At the same time, reassure them that your divorce hasn't and will not change your love for them and that you both will continue to be involved in their lives. However, don't promise your children things you can't deliver; your reassurances and promises should be more than hot air. Otherwise, your children may become distrustful of you and cynical about your reliability and honesty.

✔ **Be very clear with your children that your divorce has absolutely nothing to do with them.** Otherwise, they may feel somehow responsible for the divorce and assume that maybe if they had behaved better or gotten higher grades you wouldn't be ending your marriage.

✔ **When you tell your kids about your divorce, stay calm.** Avoid angry or irritated facial gestures and body language, and don't argue with your spouse in front of your children. Such behavior contradicts the messages you want your kids to hear from you.

✔ **Try not to get emotional when you tell your children about your divorce.** Watching a parent cry or get very upset can be frightening for children, so don't add to their anxiety with histrionics and overly dramatic behavior. You're likely to make them more concerned about your emotions than their own and, as a result, they may not let you know exactly what they're feeling for fear of upsetting you.

If you and your spouse don't plan on breaking the news about your divorce to your kids together, try to agree about which of you will tell them. This decision may be an easy one for you to make because one of you has no interest in delivering such difficult news to your kids or because one of you is emotionally incapable of doing so. Or, you may both agree that the parent who most often provides your children with emotional support should talk to them.

You and your spouse should also reach a general agreement about what that parent will tell your kids. That way, if your children later ask the other parent questions about your divorce, he or she won't tell them something contradictory. Receiving conflicting information from the two of you is apt to unsettle your children further.

If you separate before your divorce is final, your children should visit the parent who moves out as soon as possible so they're assured that they'll continue to have a relationship with both of you. However, if your children refuse to visit their other parent or act reluctant to do so, don't force them to go. Also, make sure that they have their other parent's new address, phone number, cell phone number, and e-mail address.

Finding the Right Time to Talk with Your Children

Most of us tend to put off doing things that are unpleasant or that we're nervous about doing. As a result, you may come up with countless reasons to delay telling your children about your divorce plans. However, make sure that you tell them before anyone else does. They need to hear the news from you in your own words. And, in the same breath, you need to reassure them that you will always love them and take care of them.

The right time to talk with your children about the changes to come depends on their ages and on the circumstances of your divorce. For example, if your spouse announces that he or she has already filed for divorce and is moving out next week, you should tell your children about the split sooner, not later.

Letting your older kids know sooner

Bear in mind that you usually need to tell preteens and teens sooner than very young children (assuming that you have some control over the timing of your conversations with your children), because they're more likely to learn about your divorce plans by overhearing a conversation or by coming across divorce-related papers. Also, they're better at sensing that something's up. Therefore, when you're certain that you will be divorcing and have worked out at least some of the details, especially those that affect your children, have a talk with your preteens and teens as soon as possible.

Be sure to tell your older children not to share your news with their younger siblings if there's a significant age gap between them. For example, say your teenage children have two younger siblings, ages 5 and 7. Explain to your older kids that you want to tell the younger siblings yourself in your own way. But be sure to let your older kids know when you've had that conversation so that they can talk with their younger brothers or sisters about your divorce and be a support to them.

Avoid making your kids your divorce confidantes. Seeking their advice and counsel about matters related to your divorce is unfair to them and is an inappropriate and unhealthy role for you to expect your children to play. If you need to talk with someone, talk to a trusted friend or family member, your religious advisor, or a mental health professional.

Waiting to share the news with your younger ones

If you have toddlers and elementary-age children, avoid telling them about your divorce plans too far ahead of the date that you and your spouse plan to begin living apart. Young children's sense of time is different from that of adults and older children — a week can seem like a month, and a month can seem like a year. If you tell your younger children prematurely, you risk intensifying the anxiety they have over knowing that their lives are going to change in ways they don't yet understand.

Regardless of your children's ages, whenever possible, don't wait until just before you and your spouse begin living apart to break the news to your children. Instead, tell them far enough ahead of the day you plan to separate that your children will have time to process your news, ask you questions, spend relaxing and fun time with both of you, and enjoy your affection. Being able to do those things is essential preparation for the changes to come in their lives. A week or two before you and your spouse begin living apart is probably about the right amount of time for younger children.

Deciding Whether to Tell Your Children Individually or All Together

If your children are close in age and maturity, telling them all together has important benefits:

- ✔ **It can help foster a "we're all in this together" attitude among your children.** That feeling can be a comfort and a source of strength to them.

- ✔ **If all your children find out about your divorce at the same time, each of them knows exactly what his or her siblings know.** This may not seem important to you but, if you tell each of your kids separately, they may worry that they don't know what their siblings know or that you're going to treat them differently than everyone else in the family.

If there are significant disparities in the ages, maturity levels, or emotional needs of your children, talking to each child individually about your divorce is best. Having separate conversations enables you to tailor an appropriate message for each child and to provide as much support and comfort as the child may need after hearing your news. When you meet with each child, let him or her know that you're having a similar conversation with his or her siblings.

Unless your children are very young, they're probably going to talk with one another about what you've told them. Therefore, the basic message you convey to each of your children about why you're getting a divorce and what is going to change or stay the same in their lives should be consistent, though you may decide to use different words to convey it. If you tell each child something different and they begin comparing notes about your divorce, they are apt to become more anxious and worried.

Preparing for Your Children's Responses

You can't possibly predict exactly how your children are going to react to the news of your divorce. Their reactions depend on their ages, maturity levels, personalities, emotional makeup, and the relationships they have with you and your spouse, among other things. In this section, we prepare you for what may be ahead by explaining the various ways that your children may react to the news of your divorce.

Calming your emotions

Interestingly enough, you may find that their emotions mirror yours. Those emotions may include anger, depression, disbelief, fear, rejection, and sadness.

Telling your children about your divorce is apt to trigger a new flood of emotions inside of you, even if you thought that you had them under control. For example, you may feel guilt about the fact that you couldn't make your marriage work and that now your kids are hurting; anger toward your spouse if he or she did something to cause the divorce; sadness because your news made your kids cry; and so on. Be prepared to do whatever you need to do to deal with your own emotions because if you're an emotional basket case, you're not going to be much help to your children and are likely to make them even more scared and worried than they may already be. If you need suggestions for how to meet your own emotional needs, turn to Chapter 7.

In some jurisdictions, parents who are getting divorced are required to take parenting classes taught by mental health professionals. In these classes, parents learn about children's reactions to divorce, effective parent-child communication, and resources that can help parents and their children go through a divorce.

Fielding their questions

After you tell your children about your divorce plans, give them an opportunity to ask questions. Your children's initial questions will probably relate in some way to how your divorce will change their lives and what will stay the same. For example, depending on their ages, they may want to know

- ✔ Where will they live?
- ✔ Will they still go to the same school?
- ✔ Will you and your spouse still live in the same town?

- ✔ Will they spend time with each of you?

- ✔ Will you continue to coach their soccer or little league team?

- ✔ Can they continue their music or dance lessons?

- ✔ How will you share parenting responsibilities?

- ✔ Can they still go to camp next summer?

- ✔ Will there be enough money?

- ✔ Where will their dog or cat live?

Answer your children's questions clearly, calmly, and honestly. If they ask you something that you can't answer, admit that you don't know or that it's too soon to tell. When appropriate, tell them that you will give them an answer by a certain date or as soon as you can. If your children don't ask direct questions, you may be able to intuit their thoughts through their behavior and actions or by reading between the lines when they talk to you.

Your younger children may have a hard time grasping the concept of divorce and realizing that you and your spouse will always continue to love them and care for them. They may ask you the same questions over and over, which can really tax your patience. Understand that right now they need constant reassurance.

You can help your younger children deal with your divorce by reading them age-appropriate books that deal with the subject. We recommend the following titles to help your younger children acknowledge and express their fears and worries about your divorce and the changes that are occurring in their lives:

- ✔ *Dinosaurs Divorce: A Guide for Changing Families* by Marc Brown and Laurence Krasny Brown (Little, Brown & Co.)

- ✔ *Mama and Daddy Bear's Divorce* by Cornelia Spelman (Albert Whitman & Company)

- ✔ *I Don't Want to Talk About It: A Story About Divorce for Young Children* by Jeanie Franz Ransom (Magination Press)

- ✔ *My Family is Changing* by Pat Thomas (Barron's Educational Series)

Don't be surprised if your children don't ask you many questions at first. Learning that you're getting a divorce may come as quite a shock to them, even if they're aware that you and your spouse are having marital problems and even if they have plenty of friends with divorced parents. They may need to let the news sink in before they're ready to ask you questions. Also, your older children may not come to you with questions until after they've shared your news with their close friends, especially if those friends are the children of divorce and they tell your kids what their parents' divorce was like for them.

Let your children know that you're willing and available to talk with them about your divorce and to answer their questions whenever they want. If time passes and they seem reluctant to ask you questions, take the initiative by talking with each of them individually and asking them whether they have any questions about your divorce.

Pick up a copy of *Difficult Questions Kids Ask and Are Too Afraid to Ask About Divorce* by Meg F. Schneider and Joan Offerman-Zuckerberg (Fireside). We recommend this title if you want advice on how to tell your children the truth without frightening them, how to strengthen your relationship with them, and how to keep and build their trust. Regardless of your children's ages, this book is likely to be helpful.

Divorce can be particularly difficult for preteens and teens, so you may want to purchase some of the following books for them:

- *The Divorce Helpbook by Teens* **by Cynthia MacGregor (Impact Publishers):** This book talks to teens about divorce; discusses the emotions they're feeling; and addresses many of the difficult issues they may be thinking about, such as how to deal with the sadness and depression they feel, how to tell one parent that they don't want to spend as much time with him or her, and what to do if their parents are trying to make them go-betweens.

- *How it Feels When Parents Divorce* **by Jill Krementz (Knopf):** This book can be helpful to teens as well as younger children. It shares the experiences and feelings of children whose parents have gone through a divorce. The book helps children understand that the emotions they may be feeling are normal and that other children of divorce have had to deal with many of the very same changes that they're facing now.

- *My Parents are Divorced, Too: A Book for Kids by Kids* **by Jan Blackstone-Ford, Annie Ford, Melanie Ford, and Steven Ford (Magination Press):** Written by kids for kids, this book takes on the toughest questions your older kids (ages 8 to 12 year, approximately) may have about your divorce.

If your kids act uninterested in the books when you first bring them home, leave them in a place where they can see them. When they're ready, your kids may start reading the books. Also, before you give the books to your children, you may want to read them to gain insight into what your kids feel like right now. That insight can help you do a better job of parenting them during your divorce.

Helping Your Kids Cope over Time

After you've told your children about your divorce plans, it's important that you behave in a way that reflects the promises you made to your children about what life would be like for them in the future.

Watching your own behavior around your children

Monitor your own behavior around your children. What you choose to do (or *not* do, as the following list tells you) can help reassure them that things will be okay or can add to their anxiety about the future. Consider the following tips to avoid stoking any fires of concern:

- Don't fight with your spouse when your children are around.

- Don't say negative things about your spouse to your children or to someone else within earshot of your children.

- Avoid sharing your anger or frustration about your spouse with your children. Also, don't speak negatively of your spouse to your friends and family when your children are around. They may overhear the very information you don't want them to know about. Also, the tone of voice and your body language may upset them.

- Don't get overly emotional around your children about your divorce or about what life will be like after the divorce. You risk increasing their insecurity and fear about the future.

- Don't use your children as liaisons between you and your spouse. If you have something to convey to your spouse, speak directly to your spouse or through your attorneys, not through your kids.

- Don't interfere in your children's relationship with your spouse by trying to manipulate them into thinking of you as the "good parent" and your spouse as the "bad parent."

- Don't pressure your kids to choose sides in your divorce.

- Avoid making dramatic changes in their daily routines. As much as possible, keep everything in their lives just as it was before your divorce. Children generally don't like change, and divorce is change enough.

- Don't attempt to assuage your guilt over how your divorce may affect your children by giving them special gifts or privileges or by relaxing your discipline of them.

✔ Avoid making your children your confidantes. Keep your adult worries and concerns to yourself or share them only with other adults.

✔ Don't expect your children to comfort you. You should be the one comforting them.

✔ Don't expect your child to become "the little man" or "the little woman" of the house. Your kids are kids, not surrogate spouses.

Remaining sensitive to your children's feelings

When you get divorced, you and your spouse aren't the only ones affected by the change in your marital status. Your divorce means the end of family life as your children know it, which is something that has been a key foundation in their lives and something that they've probably always taken for granted.

As a result of your divorce your children may also experience a change in their economic circumstances and/or they may have to move out of their home and neighborhood, attend a new school, and make all new friends. Therefore, even if your divorce is a good thing for you, unless you're aware of what to do and what not to do in regard to your children and unless you stay attuned to troubling changes in their moods and behaviors, and do whatever you can to help them cope with the impact of the divorce on their lives, your divorce may be emotionally devastating for them.

When parents divorce, children often fear that they will lose one of their parents or that their parents will abandon them and they'll have to fend for themselves. Therefore, both you and your spouse need to convey in your words *and* deeds that you will always be there for your kids. For example, if you promise your children that you'll do something for them, do it. Also let your children know that you love and appreciate them, and make plans with them to do something in the future — maybe a trip to the beach. And, if your children are nearing college age, start talking with them about which colleges they want to attend and make plans to visit some of those schools with them.

If you don't tend to your children's needs during your divorce (and afterward), you risk making them the innocent victims of your marital breakup. For example, you may cause them to begin having problems at school, get into trouble with the law, develop substance abuse problems, and so on.

Research also shows that parents who openly express their hatred, anger, feelings of betrayal, or desire for vengeance — feelings that many couples have toward one another during divorce and sometimes long after — unwittingly program their kids to be unhappy adults with troubled marriages of their own. Parents also harm their children by manipulating them in order to gain the upper hand in custody negotiations or to get back at the other spouse. Couples who use their children as pawns in their divorce games put their children in a terribly difficult and unfair position because most children love both of their parents equally.

If your children have gone through a divorce before, don't assume that it's going to be easier for them the second time around. The second divorce may trigger the very same emotions that they experienced during your first divorce because once again their lives are being disrupted and they're experiencing for a second time the discomfort of living with two parents who are preoccupied with the details of their divorce. Furthermore, because your children will be older than they were when you got divorced the first time, their emotions may be more intense, and they may also experience new emotions that may cause them to respond differently to your second divorce.

To help monitor how well your children are coping with the news of your divorce, try to spend some extra time with them (but not in an interfering way). For example, spend more time in the same room with them than you usually do so you can watch their behavior and be more attuned to them when they're in the car with you, when you're sharing meals, and so on. Also, the time you spend with your kids gives them an opportunity to express their feelings and concerns about how your divorce will affect their daily lives.

Although your children may appear to be coping well, don't assume that they're not having trouble or won't have trouble later on. Watch for any mood swings or changes in behavior that may signal emotional problems. Touch base periodically with their teachers and caregivers to find out whether they've noticed any problems.

What your kids may be fearing (but not telling you)

During and after their parents' divorce, children (especially the younger ones) often become fearful that terrible things will happen to them or believe that they're responsible for the breakup of their parents' marriage. Some of the most common fears and misconceptions kids have about divorce include

✔ My parents' divorce is my fault.

✔ The parent I no longer live with will leave me forever.

✔ If I am really good, my parents will get back together.

✔ I have to choose between my parents. I can't have a relationship with both of them after they're divorced.

✔ My mother's or father's new significant other will replace my real parent.

✔ My new stepbrother or stepsister is going to replace me.

Understanding the thoughts that may be going through your children's minds can keep you alert to any signs that they are having trouble coping with your divorce.

Being prepared for your children's initial reactions

After your children find out about your divorce plans, they may begin to feel isolated and cut off from their friends. They may feel as though they're the only children whose parents ever got divorced and may be embarrassed about what's happening to them. On the other hand, if you and your spouse fought openly and often during your marriage or if violence or substance abuse colored your relationship, your divorce may be a relief to your children and represent a positive change in their lives.

For a sensitive and comprehensive overview of the stresses that children commonly feel when their parents are going through a divorce, and detailed advice on what parents can do to help their kids, head to the University of Missouri Extension Web site at `http://muextension.missouri.edu/xplor/hesguide/humanrel/gh6600.htm`.

If your children are having trouble coping with the news of your divorce, all you may need to do in order to turn their frowns into smiles is to cuddle them more and give them a little extra attention. But sometimes it's not that simple. When your children need more than what you can give them, consider involving a school counselor, mental health professional, social worker, relative, or another adult who's especially close to your children. Participating in a divorce support group for kids may also be helpful to your older children.

Tell your children's teachers, babysitters, other caregivers, the parents of their close friends, and any other adults who they see regularly about your divorce plans. Your heads-up will help those adults stay attuned to any significant changes in the ways your children behave. Ask the adults to keep you informed of any worrisome changes.

Another option is to contact your state's family law court, your divorce attorney, mental health professional, or a social worker who works with children and families to find out about any public or private resources (such as classes, workshops, and support groups) that may be available in your area to help your kids cope with your divorce. Some of these same resources may also offer counseling for divorcing parents.

For valuable resources that can help your children cope with your divorce, check out

> ✔ **The Divorce Kids Web site (`www.divorce-kids.com`):** This Web site reassures kids that they're not the first kids to go through a divorce and helps them adjust to the changes in their lives. It helps kids cope with stepparents and stepsiblings. The site also helps parents understand what their children may be going through and offers advice on how to help them.

✔ **A Kid's Guide to Divorce (`www.kidshealth.org/kid/feeling/ home_family/divorce.html`):** This site provides caring explanations of divorce and why it happens, discusses the feelings kids may experience when they learn that their parents' marriage is ending, and suggests things kids can do to cope.

✔ **KidsTurnCentral (`www.kidsturncentral.com/topics/issues/ divorce.htm`):** This Web site is just for kids. It features a variety of information and other resources for kids of all ages, like links to Web sites to help them cope with divorce, a Web site for posting their divorce-related drawings, personal stories from kids who have gone through divorce, and a chat group where kids can talk to one another about how they're feeling and what they're experiencing, a children of divorce bill of rights, and much more.

✔ *The Truth About Children and Divorce: Dealing with the Emotions So You and Your Children Can Thrive* **by Robert E. Emery (Viking Books):** Written by a therapist and mediator, this book helps parents help their children as well as themselves get through divorce and rebuild their lives after divorce.

✔ *Helping Your Kids Cope with Divorce the Sandcastles Way* **by M. Gary Neuman (Random House):** This book is based on the Sandcastles workshop concept, a workshop for children ages 6 to 17 that helps them deal with their feelings about divorce through activities, such as drawing, poetry, role playing, and so on.

Chapter 7

Handling the Emotions of Divorce

*F*or better or worse, your marriage is an important part of your life. So, if you're like most people, ending it won't be easy on your emotions — whether you initiate the divorce, it's a mutual decision, or your spouse is the one who calls it quits.

As the reality of your divorce sinks in, clear and rational thinking may become difficult, if not impossible. While one part of your brain may know that getting divorced is for the best (or at least inevitable), the other part may be a jumbled and confused mess of emotions. You may find yourself distracted by questions such as, "Will I have enough money to live on?"; "Where will I live?"; "How will my divorce affect my children?"; and "Will I ever marry again?" These and other thoughts may make it difficult for you to focus on your day-to-day activities and to get a good night's sleep. You may have similar problems if you and your spouse separate.

Getting divorced can be like taking a ride on an emotional roller coaster. One day you feel angry, sad, depressed, and guilty, and the next you feel hopeful about the future and confident in your ability to handle whatever comes your way. Your feelings may even change from morning to afternoon or from hour to hour. Most likely, your emotions will be most intense at the start of your divorce and gradually lessen over time. Little things may trigger swings in your mood: you hear a song that you and your spouse used to enjoy; you go to a party by yourself and feel awkward trying to make conversation; you run across photos of you and your spouse in happier times; your child asks you a question that you find especially painful, and so on.

If you did not initiate your divorce, and especially if your spouse's desire to split up took you totally by surprise, your emotions will probably be especially intense. Whatever your situation, this chapter helps you understand the emotions that you're likely to feel and provides you with suggestions for managing them. The more you understand your feelings, the better you'll be able to put them in perspective, to handle them in a positive way, and to prevent them from making your divorce more difficult than it already is.

Understanding the Stages of Grief

Elisabeth Kubler-Ross, MD, wrote an important book about grief and loss called *On Death and Dying* (Scribner). In it, she explains that when someone loses a close loved one, that person must progress through a series of stages in order to get over the loss and to heal emotionally. Those stages, which follow, have been found to apply to the loss of anything that is especially important in someone's life, including marriage:

- Shock and denial
- Anger
- Depression
- Bargaining
- Sorrow
- Understanding and acceptance

Becoming familiar with each of the stages you must pass through in order to recover from a divorce won't make your pain go away. In fact, as you experience some of the earlier stages of grief, you may feel like you're going crazy or that life will never be normal again. However, knowing what to expect, realizing that what you're feeling is normal, and finding out that countless other people in your situation have experienced exactly what you're going through and have gone on to find happiness in life can be very reassuring.

Because your judgment may be somewhat impaired during the early stages of the grief process, avoid making important decisions related to your divorce and to your life in general whenever possible. Try to wait until you've reached the understanding and acceptance stage. If you can't put off certain important decisions until then, seek some objective decision-making advice from a trusted friend or family member, a mental health professional, or your religious advisor.

The length of the grieving process is different for everyone. For some it lasts only a few months, whereas others take a year or more to get through it. Furthermore, even after you think you've stopped grieving, something may happen that triggers your emotions all over again. When that happens, think about what helped you cope with your emotions when you were in the early stages of the grieving process and try those same things again.

Shock and denial

Even if you knew that your marriage had problems and that your spouse was unhappy, the news that he or she wants a divorce can be gut-wrenching. *Divorce?* That's something that happens to other people, not to you! If the decision to divorce is a mutual one, you may still find it difficult to comprehend that your marriage is actually ending.

During this stage of the grieving process, you may waver between thinking that your divorce is just a silly misunderstanding and that you and your spouse can work things out. You may also find yourself questioning your judgment (were you too naïve, too trusting, too ready to forgive?) and the assumptions you made about your marriage and your spouse (was he really such a great guy, did he really love you?). You may also feel anxious about and unprepared to handle all the changes that are about to take place in your life because your marriage is ending.

Anger

Anger commonly follows shock (although not for everyone). Anger is a normal response to the demise of your marriage, especially if your spouse initiates the divorce. In addition to being angry with your spouse, you may be angry with yourself for the things you could have done but didn't do that might have saved your marriage or for all the sacrifices you made on behalf of your spouse and your relationship.

Expressing your anger is actually a healthy response that can help relieve some of the pressure you feel. Keeping anger bottled up inside can lead to depression. Of course, it's also possible for you to get *too* angry. If you let your anger get the best of you, you may find yourself lashing out at your children, experiencing problems at work, and getting into conflicts with others, making your divorce far more difficult and ugly than it needs to be.

If you get angry every time you talk with your spouse or even think about her, try to figure out why. Putting your finger on the reasons may take professional help. What buttons does your spouse push for you and vice versa? The sooner you can answer that question, the quicker you can get off the emotional roller coaster ride you're on.

One suggestion for what to do when you start to get angry is to write down the reasons you feel that way or write down all the things you would like to say to your spouse. Sometimes just putting your feelings on paper can help you clarify your emotions and take away their intensity so that you can deal with them better. Another suggestion is to check out the anger tool kit available at www.angermgmt.com. It can help you dissect your angry feelings so you can deal with them constructively and move beyond them.

You may also want to talk to a close friend or relative about the anger you feel. Ideally, this person will just listen to you blow off steam and won't tell you how to think, argue with you, or take your spouse's side. Avoid sharing your feelings with someone who will reinforce your anger and convince you that feeling angry all the time is okay. Feeling some anger for a little while is okay, but harboring too much anger for too long is dangerous and destructive. Moving beyond anger is important.

When you can't seem to shake your anger, especially if you've become confrontational or violent, seek the help of a mental health professional immediately. Confiding in someone who can help you put your feelings in perspective and help you find better ways of coping with them is imperative.

Depression

Depression is another perfectly normal response to a difficult life situation. However, if your depression doesn't go away or grows worse, if you begin having problems getting out of bed in the morning and carrying out your day-to-day responsibilities, you are crying all of the time, gaining or losing weight, ignoring your physical appearance, start drinking too much or doing drugs to numb your feelings, or if you're having thoughts of suicide, immediately seek help from a mental health professional. You may need therapy and an antidepressant.

If your doctor prescribes an antidepressant, it doesn't mean that you're crazy; it simply means that you need some help handling the trauma of your divorce in the safest way possible. Many people in your same situation have needed exactly the same kind of help. Most likely, you will take the antidepressant for a limited period of time and once you are feeling better, your therapist will take you off the drug.

A correlation exists between divorce and suicide. In fact, some studies indicate that the rate of suicide among divorcing couples is three times higher than among married couples.

Right now you may not believe that you will ever feel happy again, but take heart. Over time, your negative emotions will subside and, eventually, you'll feel like smiling again.

Bargaining

At times during the healing process, you may respond to your divorce by trying to strike bargains with your spouse. In desperation, you may promise to do just about anything to keep your marriage together and to make the pain go away.

Avoid making such deals. If your spouse accepts your offer and you stop your divorce proceedings, you may only be postponing the inevitable. The promises you made to your spouse may be impossible for you to keep, and you may find that you're more miserable than ever in your marriage. If you're tempted to promise your spouse the world in order to save your marriage, talk to a trusted friend or therapist first to get an objective outsider's perspective on what you are about to do.

Sorrow

Feeling sad is another normal response to the end of your marriage. You may cry over what your relationship used to be or over the realization that all the dreams and hopes you had for your marriage won't be realized. You may mourn the loss of your role as a spouse and greatly miss the lifestyle you enjoyed as a married person.

You may also feel remorse over what your divorce may do to your children. They may have to move into a smaller house or apartment and leave behind their neighborhood, best friends, and favorite teachers, for example. In addition, you may mourn the fact that your children will be living with your spouse and you won't be as much a part of their lives as you used to be.

The realization that you're losing the wife or husband role that you greatly value may also trigger feelings of sorrow. You may feel sad about the lifestyle change getting divorced is going to bring — no longer being part of a couple, living apart from your children, moving into a smaller home, living in a less comfortable neighborhood, giving up club memberships or hobbies that you can no longer afford, and the like.

If you're feeling sad about what divorce is taking from your life, realize that no situation lasts forever. In the future, you may experience a more loving and more successful relationship, make more money, and even have more children. Use what you learned in this last relationship to make your married life better the next time around.

Understanding and acceptance

If you're like most people, eventually you will begin to accept the fact of your divorce. Ideally, you should reach this stage before you begin negotiating your divorce agreement with your spouse, but many people are not able to make peace with the fact that their marriage is ending until after their divorce is final. Regardless of when you reach that stage, you will finally begin to experience some calm in your life.

At the understanding and acceptance stage in the grieving process, although you may still feel some anger or depression, those emotions won't be as intense as they used to be and should continue to dissipate gradually. Also, your energy level will climb, and your enthusiasm for life will return. Laughter will come easier to you, you'll be ready to begin dating again, and you'll feel ready to take on new challenges.

Sometimes it's good for a trusted friend who knows you and your spouse well to play devil's advocate when you're talking about what went wrong with your marriage, especially if you're particularly wronged by him or her. By doing so, your friend may be able to help you gain a balanced perspective about your marriage and why it ended.

If you begin dating, keep it casual. Studies show that rebound marriages — marriages that occur just a short time after a couple's divorce is finalized — have a high failure rate. Divorced spouses need time to gain a perspective on why their marriages failed and to understand what they need to do (or not do) next time in order to increase their chances of marital success.

Preventing Your Emotions from Taking Over

How you handle your emotions can mean the difference between creating a fulfilling life for yourself as a single person and remaining stuck in the past. It can also mean the difference between helping your children cope with the situation and jeopardizing their happiness now and in the future. You can end up bitter, angry, and defeated, or you can emerge from your divorce stronger and more self-confident.

It's important to recognize the possible negative effects of not dealing with the emotions you're feeling. Letting your emotions go unchecked can

- Impede your ability to make sound decisions.
- Sap your energy at the time you need it most.
- Prevent you from recognizing and acknowledging how you may have contributed to the demise of your marriage.
- Make you more apt to acquiesce in your divorce negotiations, especially if you feel wracked with guilt and remorse. Conversely, your emotions may also make it more likely that you'll dig in your heels during the negotiations, refuse to give an inch to your spouse, and cause your divorce to end up in court.
- Drive away your friends and family.
- Make life more difficult for your children.

You can take some steps to help yourself move through the emotional healing process as quickly as possible.

- ✔ **Give yourself permission to cry.** Crying is *not* a sign of weakness. It can be a great way to release emotion. Plus, crying releases natural antidepressant chemicals in your brain, so a good cry can actually make you feel better! However, if you cry all the time, you probably need to see a therapist. You may be depressed.

- ✔ **Reach out to close friends and family members.** Sometimes just talking with the people you feel closest to, sharing a meal with them, or letting them pamper you a little will make you feel a whole lot better.

- ✔ **Join a divorce support group.** A support group is a particularly good idea if you're not comfortable talking with friends and family about your divorce, if you feel that you may be wearing out your welcome with them, or if you don't feel that they're giving you the support you need.

- ✔ **Keep a journal.** The process of recording your thoughts and feelings on paper can help you feel calmer and can help you gain a new perspective on your life.

- ✔ **Begin an exercise program or start exercising more.** Exercise can make you feel better about yourself, which is something you may really need if your spouse initiated your divorce. Additionally, science has shown that exercise helps release those wonderful endorphins, which help lift your spirits naturally and ease depression.

- ✔ **Be kind to yourself and enjoy focusing on your own needs instead of on your spouse or on your marriage problems.** Renew your interest in a sport you used to enjoy, pick up a new book by your favorite author, or take up a new hobby.

- ✔ **Enroll in a class, just for the fun of it, or with an eye toward future employment or a new career.** You can explore and develop new talents while making new friends.

- ✔ **Do something you've always wanted to do.** Plan a trip with a friend, take a hot air balloon ride, or sign up for ballroom dancing classes.

- ✔ **Volunteer.** Getting involved in a cause that you care about can boost your self-esteem and take your mind off your own problems. If you have trouble getting motivated to do anything other than sleep and eat, the more you can structure your life, the better. Volunteer work is one way to do that.

- ✔ **Get reacquainted with friends you lost touch with after your marriage began failing.** Renewing friendships with people you used to enjoy may be just what you need to put a little spark back in your life.

- ✔ **Focus on your career.** However, don't let your work consume your entire life. Withdrawing into your job won't make the unpleasantness of your current situation disappear.

✔ **Spend more time with your children.** Making your children an even more important part of your life than they already are helps reassure them that your divorce has not diminished your love for them and that you will continue to be a part of their lives, no matter what.

✔ **Appreciate nature.** The beauty of nature can help heal a wounded spirit. Go for walks in the park or along a waterfront, pause to take in the sunrise and sunset, listen to the birds, or smell the air after a hard rain.

✔ **Make a point of taking a break from your troubles.** Go for a bike ride or a drive in the country, go to a movie, enroll in a class, or take a short vacation if you can afford it and if the time away doesn't interfere with your divorce proceedings.

✔ **Explore your spirituality.** Become more involved in your church, temple, or synagogue. Begin meditating or studying yoga. To get started, try the video *Yoga Workouts For Dummies* or pick up a copy of *Meditation For Dummies* by Stephan Bodian or *Power Yoga For Dummies* by Doug Swenson (all published by Wiley).

✔ **Seek out the friends and family members who have a positive influence on your life.** Doing things together and sharing your thoughts with people you like and trust can take your mind off your troubles and help you gain a healthy perspective about your life changes.

✔ **Schedule time with your religious advisor or a mental health professional.** Counseling can help you put your marriage in perspective and assess what went wrong. Then you can think more clearly about what the future may hold.

If you've tried the suggestions in the preceding list and you're still feeling blue, figure out what's missing in your life and identify safe and healthy ways to fulfill those needs. For example, if you miss the physical contact you had with your spouse, a massage or hugs from your friends may help you feel better. If you enjoy restaurant meals, ask a friend to split a two-for-one meal coupon.

Use your creativity. You may discover inexpensive activities that are just as enjoyable — and maybe even more enjoyable — than some of your more costly predivorce pastimes.

Dealing with the Response of Friends and Family

No doubt most of you will share the news that you're getting divorced with your friends and family soon after you've made your decision. You may even discuss the pros and cons of divorce with your very closest friends and family members before you decide to end your marriage.

Your decision to divorce shouldn't affect your close personal relationships; your true friends will remain friendly no matter what your marital status may be. But be ready for those friends and family members who may view the divorced you a little differently than the married you.

If your friends give you the brush-off

Almost inevitably, some of the friends and acquaintances you and your spouse shared as a couple will stop calling you after your divorce becomes common knowledge. Others may act aloof and distant when you cross paths. That sort of behavior can be very hurtful, especially if you already feel rejected.

Some friends may behave as they do because they feel that they can't be friends with you *and* your spouse, and so they've decided to side with your spouse. Some of them may have business or social reasons for choosing your spouse, or they may feel some loyalty toward your spouse because they knew him or her before they knew you. Try not to dwell on their behavior. Some of those friends may come around over time, but others never will.

Some friends who act uncomfortable around you may do so because your situation reminds them of their own marital troubles. Others may feel awkward because they're uncertain how to behave when they're with you. They may be wondering whether they should tell you that they're sorry about your divorce or ignore the subject until you bring it up.

If certain friends are important to you, consider making the first move — invite them over for coffee, ask them if they want to play tennis or go shopping, or invite their children to come play with yours. They may feel awkward about your divorce and your invitation may help break the ice.

If your family disapproves of your divorce

You may also notice your relationship with some of your family members becoming chilled now that you're getting a divorce. Your relatives may disapprove of your divorce plans, maybe because no one in your family has gotten divorced before, for religious reasons, or because they're very fond of your spouse.

It's also possible that things may have become strained between you and your family (and your in-laws, if you were close) because they resent that you're relying on them for help with childcare more now than you did before. Or they may be uncomfortable with your requests to borrow money from them, or tired of complaints about your ex-spouse.

Finding humor in the end of a marriage

Gifts for the newly divorced, albeit not always in the best of taste, are part of a booming industry that is trying to put a humorous spin on the end of a marriage. They range from "happy divorce" chocolate bars, ex-husband and ex-wife voodoo dolls — pins included — and wedding ring coffins, to divorce greeting cards, tee-shirts, healing baskets, and other items just too tacky to mention here.

Divorce celebration parties are also becoming popular. Some wedding cake makers have begun making new profits by baking divorce cakes that often feature one miniature spouse figure kicking the other off of the top of the cake or positioned upside down on the cake with his or her head buried in the frosting. Also, an enterprising New Orleans resident rents out a hearse to divorcees who want to ride around town in the vehicle with their friends while partying to celebrate the end of their marriage.

Although you should expect your family to support you through tough times, don't take their support or patience for granted. If they help you out, let them know that you appreciate their generosity and stay alert for ways that you can return their favors. Also, try to be sensitive to just how much you can lean on a family member — everyone has limits — and avoid crossing that line.

If your kids enjoy a loving relationship with your in-laws

If your children have always had good relationships with your in-laws, don't let any negative emotions you may be feeling toward your spouse poison your children's relationship with their grandparents. In fact, difficult as it may be, you should do everything you can to let that relationship continue, even if you know that your in-laws are upset about your divorce and maybe even angry with you about it. The grandparent/grandchild relationship is a special kind of relationship, and your children are lucky to have it. So, encourage and support the relationship; don't interfere with it.

Part III
Deciding the Basic Issues in Your Divorce

The 5th Wave   By Rich Tennant

"The attorney said I could initiate a divorce by filing a petition. It sounds like something I'm supposed to stand outside a supermarket and get people to sign."

In this part . . .

The decisions you must make about the issues in your divorce may be some of the most difficult ones you've ever faced. For example, you and your spouse must decide how to divvy up your marital property and debt, what to do about the custody of your minor children, and how much child support one of you will pay the other. Spousal support may be another issue you must resolve. The chapters in this part of the book provide you with information and advice to help you make these important decisions, whether you and your spouse make them together in consultation with your attorneys or you rely on your attorneys to do all the negotiating for you.

Chapter 8

Dividing Your Assets and Your Debts

. . . .

In This Chapter

▶ Identifying which assets are yours and which ones you own with your spouse

▶ Figuring out the value of the assets from your marriage

▶ Dividing up the assets from your marriage

▶ Deciding what to do about your home, retirement benefits, and your joint business

▶ Determining who will pay your marital debts

. . . .

*I*f your marriage has been a relatively lengthy one, and if you and your spouse have enjoyed a reasonably comfortable standard of living, you may be surprised to discover how much stuff the two of you have managed to accumulate over the years and just how much it's all worth. Dividing up your marital property requires deliberation and possibly the advice and assistance of outside experts. How you divvy up your assets during your divorce has short- and long-term financial implications for you and your spouse.

This chapter focuses on what to do about the big stuff from your marriage when you and your spouse are deciding how to divide everything up. The "big stuff" includes your home, any retirement benefits you earned during your marriage, and your financial investments — as well as some of the smaller items. We also offer some suggestions for what to do with your marital debts — the debts that you and your spouse acquired during your marriage. For guidance and advice on negotiating the terms of your divorce with your spouse, including how to divide up your assets and debts, see Chapter 12.

Categorizing Your Property

During your marriage, you may have bought a home, furniture, vehicles, expensive computer equipment, stocks, bonds, and mutual funds, and maybe even fine art. No doubt you also own other less-valuable items, too, like kitchen equipment, a TV set, a DVD player, books, and bikes. And, don't forget that pile of wedding gifts you've had stashed in the attic for years! Now that you're getting divorced, you have to do something with that stuff.

As part of your divorce, you and your spouse can informally divide up the less-valuable stuff you own. This division is a matter of making sure that each of you gets your fair share of what you need to set up new households and that you get to take at least some of the items that have special meaning to you. Chapter 12 suggests some ways of accomplishing this division.

Distinguishing between tangible property and intangible property

When you divide up your more significant assets, you and your spouse should take into account whether those assets are *intangible or intangible assets. Intangible property* refers to assets that have no intrinsic or marketable value, but instead represent value. They include retirement benefits, stocks, and bonds. *Tangible assets,* such as your car and your home, are assets that you can touch and that have a marketable value by themselves.

Identifying separate property versus marital property

Before you can divide up the value of your property, you and your spouse must first determine which assets are *marital property,* or assets that you own together and which ones are your *separate property*. Each of you is legally entitled to a share of the value of marital property, and separate property is yours to keep. If you haven't already done so, inventory and categorize all your assets. (By the way, a closely held business or business interest may be considered marital property. You need an attorney's help dealing with such an asset.) Chapter 3 gives you some advice on how best to do your inventorying and categorizing.

The property laws of your state ordinarily determine which assets are marital assets and which ones are not. But if you and your spouse signed a valid prenuptial and/or postnuptial agreement, you may have already decided how you intend to divide up your property in the event of a split.

Detangling the confusion of commingled property

In the course of your marriage, you and your spouse may have mixed together your separate property or may have mixed your separate property with your marital property. For example, you may have used some of your separate property to improve the rental property that you and your spouse own, or both of you may have deposited your separate money into a joint account. Blending together different kinds of property is called *commingling,* and unless both of you have kept detailed records of exactly what you did with your assets, distinguishing between marital property and separate property may be difficult, if not impossible.

If you and your spouse try to decide which portion of your commingled assets you should treat as separate property and who owns that separate property, your decisions will probably be based on your best guess. But if the court decides, the standard used to make that determination depends on your state.

You can use forensic accountants to trace the commingled assets, but that can cost you more than what your attorneys may charge!

Assessing the Value of Your Assets

After you determine which of your assets constitutes marital property, you need to assign a dollar value to each of them. Ordinarily, that dollar figure is the item's *fair market value,* or the amount that you could reasonably expect to sell it for.

Although you can probably value many of your marital assets yourselves, you may need the help of outside experts, such as appraisers and CPAs, to determine the worth of particularly valuable or complex assets, such as real estate, certain types of retirement benefits, fine antiques, a closely held business, and so on. An outside expert's services can also be helpful if you and your spouse can't agree on how to value an important asset.

After you value your marital assets, you must determine their total value and then divide that amount either by applying the property law concepts and guidelines that would be applied in your state if your divorce went to trial or by applying some other criteria that you and your spouse both agree to.

When deciding which property to take from your marriage, keep in mind your personal goals for your life after divorce, the separate property you already own, and your postdivorce financial needs.

Divvying Up Your Assets

If you don't have a lot of complicated assets, like retirement plans, investments, and business interests, for example, or a lot of debt, you and your spouse may be able to divide up your assets and debts by yourselves. The information in this section provides general advice for how to do that and explains the criteria you should consider when you're doing the dividing.

Doing the dividing yourself

If you and your spouse do your own dividing, your individual judgments about what is and isn't fair and your ability to compromise with one another influence how you end up allocating the value of your marital property. (See Chapter 12 for details on how to negotiate your marital property.)

Bear in mind that if you and your spouse end up in court after your divorce is final because one of you wants your property division agreement overturned, the judge will assess the fairness of your agreement in light of your state's property laws and property division guidelines. Therefore, even when you divide your marital property yourself, keep your state's laws in mind:

- ✔ If you live in an *equitable distribution* state (see Chapter 3 to find out what type of state you live in), you're entitled to your *fair share* of the value of your marital property. Your fair share is whatever the judge decides you're entitled to based on the guidelines that your state uses to divide up marital property or whatever your lawyer negotiates for you.

- ✔ If you live in a *community property* state (see Chapter 3), the general presumption is that you and your spouse are each entitled to half the value of your marital property. But, in reality, your state probably allows the court to divide up your marital property on an equitable basis rather than splitting everything strictly 50/50, taking into account many of the same criteria that the court in an equitable distribution state would use.

If you and your spouse are handling your own property division negotiations, and especially if the total value of what you own together is substantial, it's a good idea to consult with a certified divorce planner, a qualified CPA, or a financial planner before you start dividing what you own and what you owe. These financial professionals can help you analyze the best way to deal with not only the division of your property and your debts, but also help you figure out how to handle child support and spousal support.

Why women's standard of living often decreases

After a divorce, a woman's standard of living tends to decline, whereas, on average, a man's rises. One explanation for this difference is that men usually earn more than women, so they tend to be able to afford better divorce lawyers and have more financial resources to fall back on after their divorce. Another explanation is that women are more apt to stay home during their marriage in order to raise the children (or work sporadically) and so they are at an earnings disadvantage when they join the work world after their marriage ends. In addition, women are more apt to get custody of the children and, although they may receive child support, in most divorces, the amount of the support doesn't allow the average woman to maintain her predivorce lifestyle. Of course, a significant number of women with custody of their children don't receive their court-ordered child support or receive it only occasionally.

If you find yourself in a tough financial position, the following books can help you get by on the money you have and deal with any money troubles that may develop:

- ✔ *Managing Debt For Dummies* by John Ventura and Mary Reed (Wiley)

- ✔ *The Budget Kit: The Common Cents Money Management Workbook* by Judy Lawrence (Wiley)

- ✔ *Women and Money: Owning the Power to Control Your Destiny* by Suze Orman (Spiegal & Grau)

You and your spouse can share the cost of hiring the same financial professional, or you can each hire your own. If you share one, don't hire a professional who is related to either of you, is a friend of either of yours, or is a professional associate of yours or your spouse's. If you do, the spouse who doesn't have the relationship with the financial professional may view as suspect whatever conclusions the professional reaches.

Leaving the decisions to the legal experts

If you and your spouse involve attorneys in your property division negotiations or if you look to the court to decide who gets what, your state's property laws and property division guidelines take center stage. The prejudices and preferences of the judge or jury who decide how your assets (and your debts) should be divvied up and the persuasiveness of your attorneys can also be big factors.

Although property division guidelines vary from state to state, they usually take the following factors into consideration:

✔ **How much you and your spouse each earn now and can be expected to earn in the future:** Often a judge awards a relatively larger share of marital property to the spouse who earns less money and who has the lower earnings potential. In evaluating your earnings potential, the judge may consider your education level, physical and mental health, and other factors that may have a bearing on your ability to earn a good living.

✔ **Your current standard of living:** A judge tries to allocate the value of your marital property between you and your spouse so that neither of you suffers a dramatic reversal in your lifestyle after you're divorced. But in reality, your lifestyle may change, often for the worse (especially if you're a woman).

✔ **The value of the separate property that each of you may own:** If one of you has considerably more separate property than the other, the wealthier spouse may end up with less marital property.

✔ **Your individual contributions to your marriage:** These days, most states recognize that earning money to pay the family's bills is only one way that a spouse can contribute to a marriage. Courts now acknowledge that being a full-time parent, helping your spouse advance his or her career, and making other contributions to a marriage also have a financial value.

If you worked so that your spouse could obtain a degree or professional license, your state may view that degree or license as a marital asset, and you may be entitled to a share of its value. In other states, you may be reimbursed for the value of your contribution to your spouse's education.

✔ **How long you were married:** The longer you were married, the more likely the court will view you and your spouse as equal partners. A long marriage often entitles the spouse with less separate property or a lower earnings potential to a greater share of the marital property.

✔ **Your age and health:** Older spouses and spouses who are in poor health often receive a greater share of their marital property than younger or healthier spouses.

✔ **Whether either of you squandered marital property:** If one of you wasted your joint funds by gambling or repeatedly making bad business investments or risky personal loans, for example, that spouse may end up with less marital property.

✔ **Other factors:** The court may consider other factors, too, such as whether either of you has a lot of debt from a previous marriage, is likely to come into a significant inheritance, helped increase the value of the other's separate property during your marriage, and so on. Also, in some states, the only factor the court considers when dividing a couple's property is the value of that property, with each spouse getting approximately half of that value.

Fault can be the single most important factor in the eyes of some courts in states where courts can consider fault when dividing up a couple's marital property and debts. For information on fault divorces, turn to Chapter 1.

If your former spouse agrees to pay you a substantial amount of money as part of your property settlement, securing that debt with an asset — just as a bank would do if you borrowed a significant amount of money from it — is a very good idea. That way, you increase the likelihood of actually receiving the money you're entitled to. For example, if your former spouse gets your family's home and, in return, is obligated to pay you $80,000 over the next ten years, secure that debt by placing an $80,000 lien on the house and record the lien at your county courthouse. Then, if your ex doesn't pay the money you're legally entitled to according to the terms of your divorce, the lien will prevent him or her from selling the house, borrowing against, or transferring it without paying you first. You may also want to foreclose on the home and then sell the property in order to get the money you former spouse should have paid to you.

Deciding What to Do with Your Home

When everything around you is changing, you may be tempted to hold on to your home at all costs. You probably feel comfortable living there, and perhaps you've spent a great deal of time and energy decorating it and landscaping your yard. Also, if you have young children and you're going to be their primary caregiver after your divorce, you may want to stay in your own home to bolster their sense of emotional security.

But when the matter of your home comes up, try to put your emotions aside and approach the decision about whether to keep it from a purely financial perspective. You may decide that holding on to your home after you divorce is neither wise nor financially realistic. On the other hand, with some savvy financial planning, you may find a way to hold on to it.

Here's the bottom line: Whatever you do about your home should be a rational decision, not an emotional one. If you let your emotions rule, you may end up losing your home eventually because you can't afford to keep up with the mortgage payments or the property taxes. Also, when you evaluate whether you can afford to keep your home, don't overlook the expenses associated with maintaining your home, such as interior and exterior painting, repair and servicing of the heating and AC systems, roof and foundation repair, lawn mowing, snow plowing, and so on. Such expenses can really add up, but they're essential to maintaining your home's value.

Finding out how much it's worth

You can determine the value of your home in a couple of inexpensive ways. The traditional way is to ask a real estate agent for some recent selling prices of comparable houses in your neighborhood and to advise you about how much you may be able to get for your house. However, the figure a real estate agent gives you represents only an approximation of your home's value. A better method, albeit a more expensive one, is for you and your spouse to hire a real estate appraiser to value your home. An appraiser's value tends to be more accurate. You and your spouse can hire an appraiser together as long as you select one who you both feel will give you an objective value. If you and your spouse each get your own appraisals, don't be surprised if the results are quite different. If that's the case, you and your spouse must either agree on which value is more accurate or hire a third appraiser and agree to accept whatever dollar value she assigns to your home.

Don't value your home based on its tax appraisal. Tax appraisals are always considerably less than a home's actual value.

Evaluating your options

Most divorcing couples resolve the "what to do about the house" problem in one of the following ways: by selling it, keeping it, or retaining an interest in it. Another option that some couples choose, especially in a depressed real estate market is to rent their home out for a while. Read on to find out more details about each of these options.

Selling it

If you decide to sell, remember that the selling price probably won't represent the actual amount of money you and your spouse will split between you. Most likely, you'll have a mortgage to pay off, selling costs, and possibly property taxes to deduct from the total amount your home sells for. Also, if you use a real estate broker to sell your home, you'll have to pay the broker a percentage of your home's gross selling price (that is, a *broker's fee*). After all is said and done, when you subtract those costs from your home's anticipated sale price, selling your house may not appear to be a very attractive option but may, nevertheless, be your best one.

Don't overlook the federal tax implications of selling your home, either, when you're deciding what to do with it. To understand how a sale may affect your federal taxes, talk to your CPA and read the IRS publication *Selling Your Home*, Number 523. You can order this publication by calling the IRS at 800-829-1040 or you can read it online at www.irs.gov/pub/irs-pdf/p523.pdf. You may also want to pick up a copy of *House Selling For Dummies* by Eric Tyson and Ray Brown (Wiley).

If the real estate market in your area has taken a sharp turn for the worse and the value of your home is now less than the amount you owe on it, you may want to consider a short sale, especially if neither you nor your spouse can afford to pay the note on your own and you're worried that the house will end up in foreclosure. In a *short sale,* the mortgage holder agrees to let you pay off your mortgage with the sale proceeds even though the proceeds are less than what you owe on your home. Before you can do a short sale, the mortgage lender must agree to it and you must complete certain paperwork. Be sure to get the agreement in writing and don't sign the agreement until you understand exactly what you are agreeing to. A potential drawback to a short sale is that the IRS may consider the difference between what you actually owed on your mortgage and the amount that you paid it off for as income to you, which could increase the amount of income taxes you owe on April 15.

Keeping it

Taking the house in your property settlement may be an option if you have enough other marital property that your spouse can take another asset of comparable value (or multiple assets with a total value that equals the value of your home). However, this option isn't viable for many couples; instead, some of those couples may work out a buy-sell agreement in which one spouse buys out the other's interest over time. We describe this option in the upcoming section "Retaining an interest in it."

If you want to keep the house, you'll get the mortgage that goes with it, as well. Therefore, review the household budget you projected for your life after divorce to make certain that you can truly afford the monthly mortgage payments, taxes, insurance, and the cost of upkeep on your home. If you take over responsibility for paying all these expenses without making certain that you can afford them, you may have to sell your home eventually or you may even lose it in a foreclosure. Chapter 3 tells you how to develop a budget.

If you want to keep your home and you will either take over the existing mortgage or get a new mortgage in your own name, here are some important words of advice: If your spouse is going to pay you spousal support, don't take the house under the assumption that you'll use the support payments to pay your mortgage. That assumption could be financially disastrous for you if your ex stops paying you support or falls behind on the payments. Worst-case scenario, you could find yourself facing foreclosure.

In some states, if you get your spouse's interest in the home that you owned together, your spouse will give you a special warranty deed. In turn, you'll give your spouse a deed of trust in order to secure your assumption of the mortgage loan, assuming there is a balance due on that loan.

If your spouse keeps the home, takes over the mortgage, and then defaults on the loan, the mortgage holder can look to you for payment, no matter what your divorce agreement may say. One way to handle that possibility is to add a *hold harmless provision* to your property settlement agreement, giving you the right to sue your former spouse for the money you may end up having to pay on the loan if the mortgage holder goes after you for the money due on the mortgage. However, you must go to court to enforce the provision and, even if you get a judgment against your spouse, you have no guarantee that you can actually collect what he or she owes you. A better option, if your spouse can qualify for a mortgage on the house, is for him to agree as part of your property settlement agreement to get a new mortgage and pay off the existing one. That way you have no legal obligation to pay the new loan.

In some states, a *deed of trust to secure assumption* gives you the right in the event that your spouse defaults on the mortgage after your divorce to dispossess (legally remove your spouse from the home) so that you can put a tenant in the house, or sell it in order to eliminate your financial and legal exposure on the home. However, to accomplish that, you must stay up-to-date on the status of your former spouse's mortgage payments, which may be difficult if not impossible, especially if you and your ex live in different towns or have little communication with one another.

Retaining an interest in it

You and your spouse may want to sell your home eventually, but for practical reasons you may decide to hold on to it for a while. For example, you may want your children to be able to live in the home until they complete high school or until the real estate market in your area improves. In this case, the spouse with primary responsibility for raising the children stays in the home with the kids. Your property agreement would then give you and your spouse an interest in that property.

If you opt for this sort of arrangement, be sure that your agreement addresses the following questions:

- How much of an interest do each of you have in the home?
- At what point must you put your house up for sale?
- Who will put the house up for sale?
- How will you determine the asking price?
- How will you and your spouse share all sale-related expenses?
- How will you and your spouse divide up the sale proceeds?
- How will you share the costs of repairing and maintaining the home and property taxes?

If each of you wants the option of buying out the other's interest in your home, you and your spouse should clearly define the buyout terms in your divorce agreement. If you'll still owe money on the mortgage after the buyout, your agreement should also address the following questions:

✔ How will you and your spouse pay the mortgage each month?

✔ How will you and your spouse pay the homeowner's insurance and property taxes?

✔ Who will be responsible for the cost of minor repairs and major ones, such as a new roof?

Your agreement should also specify the regular upkeep that your home requires in order to protect your investment in the property. You should specify who's responsible for doing the maintenance and how often. Enforcing this provision, however, may be tough.

Renting out your home

If you and your spouse want to sell your home, but the real estate market in your area has taken a turn for the worse, one option is to keep the house as rental property until the market improves. Renting it out may also be an option if you want to keep your home in your property settlement, but you can't afford to live there. The rental income would help defray the costs of owning the home by yourself.

If you and your spouse decide to rent out your family's home after your divorce, your property settlement agreement should addresses such issues as

✔ Who will be responsible for managing the property — selecting tenants, collecting the rent, taking care of repairs, initiating eviction proceedings against a tenant if needed, and so on. One of you may agree to act as property manager and handle such matters or you may decide that a better choice is to hire a professional property manager.

✔ If you turn a profit on the rental property, what will you do with the money? The two of you may decide to

- Keep a certain percentage of the money in a bank account so that you'll have money on hand to pay for repairs and maintenance, to help pay the mortgage on the property when you're between tenants, to cover taxes and insurance (assuming these expenses are not included in your monthly mortgage), and so on.

- Apply the extra money to your loan principal if you're still paying off the mortgage on the property. By putting extra money toward the principal, you'll pay off the note more quickly.

- Each take a share of the profit.

Understanding the capital gains tax

If you sell your house for enough money, you may have to pay a capital gains tax on your *capital gain,* or profit. A capital gain is the difference between your home's purchase price and its sale price minus the cost of any capital improvements you have made to it — for example, adding an addition to your home. However if you're single when you sell your home, you'll get a capital gains tax exclusion of up to $250,000, which means that you won't have to pay taxes on the first $250,000 of any profit you may realize from the sale. If you're married and file a joint tax return, you'll get a $500,000 exclusion. But married or single, to qualify for the exclusion, you must have lived in your home for at least two of the five years prior to its sale.

If you move a great deal, you'll be pleased to know that the capital gains tax exclusion is not a one-time thing: You can use it every two years for an unlimited number of times. Should you end up owing a capital gains tax on the sale of your home and assuming you and your spouse are above the 15 percent income tax bracket, you will be taxed at 15 percent. If you're at or below that tax bracket, you'll be taxed at 5 percent. If you don't know what tax bracket you're in, speak to your CPA.

If you and your spouse can't get along, sharing your home as rental property is probably a really bad idea, especially if one of you is going to be the property manager. It may be impossible for the two of you to agree on such basic issues as how much to ask in rent, who to rent to, how much to spend on repairs and maintenance, and so on. Arguments over such matters may create difficulties for your tenants if your disagreements mean that repairs and maintenance are delayed or not done at all, for example. Delays in tending to those things could also cause the value of your home to go down.

Dividing Your Retirement Benefits

In most states, the retirement benefits you or your spouse have earned during your marriage are treated as marital assets and should be included among the assets you have to divide up. Such benefits may include defined contribution plans such as 401(k)s, Individual Retirement Accounts (IRAs), stock-option plans, profit-sharing plans, Keoghs, Simplified Employee Pension plans (SEPs), and old-fashioned pensions, also known as "defined benefit retirement plans." Most people earn their retirement benefits by working for an employer who makes a retirement plan available to them as an optional benefit or provides it to them as an automatic perk of their job.

If you've worked for several employers during your professional career, you may have earned a retirement benefit from each. Be sure that your asset inventory reflects all those benefits.

Defined benefit or defined contribution?

Retirement benefits fall into one of two categories: defined benefit plans or defined contribution plans.

The *defined benefit plan* is the kind of retirement plan that employees used to receive along with the proverbial gold watch that they were awarded after years of loyal service to their employers. Today, however, that kind of plan is pretty much a thing of the past for the vast majority of employees, namely because it's too expensive for most companies. Typically, defined benefit plans are available only to people at the highest levels of management.

A defined benefit plan comes as an automatic job benefit — you don't choose whether to participate in it. The plan represents a promise from your employer that, when you retire, you will receive a predetermined amount of income each month or a monthly income that is based on a formula. The formula takes into account how long you worked for your employer, your salary, your age, and other factors.

You usually don't have access to the money in your defined benefit plan until you've retired. Therefore, if your spouse wants to share in your retirement benefits, he or she has to wait for that money, just like you.

A *defined contribution plan* is the type of retirement benefit that most employees are offered these days. Participation in a defined contribution plan isn't automatic; if your employer offers one and you want to participate, you have to enroll in the plan. If you do enroll, you, your employer, or both of you contribute money to

your plan. For example, your employer may agree to match your contributions 100 percent, 80 percent, or at some other level.

With this type of plan, your employer doesn't offer any guarantees as to how much income your defined contribution plan will provide you when you retire. That amount depends on how much you and/or your employer contribute to your plan and on what kind of return you get from investing the money that is in your plan.

You can take money out of this type of retirement plan before you retire, although you have to pay an early withdrawal penalty and you may have to treat the withdrawal as taxable income. When you're ready to retire, you can receive all your retirement dollars in a lump sum or you can receive payments over time.

Visit the Web site of the federal Department of Labor's Employee Benefits Administration (`www.dol.gov/ebsa`) for additional information on pensions in general and on the pension rights of spouses and former spouses in particular. You may also want to read an online version of "What You Should Know About Your Pension Rights" (`www.dol.gov/ebsa/publications/wyskapr`), a Department of Labor publication that offers a lot of useful information on employer-sponsored pension plans. You can also order a free copy of the publication by calling 866-444-3272. Yet another pension-related resource is the Pension Rights Center, which you can access by going online at `www.pensionrights.org` or by calling 202-296-3776.

Vesting and your rights

Depending on the type of retirement plan you participate in, if you leave your job, you may have to be vested in the plan in order to be entitled to the money that your employer contributed to it. (To be *vested* in a retirement plan, you must have worked for your employer a certain number of years.) However, you're entitled at any time to the money *you* contributed to the plan.

Depending on your state, if you're not vested in your employer's retirement plan when you get divorced, the money in your retirement plan may not be considered marital property. Even if you're vested, if your marriage didn't last for at least a year, your spouse is *not* entitled to your retirement benefits.

Valuing a defined contribution plan

Assessing the value of a *defined contribution plan* is fairly easy. (See the sidebar "Defined benefit or defined contribution: Which is which?" for a definition of this type of plan.) In most cases, the value is simply the amount of money that's in the plan at any given time. To find out how much is in your defined contribution plan, contact the administrator for your plan or review the plan's most recent summary statement.

If your participation in the plan predates your marriage, all your retirement dollars aren't marital property, but those that you earned after your marriage are. By reviewing the plan reports you received over the years and doing some careful calculation, you should be able to figure out for yourself what portion of your retirement plan is marital property. If numbers intimidate you or if the total value of your plan is substantial, you may want to hire a CPA or pension consultant to do the figuring for you.

If you participate in a stock-ownership plan, the value of the plan is equivalent to the number of shares you own multiplied by the current dollar value of a share. If the company you work for is *closely held* (one whose stock isn't publicly traded), the company can tell you how much a share of its stock is worth. If the stock is publicly traded, you can find the current per-share value by going to the financial pages of your local newspaper. Or, you can ask your stockbroker or financial advisor for that information.

Valuing a defined benefit plan

Valuing a defined benefit plan and determining how much of that value is marital property can be a rather complicated process. (See the sidebar "Defined benefit or defined contribution: Which is which?" for a definition of this type of plan.) Therefore, if you want it done right, you should hire a pension expert. Ask your accountant to recommend one.

Do not assume that the value shown on your plan summary statement is the actual worth of your defined benefit plan — it may not be. Contact the plan administrator to determine its exact worth.

Parceling out those dollars

This section presents three alternatives for dealing with retirement benefits. When you're considering which alternative may be best for you, you must take into account the following:

- ✔ The value of the benefits
- ✔ The value of your share of the benefits
- ✔ The value of your other marital assets
- ✔ The value of your separate property
- ✔ How much money you need now, not later
- ✔ How close you are to retirement age
- ✔ The likely tax impact of each option

If you need help analyzing your options in light of these factors, talk with a qualified CPA, your financial advisor, or a family law attorney. Working with a financial professional is especially important if you or your spouse are nearing retirement age. Not getting your fair share of those benefits could be very costly because you won't have years of work ahead of you during which you could make up for what you did not get in your divorce. As a result, you could be forced to delay your retirement or find that your retirement years are a financial struggle.

Here are the three ways you can divide your retirement benefits:

- ✔ **Let the spouse who is earning the retirement benefits retain all rights to them, and let the other spouse take an equivalent amount of other marital assets:** This option is usually the cheapest way to deal with retirement benefits and also tends to be the way most judges prefer to deal with them. For this option to work for you and your spouse, however, you need other marital property comparable in value to the value of the retirement benefits.
- ✔ **Share the benefits:** This option provides each of you with regular income after the spouse who's earning the retirement benefits is eligible to receive them. If you choose this option, you will probably need a *Qualified Domestic Relations Order,* or QDRO, to make it work. (See the following sidebar "A crash course on QDROs.")

✔ **Give the spouse who's not earning the benefits a lump-sum payment now as his or her share:** Use this option in lieu of sharing the retirement benefits later. If you go this route, make sure to transfer the money to the spouse who's receiving the lump sum so that the other spouse doesn't have to claim the transfer as taxable income. But, remember, this option doesn't work for every type of retirement benefit. In addition, talk with a qualified CPA before you agree to a lump-sum payment so that you understand the tax consequences. Otherwise, you may face a sizable tax liability.

If you take your share of the retirement benefits in a lump sum, the amount you receive is based on the present cash value of the plan, not its future value. Therefore, you may receive more or less than you would receive if you waited to take the money later.

Social Security benefits you're owed as a former spouse

Based on your former spouse's work history, if you meet certain criteria when you reach a certain age, you may be entitled to collect Social Security benefits, including retirement and survivor benefits. Whether you're entitled to these benefits is a matter that's between you and the Social Security Administration, not between you and your former spouse. Your benefits don't depend on what your divorce agreement says.

You may be entitled to retirement benefits if

✔ Your former spouse paid into the Social Security Trust Fund.

✔ You and your ex-spouse were married for at least ten years and have been divorced for at least two years.

✔ You and your former spouse are at least 62 years old.

✔ You are not remarried when you apply for benefits.

✔ You're not already receiving Social Security, spousal, or survivor benefits based on someone else's employment history.

If you meet these criteria, you can either collect the Social Security benefits you earned in your own name or you can collect dependents' benefits. The dependents' benefits equal half of the benefits that your former spouse is entitled to, even if your spouse hasn't yet begun collecting social security. However, if you're entitled to Social Security benefits based on your own work history, and those benefits are greater than the dependents' benefits, you will receive the bigger monthly benefits — the ones you earned.

A crash course on QDROs

A *Qualified Domestic Relations Order (QDRO)* is a special type of court order that directs a retirement plan administrator to disperse benefits in accordance with the terms of your divorce agreement or in accordance with the court's decision. You need a separate QDRO for every retirement plan that you and your ex-spouse share. A QDRO can also collect alimony or child support payments from a pension plan.

If you decide to share military or government retirement benefits (such as U.S. Civil Service Retirement benefits or state retirement benefits) with your ex-spouse, you need to use different kinds of court orders for these types of benefits to accomplish what a QDRO does.

QDROs are complicated legal documents, so don't try to cut corners by drafting one on your own. Hire a qualified attorney to do the job for you because a poorly executed QDRO can jeopardize the tax-deferred status of the benefits and also result in the plan administrator not dispersing the funds in the plan according to your divorce agreement.

If you delay getting a QDRO, you may lose some or all of the benefits you have a right to according to your divorce agreement. Among other reasons, this can happen if your former spouse retires, becomes disabled, or dies before you've obtained a QDRO.

Ordinarily, if you remarry after you've been collecting dependents' benefits, you cannot continue collecting those benefits. However, you can resume collecting them if your new marriage ends in a divorce or an annulment or if your new spouse dies.

If you collect benefits based on your former spouse's work history, the amount of benefits that your spouse can collect is not affected. Also, your ex will never know that you're receiving them.

There are three ways to establish your eligibility for benefits. You can fill out an application by going to https://s044a90.ssa.gov/apps6z/ISBA/main.html; calling 800-772-1213; or visiting the Social Security office closest to you. However you apply, the Social Security Administration advises you to begin the application process at least three months before you turn 62.

To find out more about the social security benefits you are entitled to, steer your mouse to the Social Security Administration's Web site at www.ssa.gov.

Social Security survivor benefits

If your former spouse dies and you were married to him or her for at least ten years, you may also be eligible to receive Social Security survivor benefits, assuming that your former spouse would have been eligible to collect Social Security benefits at retirement age or was already doing so. However, in most instances, you cannot receive them if you remarry before you turn 60, unless that marriage ends with a divorce or annulment or your new spouse dies. If you remarry after 60 (or after 50, if you're disabled), you can continue receiving survivor benefits.

By and large, the eligibility criteria for Social Security survivor benefits mirror the criteria for retirement benefits, except that you can begin receiving reduced survivor benefits when you turn 60 or full survivor benefits when you turn 65. If you're caring for a child who's under the age of 16 or is disabled, and you are eligible to receive benefits based on the work history of your deceased spouse, you may be able to begin collecting survivor benefits when you reach age 50.

If you want to receive an estimate of your survivor benefits, call the Social Security Administration at 800-772-1213 and ask for a Request for Earnings and Benefits Estimate Statement or go to `https://secure.ssa.gov/apps6z/isss/main.html` and complete an online request form. But be aware that the eligibility rules and benefit amounts for Social Security benefits are always subject to change, especially because Congress keeps trying to figure out how to accommodate retiring baby boomers. For that reason, the actual amount of the benefits you receive may be less than the estimate.

If you remarry before you turn 60, you're not eligible for survivor benefits; if your new marriage occurs after your 60th birthday, your eligibility is unaffected. However, your new marriage cannot take place within two years of your former spouse's death.

Getting Down to Business: What to Do with Your Joint Enterprise

If either of you owns a closely held business or has a share in one, or if you and your spouse own a business together, some portion of its value is ordinarily considered marital property unless you agreed to a different arrangement through a legally valid prenuptial or postnuptial agreement.

If you and your spouse have been actively involved in your business, deciding what to do with it can be especially difficult. The idea that you may have to leave the business, shut it down, or sell it can be tough to accept when your marriage is ending. On the other hand, making plans for a new career may be just what you need to get over the loss of your marriage.

Your options in a nutshell

To help you deal with the difficult decision of what to do with the business you and your spouse own, we offer you a number of options that have worked for other couples:

✔ **One spouse keeps the business and the other gets marital assets equal in value to his or her interest in the business:** Usually, the spouse who takes the business is the one who's been most actively involved in it or whose skills and knowledge are most essential to its continued success. For financial reasons or because sufficient other marital property may not exist, the spouse who keeps the business may buy out the interest of the other spouse over time. You need to formalize the buyout in a written agreement. Also, to help secure your spouse's payments to you, placing a lien on his or her real estate, on the assets of the business, or on some other assets, if there are any, is a good idea.

When you let your spouse buy you out over time, you assume certain risks because your ex may be slow to pay you, may stop paying you entirely, or may even have to file a business bankruptcy. Unfortunately, you may not be able to avoid assuming these risks, despite the steps you may take to secure his or her payments.

✔ **You divide up the business and each of you takes a part of it:** This arrangement is practical only when you have a logical way to divide up your business and if you can divide it without jeopardizing the financial integrity of each part.

✔ **You sell the business and split the proceeds:** Selling your business may be your only option if all or most of your marital assets are tied up in it. However, if the continued success of the business depends on your skills and know-how, the business may not have much worth on the open market unless it includes significant assets that would be of value to a new owner.

✔ **Liquidate the business:** If neither of you is interested in continuing the business and you cannot sell it, liquidating the business is a reasonable alternative. However, to take advantage of this alternative, your business's assets must have market value. *Marketable assets* can include such assets as machinery, equipment, inventory, real estate, or accounts receivables. Depending on the type and value of the assets you are selling, you may want to sell them yourself, hire a liquidator to sell them for you (you'll have to pay the liquidator a part of the proceeds), or auction off the assets.

✔ **Keep operating your business together:** For obvious reasons, only a relatively small number of divorcing spouses who are also business partners choose this option. Most divorced spouses don't want to continue such an important and mutually dependent relationship. In fact, doing so may actually be harmful to the business.

If you worked in your spouse's separate-property business without compensation, your contribution to the business may be a factor in your property settlement.

Assigning a market value to the business

To implement any of the options described in the previous section (except for liquidation), you have to assign a fair market value to your business. If you want to make that determination yourself, you need the following data:

- Profit and loss statements for the past three years
- Balance sheets for the past three years
- Records of accounts receivable
- Records of accounts payable
- Statements of cash flows for the past three years
- Tax returns for the past three years
- Contracts for future business
- Recent good-faith offers to buy the business, if any exist
- Information about the purchase price of businesses comparable to yours

Be aware that valuing a business isn't easy. If you and your spouse intend to do the valuation yourself, find out as much information as you can about the process. For example, you can find excellent how-to information at the Divorceinfo Web site (www.divorceinfo.com/businessvalue). Better yet, assuming you can afford it, you and your spouse can each hire outside experts — independent CPAs or business valuation professionals — to determine the market value of your business. From there, you can average their estimates. If you do, be sure to get help from an outside expert who's familiar with your particular type of business, particularly if your business is large, valuable, or complex. Be forewarned that the help of such experts doesn't come cheap. To find a qualified business valuation expert, contact the National Association of Certified Valuation Analysts at 801-486-0600. You can also search the Association's online database by going to www.nacva.com.

When valuing your joint business, don't overlook its *goodwill value*. Goodwill consists of your business's reputation, name recognition, track record in pleasing its customers, role in the local community, and other factors that make it a respected enterprise.

If you're going to exit the business you've shared with your spouse, don't leave it up to him or her to determine its market value. Either take an active role in valuing it or hire an independent CPA or business valuation expert to do it for you. As much as you may trust your spouse, it's in her best interest to assign your business as low a market value as possible. That way, either your spouse has to pay you less if she buys you out over time or you end up entitled to less of the other marital property.

When you and your spouse began your business, if you had other co-owners, you may have negotiated an upfront agreement regarding the worth of your individual shares of the business if one of you decided to exit the business. That agreement determines the worth of your share of the enterprise, and that decision isn't one that you and your spouse can make.

Dealing with Your Debts

In our credit-oriented society, you're like countless other divorcing couples if you have a lot of debt. Unfortunately, your divorce may then be more about dividing up your debts than your assets. Although you can leave your marriage behind, you can't do the same with your debts.

Some of that debt may be *secured debt,* such as your mortgage or car loan. Secured debt is debt that you have collateralized with an asset, which means that if you don't pay the debt, the creditor can take the collateral. You probably also have plenty of *unsecured debt,* such as credit card debt, for example. Unsecured debt has the potential to create a great deal of discord in a divorce because, unlike a secured debt, it's usually not associated with an asset of any significant value. For example, unsecured debts are typically associated with the purchase of clothing, gas for your car, entertainment, vacations, and so on. Therefore, you have nothing of real value to show for having incurred that debt. Read the "Owing joint debt with your ex can be dangerous to your financial health" sidebar for a review of some of the potential problems associated with joint debt and divorce.

Tips for avoiding trouble

Figuring out how to deal with the debts from your marriage is probably one of the least-pleasant aspects of getting divorced — especially if you have a whole lot of debt and a lot fewer assets of any true value. Here are some suggestions for resolving that issue:

> ✔ **Pay off all your marital debt as part of your divorce.** This solution is usually the best way to deal with marital debt, assuming that you and your spouse have sufficient cash or other liquid assets and you don't need those assets to begin your lives as single consumers. You may

also want to consider selling liquid assets that you own outright, like a vehicle you don't need, a boat, an RV, and so on, and applying the sales proceeds to your debts. The sidebar "Owing joint debt with your ex can be dangerous to your financial health" reviews many of the risks you take if you continue to owe joint debt with your spouse after your divorce is final.

- ✔ **Trade debt for assets.** If you can't wipe out all your marital debt, you may agree to take more than your share in exchange for getting more of the marital assets — the financial equivalent of taking a spoonful of sugar to make the medicine go down — because you can afford to pay more of the debts than your spouse can.

- ✔ **Take your fair share.** If you and your spouse own little, if anything, of real value, dividing up your debts may simply mean that each of you takes your fair share. For example, you may agree to pay off the balance on a credit card that was in both your names but that you, not your spouse, used regularly.

- ✔ **Pay off your debts together after your divorce.** Avoid this arrangement if at all possible. It requires too much cooperation and communication between you and your former spouse. However, if this is your best or only option, securing your spouse's obligation to pay his or her share of your unsecured debt (your credit card debt, for example) by placing a lien on one or more of your spouse's separate assets is highly recommended. Also, if you and your spouse agree to pay off your debts together after your marriage, make the details of the arrangement part of your divorce agreement. That way, you can refer to the agreement if one of you does not live up to it, and you can ask the court for help getting the arrangement enforced.

- ✔ **File for bankruptcy with your spouse before you begin your divorce.** If your finances are in very bad shape, filing for bankruptcy before you start your divorce may make sense. Bankruptcy may eliminate some of your joint debts (and cause you to lose some of your assets, depending on the kind of bankruptcy you file), which will make working out the details of your divorce somewhat easier. However, getting through a bankruptcy requires that the two of you be able to cooperate with one another, which may be out of the question if you are estranged. Don't even consider filing without meeting with a bankruptcy attorney first, and never try to handle your own bankruptcy — it's a very complicated process!

You and your spouse may want to agree that whenever either of you pays off a joint credit card debt or line of credit, you cancel that account so that each of you can be sure that the other won't run up a new balance on the account after you're divorced. The downside to this agreement is that closing credit card accounts lowers your and your spouse's FICO scores. You can minimize this negative impact by closing the accounts gradually over time, rather than all at once. However you do it, if you manage your new postdivorce credit responsibly, it won't be long before your FICO scores start to rise.

Owing joint debt with your ex can be dangerous to your financial health

If you and your spouse have *joint debt* — debt that both of you are legally liable for — the two of you should make every effort to pay it off *before* your divorce is final. One reason is that the outstanding balances on the joint debt will show up on both of your credit reports, which may make it more difficult once you are single again to get new credit in your own names, purchase the insurance you need, rent a place to live or even obtain a good job or get a promotion. (Most creditors and many insurance companies, landlords, and employers review consumers' credit histories or check out their FICO scores in order to make decisions about them.)

Another reason for not carrying joint debt from your marriage into your new life as a single person is that if your spouse takes responsibility for paying off any of those debts after you are divorced as part of your divorce agreement and then fails to pay the debts or pays them late, you may be dogged by any number of financial and legal problems. For example

✔ Your credit histories and your credit scores, not just your ex-spouse's, will be damaged.

✔ The unpaid debt could be turned over to collections, which will further damage your credit.

✔ The joint creditors your ex has not paid may come after you for their money. They may even sue you. If that were to happen you would not only have to hire an attorney to defend you, but also, if you lost the lawsuit, you could be forced to give up one of your assets to help pay the debt; your wages might be garnished (assuming wage garnishment is legal in your state); or you could end up with a lien on an asset that you own. If there is a lien on one of your assets, you won't be able to sell the asset or borrow against it unless the debt is paid off.

✔ The joint creditors may come after you for the unpaid debt if your former spouse files for bankruptcy.

If you separate before you divorce, just who's legally responsible for the debts you or your spouse may incur during your separation depends on your state. Most states presume that it's joint debt unless you or your spouse can prove otherwise. However, some states treat the debt either of you may rack up while you're separated as individual debt. In still other states, whether a debt is joint or individual debt depends on what the debt financed. For example, if it helped pay for essentials, such as food, clothing, and shelter, it may be treated as joint debt, but it probably would not be considered joint debt if it financed a vacation or a shopping spree.

If your ex falls behind on the joint debts he was supposed to pay as part of your divorce agreement, the creditors may not notify you about what has happened, or at least not right away. Your first inkling that your ex failed to pay the debts may come when you review your credit reports and notice damaging late payments associated with those accounts or you check out your FICO scores and discover that they are lower than they used to be.

Uncle Sam wants his piece, too

Ordinarily you don't have to pay taxes when a *capital asset* (such as a home, other real estate, retirement benefits, and so forth) is transferred to you in a divorce. But if you sell a capital asset later, you may have to pay taxes on its appreciated value. Also, depending on how you transfer a *tax-deferred asset,* you may incur penalties. (A tax-deferred asset is an asset that allows you to defer or delay paying taxes on the income it generates until you sell it or begin collecting the income on it.) IRAs, 401(k) plans, and Simplified Employee Pension plans (SEPs) are all examples of tax-deferred assets.

When you and your spouse are deciding how to divide up your marital property, your tax-minimization strategies may depend on the types of assets you're dividing up, the value of those assets, and your individual financial situations. Without appropriate planning, the taxes and penalties you end up paying have the effect of reducing the amount of marital property you both end up with. Talk with your CPA or a trusted financial advisor about how to minimize taxes and penalties in your property settlement.

In order to avoid the negative consequences that will result if your spouse does not pay the joint debts she agreed in take care of in your divorce agreement, you may have to pay them instead. If you do, talk with your divorce attorney to find out whether the agreement gives you the right to go after your spouse for the money. (It should, assuming your attorney was on the ball when he or she handled your divorce.)

Where the law stands on your debts

When deciding the best way to deal with the money you owe, bear in mind that the court considers the same property laws and guidelines that apply to the division of your assets in a divorce. This means that

- ✔ Any money you owed before you got married is treated as your individual debt.
- ✔ Your joint debts are "equitably" divided if you live in an equitable distribution state.
- ✔ You and your spouse may be held equally liable for the debts you acquired during your marriage if you live in a community property state. When dividing your debts, the court considers your individual abilities to pay the debts and what the debts financed, among other things.

During your marriage if you secured or collateralized a debt with your separate property, the court usually regards that debt as your individual debt.

Chapter 9

Considering Spousal Support

*D*epending on your circumstances, you may want your spouse to pay you *spousal support* (it used to be referred to as *alimony*) after you're divorced. However, the two of you may not see eye to eye regarding how much spousal support you should receive and how long the support payments should last. Of course, if getting divorced was your idea, your soon-to-be ex may bristle at the suggestion that he or she pay you any spousal support at all, regardless of the reasonableness of the amount of support you're requesting in light of your postdivorce earnings potential, the assets you're likely to take away from your marriage, and other considerations. Then again, you may be so angry and hurt by the fact that your spouse wants a divorce that you decide to retaliate by demanding spousal support — and a lot of it! You figure that paying support is the *least* your spouse should do for you after turning your life upside down!

Spousal support can be an especially emotional issue in a divorce. To help you deal with it as dispassionately as possible so you and your spouse can make decisions on the matter that are fair to both of you and to help you avoid having to have the court decide the issue, this chapter explains what factors to consider when negotiating spousal support. It also addresses the pros and cons of receiving support in a lump-sum payment rather than in a series of payments over time, and it highlights tax considerations related to spousal support.

If you and your spouse have a prenuptial agreement, be sure to review it before you begin discussing spousal support. The agreement may indicate whether one of you must pay the other spousal support if your marriage ends in a divorce, and it may also spell out the terms of the support. If you have such an agreement and it is legally valid (complies with all the requirements for a prenuptial agreement in your state), you may have little or nothing to negotiate related to spousal support. If you have any questions about your prenuptial agreement, talk to your divorce attorney.

If the court decides the issue of spousal support in your divorce, the laws of your state limit exactly what can be ordered. For example, those laws restrict how much support one spouse must pay the other. In some states, the court may not be allowed to require one spouse to purchase life insurance for the benefit of the other spouse or to pay spousal support in a lump sum. If you and your spouse negotiate your own spousal support agreement, however, you won't face such limitations.

The Times They Are a-Changing

Spousal support is the term used for the monetary payments that one spouse makes to the other after a couple is divorced. If a couple begins living apart before their divorce is final, one spouse may pay the other temporary support during the period of their separation.

Since the 1970s, *permanent spousal support* (money that one spouse — usually the man — sent to another until the receiving spouse remarried or either spouse died) has pretty much gone the way of the typewriter, eight-track tape, and rotary phone. Even so, permanent spousal support is still a part of some divorces — most often divorces that involve wealthy couples or older couples who are ending lengthy marriages. But today, permanent spousal support agreements frequently state that the payments will stop if the ex-spouse who's receiving them begins a serious live-in relationship and shares living expenses with a new love interest.

Attitudes toward spousal support continue to change as men and women's roles evolve in society. For example, women used to be the recipients of spousal support 99.9 percent of the time; today, if the wife is the primary breadwinner in a marriage, she may have to pay spousal support to her ex-husband. In fact, the spousal support laws in all states are now gender-neutral, which means that, in the eyes of those laws, men and women are equally entitled to receive spousal support. Even so, women are still far more likely to receive spousal support than men.

In terms of dollars and cents, divorce remains harder on women than men, despite the large number of women who work outside the home. Most women — even those who receive spousal support — experience a drop in their standard of living after their marriage ends. However, some divorced men experience the same financial consequences.

Another change related to the payment of spousal support is that these days the support is more likely to be rehabilitative instead of permanent support, and it's usually paid to stay-at-home parents and full-time homemakers. *Rehabilitative support* is based on the idea that most ex-spouses, regardless of their gender, can and should earn their own livings after they're divorced. It also recognizes that a spouse (either a woman or a man) may have put her own career on the back burner to raise the couple's children or to support the other spouse's career and therefore needs time to become self-supporting after a divorce. For example, she may need to acquire new job skills, get a college education, and develop the professional connections that will help her land a good job. Also, she probably needs time to find a job once she is ready to begin looking for one.

Rehabilitative support is usually paid for a relatively short period of time — long enough to help a former spouse get on his financial feet. The support payments also may include money to help an ex-spouse get the training or education necessary to earn a good living. However, in many divorces, the amount and duration of the rehabilitative support a former spouse receives are inadequate. This is particularly true when a divorced couple doesn't have a lot of money or other financial resources and when the recipient is older and may never have worked outside the home or hasn't done so in many years.

Stay-at-home moms and dads who view raising their children as a full-time job face a difficult dilemma. If they begin preparing themselves for the possibility of divorce by getting the education and training they need to be employable should their marriage end, they not only take time away from their primary job (child-rearing), but they're also likely to receive less spousal support if they do divorce. On the other hand, if they don't prepare themselves for the job market while they're still married, they may receive more spousal support than if they had, but they may not be as prepared to support themselves when the support payments end.

In these uncertain economic times, spouses who agree to pay spousal support increasingly are asking that their divorce agreements provide for automatic reductions in the amount of support they must pay each month if they lose their job, have their works hours reduced, experience a salary reduction, and so on. If you will be receiving spousal support and your spouse wants your agreement to provide for automatic reductions under certain circumstances, you and your spouse should also agree on how long the reduced support payments will last.

Don't summarily dismiss the idea of receiving spousal support out of pride or a desire to be 100 percent free of your spouse. If you believe that you need time to become competitive in today's job market, your wisest course of action may be to swallow your pride and ask your spouse for financial help. Remember, having financial help from your former spouse while preparing yourself for a job or looking for one can mean the difference between having enough money to provide yourself and your children with what you need and barely scraping by.

A limited number of states now recognize a relatively new type of support called *bridge-the-gap support*. This kind of support provides the less financially well-off spouse with periodic payments in order to help him meet his immediate basic needs, like food, clothing, shelter, and so on. It's most often paid when one spouse needs help transitioning from being married to being single or when a spouse doesn't have assets that he can readily sell for cash after a divorce in order to ease that transition.

Making a Case for Support

If you're wondering whether support is relevant in your divorce, you don't have a lot of legal precedents to go by because spousal support decisions are relatively subjective and are decided on a case-by-case basis. Furthermore, there are not many state guidelines for determining if one spouse should pay the other spousal support, the amount of the payments or their duration, assuming the support isn't permanent. The lack of guidelines combined with the fact that, technically, divorced spouses have no legal obligation to support one another tends to make spousal support a contentious issue and means that whether one spouse will pay the other spousal support isn't as clear-cut an issue as whether child support will be paid assuming the couple has minor children.

If your divorce ends in a trial, the court will determine if, when, and how much spousal support you or your spouse will receive. If you and your spouse negotiate the terms of your divorce on your own or with the help of your attorneys, you should use the following list of factors to guide your spousal support decision-making. They're the same ones that the court would take into account. If you're the spouse who wants to receive support, the greater the number of factors that apply to your marriage, the stronger your argument for getting spousal support. If you're the spouse who may have to pay spousal support, the fewer factors that apply to your situation, the stronger your argument for ot paying spousal support. However, in the end, whether or not one of you has to pay spousal support to the other boils down to need and ability to pay.

The factors to consider when making spousal support decisions in your divorce include

- **How long you've been married:** If you and your spouse have been married for a long time (and you won't find a legal definition of "long time"), you're more likely to receive spousal support. But if your marriage is less than ten years old, the court probably won't treat it as a long-term marriage — although it may feel like an eternity to you! Typically, the longer the marriage, the larger the support payments will be.

✔ **Whether your spouse makes significantly more money than you do and is expected to continue doing so, at least for the immediate future:** When one spouse makes a lot more than the other, the court is apt to order the higher-earning spouse to share some of that income with the lower-earning spouse.

✔ **Your age or health status makes earning a good living nearly impossible:** A spouse who cannot work full time, who can't work at all for health reasons, or who's older and didn't work during the marriage or worked only part-time is more likely to receive spousal support. (The definition of "older" varies from court to court, but typically a worker in his or her late 50s and beyond is considered an older worker.)

The age of a spouse is a factor because, although employers are legally prohibited from discriminating against workers based on age, anecdotal evidence indicates that such discrimination happens more often than you may think. Therefore, an older worker can have a very difficult time finding a good-paying job. Also, older workers are more apt to have physical limitations that make them unsuited for certain kinds of work. As a result, they don't enjoy the range of job options that younger workers tend to have.

✔ **The significant contributions you made to your marriage or to your spouse's career:** For example, maybe you gave up your career to be a stay-at-home parent, continued to work throughout your marriage and let your career take a back seat to your spouse's so that you could help him or her advance professionally, or helped build your spouse's business.

✔ **Your educational background and employment history:** The courts consider whether your education or your employment history puts you at a disadvantage in the job market. For example, if you didn't work or you worked part-time during your marriage so you could be home with your children, finding a job to support yourself after your divorce can be difficult, if not impossible, because your job skills are probably outdated and you don't have much work experience to put on a resume or job application.

✔ **Whether you will be your children's primary caregiver after your divorce:** If you plan to take care of your children full-time, pursuing a full-time career is nearly impossible.

✔ **Whether you have any nonemployment sources of regular income, such as income from trusts, real estate, or investments:** Receiving income from such sources can make it less likely that you'll receive spousal support, or may mean that you won't receive as much as you would have if you didn't have that income.

- ✔ **Whether you're exiting your marriage with relatively little marital property:** If you exit your marriage with little or no assets, you have nothing to borrow against or sell in order to help pay your bills and pay for the education you may need in order to qualify for a good job.

- ✔ **Whether you will have sole custody of your children and one or more of them has special needs:** Having sole custody of a child with special needs can preclude you from working or allow you to work on only a part-time basis.

If you look to the court to decide whether spousal support will be paid and, if so, how much the payments will be and how long they will last, it can take other relevant factors into account. However, those other factors may be things that you'd prefer be overlooked, like the fact that your spouse filed a fault divorce because she found out you had been having an affair or had done something else that was harmful to your marriage.

States that permit fault divorces may allow the court to take the issue of fault into account when deciding spousal support. When fault is considered, the court is more likely to punish the spouse who's at fault for his or her behavior (adultery, physical abuse, and so on). As a result, it may order that spouse to pay more than the usual amount of support, and if the spouse at fault is the one who will be receiving support, the court may award less support than what the spouse would have received otherwise.

About half the states allow courts to consider fault in negotiations related to the division of a couple's marital property.

If you and your spouse are working out the terms of your spousal support agreement together, you can take into account factors that the courts would not consider, like your religious beliefs, your personal values, and so on.

Of course, if your spouse doesn't make much money, the court may not expect him or her to pay you anything, or probably not as much as you may want or need.

Agreeing on an Amount

Deciding how much support one spouse should pay the other can be a challenge because the spouse who's going to receive the support will probably want as much as possible, and the spouse who's paying the support will probably want to minimize the amount of the payments. Furthermore, most states don't have strict guidelines for determining the minimum amount of support that a former spouse is entitled to. So, how much support gets paid is a judgment call that is usually based on what's fair given the needs of the spouse who wants support and the finances of the spouse who will pay the support.

Determining your fair share

When deciding how much support one spouse must pay another, courts ideally would like the payments to be large enough to allow the spouse who's receiving them to be able to maintain his or her marital lifestyle. But, in reality, courts know that most ex-spouses don't make enough money to support two households equally well, not even for a short period of time.

In most divorces, how much a spouse receives in spousal support boils down to financial realities — how much money the spouse paying the support can actually afford to pay and the living expenses of the spouse who's receiving the support. Assuming that the spouse who's paying the support is earning more than enough to just get by, the factors we discuss in the earlier section, "Making a Case for Support," can be taken into account when spouses are deciding on a fair amount of spouse support. To come up with an actual amount of support, spouses should gather up their budgets and other financial information and sit down with a certified divorce planner (CDP), a certified public accountant (CPA), or their divorce attorneys.

 If your spouse wants to make the amount of spousal support you receive or its duration contingent upon whether you do certain things, reject the deal unless you feel completely comfortable with it. Some spouses go to great lengths to try to control their partners, even after divorce. For example, your spouse may try to make your receipt of spousal support contingent on you not dating a particular person, on sending your children to a particular school, or on raising your children in a certain religion. If you have any questions about whether your spouse's spousal support offer is fair, consult with a family law attorney.

If you're the spouse who will be paying spousal support, you may want to negotiate an arrangement that gives your spouse more of your marital assets in exchange for your making smaller spousal support payments than you would otherwise make given your income and other factors or for an earlier than normal end to the payments. Such an arrangement may be attractive to you because you know that it will be a struggle to pay a set amount of spousal support to your ex month after month — maybe because you're self-employed or work on commission and your income varies throughout the year — or because you want as little to do with your ex as possible after your divorce is final. Another option is to ask your spouse to agree to a lump-sum payment rather than a series of spousal support payments over time. (You find out why this may make sense for you in the upcoming section "Getting your support in a lump sum.") Talk to your divorce attorney, CPA, or CDP about which option is best for you.

If you're the spouse who will be receiving support, be wary of agreeing to take more marital property in exchange for less spousal support. Unless the extra property you receive provides you with a regular flow of income after your divorce or unless the additional assets have a good market value and it won't be difficult for you to sell them if you need the money, you may end up on the short end of the financial stick.

Changing the amount later

Under certain circumstances, the amount of spousal support you receive may increase or decrease after your divorce is final. You and your former spouse can agree to change the amount, or the court may order a change if one of you makes a formal request.

In some states, a court loses its ability to change spousal support arrangements as soon as a couple's divorce decree is final.

For the court to order a change, you or your ex-spouse must convince the court that there is a good reason for the change. The court is unlikely to view your desire to share in the hefty salary increase that your former spouse just received as a good reason, nor your wish to benefit from his or her share of lottery winnings. But the court may be more agreeable to increasing the amount of the payments you receive if you can prove that you have a legitimate need for the increase; for example, you were seriously injured in a car accident and can't work. Conversely, the court may give your ex-spouse permission to make smaller support payments if she just lost her job or has become too ill or injured to work and can prove to the court that without a reduction, she will quickly land in the poorhouse. In both scenarios, however, the adjustments would probably be temporary.

Agreeing on a Payment Plan

When you're negotiating spousal support, one of the issues you must consider is how the support will be paid. Generally, the spouse who's obligated to provide support to the other does so by making a series of fixed payments over a specified period of time. Other times, couples agree (or the court orders) that one spouse must pay the other a lump-sum amount of spousal support instead. We tell you about each method in the following sections.

Receiving support over time

Most spousal support is paid in set amounts on a set schedule. This arrangement has its pros and cons. For example, if you're the one who's receiving
spousal support, the payments can provide a steady stream of much-needed
income for you while you're building a new life for yourself after your
divorce. However, the arrangement can be problematic if your former spouse
is constantly late with his or her payments or doesn't make them at all
sometimes. Not only can this situation create money problems for you, but
it can also generate a considerable amount of tension and anger between
you and your ex and cause you to constantly relive the emotions of your
divorce.

If you're not far from retirement age and you're going to pay spousal support,
stopping your payments when you retire may be appropriate, especially
if part of your divorce agreement says that you and your spouse will share
substantial retirement benefits. If this is true in your divorce however,
don't simply stop paying spousal support after you retire. Get the court's
permission to end the payments.

Getting your support in a lump sum

Some divorced spouses receive their spousal support in a lump sum rather
than in a series of payments over time. A lump-sum payment is an attractive
option if you don't trust your ex to live up to an agreement that requires him
to make payments over time, if you're concerned that your spouse's financial
situation may deteriorate after you're divorced, or that the payments will
become erratic or stop all together.

Be sure the lump-sum payment you agree to accept from your spouse is
adequate. Although the amount may sound like a lot of money and a fair
amount for you to receive, it may not be enough, especially if your spouse
wants you to take the lump sum in lieu of receiving any of your marital
property. Talk with a family law attorney, a CDP, or your CPA before you sign
any paperwork related to a lump-sum payment of support.

Consider the tax consequences of taking a lump-sum payment of spousal
support and what you can do to mitigate those consequences before you
agree to such an arrangement. You may be able to shelter some of the money
by using a trust, but you should discuss such a strategy with your CDP, CPA,
or an estate-planning attorney.

The larger the lump sum, the more important it is to have a plan for investing the money. Ideally, your plan should maximize the interest you earn on the lump sum and give you ready access to at least a portion of the money. If you simply put the lump-sum payment you receive into your checking account, you may spend it very quickly and have nothing for the future.

If you're giving your spouse a lump-sum support payment, get the help of an attorney, a CDP, or a CPA. Your agreement regarding the support must be worded so that the IRS views your payment as spousal support, which you can claim as a tax deduction, and not as a property settlement, which you can't deduct. (You can find out more about taxes and spousal support in the section "Some Important Advice about Taxes," later in this chapter.)

Ensuring that the Payments Arrive

After your divorce is final, your ex-spouse may not make the spousal support payments he agreed to make. Whatever the reason for your ex-spouse's failure to pay, not receiving the money you anticipate (and are legally entitled to) can have a devastating effect on your life. Here are some steps you can take before your divorce is final to help ensure that the support arrives:

- ✔ **Get a court order for spousal support.** If you're not already working with a divorce attorney, hire one to file your spousal support agreement with the court and argue its reasonableness so that the court will approve it and make the agreement a part of your divorce decree. If you're the one who's entitled to spousal support and you don't go through this process, and then your ex reneges on your agreement, you have no legal recourse for enforcing the agreement and collecting the spousal support you are legally entitled to.

- ✔ **Try to enforce the court order by asking the court to hold your spouse** *in contempt of court.* Assuming that your state allows you to take this step when your ex doesn't pay your spousal support, being declared in contempt of court will put legal pressure on your ex to pay you the money you are entitled to. In fact, a judge can send your ex to jail for ignoring his or her support obligation.

  In states where you cannot accuse your spouse of contempt of court for failing to pay your court-ordered spousal support, you're in the same position as any other creditor that your former spouse hasn't paid. In this situation, whether you can collect any of what your ex owes you depends on the debtor protection laws of your state, which may make all or most of your ex-spouse's property exempt from the debt-collection process. If that's the case, your past-due spousal support is uncollectible, or exempt from being collected.

✔ **Secure your payments by placing a lien on one or more of the assets that your spouse will exit the marriage with.** A *lien* is a legal right to someone else's property until the owner of that property fulfills his or her legal obligation to the lien holder. For example, if you have a mortgage on your home, your mortgage lender has a lien on your home, which means that it can take the home if you don't make your mortgage payments according to the terms of your mortgage agreement. If your ex fails to live up to your spousal support agreement, you can ask the court for permission to take the asset with the lien on it as payment for what you're owed. However, if the asset is your ex-spouse's home, you may not be able to get your money until the home is sold. Also, if you have a lien on your ex's retirement account, you may not be able to collect the money you're entitled to until he or she retires, quits his job, or is fired.

✔ **Use disability insurance to ensure an unbroken stream of spousal support in the event that your ex becomes ill or injured and is unable to work for a period of time.** The court is likely to let your former spouse pay you less during the period of her disability, so the disability insurance helps you make up for what you are not receiving in support during the period of your former spouse's disability.

✔ **Get your spouse to agree to have your spousal support payments automatically deducted from his or her paychecks.** That way, after your divorce is final, you won't have to wonder every month whether your ex remembered to mail you a support check, whether your ex is going to send you some but not all of what you're entitled to, or whether your ex isn't going to send you any money at all. With automatic deductions, the court issues an order telling your former spouse's employer to deduct a certain amount of money from his or her paychecks and send it to the court, which then sends you a check. In other words, your former spouse never sees that money.

Preparing for Life after Spousal Support

Your spousal support may end sooner than you expect, regardless of whether you're receiving rehabilitative support or permanent spousal support. Your ex spouse may die, for example, at which point the support payments will end, and you won't have a legal right to any of the assets in his or her estate unless your ex's estate plan provides otherwise. Therefore, if your spousal support payments are an important source of income for you and you have no way of compensating for that loss, the death of your ex-spouse is likely to be financially devastating for you.

Although death can come unexpectedly to people of any age, this issue is of particular concern to individuals who are ending marriages to spouses who are elderly or in poor health. One way to address it is to require, as a term of your divorce, that your spouse purchase a life insurance policy and name you its beneficiary, assuming that your spouse isn't so old or in such poor health that he can't qualify for such insurance. While you're working out the terms of your divorce, talk to a CDP, a CPA, or an estate-planning attorney about this and other options that may help protect you from the sudden loss of spousal support.

If you're worried that your ex may purchase a life insurance policy and make you its beneficiary, but then let the policy lapse, you may want to pay for the policy yourself, assuming that you can afford the expense. That way, you make sure that the policy remains in effect.

The insurance premium payments your ex-spouse makes on a policy that designates you as the beneficiary are tax deductible as spousal support. However, if he or she dies you must claim the policy proceeds paid to you by the insurance company as taxable income.

Some Important Advice about Taxes

If you receive spousal support, you must claim that money as income on your tax return. If you pay spousal support, perhaps one of the few benefits is that you can deduct the payments on your federal tax return. To qualify for the deductions, you must comply with certain IRS rules, such as the following:

- ✔ You must formalize your spousal support agreement in a divorce decree or in a separate written agreement.

- ✔ You must make your payments with a check or money order. Ordinarily, property or services in lieu of cash don't qualify as tax-deductible support.

   Paying your spousal support in cash is a bad idea because you won't have a record of your payments. Your lack of documentation can be a problem if any questions arise concerning how much you paid your former spouse or exactly when you made a particular spousal support payment.

- ✔ While paying spousal support, you and your former spouse cannot live under the same roof. No living on separate floors of the same home or in different parts of your home, either!

✔ You cannot tie your spousal support payments to circumstances or milestones in your children's lives. For example, your agreement cannot provide that when your child turns a certain age you'll reduce the amount of support that you pay to your ex-spouse or stop the payments entirely. If the IRS learns that you've done so, it may reclassify the payments you made as child support and, because child support payments aren't tax-deductible, you may end up owing extra taxes to Uncle Sam.

✔ On a related note, you cannot stop paying spousal support or change the amount that you've been paying your ex-spouse six months before or after the date that one of your children becomes a legal adult — age 18 in most states. Again, if the IRS finds out that you stopped paying spousal support prematurely, it may reclassify some of the payments you made in the past as child support, which can have negative tax implications for you.

✔ You must file your federal taxes by using IRS Form 1040, not Form 1040A or Form 1040EZ.

Don't front-load your spousal support payments. *Front-loading* is paying your ex-spouse excess money during the first two years that you're paying support. If you're audited, the IRS is going to view the excess money you paid as a property settlement, not spousal support, which means that it won't treat those payments as tax deductible. Front-loading may apply only if you paid out more than $15,000 in spousal support during each of the first two years that you made the payments and only if you claimed the full amount of the payments as tax deductions.

If an attorney, a CDP, or a CPA helps you work out the terms of your spousal support agreement, you can deduct his or her fees on your taxes. Also, if you pay the medical insurance, college tuition, mortgage, or rent payments of your former spouse as part of the agreement, you may be able to claim them as tax deductions, too.

If you earn considerably more than your ex-spouse and you intend to pay her more than your state's minimum in child support, you may want to pay that additional money as spousal support instead because it's tax deductible, and child support isn't. However, although doing so increases your tax deductions, it may also increase the tax liability of your ex-spouse. How to deal with this issue is something that you and your spouse should discuss with your CDP or CPA before either of you agrees to such an arrangement.

Chapter 10

Choosing the Best Custody Arrangement for Your Kids

· ·

· ·

*W*hen you're getting divorced, deciding how to handle the custody of your minor children can consume every ounce of your patience and resolve. In fact, this issue is very likely the most difficult one that you and your spouse grapple with as you work your way toward a divorce agreement, and if one of you isn't happy with the outcome, custody-related issues can create problems for you and your children after your divorce is final.

If negotiating your own custody arrangement seems about as likely as winning the lottery, take heart! Estimates show that 95 percent of all divorcing parents are able to work out their own custody arrangements — either by themselves, with the help of a mediator, or with their attorneys' assistance. Chances are you will, too.

This chapter prepares you to make your own custody decisions by informing you of your options (and their pros and cons) and suggesting ways that you can make your custody arrangement work for everyone's benefit, your kids' especially. We also address issues related to visitation, including each spouse's rights and limitations. If you and your spouse can't reach an agreement about custody on your own, this chapter also explains what can happen if you ask the court to decide how custody is handled in your divorce.

Avoiding the Courtroom: The Benefits of Negotiating a Custody Arrangement

If you and your spouse can decide one thing and one thing only in your divorce, make it the issue of how you'll handle the custody of your children. There are several good reasons why you should make that decision instead of a family law judge. (Every state but Texas limits custody decisions to judges when a divorce goes to trial.) You can find more information about negotiating the terms of your own divorce in Chapter 12.

Here are some of the reasons why you're better off negotiating your own custody terms:

✔ If you go to court, you have no guarantee that you'll end up with the custody arrangement you want, even if it's available in your state.

✔ Most family law judges have very heavy caseloads, so matter how well-intentioned the judge who hears your case may be, she won't be able to devote much time to deciding which custody arrangement is best for your children.

✔ Most judges rely on the input of outside experts, such as social workers and psychologists, to help them make custody decisions. Therefore, a bunch of strangers may end up having a great deal of say in where your children will live and your role in their lives after your divorce.

✔ A court custody battle can be extremely costly and time-consuming. One reason is that a variety of experts will probably be called to testify on your behalf, and you'll have to pay for their time. Those experts may include your children's teachers, the director of your children's day-care center, the personnel at your pediatrician's office, and so on.

✔ The proceedings related to the custody of your children are open to the public, so you risk having all your private "dirty laundry" aired in the courtroom for anyone to see and hear.

✔ Members of your extended family, friends, associates, people in your children's lives, your neighbors — and maybe even your children — may have to testify in court.

✔ After the judge decides what to do about the custody of your kids, you and your spouse may find it very difficult to put your differences aside for their sake, especially if your custody hearing was very acrimonious and emotional. Worst-case scenario, you and your ex could continue to do battle over your kids for years to come, which would probably take a long-lasting emotional toll on your children and add a lot of stress to your own life.

Long-term studies show that a custody battle can do long-lasting emotional damage to young children and make it difficult if not impossible for them to establish and maintain meaningful relationships as adults. If you're considering fighting with your spouse over the custody of your kids, try to analyze why you're thinking about it and, if necessary, work with a mental health professional who can help you understand your feelings and figure out what you can do to avoid a fight. After some serious reflection, you may decide that you're confusing your own wants and needs with what's in your children's best interests, or that you want to battle over your children's custody in order to express animosity toward your spouse or to hurt him.

Some states require divorcing parents to attend parenting classes to learn how to help their children adjust to divorce and to become familiar with some of the issues they're likely to face as divorced parents. Even if your state doesn't require that you attend such a class, you may want to ask your attorney or a mental health professional whether there is one in your area that you could attend. If so, let your spouse know about the class, too.

Your Custody Options in Brief

Every custody arrangement requires you to make two basic, interrelated decisions: how you and your spouse will share the legal custody of your children and how you will share their physical custody.

Legal custody refers to a parent's right and obligation to make decisions on behalf of his children after a divorce — including decisions concerning their education, medical care, religious education, and other important matters. *Physical custody* refers to the amount of time the children live with each parent after the divorce.

In most divorces, the children spend time with each parent in proportion to how involved each parent was in their lives before the divorce — that is, to whatever degree each parent functioned as the children's caregiver, life planner, and source of emotional support. In addition, each parent has decision-making authority in proportion to the amount of time that the children live with that parent. You may decide that certain types of decisions must be made jointly, such as whether your high-school senior can go to Mexico over spring break or whether your preteen can get her ears pierced.

Here are typical custody options:

- ✔ **Primary custody:** If one parent has been more involved in her children's lives before the divorce, that parent often gets *primary* (or *sole*) *custody* of the kids. (We talk more about this type of custody in the section "Understanding the Ins and Outs of Primary Custody," later in this chapter.) Primary custody means that the couple's children spend most of their time with that parent and the parent assumes more decision-making responsibilities for the children. The parent with primary custody may make all decisions for the children, or the couple may agree that they will share certain important decisions related to their kids.

- ✔ **Shared custody:** Parents who have been equally involved in their children's lives before divorce normally get nearly equal, if not completely equal, decision-making authority and time with their children after divorce. Those parents are said to have a *shared* (or *joint*) *custody* arrangement. (You can find more on this type of custody in the section "Taking a Closer Look at Shared Custody," later in this chapter.)

- ✔ **Split custody:** Few parents choose this option. With *split custody,* some or all of your children live with each of you for a part of the year or some of your children live with one of you all of the time and the rest of your children live with your former spouse all of the time. (Read more about this custody option in the section "Considering Split Custody," later in this chapter.)

Because an increasing number of today's fathers are actively involved in their children's day-to-day care and nurturing, many couples share legal and the physical custody of their children. Among the reasons for this trend in custody is that more women work outside the home, and so married couples are more apt to share child care, and the definition of what it means to be a dad is changing.

The laws in most states assume that each parent has an equal legal right to custody of their children. In reality, however, the mother usually ends up with primary custody when the court gets involved. This is because the woman is more often the children's primary caregiver and the parent who's most involved in the children's day-to-day lives (despite the increased caregiving role that many fathers have assumed). However, if the father is the primary caregiver, the courts are more apt to award him primary custody of the children. This is especially true in urban areas where judges tend to be more progressive and where precedent-setting rulings are more likely to be made.

Be sure that you and your spouse are happy with the custody arrangement before it becomes a formal part of your divorce agreement. Although you can try to change the arrangement later, if you and your ex don't see eye to eye on the change that one of you is asking for, a judge will decide whether it's merited, and most family court judges don't like to alter a custody arrangement unless the change is clearly in the children's best interests.

Consulting Your Kids

If your children are old enough and mature enough to know their own minds, especially if you and your spouse want to share custody, you may want to consider their preferences regarding how much time they would like to spend living with each of you. They may have already let you know directly or indirectly what they'd like, but if they haven't, start a conversation with them, either with your spouse or separately. Make the conversation a casual chat, and don't pressure your children to decide one way or the other. Be prepared for the possibility that some of your children may not want to live with you.

Don't try to bribe your children into spending more time with you by making fantastic promises about what their lives will be like if they do. Also, avoid "guilting" them into spending tine with you by telling your kids how sad and lonely you'll be if they don't.

Your children very much want your approval, which means you may not be able to take their "preferences" at face value. For example, your children may tell you what they *think* you want to hear, not what they really feel, and for that same reason, they may tell your spouse the exact opposite of what they tell you. Therefore, not asking your children what they want until they're old enough and mature enough to honestly assess their needs and desires when it comes to their living arrangements is a good idea. Even then, talking with them about their preferences may not be advisable if they don't feel comfortable communicating honestly with you.

Most states have laws authorizing the courts to consider a child's preferences if the child is of a certain age (typically 10 or older). However, the judge always has the ultimate decision on the matter.

Taking a Closer Look at Shared Custody

When parents share custody of their children (another way of saying that they have joint custody), they're both responsible for all or some aspects of their children's lives, depending on the terms of their custody agreement. A key benefit of shared custody is that it allows both parents to be full participants in their children's lives after their divorce and gives them equal responsibility for their children's emotional and physical well-being. Shared custody also helps facilitate a continuation of the relationship that the parents and children may have enjoyed prior to the divorce.

Generally, when parents share physical custody of their children rather than one parent having primary physical custody of the kids, the parents are more apt to share the cost of their children's financial support, too. However, child-support arrangements are decided on a case-by-case basis and depend on a variety of factors. (For the full scoop on child support, turn to Chapter 11.)

All states recognize shared custody as an option, and 37 of them as well as the District of Columbia have laws that either presume shared custody or explicitly cite it as the preferred custody arrangement. In most of these states, a judge can even order shared custody if one of the parents objects.

Bird nesting: An option that may work

A relatively new shared custody arrangement is for the children to stay in your family's home and for you and your spouse to take turns living there whenever your time comes to be with the kids. A popular name for this arrangement is "bird nesting."

The key advantage of this arrangement is that living in one place all of the time rather than having to constantly shuffle back and forth between your home and your ex's is less disruptive for your kids and provides them with a greater sense of continuity day to day.

But to make this arrangement work, you and your spouse must each be able to afford the expense of two separate residences — your own individual home or apartment where you live when you aren't living with your children and the residence where your children live full-time — or you must be willing to live in a hotel or some other temporary location when it's not your turn to live with your kids. Also, the success of this arrangement hinges on the ability of you and your spouse to cooperate with one another when it comes to cleaning and maintaining your family home, inside and out. If the two of you were in constant conflict over those things during your marriage, bird nesting could be fraught with problems. Another consideration is that tempers could flare if one of you begins living with someone or remarries and that new special someone is moving in and out of your family home.

Given the potential problems associated with bird nesting, many couples use this arrangement on a temporary basis only — while their kids finish their school year, while they're trying to sell their family home, until the real estate market in their area picks up, and so on.

If you and your spouse decide to bird nest, minimize the potential for acrimony between you and your former spouse by spelling out in writing exactly how the arrangement will work, the responsibilities of each former spouse when living in the family home, under what conditions a new "significant other" can stay overnight at the home, and so on.

Living arrangements

You and your spouse can structure a shared custody arrangement in several ways:

- ✔ **Have your children live with both of you in your individual homes on a 50/50 basis, a 60/40 basis, an 80/20 basis — whatever seems best.** If you opt for this sort of arrangement, you'll probably parent your children much the way you did during your marriage. The only difference is that now you and your spouse live under two separate roofs, not one.

- ✔ **One parent gets sole or primary physical custody of the kids, and the other parent gets liberal visitation rights:** This arrangement lets both parents share responsibility for making the important decisions in your children's lives. It can be a good option when one parent is out of town a lot, is regularly on call or works night shifts, or when work demands regularly take that parent away from home for extended periods of time.

If you and your spouse decide to share decision-making authority about some things but not others, avoid conflict and misunderstanding after your divorce by clearly spelling out the areas of shared decision-making in your custody agreement.

Your state's child custody laws may specify certain rights and duties that you and your spouse must share at all times after your divorce, the rights and duties that you can share if you want, and the rights and duties that each of you retains whenever your children are in your care. Your attorney can fill you in on what your state's laws say.

Benefits and pitfalls

The benefits of sharing physical and legal custody of your children with your former spouse are obvious: Your children get to maintain their relationships with both of you, and you and your ex are able to stay actively involved in their lives. Nevertheless, sharing physical and legal custody of your kids has some potentially serious drawbacks, including the following:

- ✔ Shared custody is relatively expensive. For example, unless you opt for bird nesting (see the "Bird nesting: An option that may work" sidebar in this chapter), both you and your former spouse must provide your children with a place to sleep and a place to store their clothes and other belongings when they're at each home (unless you want them living out of suitcases and boxes). Plus, each of you must provide your children with separate sets of clothing, bikes, toys, and other items that they use regularly unless you expect them to cart those things back and forth from your home to your former spouse's.

- ✔ For shared custody to work, you and your former spouse must communicate and cooperate with one another much more than you'd have to with other custody arrangements.

- ✔ Shuffling back and forth between your home and your ex-spouse's home can be hard on some children, particularly very young children, because it may make them feel constantly unsettled. Moving from house to house can be hard on your kids if there's a big disparity between your economic level and your ex's, if your lifestyles are very different, if you and your ex have different approaches toward child rearing, and so on.

- ✔ When children live with each parent part-time, their education can suffer unless both parents have the same attitude about homework, getting to school on time, school behavior, and doing well in their studies.

Making shared custody work

To have a successful shared-custody arrangement, you and your spouse must do something you may have had a hard time doing while you were married — get along with each other! To help you determine whether you and your spouse have what it takes to manage a shared-custody arrangement, read the following shared-custody guidelines:

- ✔ **Avoid postdivorce warfare.** Arguing in front of your children, especially about matters relating to them, can be emotionally devastating for you and the kids. When you and your ex disagree about your kids, have a calm discussion about your differences.

- ✔ **Don't use your children to try to get back at your former spouse.** Your marriage is over; it's time to move on. If you can't forgive and forget, you have no business sharing custody.

- ✔ **Respect your ex's parenting ability and style of parenting.** No, you may not like the way your ex parents your kids, but unless your former spouse puts them in danger or unless you have good reason to believe that he is harming their emotional, scholastic, or sexual development, how your ex parents your kids is really none of your business. For the sake of your children, you and your spouse should agree upfront on certain basic values or standards for raising them — curfew, bedtimes, and amount of TV they can watch, and so on. Make these kinds of agreements part of your parenting plan, which is something we discuss in the upcoming section "Crafting a Parenting Plan."

- ✔ **Support one another's efforts to learn new parenting skills.** Even if you and your former spouse were both active, involved parents, each of you probably had primary responsibility for certain things — one of you may have gotten the kids dressed in the morning and prepared their lunches while the other helped with their school projects and got them ready for bed. You may have to learn new skills so that you can do all the things you both used to share.

- ✔ **Agree on a schedule for when the children will live with each of you, and stick to it.** Children thrive on predictability. At the same time, don't be inflexible with your ex.

- ✔ **Mind your own business when your children are with their other parent.** Don't call or stop by to find out what time your ex-spouse got the kids to bed, what they ate for dinner, or to tell your ex what the kids should wear to school the next day. Your former spouse is in charge of your kids when they're at her home.

- ✔ **Support one another as parents.** Don't let your children play one of you against the other in order to get what they want, and don't criticize your ex-spouse in front of your children.

Considering Split Custody

A split-custody arrangement, where some or all of your children live with each of you for a part of the year, or some of your children live with one of you all the time and the rest of your children live with your former spouse all of the time, can make sense when

✔ One of your children has special educational or medical needs.

✔ One or more of your children refuses to spend time with you or with your spouse.

✔ One parent has special problems or limitations. For example, the parent's finances are very limited or the parent has a serious health condition.

This arrangement can also be a good option if one of your children is involved in a gang, has an alcohol or drug abuse problem, or is getting into trouble with the law, and you're concerned about his or her influence on your other children. If you or your ex will spend less time with your children after your divorce because of work, travel, or education demands, you may be especially concerned that a delinquent older child may have more opportunity to influence the younger ones.

In most instances, however, a split-custody arrangement isn't in the best interests of your children. For most kids, not living with both parents in the same house after a divorce is hard enough, but separating siblings from each other can be downright cruel.

Understanding the Ins and Outs of Primary Custody

If you get primary custody of your children, they'll probably live with you *most* of the time after you're divorced. More than likely, you will have day-to-day responsibility for them as well as the legal right and obligation to make all major life decisions on their behalf. However, you and your ex-spouse may decide that a somewhat different primary custody arrange- ment better suits your individual situations and the needs of your kids. As long as you and your spouse stay in control of your own divorce, exactly how you structure your primary custody arrangement is up to you.

If you let the court decide how to handle custody in your divorce, the judge is unlikely to give you or your spouse primary custody of your children, because the courts in most states believe that shared custody is in the best interests of kids and therefore prefer that custody arrangement. However, if one spouse has serious emotional problems, has abused his or her children in the past, has a long criminal history, and so on, the judge will probably give the other spouse primary custody of the couple's kids.

 Surprise! Child-support payments aren't tax deductible (but spousal support payments are). If you have primary custody of your children, you may want to consider working out a win-win arrangement with your spouse that gives you more child support in exchange for him or her taking the child-related tax exemptions and deductions.

If you moved out of your family home and left your children with your spouse, the judge will probably award your spouse primary custody of your children if you leave that decision to the court. On the other hand, if you moved out *with* your kids and immediately asked the court to grant you temporary custody, you'd be more likely to get a shared custody arrangement if that's what you wanted.

Visitation rights

When you have primary custody, your former spouse — the *noncustodial parent* — usually has *visitation rights,* or the right to spend time with your kids according to a predetermined, fixed schedule. Also, in most primary custody arrangements, the noncustodial parent pays child support to the custodial parent and provides health insurance for the children.

Visitation for most noncustodial parents means that they have the children every other weekend, one day midweek each week (the kids may or may not stay overnight), on certain holidays, on birthdays, and maybe during part of their summer vacations. However, if you and your spouse work out your own visitation schedule, you can agree to anything you want. For more on visitation, see the upcoming section "Making Visitation Arrangements."

Primary custody drawbacks

Having the children live with you all or most of the time and being responsible for making all the decisions about their lives makes sense if your spouse doesn't want to be or can't be actively involved with your children after you're divorced or if your spouse has problems that could put your children at risk. However, a primary custody arrangement can be fraught with problems, especially if your spouse ends up with very limited visitation rights and would prefer to spend more time with his children. Challenges associated with this arrangement include the following:

- ✔ Noncustodial parents often feel excluded from their children's lives.
- ✔ Many noncustodial parents slowly drift away from their children, especially if they remarry and start new families. When that happens, the children from the divorced couple's first marriage no longer have the benefit of a relationship with both of their biological parents.
- ✔ Studies show that noncustodial parents who don't get to spend an adequate amount of time with their children are less apt to meet their child-support obligations.

Then again, the custodial parent's situation isn't necessarily a bed of roses either. Consider the following:

✔ As most single parents can tell you, shouldering all or most of the day-to-day responsibilities of raising children can be a tremendous burden, physically and emotionally, particularly if you're working full time or even going to school as well.

✔ All of your responsibilities may mean that you have little quality time to spend with your kids, much less any time for yourself.

✔ Your children may spend more time in day care, after-school care, or at home by themselves than they did when you were married and your spouse was around to help out.

Most states have expanded the limited legal rights of noncustodial parents by allowing them to make emergency medical decisions for their children and by giving them access to their children's medical and educational records. For example, most noncustodial parents can request that their children's school send them copies of their kids' report cards.

If you find having most of the responsibility for your children to be a difficult and even an isolating experience for you, you may want to socialize with other parents in your situation. One such group is the Single Parents Association (SPA), a nonprofit organization with the mission of providing education, resources, friendship, and fun to single parents and their kids. It has chapters in various communities around the country. Check your local phone listings to find a chapter near you. Another group you may want to check out is Parents Without Partners. You can get in touch with the organization by calling 800-637-7974 or by visiting its Web site at www.parentswithoutpartners.org.

Virtual visitation helps noncustodial parents stay in touch with their kids

Some noncustodial parents are using virtual visitation to maintain ongoing relationships with their children when the custodial parent moves. They use e-mail, instant messaging, text messaging, webcams, and other electronic technologies.

Although virtual visitation is no substitute for regular physical contact between a parent and child, it provides noncustodial parents with a means of staying in touch besides phone calls and letters. Some judges have even ordered divorced parents to use various virtual visitation when one parent is moving away on a temporary or permanent basis, and Florida, Texas, Utah, and Wisconsin have passed virtual visitation laws. At the time this book was written, virtual visitation bills had been introduced but not yet passed in seven other states and efforts to get virtual visitation bills introduced and passed were underway in 27 additional states. For more information on virtual visitation go to www.internetvisitation.net or www.internetvisitation.org.

Making primary custody work

Here are some suggestions for how you can help your children maintain a relationship with your ex when you're the parent with primary custody:

- Don't place needless restrictions on their time together. Agree on a visitation schedule that's as generous as possible. Also, let your children have some control over when they spend time with their other parent.

- Encourage your children to call their other parent to share their good news and their concerns, and to get advice or help from that parent with homework. However, don't make calling a chore or a duty. Also, let your ex know that he or she can call the kids whenever they're at your house.

- Share report cards, homework assignments, school art projects, special awards, and so on with your former spouse.

- Encourage your former spouse to attend parent-teacher conferences.

- When you take photos of your children, get extra copies made for your ex-spouse. If you use a digital camera, e-mail the photos to him. Also, if you make videos of your kids, share copies with your ex.

- Let your ex-spouse know the dates and times of your children's recitals, school plays, athletic events, and other extracurricular activities.

- Invite your ex to your children's birthday parties, to go trick-or-treating at Halloween, and to share other important dates with you and your kids.

- Let your ex-spouse know well ahead of time when you will be taking the kids out of town, and don't balk when your spouse wants to take the kids on an out-of-town trip unless you're concerned that the trip is really a ruse to kidnap them. For information about childnapping, read the "Worse than a bad dream: The kidnapping parent" sidebar in this chapter, and see Chapter 18 as well.

- Keep your ex-spouse informed of your children's medical problems.

- Consult your former spouse about the important decisions in your children's lives. However, if an issue comes up, politely remind your former spouse that you're not legally obligated to act on his or her wishes or even consider them. Also, be sure that your children understand that consulting their other parent about important decisions they may be making — where to go to college, for example — is okay.

- Don't forbid your children to spend time with your ex's new girlfriend, boyfriend, or spouse. If you do, you force your ex to do things without your children, which can add to the stress they may already be feeling.

Tax Implications of Custody Decisions

Don't overlook the tax implications of various child-custody arrangements when you and your spouse are deciding which one is best for you. Depending on the arrangement you negotiate, you could lose your eligibility for certain child-related tax benefits. However, if you work with a CPA, he or she may be able to find ways to get certain tax benefits for you that you wouldn't ordinarily be entitled to. Depending on your income bracket, taking advantage of those benefits can provide you with significant tax savings.

The following items briefly explain how different custody arrangements can affect your eligibility:

- **Filing as head of the household:** You can file your federal taxes as *head of the household* if you meet certain conditions. You must have been unmarried on December 31 of the tax year (meaning you were legally separated by that date or your spouse didn't live in your home during the last six months of the year for which you're filing taxes; one or more of your children must have lived with you more than half of that year; and you must have contributed more than half the cost of maintaining your home during that year). If you and your spouse share physical custody exactly 50/50, neither of you can file as head of the household.

- **Exemptions for your children:** According to the IRS, the spouse who has custody of a couple's children gets the tax exemptions for them. However, by filing Form 8332 with the IRS, you and your spouse can trade the exemptions back and forth with one another. If you have any questions about how to complete the form or about whether one of you should always take the exemptions, talk to a CPA. When you claim a child as an exemption, you also get other tax benefits, including the right to the child credit for each child you exempt as well as the Hope Scholarship and Lifetime Learning credit.

- **Childcare tax credit:** You're entitled to this credit only if you are the custodial parent, you have one or more children under the age of 13, and your children attend day care while you're at work.

- **Deductions for medical expenses:** You and your spouse can each deduct your out-of-pocket child-related medical expenses, if the amount of those expenses exceeds a certain percentage of your adjusted gross income.

- **Earned income tax credit:** This tax benefit is for the spouse who has physical custody of the children, who works full time or part time and who has a low or moderate income. If you qualify for this tax credit, you can reduce your federal taxes and receive a refund from the IRS. To qualify, you must meet certain requirements and file a tax return, even if you're not otherwise required to file. The credit you receive can help pay your bills. However, earned income tax credit is quite complicated, so you should speak to your CPA to determine whether you or your spouse is eligible for it and exactly how to maximize its benefits.

Crafting a Parenting Plan

Nearly all states require parents who are getting divorced or legally separated to prepare a written parenting plan in addition to, or instead of, a traditional custody agreement. Even if your state does not require a parenting plan, preparing one is a good idea, because the plan can help reduce the potential for conflict between you and your ex once your divorce is final.

A parenting plan is a highly detailed description of how you and your soon-to-be ex will be involved in the lives of your children after your divorce. It spells out in great specificity exactly how each parent will be involved in their children's lives after the divorce and lists each parent's rights and responsibilities related to their children.

At a minimum, parenting plans address such issues as how much time your children will spend with you or your spouse on a regular basis; how you will share time with your children on special holidays, birthdays, and vacations; and how you will make decisions about your children's education, medical and dental care, education, and so on. Parenting plans also spell out how you and your former spouse will resolve any parenting plan–related disagreements you're unable to work out through a friendly discussion. You may want your plan to address such issues as

- ✔ Exactly how you and your spouse will share the routine day-to-day care of your children — that is, who will be responsible for what

- ✔ How you will share decision-making related to your children, including decisions related to their religious upbringing and their day care

- ✔ Each parent's access to their children's medical records, report cards, teachers, and so on

- ✔ Who will take off work to care for a sick child

- ✔ Who will care for the children when one parent is out of town overnight

- ✔ How you will deal with issues related to an older child's dating, curfews, sexuality, or what to do if that child develops a substance abuse problem

- ✔ How you will respond to your children's changing needs as they get older

- ✔ How you will share unexpected expenses related to your children

- ✔ How you will deal with any drug or alcohol, behavioral problems, and so on, that one of your children may develop

The State of Massachusetts has produced an excellent brochure that lays out the issues you should consider according to the age of your children when you're preparing a parenting plan. You can read it by going to www.mass.gov. Search the Web site for "afcc shared parenting," and you find a link to the brochure. If your state requires a parenting plan, it may have its own brochure. Ask your divorce attorney or contact the family law court in your area to find out.

Having a parenting plan provides several advantages. For example, through the process of developing the plan, parents must grapple with issues related to their kids and come up with solutions before the issues become problems, reducing the potential for postdivorce conflict and power struggles over the kids. The plan also provides parents with a framework that helps define their relationship with one another and with their children after their divorce.

States differ dramatically in the comprehensiveness and level of detail of their custody provisions. In those states where the provisions are very general, parents can help minimize future problems by negotiating a parenting plan. Some states, in fact, require that a parenting plan be included as an integral part of a custody agreement or a judge's custody order.

Parenting plans also can help make any custody arrangement work better by

- ✔ Helping both parents be more realistic about the amount of time and energy required on a day-to-day basis as single parents.

- ✔ Encouraging you to get all your postdivorce parenting issues out on the table. (Acknowledging those issues and resolving them together, before your divorce is final, is better than doing so after you have a custody agreement in place.)

- ✔ Minimizing the potential for postdivorce strife by helping you anticipate and resolve potential areas of conflict before they develop, by spelling out on paper, before you are divorced, every detail that could make or break your custody agreement.

- ✔ Letting you establish mutually agreed upon procedures for resolving any postdivorce conflicts related to your kids.

- ✔ Allowing you and your ex-spouse to express your long-term goals for your children in qualitative terms. For example, your parenting plan can state the following goals: "Our goal is to support our children to the fullest extent possible in their scholastic and extracurricular activities" or "Our goal is to limit the amount of time our children spend watching TV and playing computer games, and to encourage outdoor activities, reading, and conversation to the fullest extent possible."

Avoid making your parenting plan so rigid and inflexible that it cannot bend and change over time to meet the changing needs of your children. Remember that what your children need from each of you evolves over time, and that issues and problems that you didn't anticipate when you were preparing your plan inevitably arise. Your plan should also be flexible enough to respond to the changing circumstances in your own lives.

When You and Your Spouse Can't Agree: Taking Your Case to Court

You and your spouse may well end up at loggerheads over how to handle the custody of your children or the details of your parenting plan. After all, any number of issues and concerns can complicate your decision-making.

If you and your spouse simply can't see eye to eye on what to do about custody of your kids, consider talking with your religious advisor, meeting with a mental health professional, or trying mediation. If you take your case to court, you may be required to try to work out your differences through mediation before the court will even agree to give you a court date. (See Chapter 15 to find out how mediation works.) Other courts require couples who cannot agree on a custody arrangement to view educational videos on the subject before the courts will get involved.

Preparing for the judge's questions

If you take your custody battle to court, the judge who decides your case will probably consider most, if not all, of the following issues when deciding what custody arrangement is in your children's best interests:

- ✔ Where your children are living now
- ✔ The age and gender of your children
- ✔ How you and your spouse have shared parenting responsibilities in your marriage
- ✔ Whether any of your children have special needs and how you and your spouse deal with them now
- ✔ The kind of relationship your children have with each of you and which parent they turn to for emotional support or help with problems
- ✔ The hours each of you works, whether either or both of you have to travel for your jobs, and whether you expect your work and travel schedules to remain the same after your divorce
- ✔ Your ability to cooperate with one another on behalf of your children after your divorce
- ✔ Where each of you intends to live after your divorce and the kind of home life you can offer your children
- ✔ The stability of your finances
- ✔ Your physical health
- ✔ Your personal habits, for example, whether either of you abuses alcohol, drugs, parties excessively, is sexually promiscuous, and so on
- ✔ Your moral characters and religious beliefs

✔ Whether either of you has ever attempted suicide or been hospitalized for an emotional or psychiatric disorder

✔ Whether you or your spouse has a criminal history

✔ Whether your children have an especially close relationship with either or both sets of grandparents

Before you decide to wage a custody battle in court, compare yourself as a parent with your state's custody criteria. How do you measure up? If you fall short, think twice (and maybe three or four times) about whether a court battle is *really* worth the expense and stress it will create for you and your children. Maybe you need to resolve things with your spouse out of court.

Arming yourself for a custody battle

If you're concerned that your spouse may try to limit your right to continue playing a meaningful role in your children's lives after you divorce or if you want to limit your spouse's involvement in your kids' lives after your marriage has ended, you may be headed for a custody battle. If that seems likely, take the following actions sooner rather than later to improve your legal standing in such a battle:

✔ **Educate yourself about the general guidelines that judges in your state use to make custody decisions.** See how your situation stacks up against those guidelines. You should be able to get a copy of the guidelines by calling the family court in your area or a local family law attorney if you're not already working with one. You can also research the guidelines on the Internet.

✔ **Stay involved in all aspects of your children's lives.** When child custody becomes an issue in a divorce, most judges look to see which parent has been the children's *primary caregiver,* the parent who has been most involved in their day-to-day lives. One of the best ways to prove that you are integrally involved in your children's lives is to bring objective witnesses into the courtroom who can testify that you were there for your children in the years prior to your divorce and that you appeared to enjoy an ongoing and meaningful relationship with them.

✔ **Be there for your children so that they view you as a "go-to" parent.** As your children grow up, their parents should be available to provide them with ongoing emotional, physical, and psychological support and general caregiving.

This advice should serve as a wake-up call for those of you who think that a divorce may be in your future and have been spending too much time at the office, have been using up all your free time honing your golf or tennis game and devoting too little time to your kids, or who have always left most aspects of child-rearing to your spouse. Now may be the time to get your priorities straight. Besides, your life will be richer for playing a more active role in the lives of your children, and you're less likely to have regrets later about your role as a parent.

Custody and same-sex parents

Society's attitude toward gay and lesbian parents is evolving, but the laws are slow to reflect those changes. For example, the laws in a handful of states — Alaska, California, New Jersey, New Mexico, and Pennsylvania — as well as the District of Columbia, say that a parent cannot be denied custody or visitation because of sexual orientation. Even so, judges still have considerable discretion when deciding custody and visitation matters, and may be influenced by their own prejudices or the standards of their communities when deciding what is in a child's best interest. Other states, on the other hand, allow courts to deny custody or visitation rights to a divorced parent solely because of the parent's sexual orientation.

Realizing neither of you may get the kids

In a very small number of custody cases, neither spouse gets custody of their children. This is most likely to happen when both spouses have a history of child neglect or child abuse, substance abuse, emotional problems, or other negative behaviors. However, a judge won't consider awarding custody to someone other than a parent unless a third party raises questions about the parents' fitness to raise their kids or unless it is undeniably obvious to the judge that neither spouse is fit to parent their children.

In such cases, the judge appoints a *guardian ad litem* (someone with master's degree–level training or the equivalent in psychology, counseling, or social work) to represent the children in court and to help the court determine where the children should live. Often, a grandparent or another adult relative assumes temporary custody of the children under a court-ordered guardianship until a permanent living arrangement can be established.

Making Visitation Arrangements

Earlier in this chapter, we introduced the concept of visitation — the right of a noncustodial parent to spend time with his or her children. When you and your spouse negotiate your custody agreement, you can decide on the terms of visitation — when your former spouse will have the children, how long the kids will stay with him or her, and other terms. If a judge decides how custody of your children will be handled and he or she awards you primary custody of them, the judge sets the terms of your spouse's visitation rights. By the way, no law requires the parent with visitation rights to exercise those rights. In other words, a noncustodial parent cannot be forced to spend time with his or her children. Fortunately, most parents want to be a part of their children's lives.

Worse than a bad dream: The kidnapping parent

Although not a frequent occurrence (and we're glad of that), parental "childnapping" does happen. Some parents kidnap their children because they're afraid that the judge will deny them custody (or because they already have been denied custody). Others abduct their children to exact revenge on their ex-spouse, to force a reconciliation with their ex, or to keep their children away from what they regard as a dangerous parent. Abducting spouses may flee with their children to another state or, worse yet, to another country.

All states and the federal government have laws to prevent childnapping, and in most cases, parents who kidnap their children are committing a felony. Parents convicted of childnapping can end up in prison. (Turn to Chapter 18 for more information on the laws that apply to childnapping, the specific steps you should take immediately if your child is missing and you fear he or she has been kidnapped, and some of the organizations that can help you in such a situation.)

If you and your spouse are separated, your spouse takes off with the kids, and you have no idea where they are (and neither of you has a temporary court order for custody), immediately call a family law attorney. The attorney can initiate the appropriate legal actions to get you temporary legal custody of your missing children so that you can get your children returned to you.

Making visitation an issue for the court

When bad feelings between ex-spouses run deep, visitation can become a hotly contested issue, even if the court clearly spells out the rules of visitation. Often the only way this emotionally charged duel can end is if one parent takes the other to court.

When one parent has primary custody, a judge may order either "reasonable visitation" or "generous visitation" rights for the noncustodial parent and let the parents work out what that means. Or the judge may spell things out more specifically.

To help protect the best interests of the children and to protect the visitation rights of noncustodial parents, too, most states have guidelines that spell out the minimum amount of time that a noncustodial parent can spend with his or her children.

Burying the hatchet for your kids' sake

When you and your spouse use visitation as a vehicle for expressing your negative feelings for each other, you're likely to do serious emotional damage to your children. Children hate to see their parents fighting and, more important, they often blame themselves for the discord. Those feelings can create many problems that can follow your children throughout their lives, including low self-esteem, emotional distress, problems with intimacy, and even marital troubles of their own. Is this the kind of legacy you want to leave your children?

Your children deserve the opportunity to have both parents in their lives. Remember, a bad spouse doesn't necessarily equal a bad parent. Using your children to get back at your ex-spouse punishes your children as well as your ex. For the sake of your kids, you and your ex must act like mature adults and put them, not your hurt and angry feelings, first. If you can't work things out through mediation, seek help from a mental health professional — together or separately — so you can get beyond whatever issues are in the way of being able to cooperate with one another for your kids.

Visiting with restrictions

When you have good reason to believe that the noncustodial parent will harm or endanger your children, that parent's visitation rights should be restricted or even prohibited. Examples of when this restriction may occur include when the noncustodial parent has a history of

- Alcohol or drug abuse
- Child neglect
- Criminal activities
- Exhibiting explicit sexual behavior in front of children
- Mental or emotional instability
- Mental, physical, or sexual child abuse

Usually when a court restricts a parent's visitation rights, a designated adult must be present whenever that parent spends time with the children.

If you have custody of your children and think that the court should restrict your ex-spouse's visitation rights, ask the court to change the terms of your ex's visitation. Don't take the law into your own hands; if you do, you'll be breaking it.

As a way to deny a former spouse access to his or her children, some parents cruelly and maliciously make unwarranted accusations of child abuse or molestation. If you're unfairly accused, get legal help from an attorney.

Usually if allegations of abuse surface in a divorce, the court appoints a guardian *ad litem* or attorney *ad litem*. Ad litem is a Latin term meaning "for the lawsuit or legal action." In a divorce, a guardian ad litem or an attorney ad litem is someone who protects your children's interests in your divorce proceedings. This individual conducts an investigation into the abuse allegations and prepares a report that a judge uses to rule on custody, visitation, and what to do about the alleged abuse.

Grandparents' visitation rights

Many states have laws that give grandparents the right to court-ordered visitation when the children's parents get divorced. Those laws vary from state to state. In most states, if the custodial parent doesn't allow the grandparents to spend time with their grandchildren after a divorce or if the grandparents are fearful that the custodial parent will try to exclude them from their grandchildren's lives, they can ask the court to grant them formal visitation rights. Like with other issues related to children and divorce, the court determines whether spending time with their grandparents is in the children's best interest. If a court grants a grandparent that right and one or both divorced parents interfere with his or her exercising it, the grandparent can ask the court for help.

In 2000, the U.S Supreme Court dealt a serious blow to grandparents by severely limiting their right to sue to gain visitation rights. Since then, the high courts in 23 states have ruled on the constitutionality of their own visitation laws. Although most of them have upheld their laws, four of the states — Florida, Illinois, Michigan, and Washington — ruled that their laws were unconstitutional. Since then, some of those states have revised their laws giving parents more power to determine whether or not a grandparent can spend time with their grandchild.

Given the changing legal environment for grandparents seeking visitation, if you want the right to spend time with your grandchild, consult with a family law attorney in the area where the child lives. The attorney can educate you about the state law that applies to your situation, assess whether you have any legal standing under that law, and explain what you need to do in order to build a convincing case in favor of visitation if you decide to move forward with your efforts to get visitation rights as a grandparent. In some states, for example, grandparents are more apt to get visitation when one of their grandchild's parents has died, has become seriously ill, or is in prison; when the grandparent used to raise the grandchild; or when the grandparent can prove to the court that her grandchild would be harmed if they did not have a relationship with one another.

In order to avoid the stress and cost of a trial, your attorney may suggest that you and the other parents involved in your dispute over visitation try to work out your differences using mediation. However mediation has a chance of success only when everyone is willing to try to resolve their differences.

More and more grandparents have gone beyond trying to establish visitation rights and are seeking custody of their grandchildren instead. Usually this happens when a grandparent thinks that both parents are unfit to raise the children or when the grandparents have been acting as *de facto* parents.

If you think your ex is abusing your children

If you think that your ex-spouse is abusing your children, talk to an attorney immediately. The attorney can advise you on the appropriate steps to take, which may include any of the following:

- Contacting the police

- Filing a criminal lawsuit against your former spouse and stopping all communication with your ex

- Asking the court to prohibit your ex-spouse from having any future contact with your child until your allegations are investigated

- Having your child examined by a doctor

- Having your spouse undergo evaluation and treatment for chemical dependency, alcohol abuse, psychiatric problems, or anger management

- Taking photos of any unusual marks, bruises, or cuts on your children that you believe are evidence of the abuse or molestation

You should also report your ex-spouse to your local Child Protection Services office immediately. In fact, you may be held criminally liable if you don't report your spouse.

Chapter 11

Using Child Support to Provide For Your Children

. . . .

In This Chapter

▶ Determining which spouse pays child support — and how much

▶ Deciding the terms of your child-support agreement

▶ Providing your children with life's extras

▶ Making certain you receive your child-support payments

▶ How to include child support on your federal tax return

. . . .

*A*s a parent, you have a moral and legal responsibility to support your minor children (younger than age 18 in most states) so that at a minimum they have the basics in life — a roof over their heads, clothes to wear, enough food to eat, and an education. Divorce doesn't change this obligation, whether your children live with you or with your former spouse after your marriage ends. Therefore, if you have minor children, deciding how you and your spouse will share the cost of raising them is a key issue that you must resolve before your divorce can be final. And, if you separate and have minor children, you and your spouse should negotiate a temporary child-support agreement.

In this chapter, we explain which parent usually pays child support to the other and the role of state child-support guidelines in determining the minimum amount of support to be paid. We also help prepare you to negotiate your own child-support agreement and explain what the court may decide if you and your spouse can't work things out yourselves. In addition, we cover other child-related expenses beyond the basics that you may want to include in your divorce agreement or that the court may order one of you to pay the other, along with the tax implications of your agreement.

Defining Child Support and Figuring Out Who Pays It

Child support is a fixed amount of money that one parent pays to another parent after the couple divorces to help cover the cost of raising their minor child or children. You and your spouse can negotiate your own child-support agreement, taking into account the support guidelines in your state, or you can let the court decide how much child support one of you must pay the other if you and your spouse can't reach an agreement. (The section "Negotiating Your Own Agreement," later in this chapter, provides advice for how to work out the terms of the agreement on your own, and the "Taking state guidelines into account" section gives you the lowdown on state guidelines in general.) Contact your state's child-support enforcement office or a divorce attorney for specific information about the guidelines in your state.

If you're the parent who receives child support, you're expected to use those payments *only* for the benefit of your child or children. You are not expected to use the money to enhance your own lifestyle — to pay for your vacation, to help finance the sexy little sports car you always wanted, to pay for the cost of a personal trainer at your gym, and so on.

When one parent has primary custody

Normally, if one parent has primary custody of the children, the other parent (the *noncustodial* parent) is obligated to pay child support. The court usually considers the parent with primary custody to be meeting his or her child-support obligation by raising the couple's children. However, studies show that custodial parents typically spend up to three times the amount of money they receive in child support paying for their children's necessities.

Although some states deduct *reasonable living expenses* from the income of the parent who will pay child support before determining how much support that parent must pay, in primary custody arrangements especially, most states calculate child support based on that parent's gross income. Gross income is income before taxes and other deductions.

When parents share custody 50/50

When parents share custody of their children on a 50/50 basis, depending on their individual incomes and assets, neither parent may pay child support to the other. Instead, they may agree (or the court may order) that whenever their children are living with one of them, that parent is responsible for paying the costs of the children's day-to-day care. However, parents with a 50/50 custody arrangement should have an agreement regarding how they share the cost of the big stuff — health insurance, private school or college, private lessons, summer camp, and so on.

Depending on each parent's individual circumstances and the needs of their children, one parent in a 50/50 custody arrangement may pay the other parent child support. For example, if one of the parents earns much more than the other parent, the higher-earning parent may agree that it would be fair if she paid child support to the parent who earns less. If the parents don't see eye to eye on this matter, they may ask the court for a ruling. If the court decides that the higher-earning parent must pay child support, the amount of the court-ordered support will probably be less than it would be if the parents didn't have a 50/50 custody arrangement.

If you and your spouse decide to share custody on a 50/50 basis and negotiate your own child-support arrangement, but your incomes aren't equal or close to equal, one way to determine how much each of you should contribute toward the care of your children is to calculate the percentage of each of your individual incomes relative to your combined incomes, and then apply that percentage to the total cost of your children's day-to-day care.

When shared custody isn't 50/50

In some shared custody situations, each parent's financial contribution to child support is a function of their individual incomes relative to their combined total incomes and of the amount of time the children will spend with each parent. For example, a couple's children may spend more time with the parent who earns less — maybe because the other parent travels a lot for business. Therefore, the parents may agree (or the court may order) that the parent who is with the children less often should pay the other parent child support. Exactly how much support depends on what the parents (or the court) decide is fair and necessary to take care of their children's needs. But the amount of the payments will probably be smaller than they would be if the parents weren't sharing custody.

If you and your spouse decide to share custody of your kids but agree that one of you will stay home to care for them until all of them reach a certain age, you should negotiate child support as though you had decided on a sole-custody arrangement. (Chapter 10 discusses various child-custody arrangements.)

Calculating and Paying the Child-Support Check

You and your spouse can negotiate your own child-support arrangement based on how you will share custody of your kids, your individual estimated postdivorce budgets, and the financial needs of your children. Or, you can ask the court to decide which of you should pay child support and how much the support should be. When determining an appropriate amount of support, the court takes into account your state's child-support guidelines, and it may factor other considerations into its decision as well, such as whether any of your children have special needs, whether one of you makes much more money than the other, and so on.

Federal law now requires that your child support court order address how your minor child will be provided with health insurance. The upcoming section "Taking care of medical expenses" discusses your options.

If one of you asks to receive spousal support (or alimony) in your divorce, that request takes a back seat to child support because, in the eyes of the law, child support is more important than spousal support. Therefore, the court won't order one spouse to pay so much spousal support that he won't be able to pay an adequate amount of child support. Similarly, if you and your spouse are negotiating your own divorce agreement, you should make child support a higher priority than spousal support if you're addressing both types of payments.

Taking state guidelines into account

In the late 1980s, Congress passed a law requiring all states to establish guidelines (formulas, really) that family law courts must use to calculate the appropriate amount of child support in a divorce. One of the reasons for the guidelines was to try to bring some consistency to the amount of child support paid from state to state. Even so, a considerable amount of variability still exists among states, which means that parents in some states pay more in child support than parents in other states who make the same amount of money.

Most states express their child-support guideline amounts as a percentage of a parent's income. Usually, the more dependent children a couple has, the higher the percentage. Here are some of the considerations you may encounter:

✔ When calculating the amount of child support that one spouse must pay the other, some states consider only the income of the noncustodial parent, whereas other states consider the incomes of both parents.

✔ Some state guidelines base the amount of child support on a parent's *gross income* — his income before taxes and essential living expenses are deducted. Others base the amount on the parent's *net income,* or actual take-home pay.

✔ Some states cap the total amount of income that their guidelines can apply to; that is, the states only apply the guidelines to income up to a certain dollar amount, which means that the court doesn't consider any income a parent may earn above and beyond that amount when determining how much child support the parent must pay. Also, some states apply a different percentage to income over a certain amount. The percentage may be higher or lower depending on the state.

✔ State guidelines even differ in their definitions of income. For example, some states consider only a parent's wages, whereas others take into account *all* sources of income, including wages, investment income, trust income, royalties, commissions, government benefits, and so on.

Accessing your state's guidelines

You can find the info you need to figure out the minimum amount of child support you'll have to pay (or will receive) in several ways:

✔ Ask your divorce attorney about your state's child-support guidelines.

✔ Call your state attorney general's child-support division for your state's guidelines.

✔ Go online to `www.acf.hhs.gov/programs/cse/extinf.htm`, which is located within the U.S. Office of Child Support Enforcement's Web site. You can also access brochures and fact sheets about your child-support rights at this site.

✔ Check with the family law court in your area to determine whether it can provide you with a child-support worksheet you can use to calculate the amount of child support that you're likely to receive or may have to pay based on your state's guidelines.

If you have custody of your children and you move to another state where the cost of living is higher than where you used to live, you can ask the court that issued the original child support order to increase the amount of support that your former spouse must pay you.

Needing more than the guidelines allow

If your spouse will be paying you child support and you believe that you need more support than your state's guidelines provide, prepare a postdivorce budget for your children that clearly demonstrates just how much you need to care for them. Bring the budget to your negotiations if you and your spouse are resolving the issue of child support on your own. If your attorney is helping you determine the amount of child support that will be paid in your divorce or if you're asking the court to figure it out, make sure that your attorney has a copy of your budget.

When you're preparing this budget, include expenses such as your mortgage or rent payment, your car payment, phone service, cable, and other similar expenses as well as expenses that are directly associated with your children — clothing, day care, educational costs, and so on. Be sure to figure in your income, too.

To make preparing your children's budget as painless as possible, try using the budget worksheet found at `www.free-financial-advice.net/budget.html` or flip to Chapter 3, where you find an example of a budget that you can adapt to your needs.

Leaving special circumstances to the discretion of the court

In most states, under certain circumstances family law courts have the flexibility to order more or less child support than the guideline amounts dictate. Those circumstances may include the following:

- ✔ The custodial parent earns considerably more than the other parent or has considerably more assets, or the assets of the noncustodial parent are worth relatively little.

- ✔ The couple's children have emotional, physical, educational, or other special needs.

- ✔ During the couple's marriage, their children enjoyed a standard of living that was higher than what the guideline amount provides.

- ✔ The noncustodial parent has the ability to pay much more than the guideline amount or makes too little to pay the guideline amount.

- ✔ One of the parents must incur substantial childcare expenses in order to be able to earn a good living.

- ✔ One parent assumed a lot of the couple's debt in their divorce.

- ✔ One parent experiences a significant amount of positive or negative cash flow from his or her real or personal property.

- ✔ The noncustodial parent makes substantially less than his or her full earnings potential.

  In this case, the court may decide to order an amount of support based on how much that parent *could* earn, not on how much money the parent *is* earning. For example, if a former corporate executive trades his or her high-stress job (and six-figure salary) for less lucrative but more relaxing employment as a woodworker, the court may order that parent to make child-support payments that are more in line with what he or she earned when the parent was a corporate executive.

✔ The noncustodial spouse becomes unemployed.

The court may order the noncustodial spouse to pay less support or none at all until she finds a job. However, if the court has reason to believe that the parent's unemployment is little more than a ruse to avoid paying child support, it may set a date by which the parent must begin paying an amount of support equal to what she would pay if she were working at her full earnings capacity. Even if the court doesn't think that the unemployment is a ruse, it may order the unemployed parent to pay what the parent would have to pay if she were employed or to make up the missed payments after he or she lands a job.

✔ The children will be living full time with the noncustodial parent during a certain time of the year — for example, during the summer. In such an instance, the court may allow the noncustodial parent to pay less child support during that time.

Considering the payment method

If you and your spouse have more than one minor child, the court may order the noncustodial parent to

✔ Pay a per-child amount of child support.

✔ Make a lump-sum payment of child support (However, most courts don't like the lump-sum option because judges realize that many people have trouble managing a large chunk of money.)

✔ Purchase an annuity calculated to cover the financial needs of all your children.

✔ Set aside specific property so that it can be administered for the benefit of the children.

✔ Combine all or some of these options.

If you have only one child, many of these same methods can also apply, including a lump-sum payment, an annuity, setting aside property to be administered for your child's benefit, or some combination of these options.

Unless you and your spouse agree to a different arrangement or the court orders otherwise, a noncustodial spouse with child-support obligations must pay support year-round, not just when the custodial parent has the children.

If you pay your child support by check, note exactly what the payment is for on the bottom of each check because a canceled check provides proof of payment in the event that some question arises in the future about whether you failed to make a payment or didn't make a full payment.

Negotiating Your Own Agreement

Like most everything else to do with divorce, negotiating your own child-support agreement has its advantages:

- ✔ **You split the responsibility:** The negotiation process encourages you and your spouse to assume equal responsibility for deciding how your children's financial needs will be met.

    Mothers often end up being their children's financial advocates in child-support negotiations and, sometimes, it can appear to their husbands that they're really arguing on their own behalf instead of for their kids. If you're a mother in this situation, a good way to avoid this problem is to be prepared to justify what you ask for on behalf of your kids with receipts, check-register entries, and anything else that helps prove that your requests make financial sense.

- ✔ **1 + 1 = 2 parents:** Negotiating together reinforces the fact that, even though your marriage is ending, you and your spouse still have a relationship as parents and that you're both legally responsible for your children's welfare.

- ✔ **The child support is more apt to get paid:** Working things out together makes it more likely that after you're divorced, the parent who's obligated to pay child support will actually do so since he will have been part of the decision.

If you decide to negotiate the agreement yourself, make sure that you spell out all the details of your child-custody and -support arrangement in writing, including the amount of child support, how often each payment will come, and the date by which you or your ex must pay it. After you have a draft, hire a divorce attorney to review it so that you can be sure that the agreement covers all the bases and leaves little in question. Then file the appropriate legal paperwork in order to get the terms of your agreement court-ordered. That way if you and your former spouse subsequently disagree over exactly what you agreed to, you can refer to that document, and if need be, you can get the court to enforce the agreement.

Agreeing on how much is enough

Although you may both agree that one of you should pay child support to the other, deciding on the exact amount of the support payments can be a challenge. Start by reviewing the following: a budget that reflects the cost of raising your children; your and your spouse's estimated postdivorce budget; and your state's child-support guidelines, which you can obtain from your divorce attorney or from your state's child-support enforcement agency. But most likely, you and your spouse will want to provide your children with more than the guidelines indicate because they generally define the minimum amount of support to be paid.

Don't forget to factor inflation into your child-support agreement, because increases in the inflation rate ultimately decrease the value of the child support that one spouse is paying the other. A practical way of dealing with this issue is to build nominal increases in the amount of child support into your agreement. If those increases don't keep pace with the inflation rate, your agreement can state that you and your former spouse will negotiate a different amount of child support. (If you do, be sure to get a new court order that reflects the revised amount.) Another option is for the spouse who receives child support to ask the court to order an increase in the amount of the support payments.

If you initiated your divorce and feel guilty about how it may affect your kids, don't try to ease your guilt by agreeing to pay more child support than you can truly afford. Otherwise, if you have a tough time meeting your child-support obligation after your divorce, you may find yourself in court if your former spouse takes legal steps to enforce your child-support agreement.

If you're the parent who will receive child support, try hard to negotiate a child-support agreement with your spouse rather than have the court decide how much your spouse must pay. Your spouse is more apt to meet his child-support obligation if he had a say in the amount of those payments. And, if the support checks keep coming, you'll be better able financially to provide your children with what they need.

Adjusting as your lives change

Another advantage to negotiating your own child-support agreement is that you and your spouse can craft one that readily allows you to anticipate and accommodate changes in your lives and in the lives of your children over the years. For example, your agreement can spell out how you'll deal with possible future expenses related to your children and how any salary increases or decreases either of you may experience will affect the agreement. If the future brings any changes in the amount of support to be paid or when it will be paid, be sure to get a new order from the court that reflects those changes. Otherwise, the changes won't be legally enforceable.

When you ask the family law court to revise your existing child-support court order, assuming you and your ex-spouse are in agreement about the changes, the court will probably approve your request without any delays or problems. However, to help ensure that things go smoothly, it's best to involve a family law attorney.

State courts aren't bound to honor any provisions you may include in a prenuptial or postnuptial agreement concerning the custody or support of your children.

Being prepared for negotiating obstacles

Despite the benefits of negotiating your own child-support agreement, doing so is apt to be easier said than done if you don't ground your negotiations in reality or if you let your emotions get in the way. Before you start negotiating, therefore, get in the right frame of mind, and stay aware of the following thought patterns that can derail your negotiations:

- ✔ The spouse who will pay child support may view the payments as nothing more than spousal support in disguise. Therefore, he may argue for as little child support as possible and against any extras.

- ✔ The spouse who will receive the child support may demand an unreasonable amount of support as revenge for having to get divorced or out of fear for the future.

- ✔ Looking forward to being single again, some spouses begin dreaming about the exciting new lifestyles they'll enjoy. Because living that kind of life takes money and because money is usually in short supply after a divorce, the parent who will be paying the support often wants to pay as little as possible, while the other parent wants as much as possible.

Going Beyond Basic Child Support

Child support isn't the only expense that the court can order you, your spouse, or both of you to pay for the benefit of your minor children. Also, if you negotiate your own support agreement, child support isn't the only expense that you and your spouse may decide should be paid. For example, depending on your state, the noncustodial parent can be ordered to contribute to the cost of the other parent's work-related day care and the children's college or trade-school education (assuming that the parent can afford to do so). The court can also order the noncustodial parent to provide health insurance for the children, unless the parents have worked out another arrangement that's acceptable to the court.

Making your children your life insurance beneficiaries

If you're obligated to pay child support, you can help ensure that your children's financial needs will be taken care of if you die while they're still minors by purchasing a life insurance policy and making them the beneficiaries. If the court is involved in your divorce and orders you to purchase such a policy, you may also be ordered to provide your ex-spouse with annual proof that the life insurance policy continues to be in force. If you and your spouse decide to share the cost of raising your children, you should both purchase life insurance policies.

If you purchase life insurance, you must designate an adult to manage the policy proceeds on your children's behalf because, legally, minors can't manage more than a very small amount of money or other assets. Depending on the kind of estate planning you've done, this adult can be the trustee of the living trust you may have set up for your children, or the person you designated as their property guardian in your will. This adult may be your children's other parent, a relative or friend that you trust, an attorney, and so on. You should discuss how best to use life insurance to benefit your minor children with an estate-planning attorney.

Ensuring uninterrupted child support with disability insurance

Disability insurance pays a working parent a percentage of her income if that parent can't work because of a debilitating illness or injury. Therefore, the court often requires the parent who's paying child support to purchase this kind of insurance, particularly if the parent is self-employed.

Disability insurance is especially important if a parent's business is a sole proprietorship, a partnership, or a small, closely held corporation. In such businesses, the active involvement of the business owner is almost always critical to the business's financial success. Therefore, if the owner becomes physically or mentally incapacitated, the business can falter or fail, leaving the owner with little or no income. As a result, the owner probably won't be able to meet her child support obligations after a period of time.

Taking care of medical expenses

Having health insurance for your children is important to their well-being, so important in fact that federal law requires your child support court order to spell out exactly how that coverage will be provided. The spouse who is paying child support may fulfill this obligation by

✔ Keeping your kids on his employer's health plan or adding them to the plan. This is the arrangement that courts most often order when a couple is unable to reach a negotiated child support agreement. However, the court will probably okay a different arrangement if either you or your spouse can provide your children with comparable coverage at a lower price through a different insurance plan.

✔ Purchasing a new insurance plan for your children.

  ✔ Reimbursing the non-support-paying spouse for all or a portion of the costs of the children's health coverage if that spouse has the kids on her own health plan.

  ✔ Paying the other spouse an additional amount of support to recompense him for any ongoing medical costs the couple's children may have or for any medical costs that the other spouse's insurance may not cover.

Health plans may not cover all your children's medical expenses and don't pay 100 percent of the expenses they do cover. For this reason, as part of your negotiations, you and your spouse (or the court if it's involved) must decide how you will share those costs. If you'll be the custodial parent, don't overlook these expenses during your divorce negotiations. Otherwise, you may have to cover them yourself.

Some health plans provide a lower level of reimbursement if you use health providers outside the plan's network. This point can be important if doctors who aren't in the plan's network are currently treating your children and you want them to continue caring for your children after your divorce is over. Therefore, you and your spouse or the court need to decide how to deal with these and other possible issues related to the scope and cost of the health plan that will cover your children.

Funding a college education

These days, sending a child to a four-year college or university can cost a small fortune, and education is getting more expensive all the time. So, when negotiating your child-support agreement, don't forget to consider how you and your spouse will pay for your children's college educations. Neither you nor your spouse can afford to take on that expense by yourself, especially if more than one of your children will be in college at the same time. Among other options, one or both of you may agree to begin putting a certain percentage of your monthly incomes in a special account for your children's college educations and you may also agree that your children will have to come up with whatever college-related costs you can't afford to pay, by working and getting student loans.

Paying for life's little extras

Gifts, vacations, clothes, lessons, summer camp, and anything else that you give to your children because you *want* to (and not because you *have* to) don't necessarily count as child support when you have a court order for support. Therefore, if you're paying child support, you usually *cannot* deduct such expenses from the total amount of support that you're obligated to pay. But, to be certain, check with your attorney.

Under state guidelines, child support is essentially an average dollar amount that is presumed to provide adequate support for a child. But it really provides a minimum amount of support and probably doesn't cover the "extras" you may want your children to have — private school, special classes, summer camp, vacations, or tutoring, for example. If the court is deciding child support in your divorce and you want certain extras to be included in the court order, you must ask the court to consider those special expenditures when calculating how much child support your spouse must pay.

Even if you and your spouse agree that each of you will be responsible for paying the basic day-to-day costs of your children's care, depending on where your children are staying, you must still decide on which extras to fund and how to split the cost of any big-ticket extras you both feel your kids need.

Calculating how you will split the cost of special activities and other extras for your kids is a good idea because it minimizes the potential for disagreements about those matters after your divorce and formalizes what you agree on. One easy way to calculate the split is for each of you to pay a *pro rata share* — that is, a percentage of the cost of the extras based on your individual incomes relative to your total combined income. For example, assume that the total annual cost of the extras you want to fund is $10,000. Also assume that you earn $40,000 a year and your spouse earns $45,000 a year; this gives you a total combined annual income of $85,000. In this case, your income would represent 47 percent of the total, and your spouse's income represents 53 percent of the total. If you applied these percentages to the $10,000 total cost of the extras, in order to pay for them, you'd contribute $4,700 a year, and your spouse's share would be $5,300.

Realistically speaking, however, given the cost of maintaining two households and the amount of your individual post divorce incomes, you and your spouse may not have enough money left over to give your children all the extras they are used to — or paying for them will require some cutbacks in your budgets.

If you do *not* have a court order for child support, gifts, vacations, lessons, and so on are considered in-kind child support. Their costs may be applied to your child-support obligation.

Child-support payments aren't tax deductible. Therefore, if you're paying child support, treating any extra money you contribute to help cover the cost of extras for your kids as spousal support — not as child support — makes sense for tax purposes. Talk to your CPA about how to do this and what sort of records you should keep. For details about the ins and outs of spousal support, turn to Chapter 9.

Making Sure You Receive the Support You're Owed

You have no way of knowing what the future will bring, and, the truth is, being single again sometimes changes the priorities of a previously devoted parent. Even if your ex is obligated to pay child support, he may begin to take that obligation less seriously and fall behind on his support payments as result, or stop making them all together.

If your former spouse stops paying you child support, begins making the payments late, or sends you payments sporadically or in smaller amounts than were agreed to, don't hesitate to take action — your responsibility is to your children, and that means providing for them financially, including doing what you can to ensure that your child-support payments keep coming.

Getting a court order from the get-go

The best way to ensure that you receive the child-support payments you're entitled to on a timely basis is to submit the agreement you and your spouse negotiate to the court and to ask for it to be formalized through a court order. This precaution is critical even if you believe that your spouse is totally trustworthy and you're certain that your spouse will live up to your agreement, because you don't know what the future may bring.

Without a child support court order, you don't have the full force of the law behind you if your former spouse stops making regular child-support payments, begins paying less than he or she is supposed to, or fails to make any payments at all. (Chapter 18 has additional information on what you can do if you begin having trouble collecting your child support.)

Securing the payments with automatic wage withholding

To help custodial parents collect their child support, all new and amended child-support court orders written after December 31, 1993, must provide for each payment to be automatically deducted from the paycheck of the parent who is obligated to pay child support, unless both parents and the court agree to a different arrangement. (Legal limits in every state dictate how much can be deducted from each paycheck.) States are also obligated as necessary to apply the automatic deduction to any commissions, bonuses, workers' compensation payments, disability payments pension income, and other retirement income the parent paying child support may earn.

To initiate automatic wage deductions, the employer of the parent who's obligated to pay child support is served with a court order for the deduction. If the employer fails to comply with the court order, the *employer* is violating federal law.

If your former spouse has a stable work history, the automatic wage deduction ensures that you'll get the child support you're entitled to according to a regular schedule. But, automatic wage deductions are not as effective if your ex changes jobs a lot because each new employer must be served with a new automatic wage deduction court order and so you'll need to make certain that every new employer actually gets served. Doing so can be a challenge, particularly if you are constantly having to try to track down where your ex is working, and especially if he or she lives far away from you.

You and your spouse can agree to waive the automatic wage deduction; however, your attorney should structure your court order so that if your former spouse gets behind on his or her support payments, after a period of time, the automatic wage withholding activates without you having to go back to court.

To help deal with such problems, your divorce decree should order your former spouse to let you know whenever she changes jobs, which can be an iffy proposition for some ex-spouses. However, the court order for automatic wage deduction requires your former spouse's employers to inform you and the court of any change in your ex's employment status. Despite these safeguards, sometimes you still don't receive notification of such change or the notifications aren't sent on a timely basis.

Helping to ensure payments if your spouse is self-employed

The automatic wage deduction won't help you collect your child support if your former spouse is self-employed. If your spouse is self-employed, one good way to help ensure that your child-support checks keep coming is to ask the court to order your spouse to post a bond to secure the payments. Another option is to ask the court to order your spouse to secure the obligation with a liquid asset, such as a checking or savings account, rental income, a profit-sharing plan, or other asset. Then, if the child-support checks stop coming, you can begin drawing the money you need from the collateralized asset until the payments resume.

If your spouse has a history of writing bad checks, agreeing to accept your child support in the form of a personal check is a bad idea. However, the judge can issue a court order that requires that your ex make the payments in the form of a cashier's check or money order.

Understanding What to Do and Not Do if You're Paying Child Support

If you're legally obligated to pay child support and you fall behind on your payments, in addition to possibly creating a financial hardship for your children and their other parent, you also risk ending up in legal hot water. For example, if your former spouse takes action to enforce your agreement, your wages may be garnished, your assets, including your tax refunds, may be seized, you may be denied a passport, you may be arrested and sent to jail, and so on. Also, your delinquency will be reported to all three of the national credit reporting agencies, which will do serious damage to your FICO scores and to your financial standing, making it difficult if not impossible for you to obtain credit at reasonable terms, to qualify for insurance, to rent a place to live, or to find a job with a new employer or to get a promotion at your current place of work. Therefore, making each of your court-ordered child support payments on time is critical.

If you lose your job, quit your job or begin earning less than you were making when the court ordered your child support obligation, you're entitled to ask your local CSE office to review that obligation. If the office determines that there has been a "substantial decrease" in your income, it may lower the amount that you're required to pay if the amount that you were paying no longer fits within your state's child support guidelines. Most likely, however, the financial relief you receive will be only temporary and the court will order you to find a new job or a second job right away so that you can resume making your regular payments as quickly as possible. The court won't care that the new jobs or second jobs available to you don't match your education, training, and work experience. Its priority is that you be working at some job — any job — in order to live up to your child support agreement. (By the way, your former spouse is entitled to request that you be ordered to pay him more child support if your financial circumstances substantially improve after your divorce is final, like if you get a big promotion with an equally big increase in salary or you win the lottery, for example.)

If the court determines that you deliberately took a lower paying job or took some other action with the goal of lowering your income so that you won't have to pay as much in child support as you are currently required to pay, or that you aren't doing everything in your power to make up for the loss of income, it will deny your request to have the amount of your payments lowered.

If your situation does not meet your state's standards for a modification in the amount of child support you must pay, you may be eligible for a court hearing on your situation. It's best not to try to file your own petition for a hearing or represent yourself if you are given a hearing. Instead hire a divorce attorney.

If you meet your child support obligation each month but your ex is making it difficult for you to spend time with your kids according to the terms of your custody and visitation agreement, don't retaliate by withholding payment or paying less than you're obligated to pay. Doing so punishes your children for your spouse's actions. Instead, contact your state child support enforcement office or your divorce attorney. Although the federal Child Support Enforcement Program does not have the authority to enforce visitation agreements, many state governments have procedures for enforcing them.

Knowing When Child Support Obligations Cease

A parent's child-support obligation ends when a child becomes a legal adult (18 years of age in most states). However, depending on your state (or on the terms of your child support agreement), that obligation can continue while your child is a full-time college student or is attending a trade school. But, diploma or no diploma, your responsibility to provide child support typically ends when the child reaches his or her early 20s.

Your obligation to help support a child may end before your minor child becomes a legal adult if he or she

✔ Becomes an *emancipated minor*. Emancipated minors are children who become legal adults before they turn 18 or 21. They must initiate a legal process to become emancipated.

✔ Is on active duty in the military.

✔ Takes a full-time permanent job.

✔ Gets married.

✔ Dies.

If an unmarried dependent child becomes a parent, that unmarried child's noncustodial parent still has to help support that child. However, the noncustodial parent is *not* legally obligated to support his or her grandchild.

If you're paying child support and the minor child you're supporting moves in with you on a full-time, permanent basis, ask the court to cancel your court-ordered child-support obligation. If you do not, your legal obligation to pay child support to your former spouse continues.

Heeding Uncle Sam

As far as adjustments to taxable income go, if you're paying child support, you *cannot* claim your payments as a tax deduction on your federal tax return. If you are receiving child support, you do not have to claim it as income.

Although the IRS assumes that the custodial parent will claim his or her dependent children as tax exemptions, as part of your divorce negotiations, you and your spouse can agree to split up that deduction. For example, each of you can claim them in alternate years, one of you can claim one child and the other can claim another child, and so on.

Generally, the parent with the higher income realizes the greatest benefit from claiming his or her children as tax deductions. Discuss how to handle the deductions with a tax CPA or CDP when you are working out the terms of your divorce.

By agreement, a custodial parent can transfer his or her dependent-child exemption to the noncustodial parent by completing IRS Form 8332, which can be financially beneficial to both parents. You can use this transfer as a bargaining chip in your negotiations — possibly creating a win-win situation for both of you — if you give your spouse the deduction in exchange for getting more support. (The court cannot order this transfer, because taking the tax deduction for children is a privilege granted by the federal government.)

Part IV

Working Out the Details of Your Divorce

"I'm well aware that the court has requested a lot from you during the property division hearing in your divorce, Mr. Harvey. However, I don't remember sarcasm being on that list."

In this part . . .

Deciding the terms of your divorce can seem like a daunting undertaking. But the information in this part should make you feel more confident about your ability to meet that challenge. Here we show you how to negotiate as much of your own divorce as possible, explain when you should get the help of an attorney, and how to find a good attorney. We show you how an attorney will work with you, how mediation can help get you through sticky divorce issues, and give you a glimpse into a divorce trial.

Chapter 12

Negotiating Your Own Divorce

- -

In This Chapter

▶ Planning when, where, and how you and your spouse will negotiate

▶ Knowing an attorney's role for before, during, and after your negotiations

▶ Forging an agreement on custody, child support, and spousal support

▶ Agreeing on how to divide your marital property and debts

▶ Finalizing your divorce agreement

- -

*N*egotiating your own divorce agreement (or at least some of it) can definitely save you money on attorney fees and court costs. But it does require that you and your soon-to-be-ex work cooperatively with one another, which may be a challenge at times. There will not be a mediator in the room with you to help you and your spouse keep your conversations with one another polite and focused, nor will there be attorneys to do the negotiating for you. The success or failure of your discussion will all be up to the two of you. Even so, negotiating the terms of your own divorce can be a good way to end your marriage and it doesn't have to degenerate into a shouting match or a stalemate.

Although this chapter doesn't tell you *what* to decide (that's up to you) regarding the terms of your divorce, it does prepare you to make good decisions by suggesting how to plan and organize your negotiating sessions and by offering some basic negotiating advice. This chapter also provides a primer on the basic issues that you may have to resolve before you and your spouse can make your divorce legal.

Note: This chapter touches on negotiating spousal support, child custody, child support, and the division of your property — topics that we cover in more depth in other parts of this book. For more specific information on these topics and how the law addresses them, see the related chapters in Part III.

First, a Word of Caution

When you read this chapter, keep in mind that the plan of action it describes is an ideal scenario to shoot for. However, you may not have the desire, the time or the inclination to do *everything* we recommend, which is okay. If you just accomplish what you can, you can still save yourself some time and money.

You should also be aware that negotiating your own divorce isn't for every married couple and in fact may be downright dangerous for some of you. For example, negotiating your own divorce isn't a good idea if your spouse intimidates you, you know little or nothing about your finances, or there is some other inequity in your marriage that puts you at a negotiating disadvantage. Under such circumstances, doing your own negotiating could mean that you end up with a divorce agreement that gives you less than you're legally entitled to, a custody arrangement that is emotionally harmful to your children, an agreement that's completely unenforceable, and so on.

 What you say to your spouse during your negotiations can be used against you if you end up in court, unless you and your spouse have a written upfront agreement guaranteeing that whatever either of you say during your one-on-one negotiations is confidential. If you don't have such an agreement, what you say to your spouse could come back to haunt you.

Being on Your Best Behavior

A successful divorce negotiation requires hard work, a commitment to the negotiation process, and a willingness to act like mature adults. That can be a tall order for many happily married couples, let alone those who are splitting up. For your negotiations to be productive, you and your spouse must be able to sit down together; talk honestly; figure out in a calm, rational manner all of the details related to ending your marriage; and be willing to give as well as take.

You must also treat one another fairly and politely during your negotiations, which may be the last thing you really feel like doing. If you aren't civil to one another, your negotiations are apt to become little more than a painful reminder of why you're getting divorced in the first place.

Specifically, negotiating your own divorce means that both of you must

- Let reason, not emotions, rule.
- Avoid using your negotiations as an excuse to replay old, angry, and hurtful accusations.
- Listen to one another without interrupting. Waiting to have your say can be tough to do, especially if you don't like what your spouse is saying.

- ✔ Resist forming a response to what your spouse is saying while she is still talking. Instead, try to really listen to her words.

- ✔ Allow your spouse to express his opinions, and respect what your spouse has to say, even if you don't agree with his opinions. Ridiculing your spouse's choice of words, wishes, or suggestions is one way to put him on the defensive and shut down two-way communications entirely.

- ✔ Be open to compromise. Neither of you are going to get everything you want from your divorce, so be prepared to make some intelligent trade-offs.

- ✔ Stay cool. If something your spouse says or does during your negotiations upsets you, bite your tongue. Don't respond in the heat of the moment. Instead, take a deep breath and, if necessary, take a bathroom break, go get some coffee, take a walk around the block, or do something else to give yourself time to chill out.

- ✔ Don't use intimidation and threats to get what you want. Tactics like that will backfire on you.

Preparing for the Process

Take time before you begin your negotiations to plan how you will negotiate. Laying the right groundwork can mean the difference between progress and frustration. Ideally, you and your spouse should decide the following before you begin your formal negotiations:

- ✔ How you will structure your negotiation sessions

- ✔ When and where you will negotiate

- ✔ What issues you plan to address at each of your negotiating sessions

- ✔ The information and documentation you need and the kind of record-keeping system you're going to use to record your decisions

Unless your divorce is very simple — with little to divide up, no minor children, and no spousal support — you will probably need more than one negotiating session to resolve all of the issues in your divorce.

If you're concerned that working out the ground rules for your negotiations may lead to a fight, you may want to discuss the preliminaries in a public place, such as a coffee shop or restaurant. Your discussion is less apt to degenerate into name-calling and anger if you have it in a public place. (Wherever you meet, make sure that no one can overhear your conversation.) Of course, if you're worried that working out the ground rules will be full of conflict, you may want to reconsider whether negotiating your own divorce is a good idea. After all, deciding how to resolve the issues in your divorce is likely to be more challenging than deciding on the rules you and your spouse will follow.

Because a deadlock is always possible, no matter how hard you try to achieve a meeting of the minds, you should also decide ahead of time what to do if you reach an impasse during your negotiations. Your options include pursuing mediation or arbitration, and hiring attorneys to do the negotiating for you. You should also decide ahead of time where you will go to get the information you need when a matter of law arises that you don't understand.

If you and your spouse negotiated a prenuptial agreement prior to your marriage or a postnuptial agreement after you were married, you have less to negotiate. Most likely, the agreement has already addressed some of the issues in your divorce.

Educate yourself about your divorce-related legal rights and responsibilities before you begin negotiating. You can do that by scheduling a meeting with a divorce attorney (which we discuss in the "Involving an Attorney" section later in this chapter), by reading divorce-related literature (such as this book), and visiting divorce Web sites.

Planning a method of negotiation

There's no one right way to negotiate. A method that works for one couple may not be appropriate for another. However, prior to starting your negotiations, you and your spouse should reach at least a general agreement about how you will structure your negotiation sessions in order to make them as efficient and effective as possible. The following steps outline one plan of action that may work for you:

1. **Set goals and put priorities on the table.**

   Prior to tackling a major new issue in your divorce — child custody, child or spousal support, or the division of your debts and assets — share your divorce-related goals and priorities with one another and discuss any special concerns you have related to the issue you'll be addressing.

   Try to talk in terms of your realistic needs or your children's realistic needs, not about pie-in-the-sky needs. Then, identify where you and your spouse agree or disagree and where your shared interests lie.

2. **List possible options for settling the issue you're discussing.**

   As you develop this list, keep in mind your individual goals, priorities, and areas of agreement and disagreement. When identifying your options, try to be creative and avoid automatically rejecting any ideas that may seem silly on the surface. A seemingly silly idea may inspire a new, more practical one that works for both of you. You may each want to develop your own list of options and share your lists with one another.

3. Eliminate all the ideas on your list that both of you dislike or agree are unrealistic.

Identifying the options that you don't like or that seem impractical to both of you helps you focus on the ones that you both feel are more feasible.

4. From the options that remain, develop short written proposals for resolving the issue you're negotiating.

You can each develop your own proposal for an issue and present it to one another, and then each of you can respond with a counterproposal if you want, or you can write a proposal together. You may need a couple proposal drafts before you have an agreement that you're both happy with. Once you do, put it in writing. Each time you concur on a specific issue, remind yourselves that you're that much closer to a final divorce agreement.

The negotiating process you use doesn't have to be as formal as the one we describe. Find a method that you're both comfortable with and that helps facilitate a fair resolution of each issue in your divorce.

Choosing the right setting

When deciding on a place for your negotiation sessions, pick a quiet, comfortable (but not too comfortable) location that's relatively free of distractions. That rules out negotiating in front of the television set or any time at your home when your children are up and about. Wait until they've gone to sleep or, better yet, do your negotiating away from home in a neutral location — in a corner of your local library, at a coffeehouse, or in a park, for example.

When you negotiate in a public place, you're more apt to be on your best behavior, which means that you're less likely to yell at each other, burst into tears, or stomp away in a huff.

Scheduling the time

Negotiating your divorce agreement will probably take a couple of sessions, depending on what you have to resolve and how quickly you and your spouse can reach a consensus on things. Therefore, schedule your sessions ahead of time and make them a priority in your life. They should be every bit as important as your business meetings, doctors' appointments, parent-teacher conferences, children's soccer games, and the like.

Set a time to begin and end each session. Generally speaking, your sessions shouldn't run more than two hours. Longer sessions will probably become unproductive.

Don't back out of a scheduled session without a very good reason. (Incidentally, wanting to play golf, have dinner with friends, or "just not feeling like it" aren't good reasons.) However, the unexpected may come up. So, if one of you has a legitimate reason for rescheduling, try to provide the other with at least a few days' notice.

Don't rush your negotiations. Take all the time that you need — you're making important decisions that will affect your life and the lives of your children for years to come.

Deciding on the order of business

Develop written agendas for your negotiating sessions and determine ahead of time who will prepare them. You can take turns writing the agendas or one of you can agree to prepare them all. Whatever you decide, make sure that both of you have a copy of the next negotiating session's agenda well in advance of the session.

Plan on taking up the major issues in your divorce in the following order:

- ✔ **Child custody and support:** Your number-one responsibility in your divorce is your children's well-being.

- ✔ **Spousal support:** Assuming that any money is left after you decide how you'll meet your children's financial needs, consider the issue of spousal support.

- ✔ **Division of your marital property:** Negotiating this issue includes deciding what to do about any outstanding debts you and your spouse may owe.

Using written agendas may sound like needless work, but, in fact preparing them ahead of time means that you

- ✔ Know what sort of "homework" you need to do before your next session

- ✔ Can get down to business at the start of each session instead of trying to decide what you will discuss

- ✔ Are more apt to stay on track during a negotiating session because you have a written reminder of what you're supposed to be talking about

When you can't resolve an issue the first time out, agree to return to it later or to get outside help. An issue that initially seems irresolvable may be easier to address the next time you tackle it, especially after you and your spouse have successfully resolved a few other issues.

Chill out before you storm off

When negotiating tough issues related to your divorce, keeping your cool can be tough, no matter how hard you try. Old hurts and insecurities may resurface during your negotiations, especially if your spouse exhibits an uncanny knack for pushing your emotional hot buttons and deliberately or unwittingly hurts your feelings or makes you angry. Rather than letting your emotions get the best of you and maybe even derail the negotiations, try these alternatives:

- ✔ Take a short timeout. Go for a run, fix a snack, listen to calming music, or read a magazine. Then, resume your negotiating.

- ✔ If you need more than a quick break, calmly tell your spouse you can't continue negotiating, and reschedule for another time.

- ✔ Acknowledge that you need third-party help.

During your negotiations, keep an accurate record of what you and your spouse agree and disagree on. Without a written record of your discussions, you won't know where each of you stands in the negotiating process, and writing a final divorce agreement will be difficult, if not impossible. Decide which of you will keep a record of the decisions you make and don't make during your negotiations, the information you need for your next session, and so on. Regardless of who agrees to be responsible for record keeping, make sure that all of the records are always readily available to the other spouse. Better yet, whichever spouse is the record-keeper should mail or e-mail his or her notes to the other spouse as soon as possible after each negotiating session.

Getting expert advice

Before your negotiating gets underway, you and your spouse should determine what sort of information you need in order to make intelligent decisions about your divorce and which of you will be responsible for getting that information. First, make a list of what you need, and then take turns choosing a research topic. Next, you may need to hire any or all of the following professionals:

- ✔ **A certified public accountant (CPA):** A CPA can help you understand the possible tax implications of your financial decisions and how to plan for them.

- ✔ **A certified divorce planner (CDP):** A CDP can help you evaluate your options and make informed decisions. For example, a CDP can conduct cash-flow analyses to help you determine how much spousal support you may need or can afford to pay and how much child support is reasonable. The CDP can help you evaluate various scenarios when dividing your marital assets and debts, too.

- **A therapist or religious advisor:** At various points during your negotiations, you may need the help of a therapist or your religious advisor to cope with your emotions.

- **An appraiser:** An appraiser can help you value your home, other real estate, collectibles, fine art, and so on.

- **A financial planner:** A financial planner can help you determine what to do with the assets you may get in your property settlement.

If you and your spouse are going to share the cost of outside experts, you need to decide who to use and how to pay their fees. Any of the following options may be feasible:

- Liquidate a marital asset. For example, sell one of your cars, sell some stocks or bonds, or dip into your savings.

- Barter (or trade) your professional services, skills, or labor in exchange for outside professional help.

- One of you pays the costs associated with using an outside professional in exchange for getting an equivalently larger share of your marital property or assuming less of your marital debt.

Making your negotiations as painless as possible

Obviously, negotiating the end of your marriage isn't going to be a barrel of laughs. We offer some suggestions that may make negotiating the terms of your divorce easier:

- Start your negotiations with something both of you can probably agree on. Early success is a confidence-builder and helps build momentum for continued progress.

- Don't lose sight of your goals: a less-expensive divorce, an agreement that you can both live with, an agreement that's in your children's best interests, and a mutual commitment to making your agreement work after your divorce is official.

- Avoid overreaching, threatening, or posturing to gain control.

- When your spouse makes a concession that benefits you, acknowledge it. (Go on —

swallow your pride and do it!) By doing so, you help encourage your spouse to make yet more concessions and compromises. But don't forget: in order to keep the concessions and compromises coming, you must make some yourself.

- Be sure that your spouse doesn't mistake your willingness to concede a few points as a desire to get back together, unless that's definitely what you want.

- Try not to make important decisions in the heat of the moment or when you're feeling especially depressed or guilty about your divorce because you're more likely to make decisions that you'll regret later.

✔ One of you pays all the expenses associated with the experts you hire and gets reimbursed by the other spouse. You may agree that the other spouse will pay his or her share right away or in installments over time. Of course, if the spouse who's doing the paying back is unreliable and you're the spouse who's going to pay the experts, agreeing to either payment plan probably isn't wise.

✔ Split the expenses 50/50, 60/40, 75/25 — whatever you both agree is fair.

✔ One of you pays the full cost of hiring one expert, and the other pays for hiring another expert. However, for this agreement to be fair, the costs associated with each expert should be about the same if you both earn about the same amount of money. If you don't, the amounts each of you pay should be equivalent relative to your individual incomes.

So that you have no doubt about the fairness of an outside expert's advice, choose experts who have no personal or business relationship with either one of you or with a close relative or friend of either you and your spouse. Meet with the expert together (not separately) and make sure the expert understands that he or she is working for *both* of you.

Involving an Attorney

If you're like most people, one of the key reasons you may want to negotiate your own divorce is so that you can keep your legal costs down. However, entirely excluding attorneys from your divorce is usually penny-wise and pound-foolish. Lawyers have a valuable role to play in *all* divorces. (For information about how to shop for legal counsel, see Chapter 13.)

You and your spouse should each hire your own attorney. No ethical lawyer will accept both of you as clients. In fact, a code of ethics in most states prohibits attorneys from working for both spouses in a divorce.

Getting some basic information

Meeting with your divorce attorney prior to starting your negotiations is a good idea. Use the meeting to acquire an overview of the divorce laws and guidelines in your state, to gain an understanding of what your divorce agreement must include, and to clarify the issues and trade-offs you may want to consider during your negotiations. Unless you read law books just for the fun of it or are a divorce expert because you've done it a number of times, these are subjects that you probably know little or nothing about.

Be sure to get advice about any special concerns you may have related to the decisions ahead and find out about any potential legal pitfalls or problems you should be aware of and what you can do to try to avoid them. After talking with an attorney about the issues in your divorce, you may decide that your divorce is much too complicated to negotiate on your own.

You may also want to use an attorney to help you with specific tasks during the negotiating process — for example, to review financial documents, to provide you with feedback about a proposal your spouse has made, or to review the counteroffer you're considering. Another, and probably less-expensive option is to hire a CDP to help you with these types of tasks.

Be upfront if money is an issue for you. Tell the attorney that you can afford to purchase only an hour or two of his or her time.

Hiring an attorney to review or draft your final agreement

If you and your spouse are able to resolve all the issues in your divorce and draft your own divorce agreement, ask your attorneys to review the draft before you sign it. That way, they can assure you and your spouse that you haven't overlooked anything important and that your agreement doesn't create the potential for future problems between the two of you.

If you decide not to draft a final agreement but instead to provide each of your attorneys with a written list of everything you've agreed to, you will have to decide which of the two attorneys will draft the agreement. You can make that decision with a coin toss, or the spouse with greater financial assets can agree to pay his or her attorney to prepare it. However, both attorneys should review the agreement before you and your spouse sign it.

The lawyer you hire can tell you whether the agreement you and your spouse have negotiated is equitable to both of you under the law. For example, although the agreement may sound fine to you, your attorney may tell you that you're entitled to more than you're getting. If this is the case, you may decide that you're happy with what's in the draft agreement, or you may decide that you want to try to get more. Your attorney also can make sure that the agreement doesn't overlook issues that could create problems for you (with taxes, for instance) down the road and that it's legally enforceable.

Attorneys are conditioned to assume that each case is a worst-case scenario and to provide legal advice to prevent or mitigate all potential problems. So, if an attorney says something that alarms you or makes you question whether you should negotiate your own divorce, don't panic. The attorney is legally obligated to inform you of all possible outcomes, and the scenario you find alarming may have little chance of actually occurring.

If you and your spouse decide to go back to the drawing board to work out any problems in your draft agreement that your attorney (or your spouse's attorney) may have highlighted or to address issues you may have overlooked, you can try to resolve them using whatever approach worked for you and your spouse when you were negotiating your draft agreement. Or, you and your spouse can ask your attorneys to help resolve those remaining issues, if you feel you and your spouse will have trouble reaching an agreement on them by yourselves. However, involving your attorneys increases the cost of your divorce, and there is always a chance that if one of you is working with an aggressive attorney, the attorney could turn your amicable divorce into an angry one. Mediation is another option when you and your spouse don't see eye to eye on the remaining issues in your divorce and want to avoid spending a lot of money on legal help. Chapter 15 explains how mediation works.

Negotiating an Agreement Everyone Can Live With

When you and your spouse are ready to sit down and begin working out the details of your divorce agreement, depending on your family and your finances, the two of you may have to figure out how to deal with the custody of your children; whether one of you will pay child support to the other and, if so, how much the payments will be; whether one spouse will pay spousal support to the other and the amount of those payments; and how you will divide up the assets and debts from your marriage. The following sections provide guidance for negotiating each of these issues.

Creating an agreeable custody arrangement

If you're like most divorcing parents, you want to be actively involved in your children's lives after your marriage ends, as you should be. Therefore, your custody negotiations will probably focus on determining how you and your soon-to-be ex can each continue spending quality time with your children, how you can continue sharing parenting responsibilities with one another after you no longer live together, and the best way for each of you to assure your children of your continued love. (For more on the subject of custody, see Chapter 10.)

The custody arrangement you finally decide on may not be as good as having two parents under the same roof, but it can be the next best thing. And, if your marriage was tense and full of strife, parenting under two roofs rather than one may end up being better for your kids.

As you and your spouse evaluate various custody options and prepare a written proposal for the custody of your children, be sure to consider

- Your children's individual requirements, both practical and emotional.

  Develop a written list of your children's day-to-day needs, activities, and so on. Writing everything down can help both of you become more realistic about what it's going to take to meet your children's needs.

- Your individual strengths and weaknesses as parents.

- Your postdivorce lifestyles.

- How well you think that you can cooperate with one another as divorced parents.

Most judges approve whatever custody arrangement spouses choose, as long as it's in the best interests of the couple's children. Depending on your state, you and your spouse may be required to write a parenting plan instead of or in addition to a custody plan. The parenting plan (like a custody plan) is filed with the court and becomes part of your divorce agreement. Chapter 10 discusses parenting plans.

Calculating child support

If you and your spouse share dependent children, decisions about child support are apt to be the most important aspects of your divorce negotiations. You and your spouse must come to an agreement about the standard of living you want for your children after your divorce. Although you may agree that you want the very best for them, if you're like most couples, money may be tighter than ever after your divorce. Therefore, to provide your children with the extras that you want them to have, you and your spouse may have to agree to cut some items out of your own postdivorce budgets. It's also possible, try as you may, that you'll not be able to figure out a way to continue providing your children with everything that they're used to having. To make certain that you don't overlook any expenses related to your children, turn to Chapter 11, which discusses child-related expenses in detail.

You and your spouse can decide how you will fund college for your kids when you draft your agreement or, if they're very young, you can include a clause providing that you will return to that issue as each of your children reaches a certain age (10 years old, perhaps).

When negotiating child support, don't overlook your state's child-support guidelines. The guidelines help determine the minimum amount of support that one parent should pay the other. Chapter 11 discusses state guidelines in detail. Also, don't forget that your child support agreement must address how you'll provide your children with health insurance.

Your child support agreement will be part of your final divorce decree that you file with the court and that the judge signs, making everything in it legally enforceable. That means, for example, that if you are responsible for paying child support and fall behind on your payments, your former spouse can use the full force of the law to get you to pay up. (Chapter 11 talks more about enforcing child-support agreements.)

Before you sign a child-support agreement, hire an attorney to review it so that you can be sure what you and your spouse agree to is legally enforceable and fair to both of you.

Discussing the subject of spousal support

If you need financial support after your marriage ends and can present solid reasons why your spouse should provide it, your divorce negotiations should address how much spousal support you'll receive and how long the payments will last. (For more in-depth information on spousal support, turn to Chapter 9.) Many couples have a difficult time negotiating spousal support, so don't give up if you can't come to an agreement right away.

If you're the spouse who wants spousal support, in order to make your case, compare your postdivorce financial needs and resources with your spouse's. Note the contributions you made to your marriage or to your spouse's career. Steer clear of phrases such as "I must have," "I require," and "I deserve." (Those words won't get you the results you want.) Don't act resentful about the sacrifices you may have made in the interest of your spouse or marriage. At the time you made those choices, you probably believed they were for the best.

If possible, frame your arguments in terms of how your spouse, not just you, will benefit from any spousal support that he or she may pay to you. For example, you need support so that you can develop marketable job skills and earn a better living. You may be able to argue that once you have a good job, not only can your spouse stop paying you spousal support, but you can also begin contributing more to the support of your children. In other words, your spouse may trade a short-term sacrifice for a long-term gain!

When preparing your projected postdivorce budget and estimating your monthly income without spousal support, do *not* include any child support you will be receiving in your income figure. Child support is for your children, not for you.

Dividing up your property and debts without a court battle

If you don't have any young children to support and you and your spouse both earn good money, the only decisions you have to make in your divorce may relate to the division of your marital property and debts. Before you can actually get down to deciding who gets what, you must come to an agreement about what is and isn't marital property and what percentage of the value of that property each of you is entitled to. Obviously, developing a comprehensive inventory of your marital assets and debts and assigning accurate values and amounts to each is critical to this process. (See Chapter 3 for information on creating inventories for your personal and marital assets.)

If you're divorcing after just a short marriage, you and your spouse may have few, if any, joint assets and debts to divide up, so you may be able to divide up your property in a single negotiating session. Usually, the longer your marriage, the more you own and owe together, so the more time you will need to reach a property settlement agreement that's fair to you both.

Split it down the middle or not?

For simplicity's sake, many divorcing couples decide to split up their property and their debts 50/50. Depending on the circumstances of your marriage as well as your assets and debts, this method may or may not be fair. (For more information on ways to divide property, turn to Chapter 8.)

Unless you and your spouse negotiate a different arrangement, if you live in a community property state, you're each legally entitled to half the value of all your marital assets when you divorce. Unfortunately, you're also legally responsible for half your martial debts, too. Therefore, even if your spouse agrees to pay all or a portion of your marital debts, the creditors can look to you for payment if he or she fails to pay.

The following factors can suggest that a non-equal split is fairer than an equal division of property:

- ✔ One of you was significantly more responsible for the assets you acquired during your marriage or for the debts that you ran up.

- ✔ One of you has a greater need than the other for more than half your marital assets or less than half your marital debts. For example, one of you makes much less money than the other or has a limited capacity to earn money, maybe because he or she has never worked outside the home or has a chronic illness.

✔ A significant disparity in your ages is going to affect the ability of the older spouse to replace the assets that he or she would give up.

✔ One of you has a significant emotional investment in certain assets.

As a point of reference or a reality check, find out what criteria the family law court in your state would use if it were dividing your marital property and debts. You can get this information if you meet with an attorney.

Regardless of what percentage split you use to divide the value of your marital property and debts — 50/50, 60/40, 80/20, for example — both of you should be 100 percent clear about and comfortable with the rationale for the percentage. Otherwise, a number of things may result:

✔ One of you may feel cheated or swindled in some way and stay mad at the other or even go to court later to get the arrangement changed. If that were to happen and you share custody of your children, you could find it difficult to cooperate on their behalf.

✔ The disgruntled spouse may refuse to pay off marital debts according to your agreement, and the other spouse may get stuck paying them.

✔ The spouse who feels cheated may seek revenge by being late with his or her child- or spousal-support payments or stop making them all together. (Not paying them is illegal but, unfortunately, people do it all the time.)

Divide the big assets first

Dividing your property in two stages — one stage for significant assets and the other for miscellaneous personal property — is a practical way to deal with your marital assets.

Focus on the division of your most significant marital assets first — your home, other real estate, bank accounts, pensions, investments, vehicles, and so on. To be sure that you don't overlook the tax consequences of your decisions during this stage, consulting with a CPA is advisable. What may look like a good deal may not be so good after you factor in taxes. Be open to selling some of your marital assets if doing so will help create a win-win situation for you and your spouse. (You're most likely to need the help of outside professionals during this phase.)

When you divide assets that secure your outstanding loans — your home, vehicles, and so on — look at both the debt associated with each asset and the asset itself. Value these assets according to the amount of *equity* you have in each one, or the asset's market value less the amount you owe on it.

When you divvy up your miscellaneous marital property — household items like your CD player, big-screen TV, furniture, computer equipment, kitchenware, linens, lawnmower, power tools, and so on — assigning them specific values may be difficult. Approximate values will probably do. Also divide your credit card debts and other miscellaneous unsecured joint debts that you may have during this stage.

Don't overlook your family pets. If you have children, you may want to let the pets live with whichever parent will have the children most of the time after your divorce is final. Having family pets around increases your children's sense of stability and security after your marriage has ended.

If you and your spouse are childless but have multiple pets, you may want to share custody of the animals, giving each of you the pets on specific days, although such an arrangement may be impractical.

Dividing up your miscellaneous marital property can be as simple as

- ✔ Taking turns choosing, asset by asset, debt by debt, until each of you has an appropriate amount of assets and debts given the percentage splits you agreed to.

- ✔ Letting one spouse divide a pile of miscellaneous property in half, and giving first pick of either of the two piles to the other spouse (thus, assuring that whoever does the dividing makes an even 50/50 split).

- ✔ Preparing separate lists of what each of you wants and comparing the two. When some of the same things are on both your lists, you will have to decide what's fair. (One option is described in the upcoming sidebar, "When you both gotta have it: A negotiating secret.")

- ✔ Choosing comparable categories of assets and debts without strict regard to dollar amounts and percentages. For example, you take the dining room furniture and your spouse takes the bedroom furniture; you take the car, and your spouse gets the boat; you take the Visa card debts, and your spouse takes the MasterCard debts.

You can trade off debts for assets or vice versa. For example, you can agree to pay off more of your marital debt in exchange for getting a larger share of your marital assets, or you can agree to take less marital property so that you don't have to pay off as much of the debt.

Minimizing your postdivorce financial ties to your spouse is almost always a good idea. So consider wiping out as much of your joint debt as you can by selling marital assets. Chapter 8 explains the benefits of getting rid of joint debt. You may also want to sell joint assets to provide both of you with the cash you may need to start your lives as single people. Be careful however, that in your quest for cash you don't sell items for less than their actual values.

When you both gotta have it: A negotiating secret

So what do you do when you and your spouse both want the same asset? If the asset at issue isn't significant enough to merit scheduling a mediation session or getting legal help to break your stalemate, try one of the following simple, no-cost approaches to reach an agreement:

✔ Ask a neutral third party to take two small pieces of paper, write the name of the asset on one of the pieces, fold up both pieces of paper and put them in a hat, box, or some other container. Next, you and your spouse each pull one of the pieces of paper out of the container. The spouse who pulls out the piece of paper with the name of the asset written on it gets the asset; the other spouse gets something else in exchange — another asset or less debt of equal value.

✔ Collect all the items you both want and wait to deal with them until after you've divided up everything else. Then, take turns selecting items until nothing remains.

Just think — some people pay top dollar for this kind of advice!

Deciding what to do about your home

If you're like most other couples, your home is probably the most valuable asset you own together. What to do with it when you're divorcing can be a tough decision emotionally as well as financially. Nevertheless, deciding what to do with your home is a bottom-line issue that you should make based *only* on financial considerations. Chapter 8 provides an overview of those considerations.

To help you decide what to do with your home, ask yourself the following questions and talk over the answers with your spouse:

✔ How much does comparable housing cost in your area?

✔ What emotional ties do each of you have to your home and to your neighborhood?

✔ How much can you sell the house for?

✔ Is living in the same neighborhood or school district important to your children?

✔ Are there other houses in your same neighborhood or school district that you and your children move into?

✔ Can you afford to keep the home, taking into account the amount of your mortgage payments, insurance costs, taxes, upkeep, and maintenance? (Don't forget that mortgage interest is tax deductible.)

✔ What will your spouse get in return if you keep the house?

When you're making the big decision about your home, getting advice from a financial professional, such as your CPA or certified divorce planner, is helpful.

Don't overlook your income taxes

Don't forget to take your income taxes into consideration when negotiating your divorce agreement. If you'll still be married on December 31, you can file a separate return or a joint return for that year.

Filing a joint return is usually the better option for the spouse with the bigger income, but it can work against the spouse who earns less. Ask your CPA to determine the most advantageous filing method.

Other tax-related issues you may need to consider include

✔ How you will share any tax refund you may have coming

✔ How you will share responsibility for any taxes you may owe

✔ How you will share liability for any interest, penalties, and back taxes you may owe if you're audited some time in the future

Getting to Closure

As soon as you and your spouse think you're close to an agreement on all of the issues in your divorce, draft a final agreement that reflects your decisions so far. Then, each of you should hire a divorce attorney to review the draft. The "Involving an Attorney" section earlier in this chapter discusses what the attorneys look for when they review the agreement. After you have a final agreement, the spouse who initiated your divorce can file the agreement with the court so that a judge can issue a court order, or that spouse's attorney can file it instead.

Chapter 13

Finding a Divorce Attorney

· ·

In This Chapter

▶ Understanding the roles that an attorney can play in your divorce

▶ Knowing what to expect of a divorce attorney and finding one that fits the bill

▶ Taking the right steps when your attorney is not doing a good job

▶ Knowing your options when paying for an attorney is a struggle

· ·

*R*egardless of what you think about attorneys — that they're sage and savvy legal counselors or a necessary evil — it's almost always a good idea to hire one to help you with your divorce. However, the nature of your marital assets, the amount of your marital debts, whether you and your spouse have a friendly relationship despite the fact that your marriage is ending, and other considerations may determine the role of attorneys in your divorce. You may decide to limit your use of attorneys, or you may involve them from the start of your divorce through its end.

This chapter tells you how to go about finding a trustworthy and affordable divorce attorney. We explain the characteristics to look for in an attorney and how much you should expect to pay for an attorney's assistance as well as how to begin your search. We also highlight the key issues that you should consider when hiring an attorney and tell you what you have the right to expect from the one you hire and what he or she can expect from you.

What to Look for in an Attorney

You can involve an attorney in your divorce from start to finish or you can work with one on a very limited basis. For example, if you and your spouse are confident about your abilities to draft your own divorce agreement, you may decide to hire an attorney just to provide you with some prenegotiating advice and information so you can be sure that you're clear about your legal rights and responsibilities and the issues you must resolve before your divorce can be final. The attorney should also review your divorce agreement before it's filed with the court so you can be sure that it covers all the bases and won't create problems for you down the road. (See Chapter 12 for advice on negotiating your own agreement with your spouse.)

When you hire a divorce attorney, choosing one should be more than a matter of running your fingers through the lawyer ads in the Yellow Pages until you spot the word "divorce," using an online lawyer referral service, or simply asking the lawyer who helped you negotiate your office lease or draw up your will to help with your divorce. The right attorney can help ensure that your divorce goes smoothly and that you end up with a strong but fair divorce agreement, but the wrong attorney can increase the stress you may already be feeling and make getting divorced more difficult for you than it already is, among other possible problems.

You want an attorney who is experienced in family law, has handled numerous divorces before, and, ideally, has considerable experience resolving the very same sorts of issues that must be settled in your divorce. An experienced divorce attorney knows how to anticipate and defuse potential problems that could turn a friendly divorce into one that's not so friendly and is familiar with how the divorce court in your area tends to rule on various issues, among other things.

In some states, attorneys can become *board-certified* in family law. These lawyers specialize in family law matters including divorce. To become board-certified, lawyers must have significant experience handling family law cases, and they must pass a rigorous test. To maintain their certification, they must receive substantial continuing education in family law each year. Although a board-certified family law attorney tends to charge more and demand a higher retainer (upfront fee) to handle a divorce than one who isn't board-certified, the attorney is usually more experienced. Therefore, the attorney may be able to get things done in your divorce more quickly (and for less cost) and be more adept at finding solutions to problems in your divorce than one who isn't board-certified in family law.

You also want an attorney who

- ✔ Talks to you in plain English, not legalese. You have a right to understand what's going on in your divorce.

- ✔ Is willing to answer your questions rather than ignore them or brush them off as issues you don't need to worry about. However, if you have a lot of questions, consider directing some of your questions to one of your attorney's paralegals. Day to day, they will be easier to reach than your attorney, and if they don't know the answer to one of your questions, they will tell you to talk to your attorney.

- ✔ You can trust and with whom you feel comfortable. You may have to share highly personal and even embarrassing information about yourself and your marriage with your attorney.

✔ Is clear upfront that during your divorce you must put your children's needs first and that he or she will not pursue unreasonable demands for child support or vindictive child-custody and visitation arrangements.

✔ Is affordable.

Appropriate skills and experience

An old adage states, "There are horses for courses." In other words, what's right for one person or situation may not be right for another, and that applies when you hire an attorney for your divorce. You want one with the legal skills, knowledge, and experience required to get the job done for you. Here are some tips for finding the right skills and experience in an attorney:

✔ If you need help negotiating your divorce agreement, look for an attorney who is a problem-solver, who works well with people and is good at working out compromises. Find out what percentage of the attorney's cases go to trial. Unless the attorney specializes in difficult divorces that are likely to go to trial, attorneys with high percentages of divorce trials probably aren't great negotiators.

✔ If you know from the start that you're headed for a divorce trial, you want an attorney who has considerable courtroom experience. (Not all lawyers do.) When you're getting referrals for divorce attorneys, specifically ask for ones who are good in the courtroom.

✔ If your financial situation is complex, hire a lawyer who has a solid understanding of the issues and laws that pertain to your financial affairs or one who works closely with other lawyers or financial experts with that knowledge, such as a CPA or appraiser. Remember, negotiating your divorce agreement is as much about financial matters as it is about ending your marriage. If your finances are especially complicated — maybe because you and your spouse have a lot of investments or share a business — ask the attorneys you meet with what financial experts they would involve in your divorce and exactly what those experts would do to help your case.

Don't base your hiring decision on which attorney has the nicest office. A fancy office in an expensive building says nothing about a lawyer's legal skills, although such things may speak volumes about the attorney's rates. At the same time, don't assume that just because an attorney charges a lot of money he or she is highly skilled or will meet your needs. Also, don't let a lawyer's physical appearance influence your hiring decision — being attractive and having a great sense of fashion are not measures of an attorney's legal abilities.

Personal style

If you want an attorney to do more than simply review the divorce agreement that you and your spouse draft, be prepared to share details about your personal life, marriage, and finances. For example, you may have to let your attorney know that you have way too much credit card debt, that your spouse is a philanderer, or that you've been hospitalized in the past for emotional problems or an addiction. Sharing that sort of information with a virtual stranger can be embarrassing, yet it's almost always necessary in a divorce. Therefore, feeling comfortable with your lawyer is key.

In addition, your attorney should share and support your basic philosophy about your divorce. For example, if you want to keep things as calm, cooperative, and nonadversarial as possible, avoid attorneys who like to "go for the jugular."

Don't confuse your attorney with your therapist or religious advisor. Your attorney's clock is usually running regardless of whether you call with a legal question or to complain about your spouse. If you need emotional advice and support, meet with a therapist.

Affordability

Most family law attorneys bill for their services on an hourly basis, although some may agree to charge you a *flat fee* based on the total amount of their time they think it will take to complete your divorce. However, making such an upfront estimation can be financially costly for an attorney because he or she can't possibly know exactly how any divorce will play out. For example, a divorce can start out very cooperatively but end up being contentious and taking far more time than the attorney thought it would. For this reason, an attorney who charges you a flat fee is likely to provide you with limited services for your money and to charge extra for any work he or she has to do that is outside the scope of your original agreement with one another.

You're more apt to find an attorney to take your case for a flat fee if your divorce is 100 percent amicable and if the tasks the attorney will perform are very well defined (such as reviewing your divorce agreement or filling out and filing some legal paperwork).

Among other things, an attorney's hourly rate depends on your region of the country and whether your community is rural or urban. If you live in large cities on the East and West Coasts, you can expect to pay an attorney a higher fee than if you reside in a rural community in the Midwest. The services of a divorce attorney can cost you anywhere from $100 to $500 an hour, although some attorneys charge much, much more. Also, the attorney you hire will charge you for any expenses associated with your case and for the amount of time his or her legal staff spends helping with your divorce. Your legal expenses are likely to include court fees, copying, courier services, the cost of a court reporter for depositions, and so on.

If you don't have a lot of money to spend on legal help, you may have to hire a relatively inexperienced lawyer rather than a seasoned professional. New attorneys tend to cost less than lawyers who've been practicing law for years and already have solid reputations. However, working with an up-and-coming or novice attorney has a potential advantage, aside from monetary savings: The attorney may be willing to work a little harder for you than a more-seasoned lawyer would in order to develop a good reputation.

Finding a Reputable Attorney (And Avoiding the Bad Ones)

The best way to begin your search for an attorney is to develop a list of potential attorneys by

- ✔ **Asking friends and family members who've gone through a divorce and were happy with their attorneys.** Referrals from trusted friends or family members who've gone through a divorce similar to what you anticipate yours will be like are particularly valuable.

- ✔ **Asking attorneys you've worked with in the past to recommend some divorce attorneys.** When you contact attorneys you've worked with, be sure to explain the nature of your divorce — amicable or contentious, approximate value of your assets, minor children or no kids, and so on — and to indicate the kind of legal help you think you need.

- ✔ **Checking with your local, county, or state bar association.** Many bar associations can refer you to attorneys in your area who can help you.

- ✔ **Consulting an online lawyer referral service, like `www.lawyer.com`, (a service of Martindale-Hubbell).** When you use one of these services, you indicate your geographic location and the nature of your legal problem, and the service sends you the names of attorneys who practice law close to you. However, some online lawyer referral services charge attorneys to be part of their service so that the attorneys can build their visibility and get additional business. Therefore, a referral from one of these services is not a recommendation.

If you get a referral to an attorney by a bar association, online referral service, or other organization, make sure you meet with the attorney and check out him or her to make certain that the attorney is right for you.

✓ **Calling the American Academy of Matrimonial Lawyers (www.aaml. org, 312-263-6477) for a list of attorneys in your area who specialize in divorce and family law.** For an attorney to become a member, a substantial amount of his or her practice must be in matrimonial law. Among other requirements, the attorney must

- Be recognized by the bench and the bar in his or her jurisdiction as an excellent matrimonial lawyer

- Have considerable trial experience

- Be board certified, if his or her state certifies family law attorneys, and otherwise must have received at least 15 hours of continuing education in family law during each of the five years preceding his or her application to become an association member

- Pass a national exam and submit to an in-person interview

✓ **Asking your mental health counselor, religious advisor, or social worker to recommend an attorney.** Having counseled other individuals going through a divorce, these professionals may know some good divorce attorneys.

✓ **Asking members of a divorce support group for names.** Some group members, based on personal experience, are likely to have strong opinions about who is or isn't a good divorce attorney.

If you feel more comfortable being represented by a female attorney, contact the women's bar association in your area, if one exists, or other female lawyers in your community.

If you are interested in pursuing a collaborative divorce, make sure that you are clear about that when you ask for an attorney referral. However, a collaborative divorce is not an option in every state.

Steer clear of attorneys who

✓ Brag about themselves

✓ Don't pay attention to you when you're speaking

✓ Trivialize your questions by not answering them or telling you "not to worry about that"

✓ Ignore your questions entirely

✓ Ask you few, if any, questions about your marriage, your finances, or your divorce goals at your initial meeting

✓ Talk down to you

✓ Are constantly interrupted by phone calls or conversations with people who come into their office while you're meeting

If you don't find an attorney right away who fits the bill, don't get discouraged or give up. Some great divorce attorneys who truly care about their clients are out there. Sooner or later you will find the one for you.

Interviewing Potential Attorneys

After you compile a list of divorce attorneys, schedule a get-acquainted meeting with each of them. Don't hire an attorney just because someone you know and respect gives the lawyer a glowing review. Make up your own mind after an in-person meeting.

Many attorneys provide free 30-minute to one-hour initial consultations but, when you call an attorney's office, don't expect to be offered a free first meeting; you'll probably have to ask for it. Attorneys who don't offer free consultations may charge a nominal sum — $25 to $50 — for an initial meeting or may charge their normal hourly rate. The amount attorneys charge for an initial meeting has no bearing on their skills in divorce law.

In your consultation, don't be afraid to let the attorneys know where you are emotionally. Although you don't want to use up your entire free consultation explaining how awful your spouse is, how angry you are, or giving a blow-by-blow account of the demise of your marriage, a good attorney knows that your emotions will affect your divorce case. Therefore, the attorney will factor your emotional state into his or her assessment of your case and its likely cost. Some attorneys will even suggest resources, such as counseling and support groups, to help you deal with your emotions.

Ask the important questions

Prior to your initial meetings with the attorneys on your list, think about the questions you want answers to, write them down in a notebook and bring the notebook to each of your meetings. Don't be afraid to ask your questions when you talk to an attorney and don't feel shy about writing down in the book the attorney's answers to your questions and your initial impressions of the attorney Also, take note of an attorney's body language. As soon as possible after each meeting ends, write down your final impressions of the attorney you just met with. This information will be invaluable when you're deciding which attorney to hire.

The following questions represent some of the most important ones to ask when you meet with an attorney whom you're considering hiring to help with your divorce negotiations or because you need to be represented in court:

✔ **How long have you been practicing divorce law, how many cases have you handled, and how many trials have you been involved in?**

Look for an attorney who's been a divorce lawyer for at least three years. If you anticipate that your divorce may end up in court, make sure that the attorney has successfully represented other clients in divorce trials.

✔ **What percentage of your practice is represented by divorce cases?**

Ideally, at least 50 percent of an attorney's caseload is divorce cases.

✔ **Have you ever had a case like mine? How did it work out?**

Avoid hiring an attorney who has never dealt with the particular issues in your divorce case.

✔ **Who will actually handle my case? You, another lawyer with your firm, or both of you?**

If another lawyer will be involved, ask about that lawyer's divorce-related experience. You should also ask to meet him or her.

Don't assume that you're receiving inferior legal care if a skilled paralegal under the supervision of an attorney works on your case. A paralegal can do a good job of handling certain aspects of a divorce for considerably less money than if your lawyer took care of those details.

✔ **What do you think about mediation?**

If you and your spouse reach a stalemate on some aspect of your divorce and you want to give mediation a try, select an attorney who has often used mediation in divorces such as yours.

✔ **How do you charge, and how do I pay you?**

Find out the lawyer's hourly rate and get an estimate of how much your divorce will cost. This estimate is a best guess on the lawyer's part — the final cost depends on how smoothly your negotiations go, whether you end up in court, and so on. If another lawyer or a paralegal will be working on your case, get his or her hourly rates, too. If you're worried about how to pay for the legal help you need, express your concerns.

✔ **Will I have to pay you a retainer and, if so, how much will it be?**

Most lawyers require a *retainer,* or down payment, on the cost of their services. The cost of the time the attorney actually spends on your case is then credited against the retainer.

✔ **If the cost of your services exceeds the amount of your retainer, how am I expected to pay what I owe? Monthly billings? A lump-sum payment? Under what circumstances is the retainer refundable?**

Most attorneys do not consider a retainer to be refundable unless money is left over after they've completed a client's divorce or if you fire the lawyer and the entire retainer has not been spent.

✔ **How do you calculate your billable hours?**

Many attorneys round up fractions of hours. In other words, if the attorney spends five minutes talking with you on the phone, he or she may round it up to 15 minutes of billable time. Rounding up can really increase the total cost of your attorney's services.

✔ **Will you provide me with an estimate of my expenses and an explanation of what those expenses include?**

You may have to reimburse your attorney for the cost of long-distance calls, faxes, copying, delivery fees, outside expert fees, court costs, and so on. Some lawyers may also bill you for expenses not directly related to your divorce, such as the cost of working dinners and cabs. If you object to paying certain expenses, ask for an explanation of why you should be billed for them. If the expenses aren't essential to your case, tell the lawyer that you refuse to pay them.

✔ **How often do you bill for your expenses? Will I get an itemized bill?**

Expect to receive an itemized monthly expense bill.

✔ **If I have questions about my case, can I call you? How quickly can I expect you to return my calls?**

A reasonable amount of time to expect to have your calls returned is within 24 hours, unless you're calling with an emergency. Then, your attorney should return your call within an hour or two. However, if your attorney can't return your call promptly because he or she is in court representing another client or for some other reason, the paralegal working on your case or someone else from your attorney's office should contact you. This is common in busy law offices.

✔ **Based on what you know about my divorce, what is your game plan?**

The attorney should provide you with an assessment of the strengths and the weaknesses of your case (and your spouse's case) and a clear explanation of how he or she intends to exploit the strengths and minimize the weaknesses in order to get you the best divorce possible. Steer clear of attorneys who emphasize "playing hardball" rather than negotiating and trying mediation. Hardball tactics cost big bucks.

✔ **If my divorce goes to trial, will you continue to represent me or will you recommend another attorney?**

If you think that your divorce may go to trial, you want an attorney who has trial experience and who can handle your divorce from start to finish. Switching to a trial attorney midstream increases the cost of your divorce because that attorney will require a separate retainer to represent you. Your divorce will also take longer because the trial attorney needs time to get up to speed on your case.

✔ **What can I do to minimize my legal expenses?**

Some lawyers are amenable to letting you handle certain aspects of your case yourself — picking up documents, copying, conducting simple research, and doing other tasks that don't require special training.

Before you agree to handle some of the simple, nonlegal tasks that are involved in your divorce, be sure that you have the time to accomplish them in a timely manner. You don't want to be responsible for slowing down your divorce.

✔ **If I become your client, what will you expect of me?**

Any reputable attorney expects a client to fully disclose all facts that are relevant to his or her legal problem, provide information on a timely basis, return phone calls promptly, be honest, pay bills on time, and obey the attorney's directives for the case.

Provide financial documentation

When you meet with prospective attorneys, it's a good idea to bring along information regarding your family's finances. Although the attorneys probably won't study the information carefully, they may want to take a quick look at it. Examples of information to bring with you include

✔ An inventory of your assets and debts.

✔ Copies of your current will and your spouse's. If you've set up a living trust as well, bring your trust document, too.

✔ Deeds to your property.

✔ Recent tax returns.

✔ A copy of any prenuptial or postnuptial agreements that you signed.

Chapter 3 discusses the types of information you should have already prepared and assembled in preparation for your divorce. After you hire an attorney, he or she will probably ask you to provide additional information and documentation. For example, your attorney may request that you provide him or her with any divorce-related correspondence that you've received from your spouse or from your spouse's attorney and to fill out the forms and worksheets the attorney uses.

Answer the attorneys' questions

You won't be the only one asking questions at your initial meetings with the attorneys. They may need to ask you questions in order to get further information, decide whether or not they want to take you on as a client, and determine whether your divorce goals are reasonable and legitimate.

They may also ask you questions to determine whether you're using your divorce to get revenge against your spouse. Many attorneys want to steer clear of vindictive clients unless they really need the work; such clients tend to spell trouble for them, and they figure that the money they'll earn from working with those clients is not worth the headache of dealing with them.

Reputable attorneys also try to assure themselves that they won't have a conflict of interest if they represent you. For example, a conflict of interest would be that their law firm represents your spouse's business.

The following questions give you an idea of what you can expect an attorney to ask you:

- ✔ Why are you getting a divorce?
- ✔ Do you have any minor children from your marriage?
- ✔ Do you work outside the home?
- ✔ How long have you been married?
- ✔ Are you and your spouse still living together? If not, with whom are your children living (assuming you have children)?
- ✔ Do you and your spouse have a prenuptial or postnuptial agreement?
- ✔ What major assets do you and your spouse own, and what would you estimate that each of those assets is worth?
- ✔ What are your marital debts?
- ✔ What kind of employment-related benefits do you and your spouse have?
- ✔ Do either of you have a substance abuse problem?
- ✔ Have you or your spouse ever been treated for mental health problems?
- ✔ Are you and your spouse retired or do either of you plan to retire soon?
- ✔ What are your goals for your divorce in terms of spousal support, a property settlement, child custody and visitation, and child support?
- ✔ What kind of relationship do you have with your young children and what role do you play in their day-to-day lives as a parent?
- ✔ Why do you think you deserve to have custody of your children?
- ✔ Do any of your children have special needs?
- ✔ Has there been any violence in your relationship?
- ✔ What else do you want me to know about you, your spouse, your children, or your marriage?

Be prepared to provide honest answers to any questions you're asked, even if a question such as, "Are you having (or have you had) an affair?" and "Is your spouse aware of your affair?" makes you squirm.

If you aren't 100 percent honest with the attorney you hire and the attorney finds out later that you lied or withheld important information from him or her, your relationship with one another may be damaged and your attorney may not work quite as hard on your behalf. Furthermore, withholding important information from your attorney could jeopardize your case. Also, if you aren't honest with an attorney when you're interviewing him or her, you may not hire the best attorney to represent you given your circumstances.

Getting a Written Agreement

Be sure to get a written agreement or letter of understanding from the attorney you decide to hire before you pay him or her money, give the attorney a lien on any of your property in lieu of cash, or make any other kind of payment. The document should detail all the specifics you and the attorney agreed to, including whether the attorney is going to charge you on an hourly basis or a flat fee, the amount of the retainer you must pay for the services the attorney will provide to you, when your payments to the attorney will be due, any services you may have to pay extra for, and so forth.

Don't hesitate to take a day or two to thoroughly read the agreement or letter of understanding before signing it. Ask the attorney about anything you don't understand and keep asking until he or she has answered all your questions to your satisfaction. If you and the lawyer agree to add or delete anything to the document, make certain that it reflects the changes before you sign it. Keep a copy of the final signed document for your files.

What If You're Unhappy with Your Attorney?

Your divorce attorney is working for you, so if you're unhappy with something the lawyer does or doesn't do, let him or her know. But be reasonable; don't complain about insignificant matters or constantly call his or her office to gripe. If you become an irritant, your behavior may impact your lawyer's commitment to your case.

If you feel that your lawyer isn't doing a good job for you, you can fire him or her whenever you want. However, you must pay the attorney for any work that he or she has already performed and for all expenses that the attorney incurred on your behalf up to that point.

Also, be aware that firing one attorney and hiring a new one slows the progress of your divorce and will probably increase your legal costs. Therefore, don't take that step without giving it some thought. Try to objectively analyze why you're unhappy with your current attorney. Is it because the attorney consistently seems unprepared, ignores your wishes, or never responds to your phone calls or letters? Is it because your attorney is giving you advice that you don't want to hear or because you're letting your emotions get in the way of rational thinking?

The further you are in the divorce process, the greater the potential harm you may do to your case if you fire your attorney. Your case will grind to a halt until you find a new attorney; your new attorney will need time to get up to speed; your divorce will cost more; and your new attorney may have a different strategy than your first attorney, which could take your divorce in a whole new direction.

What If You Can't Afford Legal Help?

Not everyone can afford to pay the fees of even a relatively inexpensive attorney. If you've checked your wallet and come up short, some legal resources may be available to help you with your divorce case.

When money is tight, you may be tempted to cut corners by getting a divorce online or by purchasing do-it-yourself divorce software. Unfortunately, these options won't work for you if your divorce is contested, and they can be downright dangerous if your divorce is complicated. If you have child-custody and support issues to resolve, if you and your spouse own a substantial amount of marital property or you owe a lot of debt, or if you want to share in your spouse's retirement benefits, these divorce options aren't right for you. To protect your legal rights, to get all that you're entitled to for yourself and your kids, and to minimize the potential for postdivorce problems, you need an attorney's assistance, even if that assistance is simply some upfront advice and a review of the divorce agreement that you and your spouse hammered out together.

Try a legal clinic

You may be able to use the services of a nonprofit local, state, or federal legal clinic in your area. Not all these clinics take divorce cases though, and if they do, your household income must be very low (usually some percentage of the U.S. poverty level) to qualify for their services. Furthermore, if your divorce is complicated, you need more help than a legal clinic can provide. You can get the names of nonprofit legal clinics in your area by calling your state or local bar association.

For-profit legal clinics are another source of low-cost help. These clinics tend to rely heavily on standardized legal forms and paralegals and usually charge set fees for certain types of cases — typically in the $200 to $500 range plus court costs. However, if your case is particularly time-consuming, the amount you actually pay can be more than the standard fee. Check out your local Yellow Pages for the names of for-profit legal clinics.

Although the price may be right, a for-profit legal clinic isn't the place for you if your divorce is complicated. Its staff may not have the expertise or the time to give you the legal help that you need.

Your state or local bar association may have a program that provides affordable legal representation to people of limited financial means.

Explore alternative ways to pay

If you don't have a lot of cash, the attorney you want to hire may be willing to work out an alternative way for you to pay for his or her services:

- **Trade or barter:** If you have a special skill or talent that's worth a significant amount of money or is of particular value, the attorney may be willing to negotiate a trade — your expertise in exchange for legal services. This avenue may be a long shot, but it's worth a try. Such services may include computer trouble-shooting and repair, marketing, graphic design, Web site design, copywriting, data entry, and so on.

- **Payment plan:** The attorney may let you pay for his or her services over time, depending on your future earnings potential.

  As a condition of agreeing to an alternative payment arrangement, the attorney may require that you let him or her put a lien on any real property or other significant assets you may own that aren't marital property. The lien ensures that if you fail to live up to your end of the bargain, your attorney will be in line to receive all or some of what you owe to him or her after you sell the asset with the lien on it. Also, as long as there is a lien on the asset, you won't be able to borrow against it without paying your debt to the attorney.

You can reduce your divorce-related expenses by finding an attorney who lets you do your own copying, picking up and delivery of documents, and so on.

Chapter 14

Working Hand in Hand with Your Attorney

*W*hen you hire a divorce attorney to negotiate the details of your divorce with your spouse's attorney or to represent you in a divorce trial, the outcome of your divorce depends, in part, on how well you and your attorney work together. Because the divorce process becomes much more formal when you hire an attorney, it's helpful to become familiar with the legal procedures and processes that your attorney may use to reach a final agreement in your divorce and to understand the information and legal documents your attorney will need to help ensure that the agreement is good for you and your kids.

Chapter 3 provides a detailed list of the kinds of financial information and documents you should pull together when you prepare for your divorce, and Chapter 13 highlights some of the legal documents and information your attorney will want to review as well as the questions your attorney is likely to ask you.

In this chapter, we provide additional details regarding the kinds of information your attorney will want from you, including personal, financial, and legal information. We also explain how your attorney will use the *discovery process* to fill in the blanks if you're unable to provide him with all of the information he needs to represent you. We also get you up to speed on the actions your attorney may take right away if your divorce is hostile. Finally, we explain how settlement conferences and the draft agreement process works and what happens once you have a final divorce agreement (also called a settlement agreement).

Providing Your Attorney with Essential Information

In order to represent you well in your divorce and to get at all the facts involved, your attorney needs a lot of information. Although you probably shared some of this information with your attorney during your initial get-acquainted meeting (which we discuss in Chapter 13), when you're actually working together, she will need much more.

You'll provide your attorney with much of the necessary information through one-on-one interviews, by filling out forms, and by supplying her with as much backup documentation as you can.

Don't second guess whether your attorney really needs the information that he requests. Try to provide everything your attorney asks for, and don't withhold anything because you think the information is unimportant or irrelevant. By failing to share certain information even though your attorney asks for it, you may put your attorney at a negotiating disadvantage, derail his strategy for your divorce, or complicate your divorce in other ways. For example, if you withhold information from your attorney, and your spouse's attorney introduces that same information into evidence during a hearing related to your divorce, the case your attorney was building for you may be damaged, and your attorney probably won't be very happy with you.

If you read Chapter 3 and followed its advice, you're a couple of steps ahead of the game now that your divorce has begun. But if you're not familiar with the details of your family's finances and don't know where your family's legal and financial information is kept — maybe because pulling it together and reviewing it sounded oh-so-tedious and time-consuming (which it is), you have a lot of work ahead of you. That information is essential to negotiating the terms of your divorce and, if you can't locate what you need or don't take the time to try, your attorney will have to use the discovery process to get it, which means that your divorce will cost more. We discuss the discovery process later in this chapter and again in Chapter 16.

The following sections of this chapter provide a rundown of some of the things that your attorney needs to know.

Personal stuff

To help develop a strategy for ending your marriage and to determine what you may be entitled to in your divorce, your attorney needs information on your personal history, your marriage, and your minor children. For those reasons, among others, expect your attorney to question you about

✔ Why you're getting a divorce

✔ Whether you and your spouse are separated

✔ The history of your marriage, including the number of years you've been married, whether there has been any violence in your marriage, and so on

✔ Biographical information about you and your spouse — your ages, educations, work histories, whether either of you have any addiction problems, have been convicted of a crime, and so on

✔ Your individual health histories, including whether either of you has a history of serious medical or emotional problems

✔ Your minor children, including their ages, where they're living, whether they have special needs (educational, physical, emotional), whether they attend public or private school, and so on

Legal and financial stuff

Your attorney will also spend time studying the details of your finances and reviewing any legal agreements that you and your spouse may have entered into before or during your marriage. Your attorney will want to know

✔ Whether you have a separation agreement. If you do, your attorney will want to read the agreement. (See Chapter 4 for more details on separation agreements.)

✔ Whether you signed a prenuptial or postnuptial agreement.

✔ Whether you or your spouse have done any estate planning, such as writing wills, buying life insurance, or setting up living trusts.

✔ Whether you and your spouse own a closely held business together, have other shared business interests, or own separate businesses.

✔ What assets and debts you and your spouse have from your marriage as well as where you got the money to pay for any of the real property you may own. *Real property* includes your home and any other homes, buildings, or land that you own. If you own real property, be prepared to provide your attorney with the *deeds of record* to the property and any loan documents related to that property if you owe money on any of it.

✔ How much each of you earns annually from all income sources, including salaries, commissions, bonuses, and other employment-related income as well as from trusts, annuities, royalties, rents, and so on.

✔ Whether either of you made any special contributions to one another's career or business. For example, you may have helped finance your spouse's business or worked in the business without pay.

- Whether either of you has wasted marital assets by gambling, by having extramarital affairs, or through an addiction to drugs, alcohol, and so on.

- Your current and postdivorce household budgets. (Chapter 5 provides information about developing a budget, including a budget worksheet.)

If you file a fault divorce, your attorney will want you to provide proof that your spouse is at fault. Conversely, if your spouse alleges that you are at fault, your attorney will want you to provide proof that your spouse's allegations are untrue.

Other important stuff

Your attorney will ask you questions in order to understand what you want from your divorce and what you're willing to do to get what you want. Your attorney needs this information not just to help you get a divorce agreement that meets your needs, but also to be certain that you have realistic expectations. So, you can expect your lawyer to ask you about

- Your divorce goals and priorities

- What you are willing to give up to achieve those goals and priorities

- Why you feel you should receive spousal support, if that's something you want from your divorce

- Why you believe that the custody arrangement you want makes sense and your spouse's desired custody arrangement isn't reasonable, assuming that the two of you don't see eye to eye on how to handle the custody of your minor children

- Under what, if any, circumstances you're willing to go to trial to get what you want

Writing it all down: The story of your marriage

Your attorney may ask you to prepare a written narrative describing your marriage: how you and your spouse shared childcare responsibilities, your individual personal habits, what you think led to your divorce, what you would like from your divorce and for your life after divorce, and what you believe your spouse wants.

The narrative can be a good way for your attorney to get the facts related to your divorce that may not be apparent from a review of the financial, legal, and personal documents and other information you provide or from your client-attorney interviews. The information you write down can help fill in the gaps for your attorney and provide him or her with a fuller picture. Plus, you may find that recording the story of your marriage is cathartic and healing. The process may help you gain new insights on what went wrong with your relationship and why you're getting a divorce.

Resolving Issues Temporarily

One of the first things your attorney may do when you begin working together is to file motions asking the court to grant temporary orders on your behalf. (Your spouse's attorney may do the same thing.) *Temporary orders* are legally binding requirements that last for a limited period of time. In a divorce, the temporary orders apply until the final terms of your divorce are worked out. The temporary orders may

- ✔ Give you the right to receive a certain amount of spousal support.
- ✔ Determine how child support, custody, and visitation will be handled.
- ✔ Give you the right to remain in your home.
- ✔ Spell out how your marital bills will be paid.
- ✔ Give you the right to use certain marital assets, such as a car or the funds in one of the bank accounts you share with your spouse.
- ✔ Prohibit your spouse from certain types of improper behavior. For example, from selling your marital property, spending all of the money in one of your bank accounts, or making certain decisions related to a business you own together.

Your attorney may also request that the court issue a temporary restraining order if your spouse is threatening your safety or your children's safety or has already been physically violent. The order bars your spouse from coming near you or your children.

After your attorney files a motion with the court requesting a temporary order, a hearing is held to discuss the motion Although the judge's decisions on the motion applies on a temporary basis, temporary motions often become part of a divorce judgment or decree. In other words, some aspects of your divorce may actually be decided at the temporary-order level. For this reason, a hearing on a temporary court order can be just as stressful and nerve-wracking as a divorce trial.

If you need an immediate court order — for instance, you have reason to believe that your spouse is about to sell some of your marital assets or flee with your children — your attorney may be able to get a court order issued on an *ex parte* basis. *Ex parte* refers to a legal action ordered on behalf of one party without the other party being notified about it or having an opportunity to participate in the action. Therefore, your spouse would not learn of the court's decision and a hearing would not take place until after the court approved your attorney's motion and issued its order (assuming the court ruled in your favor). Ex parte court orders usually have very short durations. However, once the ex parte order is issued, a hearing will be scheduled to determine whether or not the term of the order should be extended.

If you request an *ex parte* order, you may have to post a bond to protect your spouse against any harm, such as a financial loss, that he or she may suffer because the court issues the order without a hearing. However, in many family law situations, the court waives the bond requirement.

Using Discovery to Get at the Facts of Your Divorce

Attorneys use the *discovery* process to help them determine the facts of a case. This process can be informal or formal. If it's *informal,* you and your spouse, working through your individual attorneys, willingly share with one another the documents and information each of them needs to work out the terms of your divorce. If discovery is *formal,* depending on what you or the opposing side wants to learn through discovery, the attorneys will obtain the information they need by using one or more of the following legal tools: depositions, interrogatories, motions to produce documents, and subpoenas.

Your attorney is apt to rely on informal discovery if

- ✔ The two attorneys agree in writing to willingly exchange all the information they need to work out the terms of your divorce.
- ✔ Your divorce is amicable.

Your attorney is likely to use formal discovery if

- ✔ Your divorce is contentious.
- ✔ Your attorney has to force your spouse's attorney to provide certain information related to your divorce.
- ✔ Either attorney needs to formally acquire additional information related to your divorce from other sources.

The discovery process may take just a short amount of time, especially if the facts of your divorce are clear and undisputed and most of the discovery is informal. However, if your attorney (or your spouse's attorney) uses formal discovery to get at the facts of your case, the discovery process can last many months and cost a lot of money. This is because obtaining information through the formal discovery process is time-consuming, and reviewing the requested information can also take time. In addition, court hearings related to your attorney's discovery requests or the requests of your spouse's attorney may occur. And other potential complications may slow down the process.

In some states, the amount of formal discovery in a divorce is limited. For example, your attorney may be able to use discovery to get at only the financial facts of your divorce.

Depending on the issues that must be resolved before your divorce can be finalized, any number of individuals may be involved in the discovery process: you, your spouse, your financial advisors, your business associates, appraisers, your children's teachers and babysitters, mental health professionals, your friends, relatives, and neighbors — basically, anyone who may be able to provide information about your marriage, your children, your finances, and so on.

Uncovering facts with informal discovery

Informal discovery occurs when your attorney asks your spouse's attorney (or vice versa) for financial, legal, medical, or other information, and the opposing attorney provides that information voluntarily. The particular types of information your attorney asks for depend on the issues in your divorce.

Ideally, most of the discovery in your divorce will be informal; the more frequently either side uses formal discovery, the longer your divorce will take and the more it will cost. For example, in formal discovery, your attorney or your spouse's attorney may have to complete extra paperwork, formulate questions to ask your spouse or others, conduct interviews, and then review and analyze all the information. More hearings take place as well.

Using formal discovery to dig for details

Formal discovery is most common in divorces involving spouses who are unwilling to cooperate with one another. Depositions, interrogatories, formal requests for the production of documents, and subpoenas are all formal discovery tools. The following list describes each of these legal tools:

- **Subpoena:** A court order requiring someone to appear in court at a specific day and time to testify about something at a court hearing or a trial. Someone who ignores a subpoena may be charged with contempt of court and face legal penalties.

- **Deposition:** A statement by a witness while under oath, taken out of court and recorded by a court reporter. Your spouse's attorney may depose you during the discovery process as well as others with knowledge about an issue in your divorce. Although you may wish you didn't have to give a deposition, unless you want to risk being held in contempt of court, you must comply with the request. However, your attorney will be by your side during the deposition and he or she may object to certain questions; you may not have to answer them as a result. The "Proper deposition deportment" sidebar in this chapter provides tips on how to behave if you're deposed.

✔ **Interrogatories:** Written questions prepared by an attorney for a witness to answer in order to obtain information related to an issue that's in dispute in your divorce. You may have to respond to an interrogatory and other individuals, such as your family's financial advisor, friends or family members, a business associate of your spouse's, and so on, may also have to respond to one.

✔ **Notices to produce documents and other information:** Your attorney may use these notices to obtain such things as the deed to your home, financial information related to your spouse's business, your spouse's cell phone records, and so on. A notice to produce documents is also known as a "request for production of documents and other tangible things."

Even if your divorce is amicable, your attorney may do a limited amount of formal discovery in order to

✔ Narrow the scope of your negotiations by identifying exactly what you and your spouse agree or disagree about. The more that you agree on, the less the attorneys must negotiate or litigate later and the less your divorce costs.

✔ Compare the strengths and weaknesses of your position versus your spouse's.

✔ Assess how well your spouse is likely to perform on the stand if your case goes to trial and your spouse has to testify.

✔ Get your spouse to admit to certain facts. If your divorce goes to trial and your spouse takes the stand and provides testimony that differs from what he or she said during discovery, your attorney can use the discrepancy to undermine your spouse's credibility.

Using Your Attorney to Work Out the Details of Your Divorce Agreement

After your attorney briefs you on key points and legal issues in your divorce, he or she may suggest that you and your spouse work out the terms of your divorce on your own instead of having him or her and your spouse's attorney do that for you (assuming that you and your spouse are communicating with each other). Doing it on your own will save you a lot of money. Chapter 12 provides how-to advice for negotiating an agreement with your spouse.

If you and your spouse put your attorneys in charge of drawing up your divorce agreement, they'll work together to try to negotiate the terms of your divorce in consultation with you and your spouse. Assuming they're able to work out the terms of your agreement, the attorney for whichever spouse initiated the divorce drafts and files a final divorce agreement.

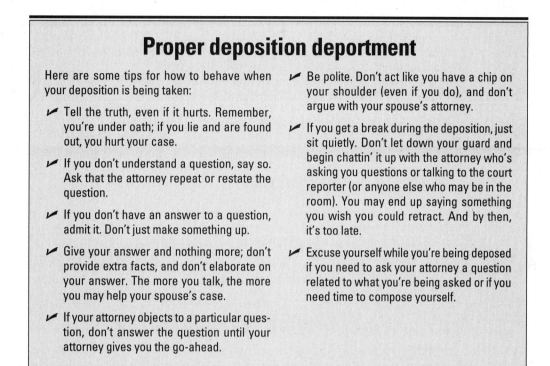

Proper deposition deportment

Here are some tips for how to behave when your deposition is being taken:

✔ Tell the truth, even if it hurts. Remember, you're under oath; if you lie and are found out, you hurt your case.

✔ If you don't understand a question, say so. Ask that the attorney repeat or restate the question.

✔ If you don't have an answer to a question, admit it. Don't just make something up.

✔ Give your answer and nothing more; don't provide extra facts, and don't elaborate on your answer. The more you talk, the more you may help your spouse's case.

✔ If your attorney objects to a particular question, don't answer the question until your attorney gives you the go-ahead.

✔ Be polite. Don't act like you have a chip on your shoulder (even if you do), and don't argue with your spouse's attorney.

✔ If you get a break during the deposition, just sit quietly. Don't let down your guard and begin chattin' it up with the attorney who's asking you questions or talking to the court reporter (or anyone else who may be in the room). You may end up saying something you wish you could retract. And by then, it's too late.

✔ Excuse yourself while you're being deposed if you need to ask your attorney a question related to what you're being asked or if you need time to compose yourself.

Working out an agreement with the help of your attorney

If you're the spouse who filed for divorce, your attorney contacts your spouse's attorney so they can begin discussing the terms of your divorce. Whenever the attorneys reach an agreement on an issue in your divorce, your attorney sends the other attorney a letter stating what they agreed to; assuming that your spouse's attorney feels that the letter accurately reflects their agreement, the attorneys put that issue aside and move on to another.

If your spouse's attorney wants to change anything, he or she calls your attorney to convey the change. Your attorney consults with you by phone before offering anything to your spouse's attorney or accepting anything he or she may offer you. This back-and-forth process continues until all the issues in your divorce are resolved or until you and your spouse reach a stalemate on one or more issues. If that happens, you and your spouse may agree to try to resolve your differences by using mediation or, worst-case scenario, you go to court to resolve whatever you can't agree on.

Expect your attorney to consult you throughout his or her negotiations with your spouse's attorney. Do not agree to anything that makes you feel uncomfortable, that you don't understand, or that you don't think you can live up to. You're not obligated to agree to anything that you don't like. You can accept or reject something that your spouse may offer to you through his or her attorney, or you can respond to the offer with a counteroffer.

You may be tempted to try to pressure your spouse to give in on certain points that are important to you by threatening her with a divorce trial. Before you try this tactic, consider which scenario is more likely: You hold your ground and your spouse agrees to a compromise, or your spouse holds her ground, calls your bluff, and you end up in court.

After you and your spouse believe that you're close to a final agreement, the attorney representing the spouse who filed for divorce drafts a formal divorce agreement. The agreement should reflect everything you and your spouse have agreed on. The two of you will approve it or send it back for additional changes.

Evaluating an offer or counteroffer from your spouse

Whenever you receive an offer or counteroffer from your spouse proposing a way to resolve one of the issues in your divorce, you must decide whether you like what your spouse is suggesting. When you evaluate your spouse's offer, ask yourself the following questions:

- How close is the offer to what I'm asking for?
- Does the offer reflect my divorce priorities? Is anything missing from the offer that's worth the cost and the time involved in further negotiations?
- Is the offer fair?
- Is it in my children's best interest?
- Can I afford what my spouse is proposing?
- Given what I know now about my legal rights and responsibilities, the value of the marital property, and how my divorce is affecting my children, am I likely to get more if I reject the proposal?
- Is my spouse likely to make any additional concessions if we continue negotiating?
- How much have I already spent on my case, and can I afford to spend any more?

✔ Am I willing to take the offer just to end this protracted and expensive legal process?

✔ Given what I know about the judge and his or her past rulings, am I likely to do better if I go all the way to trial than if I were to accept what my spouse is offering? What is the worst that could happen? (Your attorney should be able to give you a strong sense of how a judge would be likely to rule on your case.)

✔ If I really push for whatever is missing, what may I have to give up in order to get it? Is it worth it? What are the risks of not settling now?

✔ If I don't settle now, how long will it take for this case to come to trial and how long is the trial likely to last?

✔ Do I not want to settle yet because I'm unhappy with my spouse's offer, because I'm not sure that I can live up to the agreement, or because my emotions are getting in the way?

✔ What kind of financial and emotional toll is not settling likely to take on my children and me?

Discuss the pros and cons of whatever agreement you're evaluating with your attorney. Share your thoughts and concerns with him or her and find out what your attorney thinks. Your attorney may tell you that your spouse's offer is about as good as you're going to get, that you can probably get a few more concessions if you keep negotiating, or that you should not accept what your spouse is offering because it's not in your best interest. In the end, however, whether to accept the offer is your call.

Settling disputes at a settlement conference

If your divorce is very complicated and contentious and you and your spouse both feel as if you have at least the beginnings of an agreement, your attorneys may schedule a *settlement conference* to try to work out whatever issues are unresolved. The settlement conference usually takes place at one of the attorneys' offices and normally occurs after the discovery process has been completed. However, it can take place whenever you and your spouse are ready to make a deal.

The settlement conference offers your attorneys an opportunity to sit down face to face to hammer out the final details of your divorce agreement. You and your spouse may or may not participate in the settlement conference. Before it begins, you should talk with your attorney about whether you should attend. It may or may not be in your best interest to be at the conference if your divorce is contentious or if you have a hard time keeping your emotions under control. However, you may want to be there so that you can hear everything that's said and so that you can provide your attorney with immediate feedback.

A successful settlement conference involves some old-fashioned horse-trading. If you haven't been clear with your attorney about your divorce priorities and what you're willing to give up to get them, be sure to convey this information to your attorney. He will not be able to bargain effectively for you without that input.

Be patient with all the back-and-forth negotiations. It's essential that you get all the terms of your divorce agreement just right; after you and your spouse sign it and file it with the court, the agreement becomes a legally binding contract, which means that you must live up to what it says, like it or not. Although you can try to change the agreement at a later date, doing so will cost you more time and money, and you may not end up with what you want.

If you and your spouse simply cannot agree on some aspect of your divorce no matter how hard your attorneys try to craft a compromise that's acceptable to both of you, they may recommend mediation or even arbitration, both of which we describe in Chapter 15. If you don't want to give these options a try and you don't want to keep negotiating, either, your only other option — assuming that you and your spouse still want to get divorced — is to have your case tried in court. For more on what happens if your case goes to trial, see Chapter 16.

Making a deal: The final settlement

After you and your spouse have a final divorce agreement (or final settlement agreement) detailing the terms of your divorce, your lawyer or your spouse's lawyer drafts a formal document stating everything you agreed to. The final agreement includes a lot of standard provisions and boilerplate language — stuff that's in every settlement agreement. Whichever attorney does the drafting submits the agreement to the other attorney for review. The other attorney may make some minor tweaks to the agreement but, at this point, there should be no substantive changes.

After you sign the settlement agreement, depending on your state, you and your spouse (or just one of you) may have to appear at a court hearing in order to have a judge officially dissolve your marriage. In other states, this hearing takes place only in a fault divorce. (Chapter 1 explains the difference between a fault and a no-fault divorce.) If a hearing is scheduled, it's more of a formality than anything else, and it won't last long. Your attorney will attend the hearing with you.

Concluding Your Divorce: Filing the Divorce Decree

After your attorney (or your spouse's attorney) submits your final divorce settlement agreement to the judge, the court reviews its terms. Then, the judge signs your divorce decree (a final judgment of divorce).

If your divorce agreement requires that your spouse transfer certain property to you, be sure that the transfers have been completed before the judge signs your divorce decree and don't assume that your attorney has made sure that the transfer happens. Instead, ask for a copy of the paperwork deeding the property to you. If you wait until after your divorce is over to confirm that the transfer occurred and find out that it didn't, your ex may balk at turning over the property to you or ask you to make certain concessions first. In the end, your only option may be to go back to court to try to get a judge to enforce the terms of your divorce, which means spending more money on attorney fees and legal expenses.

Some states allow judges to modify negotiated settlement agreements. Others allow judges only to accept or reject an agreement. If the judge rejects your agreement, you can go back to the drawing board to work out a new, more acceptable one. A judge may reject your agreement because he or she doesn't think it's fair to one or both of you, because it's unenforceable or violates your state's laws, or because it isn't in the best interests of your minor children, among other reasons; however, judges usually accept agreements.

After the judge approves or modifies your settlement, he or she signs your divorce decree or *judgment of divorce* and enters it together with your final settlement agreement into the court records. At this point, you are officially divorced. Your attorney provides you with a copy of your approved settlement agreement and your signed divorce decree. Keep them both in a safe place. You may need them later if you have to prove that you're divorced, if any questions arise about what you and your spouse agreed to, or if you want to change something in your divorce agreement after you've had a chance to live with it. You also need this information if you decide to ask the court to modify the terms of your divorce because of changes in your life. (Chapter 18 covers the topic of modifying divorce agreements.)

Chapter 15

Using Mediation to End Divorce Stalemates

*W*hen you and your spouse are working out the terms of your divorce, no matter how hard both of you try, you may encounter issues that you just can't resolve on your own. If that happens, you and your spouse don't have to tear your hair out in frustration or toss in the towel and brace yourselves for a trial. Instead, you may be able to use mediation to resolve those issues and reach a final divorce agreement. In this chapter, we explain what mediation is and how it works, and we describe the role of a divorce mediator and of your attorney in the mediation process, if you are working with one. We also highlight the benefits of using mediation and tell you what happens next if your mediation is successful.

Deciding Whether to Try Mediation

Mediation is a noncourt dispute-resolution method that uses the open exchange of information, ideas, and alternatives to help individuals who are involved in a dispute identify a mutually acceptable resolution. The process focuses on cooperation and problem solving, *not* winning.

At the time this book was written a majority of states under certain circumstances — usually issues related to child custody and visitation — require divorcing couples try mediation before they can get a trial date. Courts believe that it's best for young children if their parents make their own decisions about how to handle custody and visitation instead of letting a court decide those matters. Spouses who can resolve those issues themselves are more apt to live up to the terms of their agreement.

Mediation is most apt to be successful for couples who are willing and able to have a calm discussion about the unresolved issues in their divorce. Therefore, if you or your spouse is having problems managing your emotions, consider working with a mental health professional before you try mediation. Otherwise, emotions may derail the process.

If you and your spouse decide that mediation is right for you, don't begin the process until each of you has met with a divorce attorney in order to gain a clear understanding of your legal rights in regard to the issues you'll be discussing during mediation. Otherwise, you may end up agreeing to something during mediation that isn't in your best interest.

Considering the benefits of mediation

It takes two to tango, to sing a duet, and to make mediation work. So, if your spouse isn't serious about mediation, you're probably wasting your time as well as the mediator's if you decide to go to mediation However, if your spouse is uncertain about whether she wants to pursue mediation, ask her to consider these important potential benefits of the process:

- ✔ **Using mediation to work out the sticky issues in your divorce is a lot cheaper than going to trial.** In fact, mediation may cost hundreds to thousands of dollars less, depending on how many mediation sessions it takes to resolve those issues and the cost of the mediator versus the cost of an attorney's help. Depending on where you live and the experience and reputation of the mediator you work with, expect most mediators to charge between $60 and $300 an hour.

- ✔ **Working out issues with a mediator is less stressful and less intimidating than having them resolved in a courtroom.** Sitting in a mediator's office and attempting to find solutions to the issues in your divorce that you and your spouse can both live with is a more informal and low-key process than being involved in a trial.

- ✔ **Your divorce will be over faster.** Depending on the caseload in your area's family court, months — or even a year or more — may pass before your trial date arrives. If you decide to use mediation, you can probably begin that process within a month, although just how long it takes you and your spouse to work things out is up to the two of you.

- ✔ **Mediation encourages you and your spouse to brainstorm creative, "outside the box" ways to resolve the issues in your divorce.** You aren't bound by the letter of the law when working out the terms of your divorce agreement as you would be if you turned over your divorce to attorneys or went to trial. The benefit of being creative? You and your spouse may come up with solutions you would never have thought of otherwise that might do a much better job of meeting your needs and the needs of your kids in your divorce.

✔ **You and your spouse are in control of your divorce.** In mediation, you and your spouse make the tough decisions, not a judge or jury.

✔ **You preserve all your options.** If mediation doesn't work, you and your spouse still have the option of continuing to negotiate a divorce agreement, with or without attorneys, and you can still pursue a trial.

✔ **Mediation maintains your privacy.** If you go to trial, everything that is said and done in the courtroom will be matter of public record and anyone who wants to can sit in the courtroom and listen while all the dirty laundry from your marriage is aired. In contrast, mediation is a private process; only you, your spouse, the mediator, and your attorneys (if you and your spouse each have a divorce lawyer), are privy to what goes on during each of your mediation sessions.

✔ **You and your spouse are more likely to be satisfied with and honor your agreement because you came up with it together.** The agreement that comes out of mediation isn't something that gets imposed on you by the court — it's a solution that you and your spouse reach together.

When mediation isn't a great idea

Mediation isn't for everyone. It's not right for you if

✔ Your spouse intimidates you.

✔ You have a hard time standing up for yourself and speaking your mind.

✔ You aren't clear about your divorce priorities and goals, and so you don't know what you want out of your negotiations and what you're willing to accept.

✔ You aren't clear about what the law in your state says regarding the issues you are going to negotiate.

✔ You don't have the information you need to negotiate on an equal footing with your spouse; for example, you don't know exactly what assets you and your spouse own and their values. (A good attorney won't let you go into mediation unprepared; see the section "How Your Attorney Can Help with Your Mediation" later in this chapter.)

✔ As hard as you try, you cannot keep your emotions under control. Angry outbursts and crying fits cloud your thinking, may alienate your spouse, and make it impossible for the two of you to reach an agreement.

✔ You and your spouse can no longer communicate effectively.

If you or your spouse don't want to try mediation, but you don't want to let a judge decide the terms of your divorce through a divorce trial, you may want to consider using arbitration, which is another noncourt dispute-resolution method. See the sidebar "Arbitration: Another out-of-court option" to find out how the process works.

Arbitration: Another out-of-court option

When you hear the word "arbitration," you may think of labor union disputes. But did you know that you can use arbitration to resolve marital disputes as well?

Arbitration is an out-of-court dispute-resolution method that's more formal than mediation but less formal and less costly than a trial. During arbitration, your attorney represents you, witnesses can testify, your attorney can present written evidence, and so forth, just like in a trial, but you're not constrained by the formal rules of evidence or the courtroom procedures that govern how a trial works. Instead, you and your spouse, working with your attorneys and the arbitrator, set your own rules.

If you want to resolve the issues in your divorce through arbitration, your attorney will choose the arbitrator who's best for you. Choosing an arbitrator is an important decision, so let your attorney's knowledge and experience work for you.

A fundamental difference between arbitration and mediation is that you and your spouse won't make the final decisions about the issues the two of you are stalemated on. The arbitrator does. Although the arbitrator is not a judge, his

or her decisions are legally binding and *can* be legally enforced. Also, you *cannot* appeal them.

Some states allow couples to have any of their divorce-related disputes arbitrated, although special arbitration rules may apply when a dispute relates to custody or child support. Other states prohibit any and all child-related issues from being arbitrated.

Arbitration can be a good alternative if

✔ You don't want to try mediation or have already tried it and failed to reach an agreement.

✔ You don't want to run up big legal bills or you want to be divorced sooner than if you have to wait for your day in court.

✔ You're willing to let an arbitrator — often a retired judge or lawyer — decide the outstanding issues in your divorce.

✔ You're willing to live with the arbitrator's decisions, even if you're not happy with them. Remember, unlike a judge's decision, you cannot appeal an arbitrator's decisions.

Working with a Mediator

If you and your spouse want to use mediation to work out the terms of your divorce, consider carefully which mediator you hire. If either of you is uncomfortable with or doesn't trust the mediator you use, mediating your divorce may not work for you.

Hiring a mediator who has experience mediating divorces is important because the issues that you want to resolve may be complicated, you and your spouse may feel very emotional about them, and you must be certain that whatever you and your spouse may decide is legally enforceable. Also, a mediator who understands your state's divorce laws and processes is better able to defuse potentially explosive situations during your mediation. For example, if your spouse threatens to storm out because you asked him exactly how much he makes, a mediator can remind your spouse that your attorney can get that information through formal discovery if he doesn't provide it voluntarily. (See Chapter 16 to find out how formal discovery works.)

Not every mediator has the skills and knowledge to help couples negotiate the terms of their divorce. In this section, we provide information and advice to help you choose a mediator who's not only qualified to help you, but who also has the trust and confidence of you and your spouse.

If you and your spouse are already working with attorneys when you decide to try mediation, the attorneys will recommend a mediator based on their past experience. Each attorney will want a mediator who has achieved positive results for their divorce clients in the past. If you're lucky, your attorney and your spouse's attorney will agree on which mediator to use but, if they don't, you may have to go to court to let a judge decide.

Selecting a great go-between

Mediators are neutral third parties who may be mental health professionals, social workers, attorneys, clergy members, financial professionals, and even volunteers. However, if you use a mediator to help with your divorce, that person should be a family law attorney or a nonlawyer mediator who has specific experience in divorce mediation.

If you and your spouse aren't working with divorce attorneys yet and are choosing a mediator on your own, the two of you should meet with the mediators you're considering to learn about their backgrounds and training and to ensure that their personalities mesh with yours. You can meet with them together or separately. Either way, you should both agree on which mediator you want to work with.

In most states, mediators don't have to be certified or licensed. Also, no national certification standards exist for mediators. Therefore, even if your attorney doesn't recommend a mediator who is certified or licensed by your state or a professional organization, that person may still be highly qualified to help you and your spouse resolve your differences.

Some mediators belong to national or state professional organizations. For example, the Association for Conflict Resolution (ACR) is a national organization that designates mediators who complete a minimum of 60 hours of family mediation training or a 40-hour class in divorce mediation as well as 20 hours of continuing education every two years and who have completed at least 250 hours of face-to-face family mediation in at least 25 different cases as Advanced Practitioner Members (APM). Someone with the APM designation has the training and the experience needed to mediate your divorce. To locate a mediator in your area with that designation, go to https:// bridge.acrnet.org/referrals.

When you meet with each mediator, ask the following questions in order to get the information you need to select a mediator who has experience mediating divorces, who you and your spouse both feel comfortable working with, and who is affordable:

- ✔ How much do you charge for your services? Do you charge by the hour or do you charge a flat fee? Most mediators charge by the hour.

- ✔ What is your professional background?

- ✔ Do you have any special mediation training and are you certified by any organizations?

- ✔ Do you belong to any national or state professional mediator organizations?

- ✔ Can you mediate all the issues that my spouse and I need to resolve? Some mediators handle the full gamut of divorce-related issues; others don't mediate financial matters or custody battles.

- ✔ How many times have you mediated issues like ours? What is your success rate, and how have you helped other divorcing couples who were dealing with the same issues that we have come to closure?

During the screening process, be sure to ask each potential mediator for client references — and check them! References can give you insights into a mediator's personality and style, which may suggest that another mediator would be a better choice for you. You wouldn't find out that information if you relied only on what you gleaned from your meeting with the mediator.

Knowing what to expect during mediation

After you and your spouse have decided on a mediator, that person will schedule a convenient time for your initial mediation session as well as a place for you to meet. Most likely, you will meet at the mediator's office, but the meeting can also take place at some other neutral location. The mediator will handle making all the arrangements.

In some states, if you and your spouse have hired attorneys, the two of you will be in different rooms during each of your mediation sessions, probably with your attorneys, and you may never see one another. The mediator shuttles back and forth between you and your spouse in an effort to help the two of you reach a consensus on the issues you want to resolve, asking questions, sharing information and conveying any offers one of you may make to the other. This style of mediation is referred to as the *caucus method.*

During a mediation session, the mediator acts as coach, consensus builder, facilitator and, if necessary, referee, with the goal of helping create an environment in which you and your spouse can feel comfortable calmly expressing your opinions, talking over your differences, and working out your problems together. The mediator won't take sides with you or your spouse, interject opinions, or provide legal advice. Also, a mediator won't make decisions for you or order you or your spouse to do anything that you don't want to do.

A mediator

- ✔ Clarifies the issues that you and your spouse need to resolve.

- ✔ Establishes the ground rules for your mediation.

- ✔ Sets an agenda for your discussions.

- ✔ Keeps the discussions moving forward.

- ✔ Provides legal information, as necessary (but not legal advice). For example, the mediator may provide you with a written explanation of your property rights so that you and your spouse have a clear understanding of what each of you is legally entitled to when the time comes to divide up your marital assets.

In some states, your attorney can accompany you to the mediation sessions and be actively involved in the discussions or be available to answer your questions. In other states your attorney may be available to you only by phone while you are in mediation. (See the section "How Your Attorney Can Help with Your Mediation" later in this chapter.)

You and your spouse may be able to resolve the issues in your divorce in a few sessions. The amount of time you spend in mediation will depend on the complexity of the issues you and your spouse are trying to work out and how well you both work together, among other factors.

How Your Attorney Can Help with Your Mediation

If you decide to use mediation, your lawyer won't simply hand you off to a mediator and wait for you and your spouse to resolve all your outstanding divorce issues. At a minimum, your lawyer will prepare you for mediation by helping you

- ✔ Develop a list of the specific issues you want to resolve

- ✔ Make sure that you understand the laws that apply to those issues

- ✔ Assess your options

- ✔ Review any information that your spouse may share with you prior to mediation so that you understand all of it and know the right questions to ask about it

- ✔ Develop a mediation game plan or strategy

Depending on your ability to negotiate with your spouse during a mediation session, the complexity of the issues you want to resolve, and your attorney's preferences, your attorney may help you in other important ways:

- ✔ Serving as a sounding board before and after your mediation sessions
- ✔ Being at your side during mediation, assuming your state's law allows this
- ✔ Providing you with information when necessary, brainstorming with you, and offering you feedback
- ✔ Confirming or denying any information that the mediator or your spouse may give you
- ✔ Reviewing any written agreement that the mediator may have drafted before you sign it
- ✔ Negotiating for you, assuming it's legal in your state

You've Got an Agreement! What's Next?

If mediation works for you and your spouse, the mediator prepares a written document that details everything you and your spouse agreed upon. The mediator gives a copy of the agreement to your attorney so he or she can review it before you sign it. After you sign it, the mediator provides your attorney with the signed agreement and does the same for your spouse and your spouse's attorney.

You and your spouse's attorneys incorporate the mediation agreement into your final divorce agreement and, after the agreement is filed with the court and the judge has signed your divorce decree, you and your spouse are legally bound to comply with everything that you both agreed to during mediation.

Chapter 16

Letting a Judge or Jury Decide the Details of Your Divorce

. . . .

. . . .

*W*e're going to give it to you straight: Resolving the terms of your divorce by going through a divorce trial isn't a pleasant experience. It's much more stressful and expensive than a divorce that stays out of court, and you get no guarantee that you'll be happy with the outcome.

Although negotiating the terms of your divorce is all about cooperation and compromise, a divorce trial is about winning and losing, and both your attorney and your spouse's attorney will do whatever they can to be on the winning side. Therefore, be prepared for your spouse's lawyer to portray you in negative terms and to use highly personal information against you during the trial. Also, people you thought were your friends may testify against you and on your spouse's behalf, and your spouse's attorney may mischaracterize or blow out of proportion things you did in the past and mistakes you made. It may be very difficult for you to sit in court and listen calmly to what is said about you. Of course, your attorney is apt to use the same tactics against your spouse, which may make you gloat or feel terrible about the way your marriage is ending.

If a divorce trial sounds like a kind of hell on earth, you're getting the picture. It's serious business. If you're headed for a trial, fasten your seat belts, because you're in for a bumpy ride. To help prepare you for some major turbulence in your life, this chapter discusses out-of-court settlement opportunities and how to evaluate any offers that your spouse may send your way. It also explains what happens prior to a trial and offers general advice about proper in-court behavior and how you should dress for a court appearance. We give you an overview of the trial process and information on when you can appeal the court's decision.

Making Certain You Really Want a Trial

Before you move full speed ahead with a divorce trial, think long and hard about its financial and emotional costs. (Remember, you can change your mind and get serious about a negotiated settlement even after the trial begins!) Now may be the time to swallow your pride and compromise with your spouse so you can avoid the pain and expense of a trial.

Weighing your options

Bear in mind that putting your divorce in the hands of a judge or jury is a gamble; the judge or jury members may not see things quite the way you do. Therefore, their decisions may not mirror what you hoped for. Most states allow spouses to decide whether they want their divorce decided by a judge or a jury; most choose a judge. However, only Texas allows a jury to decide matters related to minor children in a divorce. You cannot assume that your side of the story is so strong that the judge (or jury) will decide in your favor. Prepare to be disappointed by the results of your divorce trial.

Before you commit to a divorce trial, ask yourself the following questions:

- ✔ Because the court may not see everything my way, does the risk of not getting what I want from my divorce outweigh any benefits I may receive from having a trial?

- ✔ Would I be better off compromising with my spouse to get at least some of the things that are really important to me in my divorce rather than rolling the dice and hoping that I come up with the lucky number?

- ✔ Do I have the time to devote to a trial? Getting divorced takes longer when you go to court. Not only does preparing for a trial take a lot of time, but you may have to wait months or even a year for a trial date. If you're looking for a speedy divorce, going to trial isn't the way to get it.

- ✔ Am I willing to put my children through the emotional stress of a divorce trial? Although they may not fully understand what's going on, they will probably sense that you're under an unusual amount of pressure, which may scare them. It's even possible that they could be asked to testify.

Despite all the negatives associated with a divorce trial, sometimes it's your best or only option. This is true in situations where

- ✔ Your spouse refuses to negotiate with you.
- ✔ You and your spouse have tried and failed to negotiate an agreement.
- ✔ Your spouse is hiding information essential to a fair settlement.
- ✔ Your spouse insists on a custody arrangement that you don't think is in your children's best interests.
- ✔ You need more spousal support than your spouse will agree to.
- ✔ You want your spouse to pay more in child support than he or she is willing to pay.
- ✔ You think that your spouse may be wasting or hiding your marital property or other assets.

Don't let your selfish wishes to have your children live with you all the time, your desire for revenge against your spouse for ending your marriage, or your discomfort with having your children live with your ex and the new person in his or her life cloud your thinking about the best custody arrangement for your kids. If you do, you may end up in a painful custody battle that's totally unnecessary.

Taking a financial hit

Divorce trials aren't cheap. The exact cost depends on a number of factors: what part of the country you live in (divorcing in a major metropolitan area on either coast typically costs more than divorcing in the Midwest, the South, or in a rural area); the specific issues the court will decide; just how bitter and contentious your divorce is; your attorney's legal strategy; and the legal strategy of your spouse's attorney.

When you take your divorce to court, you can expect the amount of your legal bills to run into five or six figures — as much as four times the cost of a negotiated divorce.

At a minimum, be prepared to incur the following expenses related to your divorce trial:

- ✔ Lawyer fees
- ✔ Filing fees
- ✔ Court reporter fees
- ✔ Expert fees

✔ Discovery fees

✔ Subpoena fees

✔ The cost of hiring an outside firm to prepare exhibits for the trial

✔ Miscellaneous legal expenses — copying, long-distance charges, postage, delivery fees, and so on

Keep in mind that this list covers only the monetary costs of a trial. We can't begin to calculate the cost to your family's health and happiness if you're embroiled in an ugly divorce trial.

Deciding to Settle after Beginning Your Trial Preparations

For various reasons, most contested divorces never go to trial — although they may get as far as the courthouse steps — because more often than not the attorneys for a couple are still trying to find a way to reach an agreement even as they prepare for a trial. At the same time that your attorney and your spouse's attorney are getting ready for your trial, they will most likely try to negotiate a resolution of all the issues in your divorce so a trial becomes unnecessary. And after the reality of going to court begins to sink in, you and your spouse may both have a change of heart and decide to work together to reach a divorce agreement.

If your attorneys are trying to hammer out a negotiated settlement agreement at the same time that they're preparing for a divorce trial, the process they use is much like the negotiation process we describe in Chapter 14. In other words, the attorneys use a back-and-forth negotiating process that involves communicating via phone, e-mail, and letters in an effort to resolve the outstanding issues in your divorce. Throughout the process your attorney keeps you informed about what is going on and consults with you whenever appropriate. Eventually through this process you and your spouse may reach an agreement on the final terms of your divorce and avoid a trial.

When your attorney tells you about an offer your spouse may have made to you in order to settle one of the outstanding issues in your divorce or about a counteroffer your spouse may have made in response to an offer you made, consider carefully what your spouse is offering so that you can decide how to respond. Keep an open mind and be open to compromise unless you are dead set on a trial. Although your spouse's offer may not be close to what you're legally entitled to, what your spouse can really provide, or what you think you need, it may be close to what you want. Although your attorney should provide you with his or her opinions about what you should do, the final decision is yours. Chapter 14 provides a series of questions that should help you decide how to respond to your spouse's offer.

Working Out Your Differences through a Pretrial Conference

If you and your spouse are unable (or unwilling) to resolve your differences by negotiating and your trial preparations move forward, the next step in those preparations may be for your attorney and your spouse's attorney to participate in something called a pretrial conference. You and your spouse may or may not attend this conference.

In some jurisdictions, pretrial conferences are mandatory; in other jurisdictions, they're used rarely. And, in some jurisdictions, before a divorcing couple can get a court date for their trial, they must use mediation to try to resolve the outstanding issues in their divorce. This requirement is particularly common in custody battles.

Big business in Splitsville, Nevada

During the first half of the 20th century, divorce was legal in all states, but people generally frowned upon it as scandalous — something "nice people" didn't do. In fact, to discourage couples from divorcing, state laws made certain that the divorce process would drag out as long as possible. But the law in one state was an exception to this rule. Nevada, a freewheeling, cash-poor frontier state at the start of the 20th century saw divorce as a potential source of considerable revenue. The state allowed a man or a woman who lived within its boundaries for a minimum of six months to walk into a courthouse, tell a judge why he or she wanted a divorce, and walk out a divorced person. As a result, countless unhappy couples, including the rich and famous, flocked to Reno, Nevada, to obtain their divorces.

In 1931, to capitalize on the income potential from being the country's new divorce mecca, the Nevada legislature shortened the residency period from six months to a mere six weeks, putting a Reno divorce within the financial reach of the average person. After that point, Reno's divorce business grew steadily, reaching a peak of more than 19,000 divorces a year by 1946.

Visitors to Reno in search of a quickie divorce spent their six-week waiting period living in hotels and boarding houses or at one of Reno's "divorce ranches." Male and female guests at a divorce ranch rode horses, swam, or skied (depending on the time of year) during the day and wagered money at Reno's gambling casinos or whiled away the hours at the divorce ranch bar in the evening. Local cowboys were on hand to help the female guests forget their troubles and maybe even indulge in a little romance while they waited to end their marriages. With America's eventual acceptance of divorce and the liberalization of state divorce laws throughout the country, the divorce ranch rode off into the sunset.

During a *pretrial conference* or *pretrial hearing,* a judge (who may or may not be the same judge who will preside over your divorce trial) listens to the two attorneys present information about the unresolved issues in your divorce. The judge may ask them questions to clarify exactly what your divorce trial will focus on. Also, during the pretrial conference, your attorney and your spouse's attorney go over the witnesses they intend to call during the trial and, in cooperation with the judge, they create a schedule for discovery. (See the "Gathering in-depth information" section of this chapter for more information on the discovery process.)

After listening to both attorneys during the pretrial conference, the judge may signal to them that he or she is unhappy that you and your spouse haven't been able to agree on the outstanding issues in your divorce. Your attorney may also get the impression that the judge is apt to rule against you on some of those issues. After the pretrial conference, your attorney will convey to you this information and anything else he or she learned during the meeting. If your attorney has the impression that the judge wants you to settle your divorce out of court or may not rule in your favor on certain issues, your attorney is likely to strongly encourage you to try to reach an agreement with your spouse instead of moving forward with a divorce trial.

If you and your spouse are unable to reach a negotiated settlement in your divorce prior to the start of your trial, you can reach an agreement even after your trial begins. If you find yourself in this situation and want to know what to anticipate, see the section "Deciding to Settle after Beginning Your Trial Preparations" earlier in this chapter.

Getting Ready for the Trial

Preparing for a divorce trial is time-consuming, which is why trials are so expensive. Your attorney must gather and review all the information related to your case, develop and refine his or her legal strategy, coordinate the production of exhibits, prepare you as well as your witnesses to take the stand, and make other preparations.

Deciding on a courtroom strategy

Preparing for a trial is somewhat like staging a dramatic play, but with you and your spouse as the reluctant "stars." The witnesses who take the stand are your supporting, or not-so-supporting actors.

To help stage your trial, your attorney outlines a trial strategy. The strategy provides an overview of everything your attorney will do to try to get you a favorable out-of-court settlement as quickly as possible, assuming that's a realistic goal, or to win your case, assuming it goes all the way to trial.

Your lawyer's strategy is either aggressive or nonaggressive:

- An *aggressive strategy* involves bombarding your spouse with claims of abuse, indifference, child neglect, infidelity, marital instability, hiding or wasting assets, and so on. It also involves filing a lot of pretrial motions, interrogatories, requests for depositions, and requests to produce documents, among other things.

  The tactics used in an aggressive strategy are intended to encourage your spouse to agree to an early out-of-court settlement. Under such pressure, your spouse may cry "uncle!" and agree to settle, especially if his or her financial resources are limited. On the other hand, such tactics could backfire, causing your spouse to respond in kind and to become more determined to go all the way to trial. In the end, however, most spouses resolve the issues in their divorce either before their trial begins or after it's underway because of the financial and emotional costs of a trial.

- A *nonaggressive strategy* is less hostile than an aggressive one. It relies more on informal discovery to get at the facts of the case and cooperation between attorneys to work out the terms of your divorce. This kind of strategy will be easier on your emotions and your pocketbook and is easier on your kids.

The strategy that your attorney chooses depends on several factors, including

- Your own desires and financial resources
- What your attorney thinks is best for your case
- The strategy that your spouse's attorney is likely to use
- Your attorney's style and the style of your spouse's attorney (some are scrappy street fighters and others are wily tacticians)

If you have concerns about the strategy your attorney proposes, speak up. Find out why the attorney feels that the strategy is appropriate and express any reservations you have about it. If you speak your mind and your attorney's response doesn't quell your concerns, you may want to consider hiring a different attorney. However, changing attorneys in midstream, particularly at this stage of your divorce, is expensive and will delay the completion of your divorce. The best way to ensure that you and your attorney see eye to eye on a trial strategy is to carefully select your divorce attorney. Chapter 13 explains how to find the right one for you.

Gathering in-depth information

One of the ways that your attorney (and your spouse's attorney) gather the information they need to represent you in your divorce is through informal or formal discovery:

- **Informal discovery** occurs when you and your spouse, working through your attorneys, willingly share information related to your case with one another. That information may include legal documents, financial records, medical files, and so on.

- **Formal discovery** involves the use of legal tools, such as depositions, requests to produce documents, and interrogatories to obtain information.

The discovery that attorneys do to prepare for a trial is in addition to any that both attorneys may have already done — formally or informally — to try to work out a negotiated divorce agreement between you and your spouse. Chapter 14 discusses the role that discovery can play when you and your spouse are working with attorneys to negotiate the terms of your divorce. It also provides additional information about the legal tools used during the formal discovery process.

Discovery costs can skyrocket in a litigated divorce. Ask your attorney what he or she can do to keep those costs down.

In order to make the discovery process less overwhelming and less costly, many state legislatures have passed discovery reform laws. The provisions of these laws include requiring the parties to any lawsuit to exchange basic information and documentation upfront in the process. Usually, the parties exchange basic financial information, such as bank statements and business records.

One of the reasons your attorney may use the formal discovery process is to find out about the witnesses that your spouse's attorney will be calling. Through the discovery process your attorney may also be able to get a short summary of what each witness knows about your divorce. If you know anything about the backgrounds of your spouse's witnesses that could undermine their credibility on the stand — alcohol or drug problems, spousal abuse, or criminal records, for example — be sure to share that information with your attorney.

If you contest the validity of the prenuptial or postnuptial agreement you and your spouse may have signed, a judge must rule on that issue before the court can make any decisions regarding how your marital property and debts will be divided and whether one of you must pay the other spousal support. To save time and money, your attorney should try to resolve this matter as quickly as possible because the judge's decision about it determines exactly what issues your trial will address and influences how much discovery your attorney may need to do.

Producing physical evidence

Your attorney may use physical evidence to bolster his or her arguments on your behalf or to undermine your spouse's position on a particular issue. Your attorney also must figure out how to address physical evidence that's damaging to your case that your spouse's attorney may introduce. Among other things, physical evidence can include

- ✔ Financial records
- ✔ Property appraisals
- ✔ Doctors' records
- ✔ Photos, letters, diaries, video tapes, and audio tapes
- ✔ Psychological evaluations
- ✔ Police reports and arrest records

Calling all witnesses

Your attorney and your spouse's attorney are likely to call witnesses to testify during your trial. In fact, your spouse's attorney may even put *you* on the stand, and your attorney may put your spouse on the stand.

Attorneys use witnesses to help establish certain facts in a case. For example, if you and your spouse are fighting over the custody of your kids, the attorneys may call witnesses to help establish which of you is the primary caregiver and *go-to parent* — the parent who takes your children to the doctor, attends parent-teacher conferences, takes them to and from day care, feeds them, clothes them, and so on. Doctors, psychologists, teachers, childcare workers, teachers, and neighbors commonly serve as witnesses in establishing which parent is the primary caregiver.

Before the start of your trial, your attorney interviews your witnesses to get a sense of what they'll say on the stand and how they're likely to hold up under cross-examination. Although your attorney won't tell your witnesses what to say, he or she may advise them about the points that they should try to make and the best way to get those points across.

The attorneys may call your friends, family members, coworkers, business associates, and even your children as witnesses. The attorneys may also call *expert witnesses* who have special training, education, or knowledge related to some aspect of your divorce, such as psychologists, business valuation specialists, doctors, real estate agents, social workers, and others with professional expertise.

Expert witnesses expect you to pay them for their time. Depending on the kind of witness and his or her reputation, an expert witness may charge several hundred dollars an hour. If you and your attorney ask these witnesses to do certain things to prepare for testifying — review documents or write a report, for example — they bill you for the time they take to do that work as well as for their time on the stand. Obviously, using expert witnesses can really increase the cost of your divorce.

Courts formally order witnesses to appear and testify in court via *subpoenas*. Subpoenaed witnesses who don't show up are escorted to court by a law enforcement officer or are charged with contempt of court.

Rehearsing for your big day (or days)

Prior to the start of your trial, your attorney should prepare you for what's to come. For example, your attorney may

- ✔ Walk you through the trial process.
- ✔ Review his or her trial strategy with you.
- ✔ Explain the points that you should make when you testify, even suggesting words or phrases you ought to use to help clarify your thoughts or to add weight to your statements.
- ✔ Review the questions that your spouse's attorney is likely to ask you and help you come up with answers for the more sensitive or difficult ones.
- ✔ Do some role-playing by grilling you as your spouse's attorney might do if he or she were trying to unnerve you or make you angry. Such role-playing can help build your confidence that you can handle whatever the attorney may dish out.
- ✔ Advise you on how to dress for behave in the courtroom.

Tell your attorney about any concerns you have about the trial. Your attorney can probably help alleviate your worries.

Remaining calm and collected

Feeling nervous about what to expect as your trial date approaches is normal. One way to alleviate some of those pretrial jitters is to visit the courthouse ahead of time so that you can see the layout of the courtroom and even sit in on someone else's divorce trial. If you know which judge is going to hear your case, try to attend a divorce trial that he or she is presiding over.

You may seethe with anger, quake with fear, or feel totally defeated when you're in the courtroom, especially when you're on the witness stand, but try to keep your cool. Also, be polite to everyone — including your spouse's attorney and, yes, even your spouse!

While you're preparing for your day in court, keep a few things in mind when you take the witness stand:

- ✔ Answer the questions you're asked in as few words as possible. If you give long, involved answers, you may say something that can hurt your case. If the attorney wants to know more, let him or her ask you another question.

- ✔ Pause before you answer a question so you give yourself time to think about what to say and so your attorney has time to object to the question, if necessary. If your attorney does object and the judge sustains the objection, the judge will tell you not to answer the question. Otherwise, you're expected to answer any question that an attorney asks you.

- ✔ If you're unnerved by a question or aren't sure how to respond, buy time to compose yourself and think about your answer by pouring yourself some water and having a sip. A pitcher of water and a glass should be sitting on the witness stand. If not, ask the judge for a glass of water.

- ✔ Your attorney may tell you not to hold back your tears when you're on the witness stand. Sincere tears can work to your advantage. Fake emotion can work against you, however.

- ✔ Sit up straight; don't slouch. Keep your hands folded in front of you on your lap and avoid angry hand gestures.

- ✔ Don't be rude, sarcastic, or argumentative with your spouse's attorney, even if his or her questions are offensive or upsetting. The attorney's strategy may be to make you mad or to get you to break down in tears.

- ✔ When you get off the stand, don't send dirty looks or expressions of exasperation in the direction of your spouse or your spouse's attorney. Maintain your dignity no matter what.

Understanding the Role of the Benchwarmers: Judges and Juries

Although some states require a judge to decide a divorce trial (this sort of trial is called a *bench trial*), other states let you opt to have a jury trial or a bench trial, but only Texas allows a jury to make custody decisions for divorcing couples. When you have the choice, deciding what kind of trial to ask for is an important strategic decision that you should make with your attorney. If one spouse wants a bench trial and the other wants a jury trial, the spouse wanting a jury trial prevails. However, the basic trial process is the same whether you opt for a judge or a jury trial.

Putting the decisions on one pair of shoulders: The judge

Regardless of whether you have a bench or jury trial, the judge who hears your case is responsible for ensuring that your trial is fair and that the attorneys follow the appropriate trial procedures. The judge also

- ✔ Listens to all the testimony and the attorneys' statements
- ✔ Reviews any exhibits that the attorneys may enter into evidence
- ✔ Rules on any objections that the attorneys may make to the introduction of the evidence
- ✔ Resolves any disagreements that may develop between the attorneys and steps in if someone gets unruly
- ✔ May ask questions of some of the witnesses
- ✔ May take notes during the trial, although a court reporter will be on hand to record every word said

Like other kinds of judges, family law judges tend to have reputations for running a certain type of court and for the way they tend to rule on certain issues. For example, some run their courtrooms with an iron fist; others give attorneys a great deal of leeway. (Many family court judges used to be divorce attorneys themselves.)

If your attorney knows which judge will hear your case and is familiar with the judge's style and reputation, your attorney will take those things into account when preparing for your trial. If your attorney isn't familiar with the judge, he or she should talk to an attorney who is.

Asking a jury to make decisions

If your divorce will be decided by a jury, your attorney and your spouse's attorney must select the members of the jury from a list developed by the district clerk in your jurisdiction before they can begin presenting their cases. The attorneys do this through the *voire dire* process, which involves asking potential jurors questions in order to assess their biases and prejudices. Based on the information the attorneys obtain from their questioning they decide who they want and don't want on the jury. (Each attorney gets to eliminate a certain number of potential jurors.)

After a jury has been selected, the judge swears in the jury members. Jury members are expected to show up on time each day for your trial, to listen carefully to the testimony, and to follow any instructions that the judge gives them. They may or may not be allowed to take notes during your trial, depending on the judge's rules for his or her courtroom.

After the attorneys have presented all the evidence in your trial and each attorney has made his or her final arguments, the jury begins deliberating on the issues in your divorce according to the judge's instructions. The jury members conduct their deliberations in the jury room after selecting a jury *foreperson* — the person who's in charge of the jury's deliberations and decision-making. If the jury has any questions about certain aspects of the testimony during your divorce trial, the jury foreperson writes them down and sends them to the judge. The judge answers the questions in the courtroom in the presence of the jury as well as you, your spouse, and your attorneys.

After the jury completes its deliberations, the jury foreperson lets the judge know, and the jury members are called into the courtroom to announce their decisions to you, your spouse, and your attorneys. The jury may reach its decisions after just an hour or two of deliberation, or they may take a longer amount of time — a day, several days, or even longer. How long the jury spends deliberating depends on the complexity of the issues in your divorce as well as on how well the jury members work together.

Glimpsing Life in the Courtroom

Weeks, maybe even months, after you or your spouse files for divorce, you finally get your day in court (assuming that you haven't reached an out-of-court settlement).

In the courtroom, you and your spouse sit with your respective attorneys at tables directly in front of the judge. If you haven't seen or spoken with your spouse in a while, you may feel unnerved and upset having to be in the same room with him or her; on the other hand, you may feel just plain glad that your day in court has finally arrived and that you will be divorced soon.

In case you're wondering, the courtroom dramas that you've read about in books or seen on TV rarely occur. Instead, as anyone who's watched Court TV knows, trials often move slowly with a lot of starts and stops. And, at times, the testimony can be boring and even confusing.

No matter how long you think you'll be sitting in front of the judge, never bring food, beverages, or reading materials into a courtroom. Doing such things isn't allowed in court, and the court bailiff will tell you to stop doing them. Furthermore, eating, reading, and so on while you're in court signals that you don't respect the legal process, which can ultimately hurt your case.

Although some trials take unexpected detours, they all follow a basic sequence of events. To help you make sense of what's happening in your trial, here's a brief rundown of what to expect:

1. **Opening statements.**

   Each attorney makes an initial statement to the judge about what he or she will prove during the trial. The plaintiff's attorney goes first. (The plaintiff is the spouse who filed the lawsuit in your divorce. A plaintiff is also referred to as the petitioner.) These statements set the stage for the evidence and arguments to come. However, one or both attorneys may elect to waive making an opening statement if your divorce trial is resolving just a few issues.

2. **The plaintiff's case.**

   The plaintiff's attorney presents his or her case first. The attorney presents evidence why the spouse he or she is representing should get what he or she wants. In order to help make a convincing argument, the attorney may call witnesses to the stand and question each of them. Then the defendant's attorney will probably question each witness during a process called *cross-examination.*

3. **Redirect and re-cross examinations.**

   After each witness has been examined and cross-examined, one or more of the witnesses may have to answer follow-up questions during redirect and re-cross examinations. Redirect and re-cross examinations are most likely to occur when a witness damages the plaintiff's case during cross-examination and needs to be *rehabilitated,* that is, something he or she said needs to be clarified or explained in a way that's more favorable to the plaintiff.

4. **The defendant's case.**

   The attorney for the spouse who's the defendant presents his or her case following the same procedures used by the plaintiff's attorney.

5. **Rebuttal by plaintiff.**

   After the defendant's case has been presented to the court, a *rebuttal* may or may not take place. Rebuttal allows the plaintiff's attorney to respond to comments the defense made. However, the attorney cannot introduce any new evidence during rebuttal.

6. Surrebuttal by defendant.

Surrebuttals are rare in a divorce trial but, when they do occur, they give the defendant's attorney an opportunity to deny or counter what the plaintiff's attorney said in rebuttal. The defense attorney cannot address anything else during surrebuttal.

7. Closing arguments.

During closing arguments, both attorneys get one last chance to make their cases. The plaintiff's attorney goes first. If only a few issues need to be resolved, the attorneys may decide to waive final arguments, although that is rare.

8. The ruling.

Depending on the complexity of the case, the judge in a bench trial may issue his or her decision right away or may take time to deliberate and return with a decision later. If the judge must decide more than one issue in your divorce, he or she makes multiple rulings.

If a jury is deciding the outcome of the trial, it begins its deliberations after closing arguments. When the jury finishes its deliberations, the jury's decisions are announced in the courtroom. The jury, the judge, or a court staff person may announce them.

Listen attentively to the courtroom proceedings. Take notes and, when you hear someone say something that you know isn't the truth, let your attorney know. You're better off passing your attorney a note than whispering in your attorney's ear. Whispering may make your attorney miss important testimony, and someone on your spouse's side may overhear your comments.

In most states, after you've heard how the judge rules on the issues in your divorce, if you're unhappy with something that the judge decided you have a short period of time, typically from 10 to 20 days, to file a *motion to reconsider* with the court. (You do not have this right if you had a jury trial.) If you file this motion, you're asking the judge to revisit his or her decision with the hope that the judge will decide to rule differently. However, unless you can prove that the judge made a mathematical mistake, overlooked important evidence, or misapplied the law, the judge is extremely unlikely to change his or her mind. If the judge denies the motion to reconsider or hears the motion and decides that his or her ruling was correct, you can always appeal. The section "Making an Appeal" later in this chapter explains the appeals process.

Following the Judgment

Although you may breathe a sigh of relief (or shed some tears) when you hear the judge's (or the jury's) decisions, your divorce isn't completely over when you walk out of the courtroom. You still have some work to do before your divorce is final. For instance, your attorney and your spouse's attorney must prepare a final divorce agreement and file it with the court, and you and your spouse must do whatever the agreement requires of you. For example, you may have to transfer assets to your spouse, pay off certain debts, and so on.

Putting the terms in writing

After the judge issues his or her decision or the jury's decision is announced, usually the attorney for whichever spouse filed for divorce drafts the *divorce decree* (a legal term for the written summary of what the judge ruled and of anything that you and your spouse may have agreed to on your own). The other attorney reviews the draft decree and notifies the attorney who prepared the draft whether any changes are necessary. At this point, the changes, if any, should be very minor. When a final draft of the divorce judgment is ready, the judge signs it. This usually happens between 10 and 20 days after the judge's or jury's decision.

After the judge approves your divorce decree, expect the following to happen:

- ✔ The provisions of the decree usually replace any temporary pretrial court orders.

- ✔ Your attorney gives you a copy of your signed divorce agreement. Now you're officially divorced. You will receive a copy of the judgment at a later date after the court processes all the paperwork. Make sure that your copy is certified (which means the copy will usually be pressed with a seal or a stamp).

- ✔ The attorney for the spouse who initiated your divorce files a record of your divorce in the vital records section of your state's Public Health Department.

Tending to final details

You and your attorney should review the details of the judge's decision and any aspects of your divorce that you may have negotiated with your now ex-spouse so that you understand your legal obligations to your ex as well as what you're entitled to. Another reason to review the decree carefully is to be clear about any actions you may need to take as a result of your divorce. For example, you may need to

- ✔ Transfer titles, deeds of trust, and other ownership documents.

- ✔ Exchange cash and other valuables. If your divorce was hostile and you anticipate further problems with your former spouse, you may want to make this exchange in front of a neutral third party so that neither of you can accuse the other of dishonesty.

✔ Amend your insurance policies or purchase new ones.

✔ Revise your will (or write a new one) and review the rest of your estate planning for possible changes now that you're divorced. For example, you need to revise your living trust if your ex is one of the trust beneficiaries.

In some states, when you get divorced, your will is automatically canceled, and so you must write a new one. In still other states, only the provisions in your will that directly relate to your ex are canceled automatically.

✔ Notify your creditors and the three national credit-reporting agencies about your name change, if you take back your maiden name. (You can find information about how to contact the credit-reporting agencies in Chapter 3.)

You should also notify the Social Security Administration (SSA) and your employer about your name change so that your earnings are properly reported to the SSA and so that it records that information properly. To get a form to report your name change to the SSA, go to www.ssa.gov or your local SSA office. You need to provide the SSA with identification that shows your old name and your new name; for example, you need a copy of your marriage certificate and your divorce decree. When the SSA receives all the necessary information, it sends you a new SSA card that reflects your name change.

Making an Appeal

You can appeal the court's decisions in your divorce if you have reason to believe that that some sort of error occurred during your trial. Your attorney can tell you whether you have a good basis for an appeal. If you do appeal, it will take up more of your time, cost you additional money, and involve you with the court once again.

You must file your appeal within a certain period of time after your trial ends; how long you have to file depends on your state. Your attorney can tell you how long you have and can also advise you of your chances of prevailing in an appeal case.

You can't appeal a judge's (or jury's) decisions just because you want to. You must have a legal basis for your appeal. For example, your attorney may try to use any of the following to justify the need for an appeal, among others: Your spouse withheld information, a witness for your spouse lied on the stand, a legal procedure wasn't followed appropriately during your trial, or the judge misinterpreted a law related to your divorce.

Time, money, and more court involvement aren't the only factors to consider when deciding whether to file an appeal. Keep these facts in mind, too:

- ✔ A court may not hear your appeal for months.

- ✔ While you're waiting to learn the outcome of your appeal, you, your spouse, and your kids live in a sort of limbo. And, if the appeals court does overturn the judge's decision, its action means that you're still married. The result: You face yet another divorce trial.

- ✔ Everyone in your family may already be emotionally worn out by your first divorce trial. A second one may be more than some members of your family can bear.

- ✔ You may have to find a new attorney to help you with your appeal, especially if your current attorney thinks that filing an appeal is pointless given the facts of your case.

- ✔ The appeals court may not throw out the judge's decision. Even if it does, you have no guarantee that you'll be happy with the outcome of your second trial. In fact, you can end up with a judgment you like even less than the first one!

Rather than trying to get the judge's decision overturned, if you don't like one or more provisions in it, you can leave the judgment in place and ask the court to modify those specific provisions by filing a *petition for modification.* Such a process is faster and less expensive than trying to get a judgment overturned and, if you're successful, going to trial again. Chapter 18 talks about modifications to a divorce decree.

Part V

After You're Officially Divorced: Avoiding Problems and Handling Challenges

In this part . . .

In this part of the book, we help prepare you for life after divorce. We discuss the kinds of final divorce-related details you may need to take care of, including transferring assets to your ex, paying some of your marital debts and redoing your estate plan (or maybe preparing a plan for the first time). We fill you in on the steps you may need to take now that you are fully responsible for your own finances, including suggestions for finding a job or getting a better one. We also alert you to some of the more common (and serious) problems that divorced people face and help you build your new life.

Chapter 17

Focusing on Your Postdivorce Financial Life

*A*fter you're officially divorced, your work isn't over. For example, depending on the details of your divorce decree, (or *final judgment of divorce*), you may have payments to make and legal paperwork to complete. As you find out in Chapter 16, your divorce decree spells out everything that you and your spouse agreed to in your divorce or that the judge (or jury) decided. Also, now that you're on your own, you are totally responsible for your own financial life, including managing your money, making sure you have the right insurance, doing the appropriate estate planning, and figuring out what to do if you're having a tough time making ends meet, among other responsibilities. You may decide to seek help from financial professionals, like a financial planner and a CPA.

Handling all of these responsibilities may sound like a formidable challenge, but with the right resources and a positive attitude, you can do it. You've already started by reading this chapter. It provides you with the information and advice you need to tie up the loose ends of your divorce, take control of your financial life, and handle any problems you may face in the months ahead. Among other things, the chapter highlights postdivorce estate-planning issues you may need to consider, suggests steps you can take to do a good job of managing your money, no matter your income, and provides essential advice about what to do when you can't meet all of your financial obligations. This chapter also offers advice and information that can help you earn more money or achieve your postdivorce educational and career goals.

Abiding by Your Divorce Decree

After your divorce, you can't just put your divorce decree in a drawer and forget all about it. Read the details of your divorce decree carefully and do exactly what it says you must do. For example, the decree may require you to accomplish specific tasks by certain dates, such as closing a joint checking account, paying off certain debts for your ex-spouse, and begin making monthly spousal support or child-support payments. Depending on the terms of your divorce, you may have to take care of other details (some of which may be a little complicated), like transferring legal ownership of property to your spouse, selling assets, and so on.

If you're unhappy with something in your divorce decree, comply with it anyway. If you thumb your nose at whatever legal obligations the divorce decree sets out for you because you don't like them, the battles that may have plagued the end of your marriage are likely to continue, and your ex-spouse may take you to court for not holding up your end of the divorce bargain. Going to court again will mean more legal hassles and expenses, including the cost of an attorney and more emotional upset. If you want the terms of your divorce modified, you can ask the court to reconsider the terms. (Chapter 18 provides details on modifying your divorce decree.)

After your divorce is over, your attorney should send you a letter stating exactly which of the final responsibilities spelled out in your divorce decree he'll take care of and which ones you must handle. If you don't receive such a letter, ask your attorney to prepare one for you. Use the letter as a checklist to make sure that you don't overlook any of your legal responsibilities.

Transferring assets

If the decree says that your former spouse is to become the sole owner of real property that you owned together — your home, land, or rental property, for example — you must transfer your interest in that property to your ex by giving him or her a signed copy of the deed. The deed will be recorded in the public records at the courthouse in the county where the property is located.

If the transferred property is associated with an outstanding debt, such as a mortgage or a home equity loan, you're still liable for that debt, even if your divorce decree says that your former spouse must pay it off. In other words, if your ex does not pay the debt, the creditor can look to you for payment. (See Chapter 8 for a discussion of the legal actions that you can take to protect yourself if your ex-spouse defaults on a debt she is responsible for paying according to the terms of your divorce.)

If you transfer stocks, bonds, or mutual funds to your former spouse, you do *not* have to pay a capital gains tax if their value has appreciated since you first purchased them.

States differ in their requirements for transferring the legal ownership of vehicles, boats, and motorcycles. Your divorce attorney should be able to advise you on the requirements in your state.

Paying off debts

If your divorce decree requires your former spouse to assume responsibility for paying some or all of the balances due on any of your marital debts, it's a good idea to notify your creditors in writing of that fact and to ask them to transfer the debts into your ex's name. The creditors aren't legally obligated to comply with your request and can still collect the debts from you if your former spouse doesn't pay them, but your letters help underscore who's supposed to satisfy those debts. And, as a friendly reminder of what you expect her to do, send your ex a copy of the letters.

If you want to be sure that your ex-spouse is paying off the marital debts she is responsible for according to your divorce decree, you may want to ask her to provide you with proof of each payment she makes — canceled checks for example. However, if there is a lot of bad feeling between the two of you, she may refuse to do that, and even if your divorce was amicable and your ex is fine with sending you proof every month, she may forget sometimes.

Another option, assuming the debts are still in your name, is to call the creditors your ex is supposed to be paying to confirm that each monthly payment has been made, or to go to the Web site of each creditor to check for yourself if you know the ID and password for each account.

Arranging for your own health insurance

If you were on your former spouse's employer-provided health plan, you need to decide sooner rather than later what you will do about health insurance now that you're divorced, unless your divorce decree requires your ex to provide you with health insurance. One option is for you to exercise your federal COBRA rights, which entitle you to remain on your ex's policy for up to 36 months. However COBRA is only an option if your former spouse works for a company with at least 22 employees. If you want COBRA coverage, be sure to let the health plan administrator for your ex's employer know about your decision no later than 60 days after your divorce is final.

Before you decide to remain on your ex's health insurance plan, note that every month you'll have to pay the full cost of the insurance; in other words, COBRA does not entitle you to benefit from the same employer subsidy that you and your ex enjoyed when you were married. Therefore, the cost of your COBRA coverage may be much more than you can afford or want to spend.

Check your divorce decree to see whether it requires your former spouse to pay the cost of your COBRA coverage for a certain period of time. If it does, it may also require your ex to provide you with a monthly proof of payment so that you can be sure that your coverage doesn't lapse due to nonpayment.

Another option if you're working outside the home and your employer offers health insurance, is to enroll in its plan. If this is not an option for you, you can purchase an individual health insurance policy; however, this kind of policy tends to be pricey and may be difficult to obtain if you have any pre-existing health problems. If you do find one, the policy may not cover those problems for six months or longer, or it may never cover them at all if the problems are very serious. An insurance broker or agent can help you explore your options. The upcoming section "Making Sure You Have the Right Insurance" provides more information about your health insurance options.

Protecting your pension rights

If your divorce decree gives you the right to collect a portion of your former spouse's pension benefits, profit-sharing money, 401(k) funds, or other deferred retirement income when your ex becomes eligible to retire, your attorney must prepare a special type of court order called a QDRO (Qualified Domestic Relations Order) during your divorce and send the completed document to the bank or brokerage firm where the retirement funds are located or to the employer who's administering your ex's retirement benefits. Without a QDRO, you cannot be certain that you'll get your share of those retirement assets when the time comes. (Chapter 8 provides a more complete explanation of QDROs.)

Rethinking Your Estate Planning

If you prepared a will when you were married, you should revisit that legal document now that you're divorced. Like most divorcees, you will want to revise it so that any assets you earmarked for your former spouse will go to someone else when you die. In some states, however, any provisions in a will that relate to an ex-spouse are automatically canceled when a couple's divorce is final, while in other states, a divorce completely voids a divorced spouse's will, leaving him with no will at all. A divorce attorney or an estate-planning attorney can tell you how the law in your state works.

If your state law doesn't provide for canceling your will or its provisions related to your ex, you'll probably want to remove all mention of your spouse from your will, either by amending that document or canceling it and writing a new will. Find out from an estate planning attorney whether, from a legal standpoint, you're better off amending or canceling your will and exactly how to do whatever your attorney advises. If you don't amend or cancel your will exactly the right way, your action may not be legally valid, and your will then stands as though you never changed it.

If you set up a *testamentary trust* (a trust that is inside your will and activated upon your death) or a living trust while you were married and made your spouse the beneficiary of the trust, you will almost certainly want to change that estate planning document, too. An estate-planning attorney can advise you about how to go about amending it and about how to revise or cancel any other estate-planning documents you may have prepared that involved your former spouse. Those documents may include

- ✔ Durable powers of attorney for your finances and your healthcare, if you gave those powers to your spouse while you were married.
- ✔ Your life insurance policies, if your former spouse is their beneficiary.
- ✔ Other assets for which you designated your former spouse as a beneficiary. Those assets may include your IRA, retirement plan, and some types of bank accounts.

For an easy-to-understand primer about all aspects of estate planning, check out *Kiplinger's Estate Planning,* by John Ventura (Kaplan Publishing).

If you don't have a will, write one now

Getting divorced is a good excuse for writing a will if you don't have one already. A will is the foundation of most estate plans and spells out what you want to happen to your assets when you die, among other things. If you die without a will, the laws of your state determine which of your *legal heirs* inherits your property. Your legal heirs are the people you are related to — your children, parents and siblings, for example. If you die without a will, your best friend, unmarried partner, favorite charity, or alma mater won't receive any of your estate. By the way, regardless of which state you reside in, the law will not treat your ex-spouse as one of your legal heirs, so he or she will not inherit from you if you die without a will.

If as a result of your divorce you end up with assets that you and your former spouse owned *jointly with the right of survivorship* — real estate, for example — and the ownership documents are not changed to make you their sole owner, your ex will automatically own 100 percent of them when you die.

You cannot transfer certain types of assets through a will, including assets for which you have already designated a beneficiary. For example, when you purchased a life insurance policy, you indicated who should receive the policy proceeds upon your death — your policy beneficiaries. Regardless of what your will may say about those proceeds, the insurance company from whom you purchased the policy automatically distributes that money to your policy beneficiaries after you die. An asset that you own with someone else, like an asset that you and one or more other people legally own together as *joint tenants with the right of survivorship,* is another example of an asset that you cannot transfer to someone using your will. That's because given the way the asset is titled, it automatically goes to your co-owners when you die.

Besides giving you control over what will happen to most types of assets that you own when you die, your will is the legal document you use to designate

- ✔ **The adult you want to raise your kids if you die or become mentally or physically incapacitated while they're still minors.** This person is called a *personal guardian.* Most likely, if you're the custodial parent and your former spouse is still alive, she would raise them after your death. However, if she were already deceased at the time of your death or wasn't able to raise them for some reason (like the court decides that your ex is an unfit parent; your ex is in prison; your ex is very ill, and so on) and you died without a will, the court would decide who would raise your kids and might choose someone you don't like or don't trust or someone who doesn't share your values or philosophy about parenting. This person could be one of your family members or a close friend. If none of your relatives or friends were willing or able to raise your children, they would be placed in foster care until they could be adopted.

  If you don't want your former spouse raising your children, maybe because you believe that she wouldn't do a good job, be sure to designate a personal guardian. Provide the executor of your will with a written explanation of your rationale for wanting someone other than your former spouse to raise your kids in the event of your death. (An *executor* is the adult you choose to carry out the wishes you express in your will after you die. You must designate an executor in your will. You should name an alternate executor, too.)

- ✔ **The adult you want to manage the property you've left to your minor children.** This person is called a *property guardian.* Your children's property guardian manages their assets until your children become legal adults. You need a property guardian if the property you leave to your children is worth more than the amount your state says a minor child can own without having an adult in charge of the assets; in most states, the maximum amount ranges from about $2,500 to $5,000.

  If you don't name a property guardian in your will, and you die while your children are still minors, the court will name someone to play that role. Most likely it would designate your ex-spouse assuming he or she were still alive and mentally competent, but the court might name instead one of your relatives or close friends, a bank, or an attorney.

Parents often name the same person to serve as their children's property and personal guardian. However, this arrangement doesn't always make sense because each job requires quite different characteristics and abilities. For a personal guardian, you want someone who shares your values and is nurturing, affectionate, and a fair disciplinarian. However, the person you choose for that role may not have the financial management skills and know-how that a property guardian should have.

Considering other kinds of estate planning

A will isn't your only option for making sure that your young children are financially provided for if you die while they're still minors. We highlight some of those alternatives in this section. An estate-planning attorney can help you decide which ones are most appropriate for you.

Even if you use some of the options in this section, you still need to use your will to designate a personal guardian for your minor children and to designate a property guardian for any assets you may leave to them in your will.

Custodial accounts

One easy and inexpensive option for leaving assets to your young children is to set up a *custodial account* for each child at a bank or brokerage house. You can transfer assets that you own to each account while you're alive, or you can arrange to have them transferred after your death through your will or living trust. When you set up a custodial account, you designate an adult as the account *custodian.* This person manages the account assets and possibly disperses money generated by those assets to your children while they're minors. (While you're alive, you can be the custodian for each account you set up.) When your children become legal adults, they get full control of the assets in their custodial accounts; in some states, you can specify that your children gain control of the accounts when they reach age 25.

The particular kinds of assets you can transfer to a custodial account depend on whether your state has adopted the Uniform Gifts to Minors Act (UGMA) or the Uniform Transfers to Minors Act (UTMA). Under the UGMA, you can transfer bank accounts, mutual funds, stocks, annuities, and insurance policies to a custodial account. The UTMA also allows you to transfer real estate.

Testamentary trust

You can provide for your young children by including a *testamentary trust* in your will. This type of trust exists only on paper while you're alive and is activated by your death. In your trust document, you indicate what assets you want transferred to the trust upon your death. The assets might include jewelry, antiques, fine art, money, rare books, real estate, and so on.

In the trust document, you designate a trustee to manage the trust assets after it is activated. The trustee can be someone you know (and trust), a trust company, or a bank trust department. One of the advantages of a testamentary trust is that you can control how the assets must be managed while your children are still minors as well as when your children can take possession of those assets after they become legal adults (You may indicate in the trust document that they cannot take control of the assets until they reach age 25, for example.) and what they can use the assets for. You cannot do any of these things with a will only.

Living trust

Another kind of trust you may want to set up for your minor children is a living trust. This type of trust exists outside of your will, unlike a testamentary trust. While you're alive, you can transfer assets into and out of the trust, and you can manage and control them if you designate yourself as trustee of the trust. However, you can designate someone else as trustee, and that person is legally obligated to manage the assets according to the instructions you set out in your living trust agreement. Whatever you do, be sure to also designate a successor trustee who will manage the trust if the first trustee dies or becomes too ill to fulfill his responsibilities. Like a testamentary trust, a key benefit of a living trust is that it maximizes the amount of control you have over when your children receive the trust assets as well as how the assets can be used and how they must be managed.

A living trust can be either revocable or irrevocable. Irrevocable living trusts are most commonly used by individuals with very large estates who want to minimize the amount of estate taxes they will owe when they die. If you set up an *irrevocable living trust,* you cannot remove any of the assets you put into the trust or make other changes to the trust. A *revocable living trust* is much more versatile and flexible; while you are alive, you can change anything you want about the trust. Therefore, revocable living trusts tend to be more popular than irrevocable living trusts, even though they provide you with no estate-tax benefits.

If you want to use a living trust to help care for your children after your death (or in the event of your incapacitation), you must decide exactly what kind of living trust to set up. You have many options, including a *common* or *shared trust* that benefits all your children, a *separate trust* for each child, and a *special needs trust* for a child who's mentally or physically incapacitated, among other types of living trusts.

Do not try to decide what type of living trust is best for your children or to set up your own trust. Trusts are complicated legal entities, and so you (and your kids) are best off if you work with an estate-planning attorney who has a lot of living trust experience.

Life insurance

A very affordable way to leave your children a substantial amount of money is to purchase a life insurance policy and to designate them as the policy beneficiaries. If you die while they're still minors, their property guardian will manage the policy proceeds on their behalf; if they are adults when you die, they will have full control over that money after the insurance company pays it to them. Alternatively, you can provide that, upon your death, the proceeds must be transferred to a living trust that you've set up for your children. If that happens, whomever you designated as trustee of the trust manages the proceeds according to your instructions.

Other estate-planning options

Making your minor children the beneficiaries of your employee benefits plan or IRA are two other ways to take care of them after you die. Again, depending on the value of those assets, you may have to name an adult to manage them for your children. Whether you arrange to have the assets paid directly to your children, transferred to a trust or deposited in a custodial account, you must name an adult to manage them while your kids are still minors. Your estate-planning attorney, financial advisor, or plan administrator can provide you with helpful advice on this topic.

Taking Charge of Your Finances

After you're officially divorced, you are 100 percent responsible for the state of your finances. Having to make every money-related decision yourself may seem daunting — especially if, like most divorced people, you ended up with something less than you'd hoped for from your divorce. For example, you may have received fewer marital assets, been saddled with more debt, or received less child support and spousal support than you had wanted. On the other side of the coin, if you're the one who's obligated to make those support payments, you may be paying more than you wanted to. If you begin having trouble making ends meet as a result, read the upcoming section "Taking the Right Steps When Your Finances Are Falling Apart."

Good credit histories and high FICO scores are essential to your being able to build and maintain a stable financial life for yourself and your family. Without them, you won't be able to get credit at a reasonable rate if you want to finance the purchase of an asset that you cannot afford to buy with cash, like a new car or a home, for example. Chapter 3 tells you about building a credit history in your own name.

If you haven't done so yet, prepare a monthly budget for your household. A budget is an essential tool for helping you live within your means and make every dollar count. If you prepared a postdivorce budget in preparation for your divorce negotiations, be sure to modify that budget after your marriage has ended so that it reflects the realities of your current postdivorce finances. Chapter 5 steps you through the budget-building process.

If you feel that you need to improve your money management skills, there are many good resources, including Web sites like Bankrate.com, `www.bankrate.com` and Credit.com, `www.credit.com`, books like *Personal Finance For Dummies* by Eric Tyson (Wiley) and magazines like *Kiplinger's Personal Finance Magazine,* which covers a wide range of personal finance topics.

As you get your finances in order, you may want to get help from financial professionals like a financial planner or a CPA. The upcoming section "Enlisting financial professionals" reviews the different types of financial professionals you may want to work with and tells you how each one can help you.

If you're obligated to pay spousal or child support, managing your money is particularly important because if you fall behind on those payments and your former spouse takes you to court to collect the past due support you owe her, arguing that you "just ran out of money" won't cut it with the judge!

Enlisting financial professionals

Like many people, you may want to manage your finances with the help of professionals. Which professionals you work with depends in part on your level of financial knowledge and how confident you are about your money-management abilities, the amount of time you have to spend on financial matters, the value and complexity of the assets you own, and your financial goals. The following sections offer a short rundown of the kinds of expertise and services each type of professional can offer you.

If you're in the market for advice from any of these financial professionals, get recommendations from friends and family members, your divorce attorney, any financial professionals you may already be working with, and so on. Then interview several possible candidates. Come to the interviews with a set of questions and learn about the credentials of each person you interview. And don't forget to get references from them *and* to check those references!

Financial planner

A financial planner can help you define your short- and long-term financial goals and figure out how to achieve them.

When you're looking for a financial planner, steer clear of those who make their money from the commissions they earn selling specific financial products, like insurance. These financial planners have a financial incentive to push you toward whatever they're selling, which means that their advice may not be in your best interest. A far better option is to work with a financial planner who either makes money by charging you a percentage of the total value of the assets he or she manages or invests for you or who charges you by the hour.

Regardless of how a financial planner charges, you're best off hiring one with the letters CFP for Certified Financial Planner after his or her name. This designation means that the financial planner has received extensive financial education on a wide range of subjects, passed tests on those topics and has experience advising clients about them.

Certified Public Accountant (CPA)

A CPA is a good choice if you need help with your taxes, if you want advice about how to minimize your tax liability, or if you want to know what you can do to reduce the amount of estate taxes your heirs will have to pay when you die. And if you end up on the wrong side of Uncle Sam or your state taxing authority, a CPA can help you resolve your problem.

Some CPAs receive special training in order to become Personal Financial Specialists (PSE). PSEs offer many of the same kinds of services as financial planners do. In fact, if you decide to work with a financial planner, he or she may be a PSE.

Insurance agent or broker

An *insurance agent* works for one or more insurance providers as an independent contractor and is licensed by the provider to represent it in the marketplace. For example, the agent may work for State Farm, Metropolitan Life, AllState, and so on. An *insurance broker,* on the other hand, works for you and shops around among many insurance companies to find the best deal.

An agent or broker can help you assess your insurance needs and make sure that you purchase the policies that meet those needs. The most common kinds of insurance are life insurance, health insurance, auto insurance, and homeowners insurance. Other kinds of insurance include disability insurance and long-term-care insurance.

Estate planning attorney

An estate planning attorney can help you define your estate planning goals and then figure out the best way to achieve them given the value of your estate, the kinds of assets that you own, and your family situation. He or she can also help you write your will and can prepare any other legal documents that you may decide to include in your estate plan, such as a living trust.

Rather than hiring an estate-planning attorney to help you prepare your plan, you may decide to prepare your own will or living trust using estate-planning software. If you do, you may want to meet with an estate-planning attorney first to find out whether using such software would not be a good idea given your finances or family situation. The attorney can also get you up to speed on the different estate-planning and property laws you should be aware of before you begin work on your plan.

Making sure you have the right insurance

An important part of managing your own finances is having the right types and amounts of insurance. Insurance helps protect you in the event of a problem like a car accident, a hospitalization, a house fire, a flood, and so on. Certain kinds of insurance are mandatory, such as liability insurance for your car and homeowner's insurance if you're still paying a mortgage, while other kinds of insurance, like disability and long-term-care insurance, are optional. Life insurance can be an important part of your estate plan.

An insurance agent or broker or your financial planner can help you determine the kinds and amounts of insurance you need. As your life changes — the value of your assets grows, you open a business, you grow older, for example — your insurance needs are likely to change. Therefore, you need to review periodically the risks in your life relative to your current insurance coverage and the amounts of that coverage.

The most common kinds of insurance are

- ✔ **Auto insurance.** Nearly every state requires car owners to have liability insurance. This kind of insurance protects you if you cause a car accident that results in property damage or injury. You can also purchase additional kinds of auto-related insurance such as insurance that pays your expenses if you're hit by an uninsured driver; collision insurance that pays to have your car repaired; and comprehensive insurance that pays for any damage caused to your car by a non-accident. For example, a tree falls on your car during a windstorm.

  Some states have no-fault liability insurance, meaning that regardless of who caused an accident, your insurance company reimburses you for any physical harm you may have suffered in the accident. It may also pay for the damage done to your vehicle.

- ✔ **Homeowner's insurance.** If you're paying a mortgage, your mortgage lender requires you to insure your home for a certain amount. The cost of your insurance may be built into your monthly mortgage payments, or you may pay the insurance premiums separately.

✔ **Renter's insurance.** If you're renting a place to live, you need to have renter's insurance; most landlords have only the insurance that covers structural damage to your apartment. In other words, if your belongings are ruined because of a broken pipe or if everything you own is destroyed in a fire, your landlord's insurance probably won't help you. Renter's insurance is very affordable.

✔ **Health insurance.** This kind of insurance helps pay for the costs of your prescription drugs, doctor visits, medical tests and treatments, and hospital visits. If you're lucky, you receive your health insurance through your employer, and your employer pays for most or all of it. Otherwise, you must purchase your own insurance. (If you opt to stay on your ex's health insurance under COBRA after your divorce, that coverage lasts for only 36 months and is expensive.) If you purchase your own health insurance, choosing the best plan for you can be very confusing, so it's best to work with an insurance agent or broker.

If your income is low and you own few assets, you may qualify for Medicaid, which is a federal-state health insurance program. To find out more about the program, go to www.cms.hhs.gov/home/medicaid.asp. Also, you may be eligible to enroll your children in your state's children's health insurance program. (Every state is required to have such a program.) You can get more information about the program at www.insurekidsnow.gov or by calling 1-877-543-7669.

✔ **Life insurance.** When you purchase this kind of insurance, you designate who will receive the policy benefits when you die. Purchasing life insurance and making your minor children the policy beneficiaries is a good way to provide for them financially in the event that you die while they are still minors. If your children are already adults, making them the beneficiaries of a life insurance policy is a very affordable way to leave them with a substantial sum of money after your death.

Term and whole life insurance are the two most common kinds of life insurance. A *term policy* is pure life insurance. If you die while the policy is still in effect (during the *term* of the policy) it pays a benefit to your designated policy beneficiaries. A *whole life policy,* on the other hand, combines insurance with a tax-deferred savings account. Your monthly or quarterly premiums not only pay for the cost of your insurance but help fund the savings portion of the policy. Most financial experts recommend purchasing a term life insurance policy and building up your savings separate from your insurance plan.

You may want other kinds of insurance, as well. For example, disability insurance helps pay your bills if you become ill or injured and are unable to work, and long-term-care insurance helps pay for a stay in a nursing home if you become chronically ill or injured and contributes to costs for assisted living, home health care, hospice care, adult day care, and the like. Whether these or any other kinds of insurance are right for you depends on a variety of factors including your age, health status, finances, and so on. Your best bet is to consult with a trusted financial professional, like an insurance agent or broker or a financial planner before you make insurance-buying decisions.

Taking the Right Steps When Your Finances Are Falling Apart

Whether you're preparing a household budget for the first time by following the instructions in Chapter 5 or updating your budget to reflect any payments you'll be receiving or making as a result of your divorce, you may find that you owe more each month than the amount of income you receive. Whatever the reason for your budget shortfall, reducing your expenses so that your total monthly expenses become lower than your total monthly income is critical.

Ideally, you also have enough money left over each month that you can make regular contributions to savings. Not having money in savings is akin to walking on a financial tightrope without a safety net. In other words, you have nothing to fall back on in the event of a financial set back. If reducing your spending is not enough to erase your monthly deficit, then you should look for ways to earn more money, maybe by working outside the home, finding a job that pays more than the one you have now, or getting a second one. We tell you how to do that in the last section of this chapter, "Finding a Job or Landing a Better One."

For help putting your spending on a diet or increasing your financial IQ, get in touch with a financial planner or contact a nonprofit debt-counseling organization affiliated with the National Foundation for Credit Counseling, most of which are Consumer Credit Counseling Service (CCCS) offices. These offices offer low-cost or no-cost debt counseling, money management, and budgeting assistance. A CCCS counselor may also be able to help you negotiate lower monthly payments to your creditors if you owe more than you think you can pay given your monthly income. If you can't find a CCCS office in your local phone book, call the organization's national office at 800-388-2227 or go to www.nfcc.org.

When you are having trouble making ends meet, you need to face facts right away and take the appropriate steps to address your situation. Otherwise, your money mess will only get worse. The following sections offer strategies for getting your finances under control in addition to cutting your budget and making more money.

Pay some bills and not others

If you've reduced your spending as much as possible and increased your income but still can't make ends meet, you need to decide which bills you'll pay and which ones you'll let slide for now. You should make every effort to keep up with the financial obligations that are associated with the most serious consequences if you don't pay them. Those obligations include

- **Secured debts, like a car loan, mortgage, or home equity loan.** If you don't pay one of your secured debts, the creditor will take back its collateral eventually because it has a lien on the asset that secures the debt. For example, if you ignore your car loan, you risk losing it in a repossession. If your home is foreclosed on, you lose your home and any equity you had in it.

  Falling behind on your car loan is especially risky because in most states your auto lender can take your car without giving you any warning or opportunity to get make your past due payments. Also, depending on the terms of your auto loan, your lender may have the right to repossess your vehicle if you miss just a single payment!

  If you're paying on a boat, an RV, or a car that you don't need, or on some other nonessential secured asset, consider giving that asset back to the lender voluntarily. The lender will sell the asset and apply the sale proceeds to the outstanding balance on your loan. If you're lucky, the proceeds pay your loan in full. Otherwise you'll be obligated to pay the difference (or *deficiency*). By giving the asset back voluntarily, you avoid having to reimburse the lender for the expenses it incurs taking the asset back, and you avoid having a repossession in your credit histories.

- **Essential living expenses.** These expenses include your rent (assuming you aren't a homeowner), utilities, groceries, gas for your car if you must drive it to earn a living, necessary insurance, and so on. Even though these expenses are necessary, you still need to do everything you can to minimize your spending on each of them. For example, you may want to move to a less expensive apartment when your lease is up and keep your home cooler in the winter and warmer in the summer.

- **Federal income taxes.** If you can't pay your taxes, contact the IRS and ask for an installment plan or an *Offer in Compromise,* which allows you to settle the full amount of your tax debt for less than what you owe, but don't just ignore your tax obligation. The IRS can do just about whatever it wants to collect past-due taxes from you, and while your taxes are past due, interest and penalties grow the total amount of money that you owe. If you have a problem paying your taxes, ask a CPA to contact the IRS about the possibility of a payment plan or an Offer in Compromise instead of going it alone; you're more apt to get what you want.

- **Federal student loans.** If you ignore this obligation, the IRS can take any tax refunds you're entitled to in order to collect what you owe, or it may order your employer to take the money out of your paychecks.

- **Other important financial obligations.** Don't neglect whatever child support the court ordered you to pay, the state income taxes you owe, your homeowner's insurance and property taxes, your health insurance payments and your medical bills. Not paying these obligations can have serious consequences for you and your children.

For complete information and advice about how to manage your debts, detailed explanations of how the foreclosure and repossession processes work, and an easy-to-understand explanation of the ins and outs of filing for bankruptcy, pick up a copy of *Managing Debt For Dummies*, by John Ventura and Mary Reed (Wiley).

If you have money left over after you pay your most important expenses and debts, use that money to pay your unsecured debts — the debts that you didn't collateralize with one of your assets. Focus on those with the highest interest rates. Credit card debts are the most common example of unsecured debts.

If you can't afford to pay your unsecured debts, the creditors you don't pay may try to collect what you owe to them by

- Turning your debt over to a debt collector.

- Suing you in order to get the court's permission to take one of your assets, put a lien on one of your assets to prevent you from selling that asset, borrowing against the asset, or transferring it, unless you pay what you owe first.

- Taking a portion of your wages each month. This is called *garnishing your wages*. Pennsylvania, South Carolina, and Texas do not allow wage garnishment.

Consider paying important debts by selling assets you own outright and don't need. Doing so could help you hold on to your home, the car you use to get to and from work, and so on.

Contact your creditors

If you continue to struggle even after you've reduced your expenses, contact your creditors right away to try to negotiate more affordable debt-payment plans. If you think your financial situation will improve soon, you may want to ask for a temporary reduction in your monthly payments or for permission to make interest-only payments for a while. However, if you believe your financial problems are going to be long-lived, try to negotiate a permanent reduction in your payments.

Don't contact your creditors until you have a clear idea of exactly how much you can afford to pay on your debts each month. If they agree to let you pay less and then you can't keep up with the reduced amounts, your creditors are unlikely to agree to additional reductions.

The creditors you should contact first include

- ✔ Secured creditors like your mortgage holder and the company that has your car loan

- ✔ Your landlord if you're a renter and you've fallen behind on your rent

- ✔ Your former spouse if you have fallen behind on your child support

- ✔ The IRS and state and local taxing authorities if you're behind on any of your taxes

- ✔ The bank that gave you a federal student loan, if you're behind on that debt or about to fall behind on it

- ✔ Your utility companies

If you feel uncomfortable doing your own negotiating, contact a nonprofit credit-counseling agency in your area. Two good resources for locating a reputable agency are the National Foundation for Credit Counseling, www.nfcc.org, or the Association of Independent Consumer Credit Counseling Agencies, www.aicca.org.

Consolidate your debts

If you earn a stable income and feel that your job is secure, one way to take the financial pressure off is to consolidate your debts. This involves paying off existing debt with new debt. However, debt consolidation makes sense only if the interest rate on the new debt is lower than the rates on the debts you pay off and if your new monthly debt payment is less than the total combined monthly payments on your old debts. Also, it's almost always a bad idea to pay off unsecured debt with secured debt. For example, don't borrow against the equity in your home to wipe out credit card debt.

Never borrow against your home unless you're absolutely sure that you can repay the loan! Otherwise you risk losing your home.

Your debt consolidation options include

- ✔ **Transferring existing credit card debt to another credit card with a lower interest rate.** Read all of the fine print about the balance transfer offer. Make sure the terms and conditions are reasonable and that you can meet each and every one of them. If you fail to comply with just one term or condition, the interest rate on the transferred balances may skyrocket and you could find yourself paying more for the new debt than you were paying in total for the individual debts that you consolidated.

Be sure that the interest rate on the card you want to transfer your credit card balances to isn't a teaser rate, unless you're absolutely certain that you can pay off the new debt before the teaser rate expires. If you can't, the debt that is still outstanding when the teaser rate ends may be higher than the rates you were paying on your original credit card debts.

- **Borrowing money from your bank.** Two possibilities are to get a home equity loan or to refinance your existing mortgage and add to the loan additional money to pay off the debt you want to get rid of. A couple problems are associated with these options, however. First, if you are a poor credit risk, you may not qualify for a new loan, or the loan you're offered may have a very high interest rate. Second, if you're able to pay off unsecured debt by getting a home equity loan or by refinancing your current mortgage, you are putting your home at risk because it will serve as your loan collateral. Therefore, if you fall behind on your loan payments, you could end up losing your home.

- **Borrowing against the cash value of your whole life insurance policy.** A whole life policy includes a savings component, or cash value, that grows over time. The insurance company won't review your credit histories or check out your FICO scores to see whether you qualify for the loan; you won't have to fill out a loan application; and you won't even need to repay the loan unless you want to. However, if you don't repay the loan, the beneficiary of your policy will receive the total value of your policy minus the outstanding balance on your loan when you die.

- **Borrowing against your retirement account.** If you have a 401(k) or 403(b) retirement account, you can probably borrow against the funds that are in the account, up to a certain amount or percentage of the account's value. You won't need to fill out a credit application, and your credit histories or FICO scores won't be reviewed. However, you must repay the loan within 5 years; if you don't, you'll be charged a 10 percent penalty on the unpaid balance assuming if you're under age 59½ when you borrow the money. If you're younger than 59½, the IRS will treat whatever money you do not repay as earned income and you'll be taxed on that income. As a result, when April 15th comes around, you may not be able to afford to pay your tax debt. If you can't, you'll have even bigger financial problems than you have now, because the IRS will charge you interest and penalties on your outstanding tax debt and because the IRS has virtually unlimited powers to collect taxes owed. For most people, borrowing against a retirement account is a *really* bad idea.

If you aren't sure which debt consolidation option is best for you or if you need help evaluating credit card balance transfer options, talk with a CPA or financial planner or meet with a credit counselor at a nonprofit credit counseling agency.

File for bankruptcy

When you see no light at the end of the financial tunnel despite your best efforts to pare back your spending, increase your income, work with your creditors or deal with your debts in some other way, it may be time to consider filing for bankruptcy. If you're in danger of losing your home in a foreclosure, losing your car in a repossession, or having your utility services cut off, or if the IRS or another creditor is preparing to seize the funds in your bank account, take other assets you own, or garnish your wages, make an appointment with a bankruptcy attorney immediately.

Bankruptcy is a complicated legal process, so never try to handle your own bankruptcy. Work with an experienced consumer bankruptcy attorney. The attorney will evaluate your finances to determine whether you can avoid bankruptcy. If bankruptcy is inevitable, she will make sure that all of your bankruptcy forms are filled out correctly and filed on time, deal with your creditors for you, and help you maximize the benefits of filing. For a detailed explanation of the consumer bankruptcy process and information to help you decide whether bankruptcy is your best option, read *The Bankruptcy Handbook* (Kaplan Publishing) by John Ventura.

You must meet with a federally approved credit counseling agency sometime during the 180 days prior to filing for bankruptcy. If the agency finds that you can't avoid a bankruptcy, it will give you a Certificate of Compliance. You cannot file without that document. For a list of federally approved agencies, go to www.usdoj.gov/ust/eo/bapcpa/ccde/cc_approved.htm.

Depending on your financial situation, you will file either a Chapter 7 liquidation bankruptcy or a Chapter 13 reorganization bankruptcy. Either type of bankruptcy protects you from most creditor collection actions, gives you time to figure out what to do about the money you owe, and helps you get rid of some or all of your unsecured debts.

If you file Chapter 13 bankruptcy, your payments to your creditors are reduced to amounts you can afford, and you get up to five years to pay off what you owe. You may also be able to reduce the total amount of money that you owe to your secured creditors and get rid of some of your debts.

A Chapter 7 bankruptcy wipes out more debts than a Chapter 13 but in exchange, you'll probably have to give up more assets. Those assets will be sold and the sales proceeds will be applied to your debts. Your priority debts (like your past-due spousal or child-support obligation, any past-due taxes you may owe, as well as the wages you may owe to your employees if you're self-employed) will be in line to get paid first. Most likely, your unsecured creditors — credit card companies, for example — will get little or nothing in your bankruptcy. At the end of your Chapter 7 bankruptcy, your unpaid unsecured debts are wiped out, which means that you won't have to pay them.

Finding a Job or Landing a Better One

When you take a hard look at your budget and assess all your options, you may decide that meeting all of your financial obligations or having the kind of lifestyle you want is impossible unless you increase your income. To do that, you need to work outside the home, find a better-paying job, earn additional money with a second job, or do freelance work on the side.

If you're entering the work world for the first time or if you haven't worked outside the home for many years, you may be unsure about what kind of career you're suited for, or you may not have a good sense of what kinds of careers are available to you. A career counselor or career coach can assess your job skills and interests, suggest things that you can do to make yourself more marketable, and advise you about the types of jobs for which you may be suited. A career counselor or career coach may also help you prepare a resume and hone your interview skills or refer you to someone else who can provide you with that kind of assistance.

If you can't afford to pay for a career counselor or coach, your state's public employment office or job service office may offer job counseling, skills assessment, and resume assistance. Also, your local community college may offer a course for people who want to enter the work world but have few, if any, marketable job skills and little work experience.

If you're not sure what career path to take, check out *Cool Careers For Dummies,* 2nd Edition, by Marty Nemko, Paul Edwards, and Sarah Edwards (Wiley). Also, *What Color Is Your Parachute? A Practical Manual for Job-Hunters and Career-Changers* by Richard Bolles (Ten Speed Press) is a classic must-read for job-seekers looking to analyze their strengths and weaknesses prior to joining the work world or wanting to make a career change. Bolles also has a Web site, www.jobhuntersbible.com, where you can learn about other sites for assessing your job skills and interests, get help preparing your resume, network with others who may be able to help you find a job, do job-related research into prospective employers, salaries, and so on. The site also fills you in on the best job sites, among other things.

To find information on the "hottest jobs" — meaning the jobs with the best growth outlook — check out the *Occupational Outlook Handbook,* published annually by the federal Labor Department's Bureau of Labor Statistics (BLS). Go to www.bls/gov/OCO/ to download this resource or read it online.

Going back to school

If you already have a job but need to increase your income or find work that you like better, landing a new job may simply be a matter of updating your resume and conducting a job search, especially if you have good job skills and strong credentials that are in demand. But, if you're entering the work world for the first time, reentering it after a long absence, or if you want to change careers, achieving your employment goals probably means that you need job training or additional education.

Financing your education

Depending on your job skills and education level, achieving your career goals may require getting a degree from a four-year college or university, completing a community college program, or attending a trade or vocational school. But financing the cost of your education can be a challenge when money is tight, especially if you're trying to put money away for your children's educations. The federal Department of Education's loan, grant, or work-study programs may be just what you need to help fund the cost of your tuition, books, and other education-related expenses.

We recommend reading *College Financial Aid For Dummies* by Dr. Herm Davis and Joyce Lain Kennedy (Wiley) for help making sense of your financial aid options and filling out financial aid forms. *The Guide to Federal Student Aid,* published by the U.S. Department of Education (DOE) is another good resource. It offers an overview of the full range of federal educational assistance programs that the DOE offers and describes the application process for each program. You can order a copy of this publication by calling 800-433-3243, or you can download it at `http://studentaid.ed.gov/guide`.

Some states offer their own educational assistance programs. Call your state's department of education to find out whether your state is one of them. In addition to government educational assistance programs, you may be eligible for a special scholarship or grant. (You can find a directory of scholarships and grants at your local library or by visiting Web sites like `www.scholarships.com` or `www.fastweb.com`.) A financial aid officer at the college or university you're interested in can tell you about the school's tuition-assistance programs.

If you're going to college with the goal of getting a good-paying job after you graduate, select your program of study carefully. Some college majors provide a bigger and more immediate financial payoff than others. Talk to a career counselor or to an advisor at the school you would like to attend to find out which careers are apt to earn you a good living in the future.

Choosing a trade or vocational school

Attending a trade or vocational school can be a great way to gain specific job skills that may translate into a well-paying job fairly quickly. However, you find good schools and bad ones; enrolling in one of the bad trade or vocational schools means you get little in return for your tuition money.

A trade or vocational school is set up to make a profit, whereas a community college is a nonprofit entity funded by students' tuition and local taxes and is specifically established to provide students with an affordable education. Before you enroll in a trade or vocational school, explore what your community college offers. You may be able to obtain the same education for a fraction of the amount that a trade or vocational school charges.

The following tips can help you choose a trade or vocational school program that will give you a quality education for a fair price:

- ✔ Ask for printed information from the school about the program that you're considering enrolling in, the cost of the program, the instructors, and so forth. If the school doesn't have such information, don't enroll.

- ✔ Visit the school you're interested in and ask to sit in on some of the classes you would take if you were a student. Check out the condition of the classrooms, the computers, and other classroom resources. Is there enough equipment for all the students? Do things look well cared for? Is the equipment state-of-the-art? Does the teacher engage the students?

- ✔ Find out whether the school is accredited or licensed, and if it is, get the name of the accrediting organizations and licensing agency. For example, the school may be accredited by your state's board of higher education or by another licensing or regulatory agency in your state that accredits trade and vocational schools. Contact the accrediting organizations and licensing agency to confirm that the school is in good standing with them.

- ✔ Contact your state attorney general's office of consumer protection and the Better Business Bureau in the town where the school is located to find out whether either has received a lot of complaints about the school.

- ✔ Ask for a copy of the contract you would have to sign if you enrolled in the school. Read it carefully. Among other things, check to see whether you can cancel the contract and, if you can, what you have to do to get your money back and how long it will take. Steer clear of any school that won't give you a copy of its contract or that doesn't have a contract.

- ✔ Talk to students who are enrolled in the program you're interested in as well as students who have completed the program. Get their opinions about the quality of school. Ask the graduates how well the program prepared them for a career; if they're working in the field for which they were trained; and, if they are, what kind of salary they're earning.

- ✔ Talk with the human resources or personnel departments of the companies you'd like to work for after you complete your education to get their opinions of the trade or vocational school program you're considering. Ask them whether they'd be more or less likely to hire you knowing that you had completed that program and whether they recommend any other programs instead.

✔ Find out what job-finding assistance the school offers its students and ask about the school's placement rate. According to the Accrediting Commission of Career School and Colleges of Technology, most trade and technical schools have a placement rate of at least 70 percent.

✔ Ask about the school's default rate. This rate is the percentage of students who attend the school, borrow money to finance their education, and then can't afford to pay back the loan. A school with a high default rate may not be doing a good job of preparing its students to get a job or may be preparing students to work in jobs for which demand is low.

 Students who attend disreputable or unaccredited trade or vocational schools are often unable to find the employment they need to repay their student loans. If you default on your student loan, the lender may have a legal right to place a lien on property you own after getting a court judgment against you. To be on the safe side, find out about the loan default rate at a particular school by going to DOE's default database `http://wdcrobcolp01.ed.gov/CFAPPS/COHORT/search_cohort.cfm`.

Looking for the right job

You can use many approaches to find a job. The right method depends on your particular job skills, work experience, and the kind of job you want. Here are some job-search methods to consider:

✔ **Visit Internet job sites.** Although there are many job search Web sites, some of the best ones are

- `www.hotjobs.yahoo.com`
- `www.careerbuilder.com`
- `www.jobcentral.com`
- `www.monster.com`
- `www.dice.com`

Many of these sites offer more than job listings. You may also be able to post your resume at these sites, receive e-mails about job listings that match your job-search criteria, and get advice from career counselors.

✔ **Read the employment classified section of your local paper.** Your paper may list them online, too.

✔ **Attend job fairs.** Job fairs can be a great way to find out which companies in your market are hiring and what kinds of skills those companies are looking for. You may even be able to get an initial job interview while you're at a fair. To find out about job fairs in your area, read your local newspaper. If you're willing to relocate, you can also find out about job fairs around the country at `www.careerfairs.com`.

✔ **Talk with some of the larger job-placement or personnel agencies in your area.** They may be trying to find individuals with your exact skills and experiences for some employers in your area.

✔ **Work with an executive recruitment firm.** If you're in the market for a relatively high-level position, contact one of these firms, better known as *head hunters.* Companies and larger nonprofits hire head hunters to locate individuals who might be right for positions they want to fill.

✔ **Check your local, county, or state human resources department to learn about job vacancies.** These government departments can tell you about job openings with your local, county, or state governments. You may be able to access their information online or you may have to visit these departments to get the information you want.

✔ **Visit your state or local job service or public employment service agency to find out about job vacancies in the public sector.** Visit these offices to find out about public sector jobs in your area. These include jobs such as transportation planner, Department of Human Services clerk, social worker for your local health department, and so on. The offices may also have information about job opportunities with nonprofits and for-profits in your community and around your state.

✔ **To find a job with the federal government, go to www.usajobs.opm. gov or call 202-606-1800.** For information about jobs with the U.S. Postal Service, go to www.usps.gov.

✔ **Let your friends and professional associates know that you're looking for a new job.** Many companies fill their better-paying jobs via word of mouth.

✔ **Attend professional networking meetings.** These luncheons, breakfasts, and happy hours may be listed in the business section of your local newspaper or in your area's weekly business journal.

✔ **Contact any trade or professional organizations to which you belong.** These organizations may maintain job banks or job hot lines and provide information about available jobs on their Web sites.

✔ **Visit the Web sites of companies and other organizations that you would like to work for.** Many of these sites provide information about job openings, and you may even be able to apply for jobs at the sites. Not all businesses and organizations list their job openings in their local newspaper or on job-search Web sites.

Chapter 18

Resolving the Stickiest Issues after Divorce

*D*ivorce doesn't always end the problems that destroyed a marriage. Rather than getting on with their lives, some couples continue to replay old arguments and go out of their way to make each other miserable after their marriage ends. Consumed by anger and a desire for revenge, they fight over the outcome of their divorce, withhold court-ordered child or spousal support, interfere with each other's custodial or visitation rights, and renege on other divorce-related obligations.

Sometimes divorce creates new problems for former spouses. For example, they may develop serious financial troubles after their marriage ends and end up in bankruptcy, a move that can jeopardize the finances of their exes. Other former spouses may even use bankruptcy in an effort to avoid having to meet divorce-related financial obligations. None of this paints a pretty picture but, unfortunately, these situations are reality in too many instances.

This chapter can't solve every postdivorce problem, but it does provide specific information about some of the most common and serious problems you may face after your divorce is final. It also explains what you can do about those problems.

Your Ex-spouse Makes Seeing Your Kids Difficult (If Not Impossible)

If you're a noncustodial parent and your ex interferes with your visitation rights, he or she is violating the terms of your divorce, plain and simple. Get in touch with your divorce lawyer to discuss your options.

If you're the custodial parent, you cannot force your former spouse to exercise his or her visitation rights. No law requires a noncustodial parent to spend time with his or her minor children, although most parents want to see their children and influence their lives. On the other hand, you can use your former spouse's repeated failure to spend time with your children as justification for modifying your current custody agreement, possibly restricting your former spouse's visitation rights.

Don't retaliate by withholding payments

If your spouse interferes with your visitation rights, you may be tempted to withhold any child support or spousal support you're obligated to pay. Don't do it! Not only are you breaking the law — just like your former spouse is — but you may also jeopardize your children's financial well-being. Two wrongs in this case definitely *do not* make a right.

A far better course of action is to continue paying your child support (and spousal support) and to try working things out with your former spouse. Mediation is one option if you want to resolve the problem outside of court. (See Chapter 15 for more on the subject of mediation.) But mediation won't work unless you and your ex are truly willing to make it work. If that's not the case, your only option is to go to court.

Do file a contempt of court complaint

If you and your ex-spouse are so estranged that resolving your problems outside of court is impossible, you may want to file a complaint for contempt of court against your ex. You can do so if, for example, your former spouse is interfering with your court-ordered right to spend time with your children. If you file a contempt of court against your ex, unless your ex can prove that there is good reason why you should not be able to exercise your visitation rights — you've abused your kids, you sexually molested them, you have a drug problem, and so on — the judge will order your former spouse to allow you to spend time with them according to the terms of your divorce decree. From start to finish, the complaint process should take relatively little time — certainly less time than your divorce.

Although you must pay a filing fee and other expenses when you file a contempt of court complaint with the court, if the judge finds that your ex is in contempt, you can probably recover those costs from him or her.

 Filing a contempt of court complaint against your ex is likely to make your former spouse even angrier with you than she already is. As a result, cooperating with one another as parents is apt to become more difficult. However, if your ex is violating some aspect of your divorce decree you may have no other option.

The Child-Support Payments Don't Arrive

Millions of divorced parents (mostly mothers) with court orders for child support never receive those payments or receive them only once in a while. As a result, many of these parents struggle to provide for their children, some go bankrupt, and still others fall into poverty.

The formal term for past-due child support is an *arrearage*. According to a survey by the U.S. Census Bureau, of the 7.9 million parents with some sort of child-support agreement (in most instances, a court order for child support), only 46.2 percent received all the child support they were due in 2005 (the most recent year for which there are statistics available). In that same year, 30.3 percent received some of their payments. Twenty-two percent received none of the child support they were entitled to in 2005.

If your ex isn't paying you the child support you're legally entitled to, you can scream, cry, and tear your hair out, or you can use legal means to force him or her to pay up. If you choose the latter option, you can

- ✔ **Get help from your state's Child Support Enforcement (CSE) Program.** Although the CSE office charges you little or nothing for its assistance, don't expect overnight results. In fact, these offices tend to be understaffed and overworked; you may not get the results you're looking for until months later.

- ✔ **Hire an attorney to do much of what the CSE would do for you.** An attorney's help can be expensive, but may get you quick results. Also, you can try to recover your attorney's fees and legal costs from your former spouse. Otherwise, your attorney will probably deduct his fee from whatever money he collects for you.

- ✔ **Work with a private child-support collection agency.** If you go with this option, select the agency carefully because some agencies take a large percentage of any child support they collect as payment for their services. For solid advice on how to choose a private child-support collection agency, see the section "Using a private child-support collection agency" later in this chapter.

Getting help from the Child Support Enforcement Program in your state

The goal of the Child Support Enforcement (CSE) Program, a joint effort of the federal and state governments, is to increase the number of custodial parents receiving court-ordered child support. The CSE Program also helps parents obtain court orders for child support.

The federal Office of Child Support Enforcement (OCSE), which is part of the Health and Human Services Department, oversees child-support enforcement in the United States. Among other things, OCSE helps fund and develop state CSE programs in accordance with federal law. OCSE also operates the federal Parent Locator Service, which uses computer matching to help find noncustodial parents so that child-support court orders can be established and enforced. For more information about the federal child-support enforcement effort, go to www.acf.dhhs.gov/programs/cse.

State social service departments, revenue departments, and the offices of state attorneys general usually coordinate state child-support enforcement efforts. Most states rely on local prosecuting attorneys, other local law enforcement agencies, and family law courts to help them implement their programs.

CSE services are available free or at very little cost to any parent who needs them. However, if you seek help from your state's CSE office, be prepared for delays and frustrations given the extent of the child-support collection problem in this country, the amount of funding most CSE offices receive, and the fact that the offices tend to be chronically understaffed. Therefore, waiting for results can be a real test of your patience.

You're apt to get better results from your state CSE office if you follow up regularly with the CSE employee you work with.

CSE programs vary from state to state. To find the particulars of your state CSE Program and to get contact information for that program, click on www.acf.hhs.gov/programs/cse/extinf.html. When you do, you will see a map of the United States. Click on your state to get to the information you need.

To more fully understand how the CSE office in your state can help you resolve your child-support problems, request a free copy of the U.S. Department of Health and Human Services *Handbook on Child Support Enforcement.* You can obtain a copy of this handbook from your state CSE office or you can read it online at www.acf.hhs.gov/programs/cse/pubs/2005/handbook_on_cse.pdf.

How the CSE office collects your past-due child support

Your state CSE office can help you collect your court-ordered child support in a number of ways. It can

✔ Order your former spouse to meet with staff from the attorney general's office to discuss how your ex can get current on his or her child-support payments.

✔ Have money taken from your ex's federal tax refund by working with the IRS. If your state has its own income tax agency, federal law requires that the state's tax collection agency intercept any state tax refunds that your spouse may receive.

✔ Ask the IRS to start collection proceedings against your former spouse. (This collection process is the same one that the IRS uses to collect back taxes.) If the IRS responds to the request, it will offer your former spouse an opportunity to negotiate a payment plan to wipe out the child-support debt. If that doesn't work, the IRS may seize assets that your ex-spouse owns, including bank accounts, real estate, equipment, and other property.

✔ Place a lien on your former spouse's real and personal assets, including real estate, vehicles, computer equipment, and so on. (However, most states don't put liens on a parent's primary residence or on any property he or she needs to make a living.) Although a lien is no guarantee of payment, it prevents your former spouse from selling, transferring, or borrowing against the property with the lien on it until he or she pays your past-due child support.

If your former spouse doesn't pay your court-ordered child support and you didn't get the right in your divorce to place a lien on one or more of your ex's assets, you can sue your ex in order to get the court's permission to put a lien in place after the fact.

✔ Require that your ex-spouse pledge real or other property to you or give you a lien on any real estate (home, land, or buildings) that he or she may own as a guarantee of payment. In the case of nonpayment, your ex loses the property to you as payment for the back support.

✔ *Levy* (take) the money in your spouse's bank account and apply those funds to her child-support arrearage. All states have agreements with financial institutions that do business within their boundaries requiring those institutions to conduct a quarterly data match or *Financial Institution Data Match (FIDM)*. The purpose of the FIDM is to identify bank accounts that belong to noncustodial parents who have fallen behind on their child-support obligations. These accounts may be subject to levies as well as liens.

✔ Seize the assets of your former spouse, sell them, and use the proceeds to pay off his or her child-support debt. Because this option has issues related to the value of the seized property and transfer of ownership, talk it over with an attorney, your state CSE office, or with a private child-support collection agency, if you hire one.

✔ Use state nonsupport statutes to prosecute your ex-spouse. This option is usually a last resort, but if you do use it and your former spouse doesn't pay up, the judge can order your ex to be arrested and sent to jail until he or she pays all or some of the child support you are owed. Of course, while your former spouse is in jail, he can't work and earn an income.

Other ways the CSE office can pressure your ex to pay up

Your state Child Support Enforcement (CSE) office may use other tools to pressure or embarrass your former spouse into paying up. Depending on where you live, some of those other tools may include

✔ Automatic billing, telephone reminders, and delinquency notices.

✔ Electronic fund transfers from your former spouse's bank account to your account. This tool is good to use when the support-paying parent is self-employed, which makes automatic wage deductions impossible.

✔ Suspending or revoking your ex's license to practice law, medicine, or another profession or suspending or revoking his driver's license, hunting or fishing license, or other government-issued license. Also, the Department of State will deny a passport to your former spouse or refuse to automatically renew his passport if the amount of past-due child support he owes is at least $2,500 and the debt has been certified to be intercepted by the IRS, which means that the agency has begun (or intends to begin) taking any federal tax refunds your former spouse may be entitled to in order to collect the child support you are owed.

✔ Using local or state "most wanted" campaigns to try to embarrass parents to pay up and to flush out parents who are behind on their child support. Typically, these campaigns provide the names and photographs of those parents.

✔ Using the media to promote "amnesty" campaigns. Parents who come forward to pay their child-support debt during the amnesty period will not be prosecuted or will be punished less severely than they would be otherwise.

✔ Posting information about delinquent parents on the Internet. The information includes a parent's name and community of residence, if known, as well as the amount the parent owes in past-due child support.

Federal initiatives to help you collect what you're owed

The federal government has a variety of initiatives aimed at increasing the number of custodial parents who receive their court-ordered child support. Those initiatives include

- ✔ Mandating that court-ordered payments be withheld from the paychecks of noncustodial parents.

- ✔ Requiring that state CSE offices report all child-support arrearages of more than $1,000 to the three national credit reporting agencies. States can elect to report smaller arrearages, if they want. A parent who has such negative information in her credit histories will have a more difficult time getting new or additional credit at reasonable terms. It may also make it harder for that parent to get a new job, to rent a place to live, and to qualify for insurance.

- ✔ Using the National Directory of New Hires to help federal and state governments keep track of divorced parents who frequently change jobs in order to avoid paying their child support.

Hiring an attorney to collect your child support

Some family law attorneys specialize in helping parents collect past-due child support (and spousal support as well), but paying for more legal help may be unrealistic, given the state of your postdivorce finances. Furthermore, an attorney cannot do anything that the CSE office in your state can't do, although the attorney can probably do it a lot faster. For that reason, spending money on an attorney may make financial sense.

If you want to hire an attorney to collect your past-due support, you can minimize your out-of-pocket legal expenses by finding one who will work with you on a contingency basis. In other words, the attorney agrees to get paid by taking a percentage of whatever money he or she collects for you. If the attorney doesn't collect any money for you, you don't owe him or her a fee, although you may be obligated to pay his or her expenses, depending on the terms of your agreement.

If you hire an attorney to help you collect your child support, that attorney can work with your area's CSE office, coordinating collection efforts with CSE staff to prevent duplication of services and conflicting enforcement decisions.

Finding further resources

Although trying to enforce a child-support order on your own is usually a thankless task, knowing more about your options better enables you to make CSE's services work for you. The following books offer practical information about how to enforce a child-support court order:

✔ *Rightfully Yours: How to Get Past-Due Child Support Alimony and Your Ex's Pension* by Gary A, Shulman (Self Counsel Legal Series)

✔ *Child Support: Your Legal Guide to Collecting, Enforcing or Terminating the* *Court's Order* by Mary L. Boland (Sphinx Legal)

✔ *Deadbeats: What Responsible Parents Need to Know About Collecting Child Support* by Simone Spence (Sourcebooks)

Also, if you decide to hire a private child-support collection agency or an attorney to help you collect your past due support, the information in these books will help you pick a good agency or attorney and work effectively with the collection agency or attorney you choose.

Using a private child-support collection agency

Many parents with child-support collection problems hire private *child-support collection agencies* to help them get their money. These agencies tend to get quicker results than CSE offices and may cost less than an attorney.

A cross between a detective agency and a traditional debt-collection agency, private child-support collection agencies can help you collect your back support and track down your ex-spouse if he or she has disappeared in order to avoid paying child support. Child support collection agencies charge for their services by taking a percentage of the past-due child support they collect for their clients — usually between 18 and 40 percent. Some also charge an upfront application fee.

Although most private child-support collection agencies truly want to help, some victimize desperate parents who are already being victimized by their former spouses. These agencies may take a bigger percentage of the child support they collect than they said they would, demand exorbitant upfront fees (and do little or nothing to earn that money), or fail to turn over the money they collect to the parent who hires them. To protect yourself from getting ripped off, be sure that you get

> ✔ **Written information about the agency's services.** The information should include background on the company's management and its legal expertise.

✔ **References.** Check them out, too. Also call your local Better Business Bureau and the consumer protection office of your state attorney general's office to find out whether they have any complaints against the private child-support collection agency on file.

✔ **A written contract from the agency.** The contract should spell out clearly exactly what the agency will do for you, the terms of payment, and how the agency will receive its fees. For example, will you pay the fee directly or will the agency take its money out of the past-due support it collects? Read the contract carefully and get all your questions answered before you sign.

QDROs count: Tapping into an ex's retirement plan

A frequently overlooked option for collecting past due child support is to tap into your ex-spouse's 401(k) plan or other defined benefit plan by using a Qualified Domestic Relation Order (QDRO). A QDRO, which is a special kind of court order, directs the administrator of your ex's retirement plan to pay some portion of his retirement benefits to you right away (not when your ex retires) in order to satisfy all or some of your ex's child support arrearage. The money will either be paid directly to you or to your state CSE office, which in turn will pass on the funds to you.

You can obtain a QDRO anywhere in the country. Because QDROs are governed by federal law, they apply even if you and your spouse live in different states. Also, if your ex's arrearage is paid off through one QDRO and then he or she falls behind on his or her child support payments again, you can use another QDRO to collect the new arrearage.

In order to use a QDRO to collect the past due child support you're owed, your state CSE office has to provide you with the exact amount of child support in arrearage and you have to determine the specific retirement benefits your former spouse is entitled to from his current employer as well as any retirement benefits he may be entitled to from past employers. Also, the QRDO document must be carefully prepared in order to ensure that it meets all the requirements of the retirement plans. (Be sure that the QDRO is worded so that your former spouse, not you, must pay the taxes associated with the early withdrawal of funds from the retirement account.) You will also have to ask the court to issue a formal court order.

Never try to prepare a QDRO yourself. They're complicated, even for many attorneys, and if everything associated with your QDRO isn't done exactly right, it won't achieve your goal. Hire an attorney with specific experience using QDROs to collect past-due child support to help you with your QDRO. If your divorce attorney does not have this experience, she should be able to recommend an attorney who does. Otherwise, it may take you a while to find the right attorney because many attorneys who collect past due child support for their clients have the misimpression that QDROs can be used only to collect past due spousal support or to collect their clients' share of the marital property they're entitled to according to their divorce decrees. They don't realize that federal law also allows QDROs to be used to collect child support arrearages.

Do not sign a contract that requires you to pay a percentage of your child support until your child reaches the age of 18 or 21 or that prohibits you from seeking help from other resources.

For additional information and advice about working with a child support collection agency, go to the Web site of the National Coalition on Child Support Options, `www.childsupportoptions.org/options/consumers_guide.htm`.

Some states have laws that protect parents who have fallen behind on their child support. Among other things, these laws prohibit private child support enforcement agencies from calling those parents to try to collect the child support they owe if the calls will cause the parents to be embarrassed or inconvenienced. Also the laws bar a private enforcement agency from mailing collection and enforcement letters to the parent if the letter could be seen by a third party and could embarrass or disgrace the parent owing past due support. To find out whether your state has such a law, contact your state child support enforcement agency or talk to your divorce attorney.

Your Ex-spouse Skips Town

Unfortunately, some parents are so intent on not meeting their child support obligations that they move out of state, often without leaving a forwarding address. When that happens, enforcing a child-support court order and collecting that support can be particularly time consuming and difficult.

The federal government requires state CSE offices to pursue interstate cases as vigorously as in-state cases but, in reality, interstate cases often get short shrift given the amount of staff time they take and the many obstacles to success. Nevertheless, Congress has passed laws to help improve the effectiveness of interstate child support and collections. Those laws include

- **The Uniform Interstate Family Support Act (UIFSA).** This law gives you the right to ask a court in your state to forward your order for child support to the court with jurisdiction in the state where your former spouse now lives. The court in that jurisdiction can enforce the order and provide your ex's new employer with a copy of your child-support court order so that the employer can begin withholding the amount you are due each month from your former spouse's paychecks.

- **The Child Support Recovery Act (CSRA).** Under this federal law, a parent who refuses to make support payments to a parent who lives in another state is committing a federal crime and can be prosecuted. However, to be prosecuted under this law, the parent must

- Owe more than $5,000 in back child support or must have owed back support for more than one year

- Have been aware that he or she had an obligation to pay child support and been able to meet that obligation when it was due

✔ **The Deadbeat Parents Punishment Act.** This act amends the CSRA by making it a federal crime when a parent owes more than $10,000 in past-due child support, hasn't paid child support in more than two years, or has willfully moved from one state to another (or out of the country) to avoid paying the support. If your ex is convicted of violating this law, he or she can be fined and imprisoned.

In the past, a parent who was obligated to pay child support could avoid paying or could pay less by moving to a new state and getting that state to modify his or her child-support court order. With the Deadbeat Parents Punishment Act, as long as either parent remains in the state where the court order was originally filed, that state has continuing and exclusive jurisdiction over the court order. Also, according to the Uniform Interstate Family Support Act, if you have a court order for child support and both you and your ex-spouse move out of state, your original court order will be valid in your new state. Contact your new state's child-support enforcement office to find out about any paperwork you may need to file to ensure that your support payments continue. You can obtain the phone number for that office by going to www.acf.dhhs.gov/programs/cse/extinf.htm.

Your Ex-spouse Disappears with the Kids

If you have custody of your kids and your ex-spouse kidnaps them or refuses to return them to you, your former spouse is breaking the law. All 50 states and the District of Columbia, as well as the federal government have laws that apply to parental kidnapping. Under most circumstances, the laws treat such a kidnapping as a felony.

If your ex takes off with your kids, leave no stone unturned. The longer you wait to act, the harder finding them will be. You should

✔ **Call your local police department immediately and file a missing persons report.** Under the federal National Child Search Assistance Act, no waiting period is required before the police can issue such a report. Get a case number and ask them to enter your child into the National Crime Information Center Missing Person File (NCIC) right away. Ask the police to give you the nine-digit NCIC number related to your missing child.

✔ **Talk with your local police department about whether your missing child qualifies for a nationwide AMBER Alert.** If your child qualifies, the police will fax information about your child, a photo of your child, and any information you may have about the type of vehicle your ex may be driving to radio and TV stations around the country. Some states also use electronic billboards to alert people about missing children. For more information on the AMBER Alert, go to the National Center for Missing & Exploited Children Web site (www.missingkids.com).

✔ **Ask the district attorney for your jurisdiction to issue a warrant for the arrest of your former spouse as soon as possible.** Ask that office to use the Federal Parent Locator Service to try to locate your ex, too. Your local CSE office can also contact this service for you, but if you want to be sure that the contact happens immediately, do it yourself.

✔ **Contact the FBI.** Don't wait for your local police department to contact the agency, but let them know that you have. If kidnapping is a felony in your state, the FBI will help you.

✔ **Contact your elected representatives in Washington.** Sometimes a call from your senator or congressperson can make government offices move more quickly than they would otherwise.

✔ **Get in contact with organizations that can help you.** Those organizations include

  • National Center for Missing and Exploited Children (www.missing kids.com, 800-843-5678)

  • Child Find of America (www.childfindofamerica.org, 800-I-Am-Lost)

  • Polly Klaas Foundation (www.pollyklaas.org, 800-587-4357)

The Web sites of these three organizations feature helpful advice and information about steps you can take to minimize the likelihood that your former spouse will abduct your child and, should an abduction happen, to make it easier to find your missing child.

✔ **Contact your state's Missing Children's Clearinghouse.** Ask the staff to list information about your missing child. These government organizations collect, compile, and disseminate information about children who have disappeared and provide parents with another way of getting the word out about their missing child. Many of these clearinghouses maintain Web sites with the photos of missing children and other information about them. If you have any ideas about which state your ex and child may be in, provide that information to the organization. You'll find a directory of clearinghouses by state at www.nmclc.org/clearing houselist.php.

✔ **Provide the local media with photos of your missing child and relevant information.** The media may publicize your missing child on TV, radio, and in your local newspaper, and someone who hears or reads about your child may come forward with information about your child's location. You may want to contact the media as soon as you know for certain that your child is missing. Before you do, however, speak with the law enforcement personnel you're working with to make certain that publicizing the fact that your child is missing will not jeopardize any effort they have underway to find your child.

✔ **Ask law enforcement for the phone numbers of the border patrol for Canada and Mexico.** If you have any concern that your former spouse may take your child to either of these countries, notifying the border patrol of that fact is important so they can be on the lookout for your ex and your child and can stop them from leaving the country.

✔ **Get in touch with the U.S. State Department's Office of Passport and Advisory Services (202-955-0377) and ask that your child's name be entered into the Department's Children's Passport Issuance Alert Program (CPIAP).** If you do, the Department will notify you or your attorney if it receives an application for a U.S. passport for your child. (With a few exceptions, federal law requires that when a child is younger than 16, the signatures of both parents must be on the child's passport application, unless the parent completing the application has sole custody. However, this requirement doesn't mean that a spouse won't try to forge the other parent's signature.) Of course, this alert is useful only if an application for a passport was made using your child's real name.

If you have a court order granting you either sole custody or joint legal custody, or prohibiting your child from traveling without your permission or the permission of the court, the Department may refuse to issue a new or renewal U.S. passport for your child, but if a passport has already been issued, it won't revoke the passport.

If your child already has a passport, protect that document by asking your divorce attorney to hold it for you.

✔ **Hire your own private investigator.** *Skip tracers,* individuals who track down missing persons by using national computerized databases, are very effective at turning up missing people through social security numbers, driver's license numbers, and plenty of asking around. Plus, they're relatively inexpensive.

If you suspect that your spouse may take off with your children, contact your family law attorney, the CSE office in your area, or both to find out what you can do. One option is for your attorney to ask the family law judge in your area to issue a court order barring your ex from leaving the jurisdiction with your children. The judge may be willing to issue the order on an emergency basis.

Keeping your kids safe

There is no 100 percent foolproof way to ensure that your ex will not kidnap your children. In fact, family members, mostly parents, carry out 78 percent of all child abductions. However, there are things you can do to minimize the likelihood that a kidnapping will happen. For example, you can

- Respect your ex's right to spend time with his or her kids according to the terms of your custody agreement.

- Avoid badmouthing your former spouse or treating him or her with disrespect.

- Try to work out any problems between you and your spouse in a friendly manner. Use mediation or mental health counseling, if necessary.

- Immediately report to your divorce attorney or to the family court in your area any kidnapping threats your ex makes. Record the date and nature of each threat. You may also want to notify your local police department or district attorney's office about the threats and ask them to explain to your ex the very serious consequences of acting on them.

- Make your children's teachers, day-care center, healthcare provider, babysitters, friends' parents, and so on, aware of your kidnapping concerns. Let them know not to release your child to any adult but you without your permission. Also, give each of them a certified copy of your child custody court order. You should also keep a certified copy in a safe place at your home.

- Write down a detailed description of each of your children, including birthdates, heights, weights, eye and hair colors, distinguishing birthmarks, and so on. Update regularly. Also, take a color photo (head and shoulders) of each of your children every six months.

- Get a passport for your child, store it in a safe place, and let the U.S. Passport Office know that your child is not to leave the country without your written permission.

- Have your child's name entered into the State Department's Children's Passport Issuance Alert Program (CPIAP). For information about how to do that and more details about the program go to `http://travel.state.gov/family/abduction/resources/resources_554.html`.

- Contact your local police department about getting your children fingerprinted. The department will keep the prints on file.

- Make certain that your younger children know their full names and address, as well as all your phone numbers.

- Teach your children how to use a telephone, including a cell phone. Make sure that they know when to call 911 and how to dial the operator. Be sure that they understand that they can call 911 without having to pay anything, even if they place the call from a pay phone. Also, make sure they know your e-mail address and how to use a computer to e-mail you.

Realistically, however, if your former spouse is determined to take off with the kids, a court order may not be much of a deterrent. Even so, pursuing this option is a good idea because if your ex does violate the court order, your former spouse will have even more problems with the law than he or she already has after taking off with your kids. Those problems are likely to work to your advantage if you want to change your custody arrangement to protect your children from being harmed again by your ex. Also, alert your child's school or day-care center about your concerns and instruct them to release your child only to you or someone you specifically designate.

During your divorce, let your attorney know if you are concerned that your ex may take off with your kids. Ask that your custody court order bar your former spouse from taking your kids to another country without your written permission, or without the court's permission. You may also want as a part of your divorce agreement for your ex to be required to post a bond to help pay for the cost of locating your children if your worst fears are realized and for the cost of returning them to the United States. The bond may help deter your former spouse from kidnapping your children in the first place.

Other options include requiring that all your spouse's visitation time with your kids be supervised and that your ex leave his passport at the county clerk's office whenever he is with them. Although these are extreme measures, they may discourage your ex from kidnapping your children, help spare them the trauma of being abducted, and help you avoid the expense and emotional upset of trying to locate them if a kidnapping does happen.

Your Ex-spouse Owes You Spousal Support

Many former spouses who are legally obligated to pay spousal support fail to make the payments or don't make them consistently. Sometimes former spouses don't meet their spousal support obligation because they develop serious money troubles after their divorce and, instead of asking the court to let them pay less spousal support, they simply stop paying anything or pay only when they can afford it.

If your former spouse falls behind on his or her spousal support payments, the Uniform Interstate Family Support Act (UIFSA) may be able to help you. In addition, some courts are becoming more aggressive about enforcing court-ordered spousal support agreements.

In some states, a portion of the wages of an ex-spouse who's fallen behind on his or her spousal support obligation can be garnished each pay period until the past-due amount is paid in full. Also, the judge may order your ex to pay the legal fees and expenses you incurred trying to get your former spouse to pay what he is supposed to pay according to your divorce court order. In addition, the judge may decide to have your ex arrested and brought to court so he can tell him in no uncertain terms that he must pay you the spousal support you are entitled to.

If wage garnishment and contempt of court aren't options in your state if your spouse doesn't pay spousal support, you may be in the same boat as everyone else your ex owes money to. Making matters worse, your state's debtor protection laws may make all or most of the property owned by your ex-spouse *exempt* (that is, protected) from your efforts to collect what he or she owes you, effectively making the past-due spousal support an uncollectible debt.

When your spouse isn't living up to your spousal support agreement, your best option is to contact your divorce attorney. Your attorney can lay out your options for collecting the money that you're entitled to and can help you carry out a plan of action.

The ideal time to ask your attorney about the potential problems of collecting spousal support is when you're working out the terms of your divorce. One option your attorney may recommend is requiring that your spouse let you place a lien on some of his or her property as a guarantee of payment.

Your Ex-spouse Doesn't Live Up to the Terms of Your Property Agreement

Some former spouses do not abide by the terms of the property division portion of their divorce decree. For example, your ex may not transfer certain property into your name as your divorce decree requires or may not pay the joint debts she is supposed to pay. Your former spouse's failure to live up to her end of the bargain could spell trouble for you. For example, you may have been counting on the assets your ex has not transferred to you to help pay your postdivorce living expenses for a while and because of your ex's failure to pay the joint debts she is legally obligated to pay, you may not be able to pay them and as a result, your credit histories and FICO scores, not just your ex's, will be damaged. It will become harder for you to rebuild your life after divorce as a result.

If you can afford it, you should pay any joint debts that your former spouse is obligated to pay but is not paying while you are trying to get the terms of your property agreement enforced. Paying those debts minimizes any potential for damage to your credit.

Schedule a meeting with your divorce attorney if your spouse fails to comply with the terms of your property agreement (or the judge or jury's decision regarding your debts and assets). Your attorney may be able to rectify the situation simply by calling your ex's attorney about the situation who in turn may issue a stern warning to your former spouse about what is likely to happen if he ignores his divorce-related, court-ordered obligations.

It may take more than a warning to get your ex to meet his or her obligations to you. If that's true in your divorce, your attorney will file a contempt of court action in the same court where you were divorced. Your attorney will spell out exactly what it is that your ex isn't doing that violates the terms of your divorce and will ask the judge to order your former spouse to live up to the specific aspects of your divorce decree that she is ignoring. If you have been harmed by your former spouse's inaction, your attorney may ask the judge to order him to pay you damages as well in order to compensate you for the harm. For example, your ex could be required to pay the cost of your attorney, your court costs, any money that you paid to a creditor that he should have paid, any loss of wages you may experience because you had to take off work to deal with your legal problem, and so on. If your former spouse ignores the court's order, then he may be sent to jail.

If your former spouse falls behind on the payments he is obligated to make to you as part of your property agreement or does not make those payments at all and as part of your divorce you guaranteed those payments by putting a lien on an asset owned by your former spouse, you have the right to foreclose on the property and sell it in order to get the money that you're owed. This can be a good option if there is enough equity in the property that the sale will provide you with sufficient funds to

✔ Pay off the mortgage

✔ Pay the costs of foreclosing on the property and selling it

✔ Provide you with some or all of the money that you're entitled to according to your divorce decree

Your Ex-spouse Files for Bankruptcy

Your former spouse may experience very serious financial problems and file for bankruptcy. If that happens, the terms of your divorce agreement may be affected. For example:

✔ If your former spouse files a Chapter 7 liquidation bankruptcy, any non-support obligations to you — payments he is supposed to make to you under the terms of your property settlement agreement — will be non-dischargeable. That means that he must still make the payments. Also, he will be expected to continue meeting his support obligations (spousal and child support) while he is in bankruptcy and afterwards. If your ex fell behind on those payments before he filed for bankruptcy, you are entitled to try to collect what you are owed during the bankruptcy by using any or all of the collection options described in this chapter, despite the automatic stay. The automatic stay is a court action that prohibits creditors from trying to collect the money they are owed while a consumer is in bankruptcy. It is issued as soon as a bankruptcy begins The automatic stay doesn't apply to past-due support, however.

✔ If your ex files a Chapter 13 reorganization bankruptcy, the bankruptcy will have no effect on his obligation to pay you child or spousal support, and he will have up to five years to catch up on any past-due support and nonsupport payments he owes to you. At the end of the five years, any remaining debt related to a nonsupport obligation will be discharged.

To protect your rights when your former spouse declares bankruptcy or when you believe that he or she may be thinking about doing so, consult with a consumer bankruptcy attorney right away. For example, if your former spouse stops paying you the money you're entitled to after filing for bankruptcy, your attorney may suggest filing a motion to initiate a *contested matter* — the equivalent of a mini-lawsuit — in order to get the bankruptcy judge to order your ex to resume making the payments.

Your Children Begin Having Emotional Problems

Children often experience some emotional upset during and after their parents' divorce. After all, their definition of a family has been changed, their sense of security has been shaken, and their lives have been altered in fundamental ways. In most instances, your children can get through this difficult time in their lives relatively unscathed assuming that you keep the lines of communication open, that you reassure them through your words and actions that you still love them and that things will be okay, and that you and your spouse don't have a bitter divorce and an angry, antagonistic postdivorce relationship.

Despite parents' best efforts, some children experience serious emotional problems after their parents get divorced. For this reason, you should be familiar with the more common signs of serious emotional distress in children and stay alert for them in your own kids. If you see any signs of trouble in your children, intervene as soon as possible in order to help prevent their problems from going from bad to worse. The following behaviors are common signs that your children are hurting and need your help.

Toddlers to kindergarten-age children may

✔ Become fearful of leaving you

✔ Begin having temper tantrums

✔ Develop behavioral problems at home or with other children

✔ Have trouble sleeping in their own room or have nightmares

✔ Revert to infantile behavior, such as bedwetting, thumb-sucking, biting, and crying

Elementary-age children may

- Begin spending more time alone in their rooms and less time playing with friends
- Choose one parent to be angry with and choose another to cling to for comfort
- Cry a lot
- Get sick more than usual (headaches and stomachaches are particularly common) or act sick so that they can stay home from school
- Lose interest in activities they used to enjoy
- Participate less in classroom discussions and activities

Adolescents and preteens may

- Develop nonspecific illnesses or nervous habits, such as nail-biting and facial tics
- Develop behavioral problems (such as getting into fights) at school, outside of school, or at home
- Engage in rebellious behavior, such as shoplifting or vandalism, skipping school, smoking, drinking, doing drugs, or becoming sexually promiscuous
- Express anger toward the parent they think is responsible for the divorce
- Spend more time alone in their rooms
- Try to play surrogate spouse to the parent they feel has been wronged
- Withdraw from friends and family

Girls who are having emotional problems are more likely than boys to become extremely withdrawn and to lose interest in the things they used to enjoy or find important.

If one of your children exhibits some of the behaviors in the previous bullet lists, try to talk with your ex about what is going on and try to come to an agreement about what to do. Both of you may need to spend more time with your troubled child, have a conversation with that child about what is bothering him or her, and talk with your child's school counselor or with other adults who play an important role in your child's life. You should also schedule an appointment with a mental health professional who specializes in working with children — especially with children of divorce. The therapist may suggest that your child join a support group for kids with divorced parents so that he or she can talk about his or her feelings with other kids and listen to them talk about their own problems and feelings. Or the therapist may advise one-on-one therapy for a while or even family therapy.

You Want to Make Some Changes to Your Divorce Agreement

As time goes on after you're divorced, you may decide that the terms of your divorce no longer work for you given changes in your life or in your children's lives. For example, your employer is in financial trouble and has asked everyone to take a reduction in salary or your children have gotten older and cost more to raise. Or maybe you've never been happy with the terms of your divorce and, although you've done your best to live with them, you've decided now is the time to try to get them changed.

If you and your former spouse see eye to eye on the changes you want, modifying your agreement or the judge's court order should be relatively hassle-free, assuming that the court shares your perspectives. Just as you did when you got your divorce, you must draw up a revised agreement with the help of your attorneys to be certain that you do not create any problems for yourselves. Then the attorney of whichever ex-spouse wants to change the agreement files the revised agreement with the court so that it can be court ordered. However, if one of you wants things changed and the other doesn't, you may be in for a replay of your divorce battles.

If you and your spouse don't see eye to eye about the changes one of you wants to make to the terms of your divorce and you want to minimize your legal expenses, you may want to try to resolve your differences by using mediation. See Chapter 15 to find out more about mediation.

Courts are more open to changing the terms of custody, child-support, or spousal support agreements than they are to changing the terms of a property settlement agreement. In fact, many states prohibit such a change. States that do allow modifications of property settlement agreements usually provide only a very short window of opportunity — typically 30 days after your divorce — for requesting the change.

Demonstrating a change in your circumstances

If you want a change in your divorce agreement and you and your ex don't agree on the change and you can't resolve your differences outside of court, it's time to hire a divorce attorney (if you haven't already done so). Your attorney, working with the attorney representing your ex, may be able to resolve your differences but, if not, he or she will file a motion with the court, and a hearing will be held. At the hearing, your attorney will present evidence to the court justifying the need for the change you are seeking, and your ex's attorney will argue against the change. By the way, the judge isn't going to okay a change just because you don't like the terms of your divorce. Through your attorney, you must be able to provide the court with solid justification for the modification you are asking for.

Changing custody and visitation

If you want to modify the terms of your custody and visitation agreement, you must demonstrate a legitimate need for the change because of significant changes in your life, in your former spouse's life, or in the lives of your children. Those changes might include the following:

- ✔ You're moving a long distance from your former spouse or your ex is moving far away.

- ✔ The income of the spouse who's paying child support has increased or decreased.

- ✔ Your children aren't being properly supervised when they're with their other parent. Perhaps your former spouse has a substance abuse problem; your spouse is having to spend longer hours at work and, as a result, your children are being left alone for long stretches of time; or your spouse has turned into a party animal and isn't spending enough time with your kids or isn't providing them with enough supervision; and so on.

- ✔ One of your children has become seriously ill, and you need more financial assistance to help pay for the child's care and treatment.

- ✔ Your ex has developed a serious physical or mental illness, has become addicted to drugs or alcohol, has been arrested for a violent crime, or has been accused of child molestation or child abuse.

- ✔ You and your teenage son or daughter are in constant conflict and you're having problems controlling him or her. You feel that having your child live with his or her other parent would be in the child's best interest.

- ✔ You believe that your ex's new spouse is trying to usurp your position as parent to your children, is giving your children advice that contradicts the values you're trying to instill in them, or is allowing them to do things that you would never permit. As a result, you feel that your children are being harmed and are not being raised in a positive way.

- ✔ You believe that your former spouse is physically abusing or sexually molesting your children.

- ✔ The arrangements in your divorce agreement or judgment are simply not working out.

Regardless of what reasons you give to the court to justify your request for a modification, the judge's ruling will be based on what he or she believes is in the best interest of your kids.

Changing how you and your ex handle child support

You or your former spouse may also want to make changes in your child-support court order. If you receive child support, you probably want more money and, if you pay child support, you probably want to reduce how much money you must pay. What a surprise!

If you request a modification in your child-support court order, you must provide the court with proof that changes in your life or in your ex's life or changes in the lives of one or more of your children merit the modification. Depending on exactly why you're asking for the change, this proof may include check stubs showing that you're no longer making as much money as you once did or medical records indicating that you have a serious health problem that limits your ability to earn money. If the court denies your request, the law in your state probably limits your ability to file a new child-support modification request.

Securing a court order if you change your divorce agreement yourselves

If you and your ex-spouse decide to change your child-custody and visitation agreement and you aren't working with attorneys, be sure to put the terms of your new agreement in writing and to get a new court order that reflects all the changes. Otherwise, despite what you and your spouse agree to, the new provisions of your agreement won't be legally enforceable because, from the court's perspective, your original court-ordered agreement is still in effect. Also, it's a good idea to for each of you to have the new agreement reviewed by an attorney so you can be sure that everything is clearly stated and that you are not creating the potential for future problems. Finally, make sure that you and your ex each get a copy of the court order.

A judge may not consider the child-support-related changes you and your ex agree to as being in the best interest of your children. If that's the case and the changes involve reducing, suspending, or completely ending your child-support payments, the court can find the spouse who's legally obligated to make the payments in contempt of court. As a result, that parent can end up in legal hot water. To be legally safe, enter a new court order when you want to modify the terms of your child-support court order.

Chapter 19

Putting Your Personal Life Back on Track

In This Chapter

▶ Getting comfortable being single

▶ Having fun on your own

▶ Planning ahead if you decide to get married again

*N*ow that your divorce is over, you have entered a new phase in your life. You may feel happier than you have in a long time because you're free of the tension and strife that may have plagued your marriage and ready for the personal growth, rediscovery, and new opportunities that can go hand in hand with being single again. But, you may also find being single again an intimidating and lonely experience — particularly if getting divorced wasn't your idea or if you're unprepared for life on your own. Not being married anymore can be especially difficult if you have sole custody of your children — even if you fought for such an arrangement — because being responsible for your kids 24/7 can be exhausting physically and mentally.

In this chapter, we help you make a successful transition from being married to being single by offering you guidance and advice for how to live your life and what to do and not do in the months immediately following your divorce. We also suggest some ways to create a new social life for yourself, and because we are eternal optimists and sure that eventually, you will fall in love again and remarry, we provide some practical suggestions for steps you can take to help ensure that your next marriage will work out and be a happy and fulfilling one.

Handling Postdivorce Personal and Family Issues

The months immediately following your divorce can be particularly difficult, especially if getting divorced wasn't your idea. You must pick up the pieces of whatever is left from your old life and build a new life for yourself at the same time that you may be feeling lonely, beating yourself up about what you might have done in order to save your marriage, questioning your judgment, and worrying about the impact of your divorce on your kids and how it may affect your relationship with them. In this section, we offer you some practical advice that should make your life easier and help you gain peace of mind as you transition from being part of a couple to singledom.

Be easy on yourself

While you're adjusting to being single again, don't place demands on yourself and set unreasonable expectations for your life. Do what's necessary to tie up any loose ends in your divorce and then give yourself a chance to recover from what you've just gone through and to gain some perspective on things; in other words, spend some time regrouping mentally and physically. You have plenty of time to pursue all the big plans you may have for yourself.

While you're recovering, don't make any major decisions; this is no time to move to a new town or state, buy a home, or change careers. Making important decisions immediately after your divorce when you may be feeling especially vulnerable and your judgment may be somewhat clouded could cause you to make big mistakes that you'll regret later.

In other words, chill out and try to take life one day at a time for now. Give yourself permission to be a little lazy! Let your house get messier than usual; eat fast food occasionally; sleep in occasionally; or lay in bed for an hour or two on weekend mornings reading a good book. However, don't stop doing the things that make you feel good about yourself and about life in general, and don't give up all the structure in your life. If you get too undisciplined and don't maintain at least some of the important constants in your life, you may slip into a funk that is difficult to get out of and which will hamper your ability to get on with your life.

Take time to reflect on why your marriage failed

Spend some time trying to understand why your marriage didn't work out and how you may have contributed to the problems that caused it to end. Unless you gain some perspective on why your marriage failed, you risk another divorce if you remarry. Writing in a journal and getting therapy are two good ways to gain some insights into what went wrong and how you can avoid repeating the mistakes you made if you do marry again.

Accept the fact that your life is no longer the way it used to be. This doesn't mean that the new life you create for yourself is going to be less satisfying and less happy than the life you led when you were married; but it does mean that your new life will be different and maybe even better, perhaps better than you ever dreamed of.

Try to identify some benefits of being single again. They may be hard to find at first, but they *do* exist. For example, now you may have more privacy and time to yourself, your relationship with your children may be stronger, you may have less upset and turmoil in your life, and you may be able to sleep better because you're not feeling as stressed out as you were when you were married.

There are many books available that can help you understand why your marriage failed and appreciate what it takes to have a successful relationship in the future. A good one is *Learning From Divorce: How to Take Responsibility, Stop the Blame, and Move On* by Christine Coates and Robert LaCrosse (Jossey-Bass).

Spend time with people in your situation

Like many people in your situation, you may find it helpful to join a divorce support group. The group's members can help bolster your confidence through the inevitable down times you'll experience as you rebuild your life, celebrate your successes with you, and provide advice and feedback when you encounter problems that you're not sure how to handle. They may also be a source of new friends and a reinvigorated social life. Your church or synagogue may have a support group for divorcees, and any mental health professional you may be working with most likely can recommend one. Other resources for locating a support group in your area include Divorce Care (www.divorcecare.com) and Divorce Source (www.divorcesource.com).

Take time to find the right group for you. You may have to try out a couple until you find one that you feel comfortable with. Issues to consider when choosing a divorce support group include whether you want to be in a group of all men or all women or a mixed group, whether you prefer a large or a small group, and whether you want to participate in a group that is led by a professional with experience working with divorcees or one that has a specific orientation — a religious orientation or a twelve-step philosophy toward divorce recovery. Steer clear of groups that are full of angry, bitter divorcees because the participants in these groups tend to reinforce one another's negative emotions, which do little to help them heal and move on.

Learn how to do it yourself at home

Being divorced usually means having to take on chores around the house that you may not have had to handle when you were married — cooking, grocery shopping, balancing the checkbook and paying bills, managing your investments, taking care of home repairs, mowing the lawn, and so on. If you know little or nothing about how to accomplish some of these tasks, your friends and relatives may be able to help you get up to speed quickly, so don't be ashamed to ask them for help. You can also learn what you need to know by trial and error, reading how-to books, watching how-to DVDs, visiting Web sites and taking classes.

As you acquire new skills and knowledge and begin to feel more in control of your life, your self confidence will grow, you'll feel proud of what you can accomplish on your own, and you'll be ready to take on new challenges. However, you should also develop a list of reliable professionals that you can call on for help with more complicated tasks that you don't have the time or interest in figuring out for yourself.

Devote more of your attention to your kids

Research shows that even in amicable splits, the effect of divorce on both boys and girls tends to be greatest during the year immediately following a divorce, and that boys tend to have a harder time adjusting overall than girls do. So during the months following your divorce, be prepared to help your kids cope with the changes in their lives by giving them more of your love, affection, and attention. However, don't smother them or be overprotective, because by doing so you may create new problems for them.

If you and your spouse were separated while you were getting divorced, your kids probably began adjusting long ago, but when your divorce becomes final, they may have a new set of changes to cope with. For example, you and your children may have to move out of your home and they may attend a new school as a result and miss the friends they had in their old neighborhood.

If your children are young, watch for changes in their behavior like nightmares, bedwetting, and tantrums. If they seem to be struggling, do what you can to help them feel safe and to adjust to life after divorce. If your children are teens or preteens, keep open the lines of communication with them and make a point of spending time alone with each child. You may find that you and your older children become closer as a result of your efforts to help them cope.

For additional information and advice about helping your children cope with the aftermath of your divorce, go to www.helpguide.org/mental/ children_divorce.htm. The site also features links to other helpful resources.

Enjoy being with your kids even if you're not the custodial parent

If you're a noncustodial parent, spending time with your children in your new home or apartment and not living with each other day to day may feel awkward to all of you at first. To help you and your kids feel more comfortable and to make adjusting to your new situation easier, avoid turning every time you spend together into a special event. Instead, do the things you used to do with one another — go to the grocery store, take bike rides, help your kids with their homework, read them bedtime stories, take them to their soccer games, and so on. Keeping everything as normal and routine as possible should help bring some normalcy back into your lives and help your kids feel like things are going to be okay.

Reassure your kids that even if they no longer live with you full-time that you are going to be actively involved in their lives by continuing to attend open houses and other events at their schools, by coming to their recitals and sporting events, and being a part of their scouting activities. Even if you live out of town, try to attend some of these activities at least a couple of times a year. When you do, you give your kids moral support and reassure them that they're still very important to you.

If you're a noncustodial parent, don't be upset if your kids act nonchalant when you pick them up to spend time with you and then act sad to leave you. Their initial demeanor may be their way of protecting themselves emotionally or it may reflect their confidence that you will always be in their lives and that divorce hasn't changed how you feel about them. Don't make assumptions about the ways that your children should respond to the changes occurring in their lives or set yourself up for disappointment by having unrealistic expectations about how they will act when they are with you. Instead, simply observe your children and try to understand the true reasons for their behavior.

If your children live with you but spend some nights with your former spouse, give them time to get used to their other parent's home and the different rules your ex may expect your children to follow. Initially, they may have a hard time falling asleep when they spend the night at your ex's or may act reluctant to visit him. However, if you and your ex work together to make the transition from house to house as smooth and as easy as possible for your kids, they should adjust fairly quickly. If they don't, you may want to talk with a child therapist.

Redefine what it means to be a family

After your divorce, help your children maintain their sense of family. Doing so is especially important if your marital problems affected how your entire family functions or if your children no longer see some of their relatives as often as they used to because of your divorce.

Feeling part of a family is important to your children and contributes to their sense of security and self-worth regardless of whether you're a custodial parent, a noncustodial parent, or you and your ex share custody. In order to do that, maintain as many of the rituals you used to observe during your marriage as you can, including attending religious ceremonies with your children, celebrating their birthdays in a special way, spending important holidays with your extended family, and so on.

You should also think about establishing new family rituals (going on an annual vacation with your kids, eating pizza together and watching a movie every Friday night, taking Saturday morning bike rides, and so on). Your new traditions can help your children feel as though there is an upside to their new lives and underscore the fact that when they are with you, they're still part of a family.

Special family time doesn't have to cost a lot of money. What you do can be as simple as taking a walk after dinner, visiting a local park, playing a board game, making Christmas cookies, and decorating a holiday tree. Your children benefit from whatever you do together as long as you make it fun for them.

If your children are preteens or teenagers, be sensitive to their need for peer support, but at the same time insist that they do something with you and their siblings. Ideally, you should all have dinner together when your children are with you. Getting your older children to participate in family activities is easier if you choose activities that the entire family enjoys or if you let each of them take turns picking something to do as a family. However, if your older children balk at family togetherness, don't make it such an issue that they don't want to be with you at all. Most likely, they will come around eventually.

Building a Life for Yourself after Divorce

Okay, you've spent hours wallowing in self-pity, watching countless TV shows, and eating way more than your share of junk food. Now the time has come to get up off the couch, brush the potato chip crumbs off your lap, and begin building a new life for yourself as a single person. Yes, there *is* life after divorce! And, in this section, we offer some suggestions on how to get your social life going again and how to find people to date (as soon as you feel ready to do that).

Create a social life for yourself

It's sad but true, getting divorced almost always means losing some of the friends you had when you were married. Most likely, they will be people you knew through your spouse or people you may have socialized with only as couples. Some of those friends may feel the need to choose sides in your divorce and will side with your ex-spouse, others may side with you, and some may simply drop out of both your lives.

Your relationships with the friends who remain in your life may also be different after your divorce. For example, if your social life revolved around being part of a couple when you were married, you may feel awkward going to your friends' dinner parties and other social gatherings by yourself. Also, when you're ready to begin dating again, that new aspect of your social life may create some distance between you and your married friends, and you may drift apart from some of them as a result.

If all goes well, your most important and significant friendships will remain intact after your divorce. Even so, try to make some new friends, too. Meeting new people can be fun and can bring some much-needed energy, excitement, and hope to your life. To make new friends, join a health club, take up a hobby, join a book discussion group, take ballroom or swing dancing lessons, or pursue some other new activity that interests you and will bring you into contact with other people. View your new life as a single person as an opportunity to rediscover your community and all that it offers you and your children. Get out of your house and get on with your life!

Don't alienate your friends and family members by constantly griping about what a raw deal you got in your divorce or about the people your spouse is dating. Although they may have been willing to provide you with a shoulder to lean on while you were going through your divorce, they may be less willing to listen to you now that your divorce is over. If you need to vent, you are probably better off joining a divorce support group or getting professional counseling.

Start dating, but not too soon

The first rule of postdivorce dating: Don't begin dating until you've given yourself time to put your former marriage in perspective, pull yourself together emotionally, rebuild your self-esteem, and create a good life for you and your children. In other words, learn to be happy as a single person. When you do, you're more likely to make better choices when you begin dating again.

If you begin dating prematurely, you risk getting into a relationship that duplicates all the problems you experienced in your marriage. For example, you get involved with someone who is a user, not supportive of you emotionally or even emotionally abusive, someone who is needy, prone to violence, and so on.

Your children are another very important reason for not dating right away. They may feel threatened by the fact that you're dating so soon after your divorce. Among other things, they may fear that they'll have to compete with your dates for your attention and affection, that one of your dates is going to replace their other parent, that you'll begin a new family and they'll take second place in your life, or that your dates will create other problems in their lives.

You may find yourself attracted to people simply because they're polar opposites of your former spouse. For example, if your ex was a total couch potato, you may want to be with people who are perpetually in motion. Or if your ex was very disorganized, you may begin dating someone who's highly regimented. However, being the complete opposite of your former spouse is no guarantee that the two of you will get along.

When your fabulous single self is ready to start dating again, don't be surprised if you feel a little nervous and insecure. The longer you were married, the more likely you'll feel this way. Your feelings are totally normal however and, most likely, as you begin to feel comfortable dating, they will go away. In the meantime, don't look right away for a new Mr. or Ms. Right. Just date to have a good time; enjoy meeting new people and having new experiences. If remarrying is your ultimate goal, you will find that special someone when the time is right.

Here are some ways to meet new people to date:

> ✔ **Let your friends know that you want to start dating.** Your friends know you well, so they're in a good position to understand the kind of person you would enjoy meeting. They may be eager to introduce you to that person, maybe by inviting both of you to a dinner party or to join them on a run or a bike ride or to participate in some other low-stress group activity.

✔ **Take a class.** An auto repair class is usually a good place to meet men and women, but other options can include a music appreciation class, an art class, a dance class, or a class on any subject you would like to know more about.

✔ **Take up a sport.** Joining a softball team, a bowling league, or a running club that attracts both sexes can be a healthy, relaxed way to meet people you may want to date.

✔ **Volunteer.** Giving your time and energy to a cause you care about can put you in touch with like-minded men and women and make you feel good about yourself, too.

✔ **Join a singles group.** You may be able to find some groups listed in your local Yellow Pages or your local newspaper. Your place of worship may also have an organized singles group.

✔ **Register with an online dating service like Match.com or eHarmony. com.** For tips and advice about online dating, check out Online Dating Magazine, `www.onlinedatingmagazine.com`.

✔ **Use a dating service.** Some dating services let you create a video to advertise yourself and preview the videos of other people who've done the same. Other services use computerized databases to match you up with potential dates based on your personal profile. Still others sponsor social activities designed to help you meet potential dates and make the initial "getting to know you" process more comfortable.

Before you agree to work with a dating service or pay one any money, make sure you're comfortable with its approach to matchmaking. Learn as much as you can about the company by reviewing its litera-ture, scheduling an in-person meeting with a representative of the dating service, and asking for a sample contract to review. Also, be clear about how much the company charges for its services (fees can be as high as several thousand dollars for some!), exactly what you'll get for your money, and under what circumstances you can get your money refunded. Finally, before you sign anything, call your local Better Business Bureau and the consumer protection office of your state attor-ney general's office to find out whether they have any complaints on file about the service.

✔ **Place a personal ad or answer one.** Try running an ad in your local newspaper, singles newspaper, or magazine, or answer some personal ads run by people who sound interesting to you. For the price of run-ning an ad, you may also get to create a recorded message that callers hear when they punch in a special code. When you create your message, don't include your last name, address, or phone number. Keep your message brief and friendly and mention some of your interests.

If you use a dating service, personal ads, or go online to meet potential dates, for safety reasons, always choose a public place for your initial meetings and steer clear of bars. A meeting at a lunch spot, coffee shop, or bookstore is usually a good choice. Do not give anyone you meet this way your home phone or address until you feel comfortable and safe with that person.

✔ **Try speed dating.** In this fast-paced world where no one has enough time, speed dating has become another way to meet fun people to go out with. Speed dating involves attending a party organized by a speed-dating service where you meet multiple potential dates in one evening, but just for a short period of time — ten minutes or less. After each encounter, you fill out a card to indicate whether you'd like the person you just spent time with to contact you later. If any of the people you met is interested in getting to know you more, they indicate that fact on their own cards. The speed-dating service provides you and those interested in contacting you with a special e-mail account to communicate with one another.

✔ **Hire a professional matchmaker.** Matchmakers are professionals who provide a highly personalized service to singles looking to meet that special someone. A matchmaker will conduct an extensive in-person interview with you in order to get to know you and what you're looking for in a mate. Then she will match you up with one or more of the other singles she is working with who she feels would be a good fit for you. A matchmaker will also provide you with coaching about dating and talk to you after you have gone on a date to find out what went right and wrong. The cost of a matchmaker's services varies from a couple hundred dollars to thousands of dollars, depending on where in the country you live and the kinds of services a matchmaker provides, among other considerations. To find a certified matchmaker, visit the Web site of the Matchmaking Institute, www.matchmakinginstitute.com, or go to www.findamatchmaker.com.

Staying safe when you use an online dating service

The Internet has become a high-tech matchmaker. Millions of singles use online dating services to find people to date, especially singles who are dating again after their marriages have ended and whose lives don't make it easy for them to meet potential dates. However, although online dating is easy and convenient, it has its risks. For example, most online dating services don't run background checks on the people who register at their sites, and so you have no way of knowing ahead of time whether that handsome hunk or sexy gal has a rap sheet, is emotionally or physically abusive, or just plain weird. Also, because online dating makes it easy for people to be whoever they want to be online — handsome, rich, accomplished, single, tall, thin, and so on — without the right precautions, you may be taken totally by surprise when you finally meet in person the individual you've been communicating with online. To protect your safety when you use an online dating service, pay attention to the following advice.

✔ **Don't include any personally identifiable information in your online profile, such as your address or phone number.** And don't share that information with anyone you meet through an online dating service until you've had an opportunity to meet that person and feel that she is someone you can trust and want to get to know better.

✔ **Don't rush things.** Take time to get to know someone through e-mails and then maybe through phone calls before you agree to meet. If you have a bad feeling about someone, politely end your relationship.

✔ **If you decide to communicate directly with someone online rather than through** the online dating service, set up an anonymous e-mail account with a service like Yahoo or Hotmail and don't give out your full name. You should take this precaution because finding out personal information about you, based on the e-mail address you use all the time, isn't difficult to do — especially if you've had the account for a long time.

✔ **If you decide to have a first date with someone you have met online, drive yourself to your date location, meet in a public place, and let at least one friend know who you are meeting and where you are meeting.** It's also a good idea to arrange to call your friend or have your friend call you at a certain time during the date. You may even want to bring a friend along on your first date.

✔ **Consider running a background check on anyone you meet online who you are considering going on a date with.** Even if someone is totally charming and good-looking, that person may have some skeletons in his closet — maybe even a criminal past — that may cause you to think twice about whether you really want to date him.

Protecting Yourself if You Decide to Get Married Again

Many of you will meet the man or woman of your dreams eventually and decide to give marriage another chance. However, despite how in love you are with one another, you may feel uneasy about getting married again because of circumstances in your lives that you believe could create friction in your marriage — both of you have children from a prior marriage, one of you makes substantially more than the other, or has many more assets than the other, among other possible issues. However, you can take steps ahead of time to minimize the likelihood that such issues will be a problem in your new marriage. We fill you in on some of them in this section.

Get premarriage counseling

Talking with a mental health professional or a trusted religious advisor about the issues that make you and your future spouse feel uncomfortable and that may have already created some friction in your relationship is an excellent way for the two of you to resolve problems before your marriage, improve your communication skills, and acquire new skills and understanding that can help you work out any challenges you may encounter as a couple after you're married. In some churches, pre-marriage counseling is mandatory. Nonsecular courses that can help prepare you for marriage also are available. Some of the more established courses include: PAIRS Foundation, www.pairs.com; Preventative Relationship Enhancement Program, www.prepinc.com; and National Institute of Relationship Enhancement, www.nire.org.

You and your future spouse should be comfortable talking openly and honestly with whomever you choose as your counselor. If, for example, you would like to work with your religious advisor but your future spouse doesn't think that she can open up to him, find someone else to work with. Also, it may be best if whomever you choose as your counselor is someone neither of you already has a relationship with. Find out whether your church or synagogue has a program that helps soon-to-be married couples better understand and appreciate their individual strengths and weaknesses, ensure that they have realistic expectations for their new marriage and teaches couples healthy ways to resolve conflicts between them.

Prepare a prenup

Having gone through a divorce, you know that marriage can be something of a gamble and that it can drain your emotions as well as your pocketbook if it ends. If you are wondering what you can do now to make splitting up a little bit easier if don't work out in your next marriage, you and your future spouse should sign a legally enforceable prenuptial agreement.

A prenuptial agreement is a legal document that, among other things, enables you and your future spouse to work out some of the details of your potential divorce *before* you get married. A prenup is an especially good idea if you're going into your marriage with substantially more assets than your future spouse or if you own your own business; you can use a prenup to protect those assets from the financial repercussions of a possible divorce.

Each state has its own rules for what makes a prenuptial agreement legally binding and enforceable. Although the rules differ somewhat depending on the state, they require that

✔ The agreement be written.

✔ You and your future spouse sign the agreement — and sign it because you want to, not because you're being threatened or coerced.

✔ Both of you be involved in negotiating your agreement, although you can use attorneys to do the negotiating for you. Using attorneys (one for each of you) is highly recommended because their involvement greatly increases the enforceability of your agreement, which would be important if, down the road, your spouse tries to contest its legitimacy. In fact, some states require attorneys' involvement in the prenuptial agreement process.

The attorney you hire should be a family law practitioner with specific experience in the area of prenuptial planning (not all attorneys have this expertise). Depending on the circumstances, you may also need the assistance of a lawyer with special expertise outside the area of family law or the help of other professionals. For example, if you own a business, you may want a business law specialist or a business valuation expert involved in your prenuptial planning. Or, if you want to set up a trust as part of your planning, the assistance of an estate-planning attorney is advisable.

✔ Each of you is 100 percent forthcoming with the other about what you own and owe coming into your marriage. Detail all your assets — homes and land, vehicles, stocks and mutual funds, insurance policies, and so on — as well as their values. Be frank about how much you owe and who you owe the money to, even if you're embarrassed by your debt.

Some states require that your final agreement be notarized. Also, it's a good idea for you and your future spouse to negotiate and finalize your agreement well before the date of your marriage so that neither of you can later say that you were pressured by the pending date of your marriage to sign on the bottom line. Generally, the more distance between the date of your marriage and the signing of the agreement, the better.

Doing most of the end-of-your-marriage negotiating at the start of your relationship — when everything's still rosy — can make your divorce easier, less emotional, and cheaper and can help protect important assets in the aftermath of divorce (should one occur).

Some couples also use a prenup to establish the "rules" of their marriage, even though most courts don't enforce such lifestyle provisions. Still, spending time discussing many of the seemingly minor issues that often scuttle a marriage can help solidify your married relationship.

Keeping the peace after your marriage with a postnuptial agreement

If you do not negotiate a prenuptial agreement before your marriage or if your agreement does not address an issue that surfaces after your marriage, you and your spouse may want to consider negotiating a postnuptial agreement. A postnuptial agreement can address the same kinds of issues that a prenup might address.

Postnuptials are recognized by most states. Like a legally valid prenup, what makes a postnuptial legally valid varies somewhat by state; however, in every state where such an agreement is recognized, it will not be legally enforceable unless

- ✓ You and your spouse are completely honest with one another about your individual assets and debts.

- ✓ The agreement is fair to each of you.

- ✓ Neither of you felt under pressure to agree to a specific provision during the postnuptial agreement negotiation process or to agree to negotiate in the first place.

Part VI
The Part of Tens

The 5th Wave — By Rich Tennant

"I knew they were writing their own vows, but I expected quotes from Robert Frost poems, not the Geneva Convention."

In this part . . .

The Part of Tens features quick and handy bits of advice and information, packaged ten to a chapter, including ten divorce-related blogs to turn to for advice and information. We give you ten tips for making sure your children feel safe and happy before, during, and after your divorce, and we give you suggestions for moving on with your life after your divorce is behind you.

Chapter 20

Ten Divorce Blogs to Check Out

● ●

In This Chapter

▶ Obtaining practical information about divorce through blogs

▶ Learning about the divorce laws in your state

▶ Reading blogs to feel better about the end of your marriage

▶ Using blogs to help you move on with your life after your divorce

● ●

*W*e roamed the Internet in search of helpful, funny, and irreverent blogs about divorce. During that process, we read a lot of bad, boring, and outdated blogs, but we also read a lot of good ones. In this chapter, we present our picks for the ten best divorce blogs.

Some of the blogs we feature here are written by people who are going through a divorce or recently went through one and want to share their experiences, emotions, and advice with other divorcees. Other divorce blogs in this chapter are written by divorce attorneys interested in sharing their expertise and advice with individuals who are considering divorce or in the middle of one. Still other blogs provide information on high stakes, high visibility celebrity divorces. Reading these blogs may make you feel like your divorce is a piece of cake.

Some of the blogs we tell you about in this chapter will help you make wise decisions as you go through your divorce and begin to rebuild your life afterwards; others will provide you with emotional support and maybe even inspire you; and still other blogs will surely make you laugh.

ABA Journal Family Law Blogs

http://abajournal.com/blawgs/family+law

In addition to featuring blogs that specifically relate to divorce law in a particular state, this site offers blogs written just for divorcing women, blogs about collaborative law, and blogs about the ins and outs of international divorce, to name but a few. In addition, you'll find blogs that focus on issues related to same-sex divorces as well as blogs that feature various divorce attorneys musing about divorce law, their divorce practice, and other divorce-related topics.

Celebrity Blog

www.myfamilylaw.com/celebrityblog

If you're looking for the *People Magazine* of divorce, this is the blog for you. Celebrity Blog tells you all about the dramatic twists and turns and high stakes legal maneuvering that characterize the divorces of many movie stars, athletes, executives, and politicians. Wanna know how much New England Patriot star quarterback Tom Brady is paying in child support to his former girlfriend? Need to stay up-to-date on Britney Spears's efforts to regain custody of her kids? Curious about the biggest celebrity divorce settlements ever? This blog tells you all about those things and more.

Daily Stories on Divorce and Family Law

www.divorcenet.com/Members/divorcenews/weblog

This blog describes itself as the "leading provider of consumer-focused divorce information." Here you find articles, editorials, and questions and answers to a wide array of issues related to divorce and separation that have been culled from news sources around the country.

Divorce Without Dishonor

www.divorcewithoutdishonor.com

You can see from the quality of the postings here that the author, a divorce attorney who went through his own painful divorce, puts a lot of thought and effort into his blog. He not only provides compassionate, practical advice about the major aspects of divorce but writes about such topics as how to overcome the guilt you feel because of your divorce and how to help your child cope with the emotions he or she may feel because of your divorce, tips for moving out of your family's home when you separate, and why some divorced fathers become ghost dads after their divorce — fathers who pay the child support, but drift out of their children's day to day lives. The blog also highlights interesting divorce-related Web sites to check out, studies to learn from and divorce books to read, and even features quotes that will make you laugh or inspire you as you go through your divorce.

Fathers' Rights

www.mddivorcelawyers.com/fathersrights

Written by a divorce attorney, this blog provides thoughtful comments, insights, and advice to divorcing dads who want to ensure that they are treated fairly during their divorce process and who are anxious to maintain ongoing relationships with their young children during and after their divorce. This blog covers the gamut of issues faced by many divorcing dads, including alimony, child custody and visitation, child support, and the emotions of divorce. It also addresses other topics like parental alienation and kickout court orders. We believe that many divorcing moms as well as dads can benefit from reading this blog.

First Wives World

www.firstwivesworld.com

This site features a wide variety of well-written blogs by women in the midst of divorce, contemplating divorce, or recovering from divorce. Most of the blogs are informative and entertaining.

The bloggers comment about everything, including their struggles with their exes, therapy sessions, concerns about money, and legal issues. Other bloggers write about the challenges and pleasures of traveling as single women, their struggles to manage the guilt they feel because they initiated their divorces, the challenges of raising young kids postdivorce, and the perils and rewards of blended families.

Just Divorce

www.justdivorceblog.com

Written by a Chicago family law attorney, this blog provides short, well-written bits of practical advice and information about divorce as well as comments on recent news articles related to divorce, including celebrity divorces.

Recent posts at the time this book was written included information about the signs of a bad divorce attorney and the importance of having a Qualified Domestic Relations Order if you're dividing retirement funds in your property settlement. Periodically, the author of the Just Divorce blog posts thought-provoking quotes and poems related to divorce. Although the focus of this blog is on divorcing spouses living in Chicago and other parts of Illinois, many of the posts are equally relevant to divorcing spouses in other states.

Life After Divorce: New Horizons

http://lifeafterdivorce.wordpress.com

Written by a divorce coach, this blog helps you turn the end of your marriage into a growing experience. It provides caring advice and information to help you move forward rather than staying stuck in the past. The blog covers issues like financial rebuilding, surviving your first Christmas on your own, dating, and rebuilding your self esteem.

The Modern Woman's Divorce Guide

www.themodernwomansdivorceguide.com/blog

This blog is an interesting mix of practical articles about divorce, ranging from the frivolous to the informative. They include compilations of online divorce-related stories, a detailed weekly divorce tip, and comments that the author claims, "you may find interesting or annoying or that might just make you smirk."

Women's Divorce

www.womansdivorce.com/divorce-blog.html

Written by a woman (a former attorney) for women, this blog puts the emphasis on straightforward practical information. Posts provide news and information about the divorce process, offer advice about how to keep your emotions under control, discuss issues related to children and divorce, and offer tips for making ends meet financially after your divorce.

Chapter 21

Ten Ways to Help Your Kids Handle Your Divorce

In This Chapter

▶ Showing your kids that you still love them

▶ Minimizing the amount of change in your children's lives

▶ Helping your children feel emotionally secure

Children of divorce often feel as if their lives have been turned upside down and that everything that they knew and loved has been taken from them. In other words, your divorce is your children's divorce, too. So, as a parent, you're responsible for helping your kids cope with the profound changes that are happening in their lives. In this chapter, we provide suggestions for how you can do that. If you would like to talk with other parents in your same situation, visit the award-winning Web site www.parentsoup.com.

Spend Time with Your Children

As you go through your divorce, spend time with your kids, show them affection, and listen when they want to talk with you about their feelings. Take time to do something special one on one with each of your children, even if it's just taking a walk around the block together or running errands with one another. If you live too far away from your children to see them regularly, get in touch with them at least once a week via the phone, e-mail, webcam, or even an old fashioned letter. Also, if you know that something important coming up for them — the SATs, audition for the school play, or the prom, for example — check in with them before the event to tell them good luck or have a good time and check back with them afterwards, too.

If you are a noncustodial parent and dread seeing your children because telling them goodbye and returning them to their other parent at the end of each visit is painful, try to take comfort in the fact that, over time, doing so will get easier. Don't let these feelings prevent you from seeing your children. Staying involved in their lives is important.

Speak Well of Their Other Parent

Don't paint such a negative picture of your ex for your children that they feel guilty about loving their other parent. Speak positively about your ex and help your children feel comfortable talking about him or her in front of you. Tell them funny or touching stories about your ex or share photos from your wedding day, photos of your children with their other parent, or photos of all of you in happier times. By doing so, you demonstrate to your children that you're comfortable talking about their mom or dad, and you give them permission to talk with you about him or her. You also provide your kids with a sense of family history, something that all children need.

At first, saying nice things about your former spouse and hearing your children do the same may be difficult for you, but eventually it should get easier. If months go by and you are still having problems, consider counseling.

Don't Cry on Their Shoulders

Don't treat your children like grown-ups, even if they have to assume more responsibilities after your marriage ends. Never forget that they're still kids. Don't share your problems and worries with them. Do that with your close friends and family members or with your therapist. Although your children may sense that you're going through a challenging time in your life, you don't need to tell them that you're struggling. If you do, they're apt to become scared, develop emotional problems, feel like they need to take care of you, and so on. Even if you're feeling overwhelmed and having a difficult time hiding it, do everything you can to assure them through your words and actions that everything is going to be all right.

Come to an Agreement with Your Ex about Child-Rearing Basics

If you and your former spouse share custody of your children, try to reach an understanding with one another about how the two of you will handle such child-rearing matters as discipline, homework, bedtime, and curfews. Consistency makes children feel safe; living by one set of rules in your home and by a totally different set of rules in your ex's is apt to confuse your kids and make their lives feel unsettled and needlessly complicated.

On the other hand, if your former spouse doesn't parent your children as you do, don't complain about it to them or argue about it with your ex within earshot of your kids. However, you should definitely speak to your ex if you feel that his or her parenting style is clearly harming your children emotionally or putting them at risk for physical harm. If you are unsure how to have get your message across your ex in a way that he is apt to hear, ask a mental health professional for advice about what to say.

Make Your Children Feel Your Home Is Their Home

Because of your divorce, you may have to move out of your home and into a new home or apartment. If you do, try to make your children feel comfortable in their new home. (If they live with you only part of the time, giving them a place to call their own is particularly important because, otherwise, they may not want to spend time at your place.) If your finances allow, let your kids decorate their new space or at least select a few items for it. And agree with your ex to maintain a supply of clothes, toiletries, and toys for your kids at each of your homes. Then your children won't have to pack and unpack items every time they move from one parent's place to the other's.

Don't Put Your Kids in the Middle

Don't argue with your ex in front of your children, don't use your kids as go-betweens if you're fighting with your ex or just don't want to communicate with him or her, and don't try to prevent your ex from seeing your kids. And if your ex starts dating, don't try to sabotage that relationship or make your children think that it's not okay with you if they like your ex's new beau. These days, kids can't have too many caring adults in their lives. Also, if you act angry or resentful about your ex's new love interest, you inadvertently give your children a lesson in jealousy.

Do What You Say You Will Do

Make your children's lives as predictable and secure as possible by keeping the promises you make to them. Although following through on your promises to your children is always important, it's especially important, after your divorce when they may be feeling very insecure. Therefore, if you tell your kids that you'll pick them up at a certain time, be there. And if you tell them you're going to do something specific with them, do it. If you're not able to keep a promise, let your children know as soon as possible and make an alternative plan with them.

Also, don't make big promises to your children to try to buy their affection, drive a wedge between them and your ex, or to assuage your guilt about the changes that your divorce has created in their lives. Building up their hopes about something that you know won't happen is unfair and emotionally cruel.

Hold Off on Dating

Don't bring home dates in the months immediately after your divorce is final. When you first begin dating, your children may resent the time you spend with your dates or may feel threatened by them. Also, at least at first, try to schedule your dates for a time when your children will be with their other parent. (For more dating advice, turn to Chapter 19.)

Maintain Your Children's Routines and Traditions

Children thrive on predictability so, after your divorce, try to maintain the routines, rules, and traditions that they're used to. For example, try to eat at the same time, let them keep their pets, expect them to perform the same household chores, and take them to religious services. And, as much as possible, make holidays and other special days like they've always been.

Also, don't try to end or interfere with your children's relationships with their other parent, siblings, and other relatives of your former spouse. Your children have already experienced a significant loss; don't compound it by attempting to ruin the important relationships in their lives.

Don't Become a "Super Parent"

If you feel guilty about the effect your divorce may have on your kids or if you're angry because your spouse has custody, don't try to deal with your feelings by becoming a "Disneyland Dad" (or Mom), lavishing them with gifts and money. Try to maintain the same relationship with your children that you had before the divorce. Right now, your kids don't need grand gestures; they need predictability, stability, and love.

TIP

Reading up on postdivorce parenting

Here's a list of some helpful books that you may want to check out:

✔ *My Parents Are Divorced Too: A Book for Kids* by Jan Blackstone-Ford, Annie Ford, Melanie Ford, and Steven Ford (Magination Press): Written by kids for kids to help your preteens/early teens start talking about their feelings about your divorce.

✔ *Vicki Lansky's Divorce Book for Parents: Helping Your Children Cope with the Aftermath of Divorce* (Book Peddlers): If you need practical advice about how to help your children cope with your divorce while it's happening and afterward, try this title.

✔ *What About the Kids? Raising Your Children Before, During and After Divorce* by Judith S. Wallerstein and Sandra Blakeslee (Hyperion): This resource contains great advice for helping your kids deal with your divorce.

✔ **Difficult Questions Kids Ask (And Are Too Afraid to Ask) About Divorce** by Meg Schneider and Joan Zuckerberg (Fireside). The authors of this book help parents understand the real meaning behind the questions their kids may ask them related to their divorce and provide advice for how to deal with the issues their children are really bothered by.

✔ *Surviving the Breakup: How Children and Parents Cope with Divorce* by Judith Wallerstein and Joan Berlin Kelly (Basic Books) and *Second Chances: Men, Women and Children a Decade after Divorce* by Judith Wallerstein and Sandra Blakeslee (Houghton Mifflin Company): These books chronicle the results of the groundbreaking study clinical psychologist Judith Wallerstein conducted on how divorce affects children.

Chapter 22

Ten Tips for Getting On with Your Life

*L*ife goes on after a divorce and, believe it or not, things usually get better (sooner rather than later, we hope). Who knows, you may even fall in love again, and your next marriage may be everything you've ever dreamed of and more. In this chapter, we provide ten suggestions for actions that can help boost your spirits and make it easier for you to start looking toward the future with optimism and hope.

Try Something New and Different

During your marriage you may have postponed (or given up) an activity that you always wanted to try. Being single opens the door to your trying it. For example, maybe you've dreamed of learning to hang glide, running a marathon, learning how to ballroom dance, or taking a cross-country trip on Route 66. Or maybe you would like to pursue yoga, take up painting or sculpting, or even work on the novel you've always dreamed of writing. Now may be the time! Pursuing a new activity can enrich your life, help you meet new people, and take your mind off of your failed marriage.

Share Your Feelings with a Friend

When your marriage ends, having someone in your life with whom you can honestly share your thoughts and emotions and on whom you can rely for solid advice helps you cope. Whoever you choose should be a good listener, trustworthy, and someone who has given you good advice in the past. But don't rely on your special confidant so much that you "wear out your welcome" and jeopardize your relationship as a result. Also, don't dump your worries, frustrations, and anger on your kids. They are your children, not your friends, and sharing your concerns and emotions with them may not only put them in an awkward position but may also harm them emotionally.

Record Your Thoughts in a Journal

Keeping a journal is a great way to cope with your feelings. Before and after your divorce, writing down how you feel and what happened to you each day can help you work through your emotions, make you feel better about your life, and become less reliant on your friends and family.

Try not to be self-conscious when you write. Remember, your journal is just for you. You don't share it with anyone else unless you want to, and no one is going to grade you on your prose. Relax and express your thoughts on paper without judging yourself. When you write, pretend that you're sitting opposite your best friend or a close family member, or that you're talking to yourself. Draw pictures to illustrate your thoughts, if that helps.

Every week or two, read what you wrote the previous week. You may be surprised at the depth (or the silliness) of your emotions and the clarity of your insights. In addition, you may discover that in just a relatively short time, your perspective on something that was really bothering you has changed considerably and what you saw as a big deal then isn't anymore.

Talk to a Therapist

If you're crying all the time, full of anger toward your ex, or struggling with depression, schedule an appointment with a therapist or social worker. This person can give you the advice and feedback you need to get on with your life. If you don't know a good mental health professional, get a referral from a friend or relative, your family physician, or your divorce attorney.

If you have a good relationship with your religious advisor, you may want to talk with him rather than with a mental health professional.

Resist the Urge to Return to Your Ex

If you become desperately lonely after your divorce, don't begin dating your ex or start living together again. Although you may be tempted to resume a relationship with her, especially if you didn't want your marriage to end, it's time to move on. Spending time together isn't the way to end your pain or ease your loneliness; the reasons behind your divorce probably continue to exist. This advice doesn't mean that the two of you can't reconcile sometime down the road; but for now, you're both probably better off focusing on the future and addressing the issues that contributed to the end of your marriage (and may create problems in any relationship).

Focus on Your Job

Your professional life may have suffered while you were going through your divorce because ending your marriage took every ounce of your energy and concentration, and so you did the bare minimum at work. Now that you're divorced, refocusing your energies on your job can help distract you from your troubles and provide you with the structure and routine you may need in your life right now. Plus, your professional accomplishments can make you feel good about yourself, providing you with what may be a much-needed ego boost — and you may even get a pay raise or a promotion as a result.

Although working hard can be good temporary therapy, don't turn into a workaholic to fill a void in your life or to avoid facing your emotions. Finding balance in your life and doing some things just for fun are more important than ever now.

Connect with Your Spiritual Side

Many people who experience challenging times find solace and strength through prayer or meditation, and so you may want to begin to begin praying to a higher power, attending religious services or meditating. Others find inner calm through yoga. If you want to explore some of these options, pick up a copy of *Meditation For Dummies* by Stephan Bodian (Wiley) or *Yoga For Dummies* by Georg Feuerstein, Larry Payne, and Lilias Folan (Wiley). Another great resource is *Mind Like Water: Keeping Your Balance in a Chaotic World* by Jim Ballard (Wiley), which can help you stay centered and calm when it feels like your life is falling apart.

Pay Down Your Debts

If you owe lot of money to your creditors, get it paid off as quickly as you can. The last thing you need right now is to be worried about unpaid bills and debt collectors, and the faster you get out of debt, the sooner you can start putting money in savings for your future. If you need help figuring out how to deal with your debts, schedule an appointment with a reputable nonprofit credit counseling agency, like one affiliated with the National Foundation for Credit Counseling (www.nfcc.org). Also, make sure that you have a realistic household budget. It can help you live on your monthly income so you don't take on additional debt and pay off your existing debts as quickly as you possible. Chapter 5 provides advice and information about how to develop a budget, but you can also get budgeting advice and assistance from a good nonprofit credit counseling agency.

Live with a Roommate

If money is tight, maybe it's time to get a roommate. Not only will sharing your space with another adult reduce your monthly expenses, but it gives you someone to eat meals with, watch TV with, and so on. In other words, your living space will seem less lonely. Of course, you need to choose your roommate carefully; go for someone with whom you feel compatible.

Sharing your space with a roommate isn't out of the question if you have kids, but be sure that whoever you're considering living with likes being around children and has no problem with the noise and mess that they can create. If your home or apartment is large enough, you may even want to consider a roommate who has children about the same ages as yours. That way you and your roommate can share some of your parenting responsibilities, which should make being a single mom or dad easier.

Get Your Social Life Going Again

Doing fun things with your friends and meeting new people that you enjoy is good therapy. So, get out of the house once in a while just for fun. Consider joining a divorce support group or a singles' club for example. Chapter 19 tells you about some Web sites for locating a support group in your area. If you used to enjoy entertaining but stopped when your marriage started to falter or after your divorce began, invite friends over for brunch or dinner again. If money is tight, make the meals potluck.

At some point, you may want to begin dating, but don't start too soon. Give yourself time to get some perspective on what caused your marriage to end and to heal emotionally. Most mental health professionals suggest waiting to date for at least a year once your divorce is final. When you feel that it's time to begin dating, you may be at a loss about how you can meet people you might like to go out with, especially if you were married for a long time and don't know many single people your own age. Chapter 19 offers some suggestions for finding people you may enjoy dating.

Index